12-92
20.00
B&T
VER

W9-ANJ-546

# A Theory of Freedom

JC        Benn, S. I.          27,640
585
.B378   A theory of freedom
1988

| DATE |  |  |  |
|---|---|---|---|
| JA 20 '95 |  |  |  |
| FE 2 '96 |  |  |  |
| SE 14 '99 |  |  |  |
| OC 5 '99 |  |  |  |
| OC 25 '99 |  |  |  |
| JA 26 '00 |  |  |  |
|  |  |  |  |
|  |  |  |  |
|  |  |  |  |
|  |  |  |  |
|  |  |  |  |

A theory of freedom
JC585.B378 1988          27640

Benn, S. I. (Stanley I.)
VRJC/WRIGHT LIBRARY

DEMCO

*Dedicated with all my love to Miriam Benn*

# A Theory of Freedom

STANLEY I. BENN

*Late Professorial Fellow in the Social Sciences,*
*Australian National University*

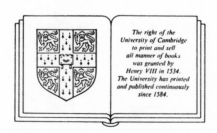

The right of the
University of Cambridge
to print and sell
all manner of books
was granted by
Henry VIII in 1534.
The University has printed
and published continuously
since 1584.

## CAMBRIDGE UNIVERSITY PRESS

CAMBRIDGE
NEW YORK  PORT CHESTER
MELBOURNE  SYDNEY

VERNON REGIONAL
JUNIOR COLLEGE LIBRARY

Published by the Press Syndicate of the University of Cambridge
The Pitt Building, Trumpington Street, Cambridge CB2 1RP
40 West 20th Street, New York, NY 10011, USA
10 Stamford Road, Oakleigh, Melbourne 3166, Australia

© Cambridge University Press 1988

First published 1988
Reprinted 1990

Printed in the United States of America

*Library of Congress Cataloging-in-Publication Data*
Benn, S. I. (Stanley I.)
A theory of freedom / Stanley I. Benn.
p. cm.
ISBN 0-521-34260-0. ISBN 0-521-34802-1 (pbk.)
1. Liberty. I. Title.
JC585.B378   1988
123'.5—dc19          87-37492
CIP

*British Library Cataloguing in Publication Data*
Benn, S.I. (Stanley Isaac)
A theory of freedom.
1. Freedom – Philosophical perspectives
I. Title
123'.5

ISBN 0 521 34260 0 hardback
ISBN 0 521 34802 1 paperback

# Contents

# Foreword

Stanley Benn completed *A Theory of Freedom* shortly before his death in July 1986. Each chapter had been rewritten several times, and he considered the arguments as sound as he could make them. He was, however, unable to make the final stylistic revisions he had intended, and in preparing his text for publication we have generally refrained from doing this for him. For the sake of clarity some punctuation has been adjusted and the occasional sentence reshaped, but we have altered his words as little as possible. Consequently his use of *man* and of masculine pronouns to refer to humans in general remains; he was never happy with this feature of English but rebelled when asked to use substitute expressions he considered clumsy. We had no wish to alter his prose in a way he would have resisted. *A Theory of Freedom* is not merely Stanley Benn's last philosophic work, it is the summation of those beliefs by which he lived. The book speaks with the author's voice, not ours; those who knew him will recognize it.

Miriam Benn
Gerald F. Gaus

# Preface

I can say, in retrospect, that I commenced work on this book some twenty years ago, though I little realized that at the time. I had undertaken to write a book on power, an enterprise I was unable to pursue very far. Having narrowly escaped being sucked into that morass, and having seen better men flounder for years striving to write on freedom, I had resolved to eschew both topics thereafter. One part of the power project did mature, however, namely, a paper published in the *Australasian Journal of Philosophy* in 1967 entitled "Freedom and Persuasion." A little later I met W.J. Weinstein, who had also recently written a piece on freedom, and we agreed to collaborate on a paper entitled "Being Free to Act and Being a Free Man" (*Mind* 80, [1971]: 194–211). Students familiar with that paper will recognize sections of it which, with Bill Weinstein's permission (granted so many years ago that he has probably forgotten it), I have adapted for use in Chapter 7 of this book, on freedom of action. The enterprise took off from there, and the papers listed below mark the various stages in its growth. One crucial stage was the writing of "Freedom, Autonomy, and the Concept of a Person," which owed a great deal to long conversations in the early 1970s in Canberra and in London with Richard Peters, whose profound influence on my philosophical development began with our collaboration in the 1950s on *Social Principles and the Democratic State*. The theory of freedom that began to emerge became, by stages, so integrated and extensive in its scope that, in recent years, I have found it impossible to write yet another paper in the general area without devoting about a quarter of it to summarizing previously published work. When that happens, nothing remains but to set it all out systematically in a book. That was not at all like anthologizing previously published work. Quite a lot of the present book is new; of the rest, all, I think, has been enriched by being located within an embracing theory.

I must acknowledge an enormous debt to one other collaborator, whose help has become ever more important to me as the book has neared completion. Dr. G.F. Gaus and I first worked together in 1979, when we began planning a research project which resulted in

ix

a book – *Public and Private in Social Life* (London: Croom Helm, and New York: St. Martin's Press, 1983) – to which thirteen scholars contributed, and of which Jerry Gaus and I were joint editors. We also collaborated in the writing of two key chapters. Having become accustomed to exchanging ideas (we occupied adjacent rooms in the Coombs Building of the Research School of Social Sciences of the Australian National University and enjoyed daily philosophical lunches), we discovered that we had arrived, by a kind of intellectual symphysis, at a theory of practical rationality which provided a common underpinning to the different projects on which, by now, we were separately engaged. Although our applications and interpretations of parts of the theory diverged at certain important points, we were able, within the area of substantial agreement remaining, to write a joint paper, published as "Practical Rationality and Commitment" (*American Philosophical Quarterly* [1986]). I have included this paper with very little amendment as Chapter 2 of the present volume, where it occupies a core position in my theory of freedom. I am deeply grateful to Jerry Gaus for so generously permitting me to take it over holus-bolus in this way.

But this is perhaps the least of the debts I owe to Jerry Gaus. He has read and discussed with me at length each chapter as it has been written, often in several versions, and has made invaluable suggestions and criticisms. His friendship and encouragement during the final months of writing, when I have been afflicted with illness, have given me enormous support. In particular, a promise that he would see it through should I be unable to bring the book to the point of publication has removed much of my anxiety and has unquestionably helped me to reach the present stage at which I am writing this preface.

My intellectual debt to my wife, Miriam Benn, is of a different order. Over some thirty years we have been companions in our respective adventures of ideas as in all our other modes of experience. Her criticism of my work has always been shrewd, and she has pointed the way out of many an impasse. But I have relied most on her common sense and moral insight, which have so often steered me in the right direction and have saved me from errors of rigidity (without loss of rigor), into which I should otherwise have fallen. Beyond that, my dedication must stand in lieu of a full acknowledgment of a life's debt.

In the course of twenty years, in which one has had the privilege of discussing seminar papers with one's colleagues and students in three continents, the amount of indebtedness one has piled up is impossible to enumerate. I hope all those other friends and colleagues to whom so much is owing will forgive me if I do not try. Perhaps I can best acknowledge it by recording my gratitude that there was a vigorous tradition of philosophical speculation into which I was privileged to be inducted (if by a somewhat unorthodox route), and to which the Australian National University has enabled me to make some contribution over a quarter of a century. I have been provided with conditions as favorable to scholarship as any that exist, to my knowledge, anywhere in the world. And in learning to be a philosopher I have learned one way of living a good life.

Australian National University                    S.I. Benn
Canberra, Australia
1986

# Acknowledgments

I have included in this book passages previously published in the following articles, either by direct quotation or by substantial paraphrase. I am grateful to the editors of the journals concerned for having given them their first lease of public life.

"Egalitarianism and the Equal Consideration of Interests." In *Equality–NOMOS IX*, edited by J.R. Pennock and J.W. Chapman, 61–78. New York: Atherton Press, 1967.

"Freedom and Persuasion." *Australasian Journal of Philosophy* 45, (1967):259–75.

"Privacy, Freedom, and Respect for Persons." In *Privacy – NOMOS XIII*, edited by J.R. Pennock and J.W. Chapman, 1–26. New York: Atherton Press, 1971.

With W.L. Weinstein. "Being Free to Act and Being a Free Man." *Mind* 80 (1971):194–221.

"Abortion, Infanticide, and Respect for Persons." In *The Problem of Abortion*, edited by Joel Feinberg. Belmont, Calif.: Wadsworth, 1973, 92–104.

"Freedom, Autonomy, and the Concept of a Person." *Proceedings of the Aristotelian Society, 1975–76* (1976):109–30.

"Personal Freedom and Environmental Ethics: The Moral Inequality of Species." In *Equality and Freedom: International and Comparative Jurisprudence*, vol. 2, edited by G. Dorsey, 401–24. Dobbs Ferry, N.Y.: Oceana, and Leiden: A.W. Sijthoff, 1977.

"Human Rights – For Whom and for What?" In *Human Rights*, edited by E. Kamenka and A. Tay, 59–73. London: Edward Arnold and Son, 1978.

"The Protection and Limitation of Privacy", Parts I and II. *The Australian Law Journal* 52 (1978):601–12, 686–92.

"Human Rights and Human Nature." In *Teaching Human Rights*, edited by A.E.-S. Tay, G. Connelly, and R. Williams, 103–9. Canberra: Australian National Commission for UNESCO, 1981.

"Individuality, Autonomy, and Community." In *Community*, edited by E. Kamenka, 43–62. London: Edward Arnold and Son, 1982.

With G.F. Gaus. "Public and Private – Concepts and Action." In *Public and Private in Social Life*, edited by S.I. Benn and G.F. Gaus, 3–27. London: Croom Helm, and New York: St. Martin's Press, 1983.

"Persons and Values: Reasons in Conflict and Moral Disagreement." *Ethics* 95 (1984):20–37.

With G.F. Gaus. "Practical Rationality and Commitment." *American Philosophical Quarterly* 23 (1986): 255–66.

# 1

## Persons and values

### 1. Reasons and justification

Philosophy is about what, if anything, can count as a reason in appraising beliefs, arguments, actions, and proposals to act, for valuing or disvaluing activities, situations, objects, characters, and so on. Its concern is not primarily with the adequacy of particular reasons for particular beliefs, other than philosophical beliefs, for philosophy scrutinizes the methods and procedures and the conceptual structures of all forms of inquiry, including its own, as well as those of other systematic practices, or what Wittgenstein called "forms of life." Philosophy is thus concerned with those more general conditions which reasons must satisfy to be adequate, if particular beliefs and actions are to be appropriate to the context or the logical environment of beliefs in which any new belief or action is set. Consequently, consistency and coherence are regulatory principles governing such judgments of appropriateness.

Philosophy is also concerned, therefore, about the relations between reasons – for instance, about the ordering of reasons. Further, it asks whether appraisals can be true or in some other way correct, or at any rate defensible, or whether they should be understood, as the more naive of emotivists would have it, as simply registering approval or disapproval. If the emotivist were correct, reasoning would have only a minor part to play in our practical discourse and experience. At the level of first-order ethics, it could mount a critique of practical, instrumental calculations, and at the level of metaethics, of the logic of moral discourse. It would then be the task of moral philosophy to remove the illusion that there was more to do.

If, *pace* the emotivist, appraisal processes or moral thinking are governed by rationality criteria, there must be some kind of consistency requirements which regulate them. If moral life consisted only of a succession of groans and smiles, one might still be disposed to see whether some regularities could be detected in one's

1

own moral life, by grasping what types of situations evoked groans, and which, smiles. That might be the beginning of rule-like consistency; for then one could begin to offer as a reason for smiling not only that the occasion was of such a kind rather than another, but that a rule picked out some feature of situations that was smile-worthy, and that this feature was consistent with other smile-evoking features.

It would be strange if, as planners and project makers, we were quite unconcerned about consistency – if, for instance, caught out in a contradiction or in some practical incoherence of belief, attitude, and action, we saw no occasion to reconsider our beliefs. A disposition to consistency is, in general, a condition for understanding and dealing efficiently with the world. We have, besides, at least two reasons to be concerned that our appraisals be rational. In the first place, appraisals are closely connected to action. "What is to be done?" calls for a rational appraisal of alternative possibilities, and of reasons for adopting one rather than another in terms of ends, values, principles, or rules. These provide the canons for consistency in action; without them, the question "What is to be done?" will be met by altogether too many, and some mutually excluding, prescriptions, with no way of selecting between them.

There is a second concern, related but still distinct from the first. Because we require the cooperation of other people, as well as the benefits of their wisdom and their approval, it is important that we be able to justify ourselves to them, which involves persuading them to think as we do. One way of doing that (though not of course the only way) is by adducing reasons which demonstrate that our critics and opponents are committed to our appraisals by premises or evaluative beliefs they already share with us, but of which they have not properly appreciated the implications. If that move fails to change their minds, it gives us, at worst, the satisfaction of knowing that they, not we, are at fault. For if they have failed in rational discussion to persuade us, we are bound, if we have argued so far in good faith, to believe that their arguments were bad or at least insufficient. Part of the pressure in ethics towards objectivism is no doubt our need to believe not only that there are right answers to practical quandaries, but also that people who arrive at answers different from our own are not merely choosing differently but also exhibiting a defect, either of reason alone or, worse, of reason and character, this being the perverting or distorting cause of their faulty choice.

Too much can be made, however, of this interpersonal concern.

2

If it should turn out that, even when I am thinking straight, there is no certainty that every right-minded person would think as I do, nevertheless there may yet be canons of rationality which commit me to some beliefs and actions and not to others, and which entitle me to say that what I have decided is indeed the right thing to do or to believe. An uncertain foundation, such as some kind of subjectivism, for the second, interpersonal concern for rationality need not weaken the first. And if there is indeed no way of knowing in advance whether agreement between persons initially in disagreement is nevertheless possible, equally there is no reason to suppose, in any particular instance and in advance of trying, that it is not. So we have no reason, save perhaps a shortage of time, energy, or patience to abandon the pursuit of agreement before the arguments run out – if in fact they ever do.

## 2. Practical quandaries – real or apparent?

Unfortunately, the reasons with which we seek to support our appraisals do not always speak with one voice, nor do they come ready-tagged with priority labels. Even in our private deliberations reasons conflict, and there may be no simple procedure for determining the thing to do. Some philosophers, such as Isaiah Berlin, Bernard Williams, Stuart Hampshire, and Michael Walzer, take a frankly pluralist view: There are situations in which not only are there reasons for and against all the available and competing courses of action, but also the reasons will not assume an ordering such that these clearly override those. Consequently, if one cannot avoid action of *some* sort (and inaction can also be a kind of action, bearing conclusively on the outcome of a situation), then *whatever* one decides to do, one will simply have to disregard all the reasons against doing that and for doing something else instead and so one cannot avoid doing wrong. Such dilemmas spectacularly abound, for instance, in war: A soldier driving through a hostile city sees a child by the roadside aiming a gun at the next truck in the convoy; should he shoot the child? In Bernard Williams's well-known parable of Jim and Pedro, Jim is offered the choice of shooting one innocent Indian to save the lives of another nineteen who will otherwise be shot by Pedro's firing squad. In Williams's view – and a very similar judgment emerges, *mutatis mutandis*, in examples given by Hampshire and Walzer – whatever Jim decides to do, it would be appropriate for him not just to regret the high cost of doing right, but also to feel remorse for doing

3

wrong. And they would presumably say much the same of the soldier and the child.[1] (For a full discussion of the moral problems of practical quandaries, see Chapter 3.)

One way to deal with such problems is briskly to deny that moral dilemmas of this sort are genuine.[2] If there appear to be reasons why one ought to do *A* and others for not doing *A*, the principle that *ought* implies *can* ensures, according to some philosophers, that we cannot have an obligation to do both. Terrance C. McConnell says that moral theorists have traditionally held that "an adequate ethical theory must not allow for genuine moral quandaries"; if a theory does so, "then there is some sense in which it is incoherent or inconsistent."[3] This is my own view, spelled out in Chapter 3, though my conclusions differ from McConnell's. R. M. Hare's recent work has had as at least one of its objectives the formulation of a metaethical theory to overcome just the kind of dilemma allegedly generated by our having intuitions pointing to inconsistent moral duties.[4] (However, I prefer "quandaries" to "dilemmas"; a dilemma is strictly speaking a form of logical argument, and though our quandaries might be formulated to conform to logical specifications, they as likely might not; so it is better not to use a possibly confusing terminology.)

According to Hare, philosophers' quandaries are so out of the ordinary as to be philosophically uninteresting; they are perplexing, he claims, only because writers insist on accepting intuitions as incontrovertible. One can easily concoct a quandary, in Hare's opinion, by constructing some highly improbable situation, including in it carefully chosen features which a selection of intuitive rules pick out as relevant for action; however, the situation is set up so that the features highlighted as the prescriptively relevant ones yield diverse prescriptions, all of which cannot be satisfied, so the rules leave the agent with no way of acting without breaking some of the rules. What makes the quandary unusual, in his opinion, is the particular conjunction of features. Our intuitions are formed for everyday use; if they leave us perplexed when submitted to extraordinary tests, that is no great matter.

Hare's program depends on relegating such moral intuitions to "first-level" moral thinking, which is normally sufficient to pick out the thing to do, but which is not to be depended upon when the intuitions come into conflict. Then, according to Hare, we have to switch to the second level, the level of "critical thinking," "imposed on us by the logical properties of the moral concepts [which] requires us to pay attention to the satisfaction of the preferences of people (because moral judgments are prescriptive, and to have a preference is to accept a prescription); and to pay attention equally to the equal preferences of all those affected."[5] Ultimately, the thing to do will depend on which rules maximize preference satisfaction.

Intuitions – or first-level principles – are all prima facie principles. Our moral education has equipped us with them, and they are simple because the part they play in moral education and as ready guides to daily life requires that they should remain so; that is why they will not resolve the unusual situations that philosophers fabricate. The reason why they did not serve the soldier confronted by the problem of the child with a gun (*not* a philosopher's fabrication, but an incident that actually occurred in Lebanon, and could well occur any day of the week in Northern Ireland or Central America) is that guerilla warfare is even yet not sufficiently institutionalized for its morality to have been codified either in institutional principles or in intuitions.

To know when and how it is appropriate to override first-level intuitions, we must ascend, according to Hare, to the level of critical thinking where the intuitions themselves come under critical review, and cannot be relied on, therefore, to warrant or to test moral appraisals.

> Critical thinking aims to select the best set of prima facie principles for use in intuitive thinking. . . . The best set is that whose acceptance yields action, dispositions, etc. most nearly approximating to those which would be chosen if we were able to use critical thinking all the time.[6]

Principles at the level of critical thinking are not prima facie and cannot be overridden. At this level, given full knowledge of the facts (which will include a full catalogue of human preferences), moral judgments are, in Hare's opinion, fully determinate. Moreover:

> . . . if we assumed a perfect command of logic and of facts, they would constrain so severely the moral evaluations that we can make, that in practice we would be bound all to agree to the same ones.[7]

At the critical level, according to Hare, we do indeed have a rationally cogent method for ordering the intuitive principles accepted for first-level operations.

Hare's argument has as its two premises (i) that preferences are prescriptive[8] and (ii) that the universalization principle requires impartiality between my own and other people's preferences. The conclusion is (iii) that preferences must be understood as grounding moral reasons for action. It is not just that someone's reason for acting can always be presented as expressing a preference for the action, or for things being made this way rather than that; rather, someone's preferring that something rather than its opposite be the case must be, for anyone else, a reason (though not necessarily a conclusive one) for making it so. Anyone's preference would then furnish a reason for action for everyone else.

This is, in itself, an implausible claim. But even allowing it, it would not follow from it, as Hare seems to assume, that *all* reasons must be grounded on preferences. Some environmentalists, for instance, regard environmental objects, such as ecosystems, as having a value capable, quite independently of anyone or everyone's preferences, of underpinning appraisals of action and policies. The environmentalists themselves prefer, of course, that the systems survive, but that follows from their valuing them. They value them because they have reasons for seeing them as valuable – appropriate to value – and therefore as objects whose survival it is appropriate to prefer to their destruction; it is not that their preference for the survival of the systems is what gives the systems their value. The reasons for ascribing value to an object will have to be something internal to the object, not its being the object of someone's preference. Similar claims might be made for the value of sacred objects – and perhaps for art objects, too, if one takes the view that their value is intrinsic to them, and not dependent on there being viewers or auditors who enjoy them.

Now it is possible that Hare might simply exclude such valuings from the category of moral reasons. But if the implication of that exclusion is to be that such reasons cannot override preference-related reasons, one is bound to ask why moral reasons in that *constrained* sense must be taken to override value-centered reasons. To call something a *moral* reason is, indeed, according to many (but not all) philosophers to give it overriding status, but one cannot justify giving a type of reason an overriding status merely by calling it "moral."

## 3. Reasons of concern and reasons of respect

Our moral tradition, *pace* Hare, generates reasons for action, then, that are not merely conflicting but also of profoundly differing kinds. In debates on what are frequently called "moral issues" or "issues of conscience" – abortion, contraception, capital punishment, conscription, in vitro fertilization, consumer protectionism –

reasons are frequently advanced on each side of an issue which seem not to engage at all with reasons advanced by the other side. Sometimes this is because arguments are being exchanged by people who differ so profoundly in their metaphysical and religious beliefs that what counts for one as conclusive, may carry no weight for, or even be quite unintelligible to, the other. Differences over the morality of abortion offer an example. Some Catholics believe that an immortal soul is incorporated at the moment of conception; for others, it is at the quickening of the fetus. However, since for many infidels there are no incorporeal immortal souls, and there is no such event as an ensoulment, the very notion being quite incoherent, conception must be a strictly physical event governed by natural laws, and the reasons for not aborting a pregnancy grounded on the immortal soul of the fetus simply pass them by.

I am interested, however, in a different kind of nonengagement of reasons. It commonly happens, even to people whose moral beliefs are squarely in the secular, rationalist tradition, that on topics such as these they do recognize the force of the opposing arguments as reasons for action or practical belief but can see no way of reconciling them with their own. We resort to words like "weighing" and "balancing" in our efforts to rank the arguments, but we are hard put to it if asked to cash these metaphors out. How weigh with no scales? In what units, such that the weighing settles which argument is the weightier? How demonstrate that it is so, to someone else? Sometimes we can do cost/benefit calculations that can actually be expressed in monetary units: Nuclear strategists weigh policies in terms of megadeaths discounted by estimated probabilities. But even within this restricted range of cases, there is an assumption of homogeneity in the unit of measurement. Is the death of every person equally deplorable, or are some a greater loss than others? This doubt apart, when such convenient currencies are unavailable and, even more, when some of the reasons do not depend for their cogency on the expected outcome but upon some deontic principle, what kind of weighing is possible?

A contrast familiar in the philosophical literature is that between deontological theories of ethics, with their corresponding reasons for action, and teleological theories and their corresponding reasons. I shall work with a related but somewhat different distinction, between reasons of respect and reasons of concern, the former being *person-centered*, the latter *value-centered*. Reasons of concern look primarily to the good consequences of an action, to whether it will bring about or preserve some valued and valuable

7

state of affairs, sustain some valued and valuable activity, or promote the survival and well-being of some valued and valuable object. Such objects, which I call *axiotima* (things to be valued), may be animate or inanimate. Among the former I include human beings, or such of them as are valuable (for I do not want to beg the question whether humanity is intrinsically valuable or valuable only by virtue of certain properties typical of members of the species in general, but which particular members of the species may or may not possess). Concern for human happiness, the sole reason for action admitted by utilitarians, is a subclass of value-centered reasons; happiness is a constituent of well-being for certain kinds of axiotima, but not, of course, for inanimate kinds.

Value-centered reasons require that we optimize – that we make the world as good as it can be made. Hare's preferentialist utilitarianism seems to be conceived in this way, provided that the preferences to which we are required to attend are not necessarily the ones people actually have, but are such as they would have if their actual preferences (which may be based on false beliefs, or arrived at by faulty inferences) were exposed to facts and logic.[9] In Hare's opinion, the world would be as good as it could be made if everyone's preferences, their incoherences duly ironed out, were satisfied to the greatest possible degree. For Hare, therefore, preferences are not *for* the good as one sees it, but *constitute* the goodness of states of affairs, which are presumably preferred for reasons other than their goodness.

Person-centered reasons have to do with principles, such as freedom, justice, equal respect for persons' rights, and fidelity to truth, inasmuch as we are committed to these principles in our dealings with any other person, simply by virtue of that subject's being a person, and quite irrespective of the outcomes of our conforming to or departing from these principles. The notion of a *natural person* is fundamental to such principles. I use the term to refer to anyone who has the natural capacity to plan and bring about a future that is different, by reason of his choosing that it shall be different, from what it might otherwise have been.

These ideas call for a much fuller treatment than I can present in an introductory chapter. I shall discuss at some length in Chapters 5 and 6 what is implied by this notion of natural personality, and its corollary, moral personality; and the chapters following these two explore notions of autarchy and autonomy closely related to the notion of personality, the notion of someone who is a minimally rational, self-determining project maker and chooser who is aware of himself under that characterization. Suffice it to say, for the moment, that recognizing in someone else the character of a chooser like myself, I would be likely to resent it if, in his conduct towards me he failed to take account of the impact his actions would have on my projects, and if he took no account of how they appear from *my* standpoint. And if that is how I respond to him, I am committed by the universality of reasons, which commits me to envisaging our roles reversed, to viewing his projects, and my actions in relation to them, from his standpoint. How he sees the world then becomes a relevant consideration for me to entertain in answering the question, "What is the thing to do?" The minimal implication of respect for persons is thus a kind of forbearance that one could not owe to nonpersonal entities, however much one valued them.

Identifying a natural person as a moral person is to recognize him as a bearer of rights. Rights (a subject tackled at length in Chapter 13, in the context of human rights), are resources deriving from norms, at the disposal of persons to deploy (subject to overriding reasons which may arise in particular cases) at their discretion in the pursuit of their own projects. They are reasons for action that bear on other people, at the behest and discretion of the right holder, irrespective of whether their being exercised will optimize the outcomes. To the extent therefore that we ascribe rights to entities other than persons we use the term in an extended or secondary sense which will require a grasp of the relevant institutional norms, such as norms of law or etiquette, to understand.

To respect someone as a person does not imply that one also values him. One acknowledges that, simply as a person, he is entitled to a kind of consideration that we do not accord to nonpersonal axiotima, such as trees, cattle, works of art, or the practice of scientific research. Nevertheless one might without inconsistency attach greater value to such nonpersonal axiotima (which in the nature of the case we cannot respect, since respect implies consideration of the subject's point of view, which these do not and logically cannot have) than to some human beings, even human beings who are genuinely persons. But assigning greater value to nonpersonal axiotima does not imply, either, that the value-centered reasons deriving from them will necessarily override the person-centered reasons of respect, not even if the world would be made a better place by the overriding in the particular instance of the person-centered by the value-centered reasons.

Certain values, it is true, can be ascribed only to persons, because they depend on those capacities that are also conditions for respect. A person, as a maker of projects, is also in some measure the maker of himself. Whether or not he explicitly entertains some future self as the goal of his present self, what he actually becomes depends, if only in part, on what he sets out to do with the world and on his own understanding and appraisal of his achievement. Not that he could be the sole cause of his future nature, but whatever storms he encounters, there is always a decision to make: Which of the possible ways of weathering shall I make my own? Some people are better than others at making such decisions, and some have a better reason than others for calling them their own. The autonomous person is the one who makes the choice of his own life and, by a process of reasoned internal criticism, creates for himself a coherent set of principles and standards by which he regulates it. The autonomous person – the truly "self-made man" – is an ideal deeply rooted in the liberal tradition and is clearly one of the threads woven into the complex notion of a free man. (The conditions for autonomy and its relation to other human ideals, such as personal integration and community, are discussed at some length in Chapters 9 to 12.)

As an ideal, autonomy belongs to the realm of value-centered reasons, even though it is a property that can only be ascribed to persons. But, other things being equal, a world in which everyone was autonomous would be a world more to be valued than one in which some people were autonomous, some heteronomous, and some anomic. To be the proper object of respect, however, one does not need to satisfy the exacting requirements of the ideal of autonomy. Autonomous or not, persons qualify for respect under the characterization of beings who satisfy certain minimal conditions of rationality, who make conscious choices backed by reasons and are not merely impelled by causes that have no place in consciousness as requiring the action as *appropriate*, but only produce it as an effect. They are not, on that account, equally admirable or worthwhile, for that is a question of their value, not of their ontic status. Some human beings – those of whom one can truly say that the world would have been better had they never been born – are worse than valueless. But the reasons of generalized beneficence that would warrant our improving it by removing them from it are opposed by reasons of respect for them as persons. Optimizing is not everything, and we only confuse ourselves if we try, like thoroughgoing consequentialists, to bring our moral intuitions into line by fabricating general welfare-promoting reasons that might

10

account for our reluctance to deal with homicidal maniacs and ruthless and bloody tyrants by simply killing them. This might in the end be the only thing to do, but it should not be done without an appreciation of the cost in terms of respect: Killing a tyrant is to dispose of him totally in the interests of other people, conceding nothing to his view of what is being done to him, as one might kill a man-eating tiger in the forests of Bengal.

The principles of freedom, justice, fidelity to truth, and equal consideration of interests are all closely connected with the respect due to persons, even though the reasons for particular freedoms and other rights may certainly be reinforced by value-centered ones too. Freedom has to do, in the first instance, with not interfering with someone's actions; justice, with giving someone his due, whether or not that is the best thing for the world in general, or even for him in particular. Fidelity to truth has to do with not deceiving him, since to deceive someone is to manipulate his responses and his actions by deliberately falsifying the way he pictures the world and the options it makes available between which he must decide. Such considerations are quite different from a concern not to cause someone pain, to promote his well-being and safety as an axiotimon (which might be best achieved by lying to him), and to make the world better for that being's remaining part of it, intact and well. Concern attends to a being's needs; respect, to his rights. (In Chapter 13 I shall consider under what conditions needs may also generate rights, as in the case of welfare rights.)

## 4. Paternalism, respect, and value

The conflict that can develop between person- and value-centered reasons is well illustrated by debates on paternalist measures, at least outside the eponymous reference area of relations between fathers and their young children. Paternalism is a term of moral ambiguity only when the subjects are not young children but rational adults, who are treated, as small children are, as if they were incapacitated from making rational decisions in their own interest and who are therefore properly under paternal (or maternal) tutelage. To protest against paternalism is not therefore necessarily to claim that the subjects are being treated contrary to their own best interests, but that they are deprived of their right to decide for themselves what their interests are, and how best they would be served. Safety restrictions on the manufacture and sale of motor cars add to their cost; the purchaser might prefer after all to choose a cheaper if riskier car, especially if it was the only car he could afford. According to the antipaternalist, the trade-off between safety and walking is one that the poor would-be car buyer ought to be at liberty to decide for himself.

Paternalist measures include consumer protectionism; the control of dangerous drugs; legislation to compel the wearing of seat belts, safety helmets, or protective clothing; the imposition of safety standards on automobiles; and hire-purchase legislation to provide the consumer with protection against high-pressure salesmanship by requiring a cooling-off period in which the purchaser may change his mind. These are all cases in which the subject is being protected against himself – against his own rashness or indiscretion.

Admittedly, these interferences may be justified by appeal to the interests of people other than the subject of the restraint – his family, for instance; nevertheless, there is in each instance a strong element of paternalist protection, designed to save the subject from the consequences of his own imprudence.

It might be argued, on the paternalist's side, that if we value the lives and happiness of our fellow men and women, as axiotima, we surely have as good a reason for looking to their welfare and for protecting them from harm, even self-inflicted harm, as we have for protecting our domestic animals and pets, our pictures, or a forest. Nevertheless, if we set out to do good to persons or to protect them from harm despite themselves, we are very likely to be met with the indignant challenge: "What has it to do with you? What right have you, or has anyone else, to make my life better – or safer – than I choose to make it myself? I have projects of my own, and mine is the prime responsibility for judging their advisability, and for assessing what I make of them and of myself. I'll thank you not to interfere."

Such a response invokes the principle of respect for persons as a way of blocking action based on value-centered reasons of beneficence, the latter depending not on the status of persons but on the value attaching to human beings as axiotima, as objects to be cherished and protected from harm. The principle of respect for persons, by contrast, constitutes a reason for taking account of a person's own view and assessment of his life. It is a reason for not attempting to shape it for him differently from the way in which he, as subject, chooses to shape it for himself, however poor that shape would be. To interfere with a person, so conceived, one must show standing, that is, that one has a special authority to go beyond mere benevolence to beneficence. Because young children are deemed not to be fully competent as rational persons, parents and schoolteachers are recognized as having the requisite standing. Prior authorization and consent may confer it too, as when Ulysses authorized his crew to bind him to the mast and to ignore his demands to be released so long as the Sirens were within earshot. It is arguable that a spouse may possess standing to interfere, by virtue of the special rights and duties of the marital relationship. But I think this should not be too readily conceded. I discuss the relation between autonomy and mutuality in Chapter 12.

The relation between person-centered and value-centered reasons is not at all like a trade-off between competing values, such as health and education, one of which can be offset against another in a cost/benefit analysis. Even when the axiotima are of different kinds – a human being and a lyrebird, let us say – one can decide in principle which of them one values more (even how much more) and how much the actions in question would contribute to the well-being of each, trading off increments of welfare discounted by the relative value attached to each subject. Such trade-offs answer the question, "Would the world be better with one package rather than another?" To insist on the priority of respect for persons is, by contrast, to claim that the principle is a constraint on beneficent action whatever the outcome.

A person-centered reason affects deliberation quite unlike a value-centered reason. One sort of effect has already been suggested: A person-centered reason can impose a constraint on an otherwise appropriate action without there being any alteration in the evaluation of expected outcomes. If a person-centered reason is at issue, it is not enough to show how much better things would be overall if the principle were set aside. To deny a person his rights for the sake of a good outcome is not like investing a dollar to gain five. Instead, one must find a reason why at just this point the constraining principle fails to constrain, and why reasons of benevolence break through. True, if a benevolent paternalist interferer chose to disregard the constraint and thereby prevented a disaster which would otherwise have struck, it would be churlish for the beneficiary to complain. But should things go badly, the interferer may justly be reproached not merely for having made things go wrong, but also for interfering where he had no standing. If that reproach seems out of place when things go well, it is not because the ground of complaint has been removed or the right to noninterference has been extinguished; nor does the success of an intervention demon-

13

strate that the benefactor had after all a right to intervene. Rather, the beneficiary's reason for gratitude is a reason also for not exercising his right to object to uninvited interference.

This analysis of the case for a constraint on paternalist interference enables me to distinguish my principle of respect for persons from Hare's rationalized preferentialism. Hare's theory is really value-centered and not, as one might suppose, person-centered, even though its central value is the preferences of persons. True, respect for persons requires that we attend to persons' preferences and that we forbear in the face of their preferred projects. Or at least that we forbear in the face of their chosen courses, which is not necessarily quite the same. For Hare it would be a reason to set aside a person's choice, his expressed or revealed preference, that it was inconsistent with something that he really wanted more. Respect for rationalized preferences is quite consistent with a paternalist arrangement of someone's life to maximize his satisfactions, whether or not that is the way he chooses to do it himself. Respect for persons, by contrast, demands of us that we forbear from putting obstinate people right against their worse judgment. Broadly speaking, persons are entitled to make the mistakes they choose, if they themselves are the only losers.

Objectors to paternalism have commonly combined, and sometimes confused, the argument from respect with utilitarian or self-developmental arguments. It has been said (by J.S. Mill, for instance) that it is better for a person to discover and to learn from his own mistakes than to be protected from their consequences, and that in any case the individual is generally the best judge of his own interests. These are value- not person-centered reasons for letting him alone, although that does not preclude adducing them to reinforce reasons of the other kind. They depend, however, on assumptions of fact, as the other kind does not, and these assumptions may be challenged. Are consumers always the best judges of their own interests, and is the provision of technical information about a dangerous product sufficient protection? Or do we need legislation to ban dangerous products for the sake of the imprudent or unwary? The principle of respect for persons would provide a ground nonetheless for resenting Big Brother's intrusion, even when he really does know best.

I have dealt at some length here with the case against paternalism because it illustrates most clearly the difference in thrust of reasons of different kinds, and exhibits how the principle of respect can generate reasons that may block beneficent interference. It is,

14

however, a very special case; not all conflicts can be so neatly anatomized. On the one hand, person-centered reasons may themselves conflict, as when one has a reason to intervene to prevent Smith from bullying Jones. More challengingly, however, value-centered reasons may override person-centered reasons; interference to prevent cruelty to an animal would be a case in point. Under some conditions, the needs of axiotima – value-centered reasons – are clearly reasons enough to override the forbearance due to persons in the pursuit of their chosen projects. These are complex questions to which I return in Chapters 3, 5, and 7.

## 5. Symbolic reasons

There is no reason to suppose that value- and person-centered reasons exhaust the range of possible types. There is, indeed, a range of different reasons employed in many controversies over medical ethics, and particularly over the use of fetal material for experimental purposes and the freezing of fertilized ova for storage and later implantation. There are also reasons relating to the disposal of corpses and to the implementation of the projects or wishes of dead persons. I treat these problems at some length in Chapter 13 in relation to theories of rights, and particularly human rights. Suffice it to say, at this stage, that the reasons we have for treating a corpse with a kind of consideration cannot be reasons of respect, person-centered, in the same sense that we owe respect to persons as project makers; and they cannot be reasons of concern, in that corpses cannot be cherished, and have no well-being which can be promoted or sustained. The reasons may therefore be of a generally symbolic nature.

We accord corpses a kind of dignity that arises from our seeing them, not simply as dead meat and bone, as we see the carcass of an animal, but in the light of their humanity and former personality. Because we breed animals for food and use their skins and other parts of their anatomies for a variety of purposes of our own, we have in our culture ready-made ways of conceptualizing dead beasts that ascribe to them a nature more or less independent of the living animal. The idea of a pig-bristle hairbrush, for instance, is fully intelligible without our having to consider the function of the bristles as parts of total pig. The reference to its porcine origin is little more than a way of setting this sort of bristle in a context of nylon and other stiff-fibered hairbrushes, from which it is thus differentiated. A human corpse, however, is nothing but a dead

15

human person; *that* description nominates the form which gives it significance for us. True, many medical students and research workers – and paleontologists too – seem to lose this consciousness of the universal form of human personality instantiated, albeit defectively, in the human remains on the laboratory or mortuary bench, just because, perhaps, they do see them as functioning as a resource independent of personality and humanity. In place of a dead human being who once acted, thought, and felt in the same fashion as the ones we cherish as now living and respect as the subjects at present of their own projects, they see only specimens to be used to achieve a very limited understanding of what it is to be human. To grasp the humanity in a corpse or a dead fetus – to see it as defective because dead, but in the light of its essential humanity as a sad symbol of human fears and aspirations, frustrated and cut short – is to be committed to treating it with a kind of respect or a kind of concern, although, logically speaking, it cannot be either the one or the other, but only a kind of shadow or reminiscence of both.

Such symbolic reasons for action derive from our notions of respect and value but cannot be identical with them. They are capable of coming into conflict both with value-centered and with person-centered reasons – in their own right as it were, without there being any immediately apparent lexical ordering of reasons, merely by virtue of type. And if it is possible to identify three or indeed four such types of reasons, it is at least possible that there may be more, none of which is a basic type to which all the others may be reduced; and further, there is no common currency, such as happiness or utility, in terms of which all of them can be re-expressed. If such a reduction is not possible, one cannot look for a resolution of conflicts between reasons by a quasi-arithmetical off-setting of gains and losses that would be compelling for all rational appraisers, like an accurate financial balance sheet.

## 6. Moral conflicts and the fragmentation of moral culture

I claimed in the first section of this chapter that, if moral appraisals were to be rational, they would have to satisfy conditions of consistency, and that, in one view at any rate (a view that I share), a satisfactory moral theory must exclude genuine, irresoluble moral dilemmas. I then scouted a notion that all moral reasons could somehow be expressed in a common currency, of preference satisfaction or utility, which would resolve the apparent dilemmas, not

16

only because values are diverse, but also because some important reasons are not value-centered at all.

The plurality and diversity of moral reasons – or of reasons claiming to be moral reasons – have led Alasdair MacIntyre to suggest that our moral culture is indeed incoherent, that the supplanting of traditional theism and teleological thinking by individualism, secularism, and positivism has resulted in the collapse of morality into rhetoric. It no longer provides a form of discourse out of which comprehension and agreement could issue.[10] But conflicts are not really peculiar to modern consciousness. Admittedly, the centering of reasons on individual personality is indeed a feature of the post-Renaissance world. The Greeks, however, were very much alive to the possibilities for moral conflict; their tragic drama relied heavily on it. The *Antigone*, the *Oresteia*, *Agamemnon*, and *Seven Against Thebes* are all about conflicts of duty, of obligations to family and to city, of duties to avoid matricide and not to let a father murdered by one's mother go unavenged, and so on.

Much Greek tragedy, and much of the *Iliad* too, can be put in terms of the conflict between the demands of the public sphere and those of the private. And this is true of much modern drama, too, except that the locus of privateness is significantly different.[11] For the modern liberal mind that locus is ultimately the individual person, and only at the second or derivative stage the family and the domestic hearth. For the Greeks, the private meant the domestic. Consequently the tragic conflicts of Greek literature are essentially role conflicts. For us they are often conflicts among the principles we see as constitutive of the individual self – matters, as we say, of conscience. The demands of one's social roles may or may not figure among them, but if they do, they figure as one kind of conscience-sanctioned claim alongside others. (I develop this point in Chapter 3.) And using the critical thinking of Hare's analysis, one is sometimes bound to inquire whether they are properly there at all, as when someone inquires whether, soldier or no, he really ought to go on shooting people. The secularized notion of conscience locates the center of conflict for the modern in quite a different way and in a different place from any previous culture.

MacIntyre is, however, right thus far; a post-Renaissance speeding up in the tempo of technical and social change has increasingly highlighted the possibilities for conflict in our tradition. So long as the situations confronting people in their daily lives remain reasonably familiar and expected, and the range of possible happenings fairly confined, a culture will develop a repertoire of acknowledged

17

ways of responding to each situation as it occurs. People will have clear intuitions, in Hare's sense, and little occasion for critical thinking. They will begin to be conscious of life as calling for decisions and of decisions being governed and in need of justification by reasons and principles precisely when they are in doubt about the thing to do. Such doubts arise more acutely as developing technology introduces new possibilities, new ways of manipulating our environment and one another. Because, more than any other human activity, war generates rapid technological change, and it presents starker and more basic value alternatives, it seems to generate the most tragic of moral quandaries. While the rate of innovation is slow, a society can digest each novelty, can develop an appropriate response that becomes accustomed and familiar – an intuition – before being afflicted with uncertainty and anxiety at the emergence of the next. When intuitions present no difficulties, we do not need to reflect on principles. The speeding up of social change drives us, however, to reflect searchingly on our moral principles and values in much the way that Hare recommends as critical thinking.

Not needing to reflect on principles is not at all the same, however, as being without principles. We can have and act on principles that we are quite unable to articulate; they can be inferred from some consistency in our responses to events as "the things to do," rather than in the words we utter. But though we may be driven to articulate principles only when they run into difficulties and present us with quandaries, it does not at all follow that we then lack any further resources for resolving our quandaries. (The role of principled beliefs, whether articulated or otherwise, in our rational practices is discussed fully in Chapter 2, and the status of quandaries and how they might be resolved, in Chapter 3.)

Now it is true that, given the diversity of principles and values that can count as moral reasons, what Jacob sees as conclusive may not appear conclusive to Esau, even though Esau sees the point of it as a reason. Each person is supplied by his upbringing in a complex cultural environment with a variety of principles and ideals, and in putting together a consistent character as he faces innovation and diversity of experience, he may well be able to impose on it an order which constitutes the person he is. But he will never be quite sure that the priorities he assigns, the trade-offs he deems admissible and the ones which for him are monstrous and unthinkable, will appeal in the same way to his critics. But then, *pace* MacIntyre, was it ever otherwise? Did Antigone fail to convince Creon through some defect of reason? Creon grasped well enough the reasons of family piety that moved Antigone, and she, on her side, was perfectly able to grasp the reasons of civil policy that moved him. What put them in opposition was their different ordering of the reasons in that particular situation. Still, Antigone's case is really very different from the modern. Though the actors were committed, by their identification with the particular roles they bore, to the priorities they assigned to the different considerations, both the roles and their duties were constituted by a common culture, albeit one, as MacIntyre points out, in which "different virtues appear as making rival and incompatible claims."[12] Each understood perfectly well the reason that the other found compelling, even if each, carrying his or her own moral burden, was bound to repudiate the other's conclusion as wicked or contumacious. Had their roles been reversed, the strengths of their particular commitments to action might have been correspondingly different. We could not say the same with confidence today. Our conflicts go deeper than theirs; they arise not only from conflicting role commitments but also from the absence of agreement on how such commitments should be ranked, even by the bearers themselves.* Greek tragedy is generated within the common culture, modern anxiety by tensions within the individual's conscience that the individual can relax only by reworking his plural heritage, in the pursuit of autonomy.

## 7. Reason and morality

Within the modern consciousness, practical reason is located in the first instance not in the mustering of knockdown arguments to persuade or justify oneself to others but in the process of individual choice and judgment. Each person's moral consciousness is something he has to keep in reasonable shape; conflicts are resolved by reviewing the ordering of, and the constraints imposed by, the principles and values which make considerations into practical reasons. Those principles and values are not, of course, the individual's inventions *ex nihilo*. They have been adopted, inculcated, absorbed from an enveloping social environment. And the more stable, integral, and coherent that environment is, and the more secure the ranking of reasons, the less the room for conflict and the

---

*Even this difference needs to be qualified. Though Ismene has a social role equivalent to her sister Antigone's, Ismene believes that Antigone, not simply as a subject but as a woman, ought to accept Creon's authority. This is evidently a case in which, as MacIntyre says, the self "transcends the social roles."

19

 VERNON REGIONAL
JUNIOR COLLEGE LIBRARY

less, therefore, the experience of irresolution in the individual's experience. Equally, the greater will be the measure of agreement in the society about how someone is to go about justifying himself. Moral assuredness in the individual will be matched by basic moral certainties in public debate. Conversely, the greater the scope for conflict and perplexity, the more conscious we are likely to be that each must do his own moral work, making over his socially endowed moral resources into a pattern as coherent as he can make it. Ironically, autonomy – living by a law, in Rousseau's phrase, that one prescribes to oneself – is an ideal for an age and culture like this one, not for the Spartans and Roman republicans that Rousseau so admired.

I do not mean to suggest that this critical process cannot be a shared experience or that one's moral life must be shut away; our moral convictions, like any other of our beliefs, can properly be subjects for discussion. However, we have no way of knowing, in advance of trying, whether our moral orderings are enough alike to make such discussion illuminating and profitable. In this respect, however, we are in principle no worse off than the most monolithic of cultures, though in such a culture one might be less able to grasp the point. If it appeared that we were all equipped with precisely the same moral resources identically ranked, we should no doubt have reason to expect that, with intelligence, patience, and good will, agreement would emerge on the things to do, to admire, and to praise. And we might be inclined to project these, or the moral resources that informed such particular judgments, into a Platonic universe, as necessary truths that everyone of sound intellect and good faith must surely recognize and agree on. All the same, it would still be a contingent matter whether, with each operating with the moral resources at his own disposal, agreement would really always emerge. For there would be no way to prove, in advance of specific inquiry, that the appearance of identity in moral equipment was not illusory. Only by exploring each disagreement as it arose could one be sure that there were no hidden differences in principles or values to generate irresoluble conflicts. But, equally and conversely, we ought never to suppose that the conditions for fruitful exchange are never more than delusively there, and that moral discourse is mere rhetoric. We cannot know until we try, and there is no call to abandon the quest for agreement until time or the arguments run out.

Nevertheless, although some measure of consensus may develop in subcultures, when a culture possesses moral resources as complex and diverse as our own and suffers rapid technological innovation, the institutions for public decision making in national politics, government, and law are unlikely to rest firmly on a shared morality. The United States Supreme Court, says MacIntyre, must be understood rather "as a truce-keeping body . . . negotiating its way through an impasse of conflict, not by invoking shared moral first principles."[13] But that does not throw doubt on the possibility that one can be a rational moral person within the culture; it is only to say that there is no shared morality – rational or otherwise – which will serve as a foundation on which to build an acceptable jurisprudence. That acceptance must come from compromise, from the recognized need – itself a moral reason, of course – to get along together, albeit without a universal conviction that outcomes are, morally speaking, all that they should be. The jurisprudence of natural law, despite its lusty resurgence since World War II, is not, perhaps, ideally suited to the twentieth century, depite the rediscovery of natural rights in the guise of human rights.

I have tried in this chapter to give the reader the overall feel of this book. Many of the topics discussed here swiftly and cursorily will be taken up again, and discussed in depth. Their introduction into this chapter is designed to provide a kind of a sketch map to the theory of freedom, which is the ultimate theme of the book, enabling the reader to locate himself in the theory as he goes. I have referred little to the content of the final three or four chapters; by the time the reader arrives there, he or she will have gotten the general idea anyway.

# 2

# Practical rationality and commitment[1]

## 1. Two Humean accounts

Contemporary analyses of practical rationality generally adopt one of two accounts of how desires, reasons for action, and the explanation of action are related. The dominant view[2] insists that something can be a reason for a person only if it relates in some way to his wants, desires, or pro- or con-attitudes. "[I]t is supposed to be a necessary condition of something's being a reason for an agent . . .," writes E.J. Bond, "that it be a *motivator*, and motivations require *wants* (Hume's principle) in the broadest sense of that term. (No want, no reason)."[3] According to this Humean orthodoxy,[4] without a motivating desire or attitude[5] one could never have more than a conditional reason to perform some act Φ: "there is a reason to Φ if you want to Φ or if Φ is a means to satisfying some other desire that you have." So the desire believed to be necessary for a reason for action also provides the drive to get the agent moving. Reasons are then not merely justificatory, but, because they are causally effective, explanatory too.

Now it is clear that a reason cannot move a person to act unless it is what has been termed "an internal reason." Though Smith's owing Jones $100 is a reason for Smith to give Jones $100, it is not a reason that can move Smith to pay up unless Smith believes that it is a reason for him. He must believe, say, that debts ought to be paid, or that he will lose Jones's friendship or damage his credit rating if he doesn't pay. And these are reasons for him, according to the orthodoxy, only because they include a desire (or pro-attitude) of Smith's which is a motivator. Of course, not every reason recognized is a reason acted on. Sometimes there are contrary reasons; sometimes, akratically, we fail to do the things that we have reasons for doing. Nevertheless, for the orthodox Humean, explanation begins with a desire, which picks out, from all the many things

22

that the agent believes, just those beliefs which explain how the agent comes to act as he does to satisfy it.

A variant of this account, proposed by David A.J. Richards, suggests that, while reasons are not necessarily grounded in desires, they move someone to action only if he has the desire to be, for instance, rational or reasonable.[6] Richards concedes that the agent's belief might supply him with practical reasons that nevertheless do not move him to act, just because he has no related desire – a concession which must be unintelligible to the orthodox Humean, according to whom the idea of a practical reason cannot get going without a desire. But if one takes seriously the notion that principles, for instance, can furnish reasons for action, and if one recognizes that a person has some principle as one of his beliefs, then one has to say that he has a reason to act as that principle indicates, whenever the situation is one to which the principle applies. For Richards, however, to have a principle is to take up only a theoretical position. One still needs a desire to motivate one to act on it.[7]

## 2. Belief, action, and commitment

I reject both the orthodox and the revised Humean accounts. I hope to show that desires and attitudes are neither basic nor necessary to explanations of action as rational. I do not say, of course, that people do not have desires; rather, the explanatory work done by even paradigmatic desires, such as sexual desire or the desire for food, can be adequately accommodated in an alternative explanatory framework, the primary components of which are beliefs and the commitments that follow from them. I shall avoid the phrases "reason for action" and "reason for belief," except when they are pretty neutral as between theories; instead, I shall refer (1) to *action commitments* and *belief commitments*, and (2) to a rational action as being, under certain conditions, *the thing to do*, and to a rational belief as *the thing to believe*. This is not mere quirkiness. This terminology avoids some of the obscurities which arise from the ambiguity of "reason to . . ." as between external and internal reasons. A person holding certain false beliefs might be said to have a reason for holding certain other beliefs those false beliefs entail, though just because they are false there is also a reason not to hold them or their entailments. Equally, if certain propositions are true, there is a reason to hold what they entail, but someone who doesn't believe the premises has, in one sense at least, no reason to believe the conclusion. And correspondingly with action. However, using my terminology, I can say that a person is committed by his other beliefs to believing $p$ even though, $p$ being false, it is not the thing to believe. Similarly, someone may be committed by his belief $p$ to doing $\Phi$, even though $\Phi$ is not the thing to do, for again, $p$ may be false. Conversely, though $\Phi$ may be the thing to do, a person without appropriate true beliefs may not be committed to doing it.[8]

Another reason for avoiding "reason for action" is that it is too closely associated with Humean instrumentalism. It is easy to presume that means/end rationality is somehow the paradigm of rational action and that all reasons will therefore be of that form. This is a presumption I am particularly anxious to avoid, because I want to give those acts done for the sake of a principle, such as respect for persons, at least equal standing as rational. Rather than being performed for the sake of an outcome in which the principle is somehow realized, or a state of affairs brought about in which it is preserved, such acts, in my view, express or instantiate the principle, somewhat as token to type. It is difficult, within a basically instrumentalist theory of rational action, adequately to distinguish value- or goal-oriented action from principled action.[9]

"Commitment," however, is itself ambiguous. In theological and existentialist contexts, a commitment is something that one makes, as one makes a promise or decides to become a nun. It involves voluntarily assuming a special set of obligations and responsibilities, as part of an affirmation or a committing of oneself to someone, to a cause, or to a way of life.[10] That is not the sense of "commitment" I shall make use of in this theory of rationality. The verb is to be understood in the passive voice; I speak of an agent "being committed" to an action or a belief, rather than of actively committing himself to it. One cannot be committed, in this passive sense, by the action of someone else, as one partner's signature on a check commits another; for one is not committed, in my sense, by actions at all, but only by beliefs. And one cannot be committed by what someone else believes.

To be committed to believing $q$ by virtue of believing $p$ means that, on account of the logical relations between $p$ and $q$, one's beliefs would be inconsistent if one believed $p$ and also not-$q$. One of the things that we mean when we characterize someone's belief as rational is that it is consistent with his logical commitments, and one way of being a rational person is to respond, when one's

24

belief structure is shown to be inconsistent, by trying to revise it to eliminate the inconsistency.

Now it is widely held that such an analysis cannot be applied to action. The difference may be attributed in part to the alleged fishiness of the practical syllogism. Because an action is an event, not a proposition, it has no truth value and cannot be the conclusion entailed by a set of premises. Propositions entail only propositions.[11] So the conclusion to a practical syllogism can be only a proposition about an action; it cannot be the action itself. Consequently, not acting on such a conclusion is not considered a failure in rationality in the same sense as not believing what is entailed by premises believed to be true. But consider

(i) If $p$, then $q$;

(ii) $p$;

(iii) $q$;

(iii) does not entail anyone's actually believing $q$.[12] Since one can hold onto a belief in the face of evident entailments, the best one can get from (i) and (ii) by way of belief is

(iv) $q$ is the thing to believe.

Rationality in belief is no more and no less a matter of logical necessity than is rationality in action. Just as a practical syllogism yields not an action but an action commitment as its conclusion, so a theoretical syllogism yields not a belief but a belief commitment. In both cases the commitment follows only if both premises are believed. Why then should one ask for a motivator, a want, a desire, or an attitude only in the case of action? If we don't seem to need to interpolate a desire – say, the desire to believe only true propositions – to explain why a credent's belief changes from not-$q$ to $q$ when confronted by (iv), why can't we do without a desire in explaining an action? If a credent's epistemic rationality depends precisely on his making such a change, given that he believes (i) and (ii), why should there be a problem in making an agent's practical rationality depend on his acting in accordance with a conclusion "Φ is the thing to do" derived from corresponding premises?

Bernard Williams suggests a possible asymmetry between belief and action in his treatment of the motivation for believing and acting. According to Williams,[13] 'wanting to believe,' in the sense of willing to have a certain belief, is an impossible and incoherent project. Belief is standardly 'truth-centered.' Someone who wants to believe $p$ (for example, that his son, reported dead in an accident, is actually alive) really wants that his belief be true; he does not and cannot want simply that he believe it, for that would be to want to believe that something is true, knowing at the same time that one believed it only because one had so chosen, and that choosing cannot make true what might otherwise be untrue. Admittedly, there are also nonstandard, non-truth-centered motives for belief, such as social conformity. Such motives, however, are parasitic on truth-centered ones; if the bulk of our beliefs were not truth centered, those prompted by other interests could not be held as beliefs at all; that is, they could not be held *as true*. Such nonstandard cases involve a kind of self-deception: To believe the thing one wants to believe, one must hide from oneself that the grounding of one's belief is a non-truth-centered motive. So either through drugs, hypnosis, or repression one must forget one's motives for holding the belief and come to believe – or at least take for granted – that one's belief really is truth centered.[14]

Williams claims, rightly in my view, that rational beliefs are caused by the reasons which are their grounds. The rationality of a species is constituted (in part at least) by its propensity to believe what there are grounds for believing; that is, a belief which is a reason for holding another belief can also be, for a member of such a species, the cause of his having that second belief. So one requires no special epistemic volitional or conative condition, such as a desire to believe only true propositions, to account for a rational being's having or accepting well-grounded beliefs. But Williams sees no analogy between reasons for belief and reasons for action. In respect to action he shares the orthodox Humean view, that the recognition of a belief as true could not explain an action without a related desire.[15]

However, there does seem to be at least one clear instance of an action commitment following directly from holding a belief. Suppose that Alan believes that today is Wednesday. Presumably an orthodox Humean such as Williams would insist that, without some desire to tell the truth, inform, be helpful, and so forth, this belief has no relation to action; in his terms it provides no reason for action. But this would be strange. A reasonable onlooker who heard Alan tell Betty that it was Tuesday, knowing that Alan believed it to be Wednesday, would certainly suppose that as a competent adult speaker of English, Alan had some other belief committing him to saying, "Tuesday." He would hardly know what to make of it if Alan insisted that, since he lacked any relevant desire, his believing that it was Wednesday provided no reason at all to refrain from saying, "Tuesday." If Alan asked, "What has the one to

26

do with the other?" the onlooker would take him to be joking, crazy, or not to understand the words he was using.

Of course, believing that it is Wednesday does not commit Alan to saying so every moment of the day; he can reasonably keep quiet. But it does commit him (1) to refraining from saying anything inconsistent with his belief, (2) to denying that it is any day other than Wednesday in circumstances in which to remain silent would standardly be interpreted, according to the prevailing speech conventions, as assenting to such a proposition, and (3) to saying what he believes to be the case, should he give any further information on the subject. I call such commitments which derive immediately from belief *epistemic action commitments*. Failing to act in accordance with them provides grounds for supposing that Alan does not in fact hold the belief, or does not really grasp its implications, and therefore suffers from a defect either of understanding or of rationality. To rebut that supposition, Alan would have to point to other beliefs with countervailing action commitments overriding his epistemic ones. For instance, not everyone who tells a lie suffers from such a defect. Typically, a liar grasps that a particular belief calls for certain truthful utterances (which is why he can expect to be believed), but has some other belief – about what statements would serve his interests, perhaps – with an overriding action commitment of its own.

Epistemic action commitments may well derive from two conditions of human life: (1) the propensity of human beings, as rational creatures, to seek to have true beliefs, that is, from their 'truth-centered motives,' and (2) the social character of the quest for truth, which uses the resources of language. These conditions together would explain why a commitment to saying what one really believes is one of the constituents of rational epistemic and linguistic practice.

Typically, human beings are conscious and purposive manipulators of their world. Effective manipulation requires the capacity to grasp what really is possible and the conditions for actualizing the better. It is understandable, therefore, that a practical species which is also capable of social intercourse and collaboration would develop a practice of rational discourse which is truth centered, with just the kind of basic epistemic action commitments that I claim arise in our own linguistic practices. One might say then that a basic human interest in truth is a necessary constituent of our practical nature, but this would not at all be the same as saying that there is a universally held desire to prosecute the quest for truth. An interest of this kind might be represented, perhaps, as a kind of ideally rational desire, but only in the sense that practically rational beings who understood their own nature would see that their beliefs about themselves committed them to truth telling.

This suggested connection between belief, truth telling, and practice points to what is perhaps the most fundamental difference between the Humean view and my own. For Hume and his present-day followers, the perceiving mind is at best a data bank in which sense-impressions are recorded against future recall for profitable employment. Hume himself saw mental events as gradually decaying motions, initiated by impact on a sense organ. His modern disciples repudiate the physiology no doubt, but they still understand perceptions as interest-neutral and motivationally inert. This permits a sharp distinction between theory and practice, belief and action, indicative and imperative. Belief alone could never lead to action just because belief reflects a world unrelated to human interests and purposes. And because of this, some desire, some indication of human purpose independent of the account given of the world, is always necessary to explain action.

By contrast, the perceiving mind is envisaged, in the present theory, not as a passive, neutral recipient of imprints, but as being already equipped or formed with basic interests, affective responses, or propensities that structure the world it apprehends. Our mode of existence as a practically rational species ensures that our beliefs and theories about the world are informed throughout by basic human interests. We are equipped with species-preserving propensities that enable us to form concepts, such as food, copulation, and male and female, without which we should be unable to act rationally and in ways appropriate to these interests. The human mind reaches out to make intelligent use of the *noumenon*, the "raw stuff out there," human animality included, mastering it by imposing its cognitive order upon it. Accordingly, to the degree that the world can be described at all, it cannot be divorced from the interests which the perceiving mind has in it, and which shape the concepts in terms of which it is apprehended. Such an epistemology will not accept, therefore, the sharp Humean distinctions noted above, and has no difficulty in accommodating the thought that gerundival sentences, of the form "Φ is the thing to do," are not simply hidden imperatives, but are genuinely propositional and may be implied by descriptive accounts of the world.

This account of the practical interests that inform our apprehension of reality is not a way of smuggling in Humean free-floating wants by a back door. Agents are said by the Humean to bring such wants to a world which confronts them ready-made as a datum. But the Humean description of a wanter confronting such a world already takes for granted the concepts in terms of which such wants are formulated. Objects, such as tables, for instance, are located in a world of cups, fluids, and so forth, and given a basic interest of human beings as drinkers in controlling the location of fluids, cups must rest on horizontal and not inclined planes. Nothing, therefore, that slopes sharply can count as a table. So far from recording a passive impression of how the world is, describing something as a table tells us how things stand in this part of the world in relation to such basic and enduring concerns. So our beliefs and theories, as well as our actions, have a practical bent. For that reason, they cannot be arbitrary. Just because our manipulative practice is intelligent, involving thought and planning, the world we conceptually constitute has to be congruent with the *noumenon*. Imagination, invention, and creativity, exercised characteristically in the devising of theories, are therefore constrained by practical regulative considerations, by truth and consistency, that is, by conditions of epistemic rationality required by just those manipulatory interests for the sake of which we reach out, both cognitively and practically, to grasp and master reality.

## 3. Towards a general account of rational action

Thus far I have argued that no personal affirmation is required for beliefs to yield epistemic action commitments. But these may be thought to be very special cases. For the remainder of the vast range of our action commitments – political, religious, selfish, or altruistic – some kind of personal affirmation or active commitment to an end may still be thought necessary. After all, one may understand that friends help one another when in need, and one may believe that Alan is one of one's friends and is in need, yet it may be thought nevertheless that no commitment to help Alan follows from this, unless one is also committed to friendship by some kind of personal affirmation or by virtue of having a pro-attitude to friendship, or affirming that friendship is a good thing.

Julius Kovesi has pointed the way to a truer understanding of our action commitments (without, however, using this term). According to Kovesi, it is neither a personal affirmation of the goodness of friendship nor a pro-attitude to it that is required to generate the action commitment, but simply a belief that one is properly described as a friend. "In analysing the concept [of a friend] we work out what is entailed in being a friend. . . . And when I am a friend, I have to act out in my life the implications of the concept."[16] So for Kovesi the beliefs (i) that I am properly described as a friend and (ii) that a friend helps a friend (which follows from the concept of a friend) together generate a commitment for me to help a friend in need.

Kovesi shares my conviction that relations of consistency among beliefs are capable of generating action commitments. To be a friend, one must act like a friend. A friend is someone who entertains beliefs concerning the nature and value of friendship and believes that certain identifiable people are his friends, who experiences appropriate emotions, such as grief at a friend's misfortune and joy in his success, who recognizes the action commitments implied by the relevant beliefs and does the appropriate things. The commitments are entailed by one's actual beliefs concerning friendship, both general and specific ("Alan is my friend"). However, this is not at all like acting out the part of a friend because one wants to be true to the way one conceives of oneself. That would put one's self-conception altogether too close to the center of the action: It would be too much like saying that it is the desire to perform consistently with the notion of the friend one likes to think one is, and the desire not to have to give up that description, that motivates the friendly act. Acting for the sake of friendship is not necessarily acting because one wants anything at all, nor in order to do anything else but to act like a friend.

This analysis of friendship suggests three conditions for practical rationality.

(1) The rationality of a belief system depends on the consistency of the propositions held true. The beliefs constituting such a system will be both evaluative and descriptive (though, as we have seen, even nonevaluative ones, such as beliefs about days of the week, can have their action commitments). A belief that something is good or right or that this is more important than that, while evaluative, is nevertheless a belief to which a credent may be committed by other beliefs of his system, and the relations between them must satisfy standard consistency conditions.

(2) A further condition of practical rationality is that one acknowledges the action commitments implied by one's beliefs. Believing today is Wednesday does seem to commit us not to say, "Today is Tuesday." Now as one proceeds from the epistemic com-

mitments to moral, political, and religious ones, the implications become less tight; that is, they are more open to doubt and disagreement. Still, the language of 'implication' is not out of order. Someone who believed in an omniscient, benevolent, and omnipotent God would be committed to paying some heed to rules that He had provided for our good, and if one did not acknowledge this, there would be grounds, whatever one professed, for doubting whether one really held these beliefs and understood their implications. Of course, one may have contrary commitments as well (arising, perhaps, from the belief that God's paternalism takes all the fun out of life), but that would be quite consistent with the claim that certain religious beliefs imply certain action commitments.

Nevertheless, to be committed to the actions implied by a set of propositions one must not only grasp what they are, but also believe the propositions. A student of religion who knows what a Catholic is committed to by his beliefs – confession, attending mass, taking communion – is not himself committed to those actions merely by understanding the propositions. They must figure in his own belief system, not merely as beliefs about the meaning of other people's beliefs, but as propositions held true. By contrast, a pacifist conscript soldier not only knows well enough the action commitments of the soldier's role, he also knows that in one obvious sense he is himself a soldier, in a way that the student of religion is not himself a Catholic. The soldier's notion of civic duty may well support these commitments; so too will his broadly prudential belief that jail for refusing to obey orders would be unpleasant. Yet he also has beliefs committing him not to be a soldier that nullify the commitment that follows simply from his believing that he is one. The prudential consideration, however, would not be so easily nullified and generates its own commitment not to make a stand on pacifist principle. (Action commitments are not necessarily heroic: Whether they are heroic or craven depends on the beliefs from which they derive.) So he has a conflict of commitments.

A conflict of commitments does not imply, however, that one must make a reasonless choice, nor is it like being confronted by a contradiction or a paradox. One does not have to choose one horn of a logical dilemma. It is more like deciding what to believe when there is some evidence in support of one theory and some of another, yet both cannot be true. The conflict is set in the context of a set of wider beliefs, and the materials for its resolution are to be looked for from among these. Precisely because the rationality of an action is taken to depend on its consistency with the whole of one's belief system, an action commitment arising from one belief can be overridden only by one arising from another. One belief may be rationally preferred on account, perhaps, of some further regulative belief which commits one to this ordering of commitments rather than the converse or on account of the key role of a belief in the system, such that to surrender this one would be to leave the rest in tatters. A rational belief system will involve, then, a reasoned ranking of commitments; but it should not be supposed that 'ranking' is something different from working out what one's existing beliefs commit one to.

Not all such conflicts are capable of resolution, however, within an existing belief structure. Someone who held that certain beliefs implied absolute action commitments would be in trouble when those commitments clashed. But equally, someone understanding his belief commitments as absolute could be in similar trouble. It is arguable that for just this reason absolute commitments of either kind are irrational. Conflicting action commitments are not so different, then, from conflicting belief commitments. In both cases, coping with conflicting commitments is a process of minimizing the damage done to one's total belief structure, in acknowledging this commitment and not that as the one requiring action or belief in this situation. Admittedly, it is not always easy to know what is the thing to do, but then, it is not always easy to decide what to believe, even in those temples of epistemic rationality, the physics laboratory and the jury room.

(3) The third condition for practical rationality is consistency between action commitments and action. There is no problem with the idea that an action may be inconsistent with an action commitment. Alan's murdering Betty would be prima facie inconsistent with his belief that his part in her pregnancy commits him to looking after her, and we should expect him to abandon the project when this was pointed out to him, unless he could point to an overriding commitment. Otherwise we might properly conclude either that he did not really appreciate that his beliefs did indeed commit him to looking after Betty or that he didn't grasp what looking after someone really amounted to.

There is, however, another kind of inconsistency between action commitment and action which is notoriously problematic, namely, the problem of weakness of will. A smoker who is trying to kick the habit is committed, by his belief that his immediate unpleasant cravings would be assuaged, to lighting a cigarette.

Suppose, however, that he also has beliefs about smoking-induced diseases which commit him to not doing so, and that he has, further, more centrally grounded beliefs, about the relative importance of short-term craving assuagement and a long and healthy future, which commit him overall to abstain. The akratic person is unable to attend to these more centrally grounded commitments; his attention is dominated, instead, by the commitments of the beliefs associated with his immediate sensations. And this is irrational precisely because he has beliefs within his own belief structure, committing him not to act in accordance with the ones that dominate his attention. But precisely because he is acting on the commitments of a belief, what he does, though irrational, must count as action, and not as a bit of automatic behavior generated by the somatic cues referred to as "cravings."

The way in which an akratic action is rationally defective as a volition can be adequately captured within the present model of rational action: Its defect arises from the act's conforming only partially to the agent's action commitments. And this is analogous to a kind of irrationality in belief, such as when a jealous lover, attending to only some of his belief commitments, misinterprets the behavior of his beloved as infidelity. Explaining akrasia, whether of action or of belief, requires no resort to a faculty of will captured by a desire which overwhelms the cognitive faculty. It requires only that a person's cognitive faculty can malfunction, whether as a result of nicotine addiction or jealousy, and select irrationally from among his commitments.

It may be thought, however, that the forming of an intention, without the simultaneous performance of the act intended, is a more recalcitrant volitional phenomenon. To make up one's mind to do something tomorrow is not, after all, to act on an action commitment, just because, so far, nothing has been done. But this, too, can be captured within this belief-centered action-commitment schema. Forming an intention to Φ tomorrow can be analyzed within the schema as (1) recognizing the commitment arising from one's present beliefs that Φ is the thing to be done tomorrow, (2) believing at the same time that one will in fact Φ when the time comes, and (3) believing that one will do it just because one will still hold the beliefs committing one to Φ. Forming an intention thus includes a prediction about how one will see one's action commitments when one actually comes to acting on them. Someone who says, "I intend to do it, but I don't know whether I will when it comes to the point," is doubting whether

33

the belief he has formed at the present point in his deliberations will remain firm. Or he may know himself to be weak-willed.

## 4. Desires and commitments

Whereas the paradigm of rational action for the Humean is an agent's efficient satisfaction of his desire, my own focus has been on acting in accordance with one's commitments. It remains to be considered whether the desire model can be translated without loss into the commitment model.

Because the Humean's conception of desire is not homogeneous, it is necessary to understand how the commitment model relates to several distinct types of desires that appear in Humean accounts. Thomas Nagel, for example, has argued that many discussions of desire confuse what he calls "motivated" and "unmotivated desires."[17] As Nagel depicts them, unmotivated desires such as hunger "simply assail us." By contrast, Nagel holds that motivated desires "are *arrived at* by decision after deliberation."

> Hunger is produced by lack of food, but is not motivated thereby. A desire to shop for groceries, after discovering nothing appetizing in the refrigerator, is on the other hand motivated by hunger.[18]

Consequently, Nagel argues that whereas unmotivated desires do not require any "rational or motivational explanation," motivated desires do.

Consider, then, Nagel's unmotivated desire for food. On both his and the orthodox Humean account, such a desire seems primitive: The explanation of the rational action of procuring food starts with the desire for it, adds a set of beliefs about how and where to find it, and then shows that the action was instrumentally efficient to the satisfaction of the desire. But suppose instead that, recognizing by certain familiar somatic cues, or maybe just by looking at the clock, that it is time for lunch, one forms the belief that one would enjoy food; one is committed accordingly to eating or to taking whatever steps would lead to it. Acting from a desire to eat amounts, in my terms, to acting in the way to which one is rationally committed by having the belief that one would enjoy eating and by one's other beliefs about the state of the food-providing world. To be sure, this is not the sort of commitment that takes a heroic effort to live up to, but I do not mean to suggest by "commitment" something necessarily opposed to inclination. Indeed, precisely because I want to include within this explanatory frame-work inclinations to bring about envisaged states of affairs, it is important that it should not be so opposed.

An action commitment is a course of action appropriate to be-lief, and seeking food to eat is standardly appropriate when one believes that one is hungry. One can be wrong about that, of course; one may have misinterpreted the somatic cue, as when someone *feels* hungry when the real trouble is a peptic ulcer. Still, given the mistaken belief that one is hungry, it is standardly appro-priate to seek food. One's belief commits one to doing so, even though it may not really be the thing to do.

But there are other nonstandard cases. For someone who is fast-ing for the sake of his health or on account of some religious belief, the appropriate response to the belief that he is hungry might be to watch television to take his mind off the unpleasant gastric sensa-tions. There are two possibilities here, too. Recognizing the sensa-tions of hunger, one might well believe (and rightly) that one would enjoy eating but also believe that, for overriding reasons, eating is not the thing to do. That would be a case of conflicting commitments. But someone who was truly devout might well be-lieve that, however hungry, he would not enjoy eating in the light of his commitment to fasting. Embedded in a nonstandard frame-work of beliefs which undermine the standard expectation that eating would be enjoyable, the bodily sensation, though truly recog-nized as hunger, would simply not generate an action commitment to seek food.[19]

In contrast, then, to Humeans, and indeed to non-Humeans such as Nagel, I do not take unmotivated desires to be primitives in the explanation of rational action. They, too, presuppose belief. And the puzzlement one feels when confronted by instances of appar-ently intentional behavior to which, however, the agent seems com-mitted by no obviously relevant belief is better captured by an account in which unmotivated desires are not taken as primitives, and in which to have a desire is understood as to have a forward-looking, self-related belief implying certain action commitments. I have in mind the puzzlement we feel when we encounter instances of neurotic behavior, such as that of the compulsive handwasher. What is deviant about such a case is not the absence of a desire, but rather that there is a very strong desire that makes no sense. So far at least as the conscious beliefs of the subject are concerned, the action is not instrumental – if he claims that his object is to clean his hands, it doesn't affect his desire if one reminds him that he washed them only seconds ago. Characteristically, his beliefs are fabricated to make sense of his desire.

It may be objected, however, that a Humean explanation of an action need not be instrumental; the end need not be distinct from the action, but realized in the performance of it, as in playing games. The Humean might say that he desires the pleasure of the game, which is another way of saying that he enjoys playing it. And according to Humean motivational theorists, this means simply that he wants to play it, to go on playing it, and to do nothing instead.[20] This account of enjoyment, however, cannot distinguish the case of the compulsive handwasher from the akratic binge drinker. Since each has a desire not to be doing what he is actually doing, neither could be enjoying it. In fact, however, the drinker may be having a good time while it lasts, whereas, as Freud says of the handwasher, he has impulses that lead him "to actions the performance of which give him no enjoyment, but which it is quite impossible for him to omit."[21]

The compulsive's problem is that his desire seems unrelated to any expectation of enjoyment, or to any other explanatory belief. Accordingly, when the psychoanalyst sets out to diagnose the causes of free-floating anxieties and compulsive desires, he looks for the beliefs which make the patient's anxieties and compulsions comprehensible and his neurotic behavior appropriate to those beliefs. Apprised, as it were, of his unconscious beliefs, the patient can judge for himself whether these beliefs, and consequently the desires and emotions they evoke, are well grounded. This is the therapeutic strategy of enabling the patient to free himself from irrationality by first transforming nonrational behavior into irrational action; by bringing hitherto unconscious beliefs into consciousness, it exhibits the neurotic action as consistent with commitments hidden, as it were, in these beliefs. But once the patient discovers in what sense he is committed to his neurotic acts, he is encouraged to assess the consistency of these beliefs with the rest of his belief structure and to appreciate his belief commitment to abandon them as irrational beliefs, therefore to abandon his neurotic acts as inappropriate to his belief structure as a whole. So he comes to appreciate the irrationality of desires that are grounded in irrational beliefs, and, it is hoped, divests himself of them.

From an explanatory point of view, then, it seems inadequate to see any desires, including such basic ones as hunger, as primitives never requiring further explanation. Typically, of course, such unmotivated desires, as well as desires motivated by one's own well-being, pleasures, suffering, and so on, do require no further explanation. We understand well enough why hungry people eat and thirsty people drink. One strength of the Humean model is that it is tailor-made for these basic cases. It does not become apparent that such desires are constituted by beliefs about one's enjoyments, together with corresponding commitments, rather than being non-epistemic primitives, until the exceptional case arises when the relation between enjoyment and commitment is obscure.

As with all theories that understand desires as intentional, the present account is cognitive in the sense that it requires a desirer to be able to identify the object of desire by forming a belief about it. This condition is generally met by human adults; however, it seems inconsistent with our intuition that infants have desires. While we say of a newborn that it wants to be fed, it would be odd to claim that it believes it would enjoy it. Now just because it is implausible to ascribe beliefs to the neonate, it is indeed difficult to make sense of the presumption latent in the common account that the infant desires *something* – that it has an identifiable object or goal. In attributing desires to it, we are assimilating its behavior to the actions of rational agents, rather than, for instance, to the behavior of Venus flytrap plants, which we put down to mechanical responses to physical stimuli. But if the belief conditions that are standard in the rational-action model cannot be met by the infant, then intentionality, and therefore desire, cannot be present either. If the infant stops crying we suppose that "it has got what it wanted," but all that we are entitled to say is that it was formerly reacting in a programmed way to uncomfortable sensations in its digestive tract, whereas now it has stopped.[22] The residual element, felt homeostatic imbalances that trigger programmed patterns of behavior, are insufficient to do the explanatory work required of desire by the Humean model of rational action.

By contrast, the intuition that mature higher animals, such as dogs, are desiring agents seems better grounded, just because it is at least plausible to suppose that they entertain beliefs about objects. It puts less of a strain on the concept of desire to say that a dog wants to be fed, or if, seeing its lead, or being invited in so many words "to go for a walk," it exhibits every sign of pleasurable anticipation appropriate to a desire. Given its greater range of responses to diverse familiar situations, it is more reasonable to suppose that a dog is equipped with a conceptual map by which it apprehends its world and which provides a field on which desires can be directed. Of course, as the infant's intellect develops and it begins to form concepts, it becomes as plausible a candidate for desire-attributions as the adult dog – but by then it will also have beliefs. Up to that point, however, all that one can say for sure is that the child has been behaving in ways that in a somewhat older child would indeed be the outcome of beliefs about the proper interpretations of its own inner sensations and experiences, which could properly be called "desires." But in the case of the newborn all one can reasonably say is that it is responding standardly to a primitive, unconceptualized experience – to a homeostatic imbalance.

Responses to unconceptualized stimuli of this sort are not confined to neonates. There are people of whom we say, in exasperation, "He doesn't know what he wants." A state of discontent, crossness, or anger generated by certain somatic cues or by a state of anxiety which may be accounted for by an organic chemical imbalance and remedied by purely physical treatment, is not properly described as a desiring state or even as a pro- or a con-attitude. This is not however because it has a physical cause, but because the subject does not know what he desires or what it is that he has an attitude towards. For that he must have beliefs about the object of his desire, know under what description he wants it, and be able to identify a form of action to which it commits him – enjoyment seeking, fear allaying, pain removing, and so on. Only then could his desire enter into a rational explanation of his behavior as intentional action. With no intentional object in the patient's belief structure, there are only somatic stimuli and physical emotive responses, such as chronic depression, but nothing that could figure in a rational explanation of action. Such cues may figure in rational action, too, but as the causes of the subject's belief implying some action commitment, which he is able to interpret and identify within the resources of his belief system, as a desire for an identifiable and distinguishable $x$.

I have argued so far (i) that no desires are primitives in the explanation of action, (ii) that Nagel's "unmotivated desires" as well as "motivated" ones regarding one's own well-being, pleasure, enjoyment, and so forth can generally be best understood as self-regarding beliefs and their action commitments, taken jointly, and (iii) that some Humean "desires" (for example, the desires of infants) do not qualify as action commitments on my account because they are not implied by beliefs. And for precisely that reason they cannot figure in explanations of action as *rational*. However, I differ from the Humean on another count. I claim not only that some desires cannot be expressed as action commitments but that many action commitments cannot plausibly be expressed in the language of desire. "I am hungry" or "I enjoy playing pushpin" are not the only sorts of belief that generate action commitments. Limiting the role of desire in the explanation of rational action seems a real strength, for we are no longer forced to posit a desire to explain every action. Someone who believes that it is right to help the poor has a reason (an action commitment) to do so whenever he can, and this reason sufficiently explains his doing so. But the Humean has to get a desire in somewhere.

Several candidates are available to him. The most obvious for his purpose is the immediate desire to help the poor. And to be sure, sometimes people help the poor because they expect to enjoy doing it or to be miserable if they don't. But one may also do it grudgingly because one believes it is the decent thing to do – a moral duty, we might say – knowing that, with this person at this time, one has no desire whatsoever to do it. The Humean may say that the agent desires to be good, to do the right thing, or to maintain consistency between his conception of himself and his actions. But all these desires seem quite otiose, extra wheels speculatively inserted to keep the creaky philosophical model running. The recognition of something as good or right, or as profitable or health giving, is quite sufficient to explain why a person who believes it to be so believes also that it is the thing to do, and to explain why he does it.

The curious persistence and apparent unshakability of the Humean model is due not only to its being tailor-made for a wide range of cases in which reasoning is clearly instrumental, but also to a less obvious feature. Adding some general motivating desire to what might be an already adequate explanation does not obviously falsify the account, especially if it is hard to tell whether such a desire is really there or not. If its presence cannot be tested, it is too easy to declare it to be necessary.

## 5. Acting rationally

The conditions for rational action implied to this point by the theory are arguably too strong. I have appeared to suggest that when acting rationally one must always be fully aware of one's beliefs and commitments. Certainly, such cases are important instances of rational action: One deliberates about them and acts with one's commitments firmly before one's mind. But if this condition were necessary to rational action, habitual action, where the beliefs committing one to the action are not reviewed each time, could not also be rational. Fortunately, the theory does not require so strong a condition. Since rational action is action grounded in the action commitments implied by one's belief system, to include habitual action within the realm of the rational requires only the concession that one can act on the basis of a belief without actually thinking about it – without its being present, that is, to the conscious mind. This concession is really not very demanding: Rational action needs no more deliberation than we habitually show in making for a door instead of trying to push through a wall.

Of course, habitual action can be irrational, too.[23] Rationality breaks down when, through inattention, a person mistakes the cues that trigger the routine performance or allows the habit to govern action when the routine is inappropriate, given the full range of his commitments. Forming a habit may still be perfectly rational, however, as a condition for efficient action, provided it includes a monitoring capacity to ensure that the routine will not prevail regardless of any countervailing action commitment whatsoever that the agent may have. Someone accustomed to turning right at a certain crossroad on the way to work acts irrationally when, through absence of mind, he fails to turn left when he is going on holiday. Because he has failed to organize his attention properly, his acts do not correspond to those to which he is committed by what, on reflection, he would recognize as a belief regulating the habit overall, that is, that today is the day for going on holiday, not for going to work.

Some philosophers, while accepting that habitual action may be rational, make it a condition of an act's rationality that the agent be able to give at least an *ex post facto* account of the beliefs that committed him to the action. But this seems much too strong a requirement. A craftsman may know very well how to meet the various contingencies encountered in his practice, based upon true beliefs, acquired through long experience, concerning the properties of his materials, and yet be quite unable to articulate those beliefs. There may be abundant evidence, despite that incapacity, that he understands what he is about, that he can recognize his beliefs when they are put to him, and that if need be he can give his work his full attention, rationally suiting his performance to a conscious grasp of the problem.

Freudians have gone much farther than this, however, insisting that you can act on the basis of beliefs of which you are totally unaware and indeed might not even recognize if they were pointed out to you. Their explanations of many habits, slips of the tongue, and so forth depend on showing them to be grounded in unconscious beliefs which commit the agent to performing them; they thus cash out as actions, satisfying at least minimum rationality conditions. It is an advantage of the present analysis of such behavior that it captures precisely the extent to which it is rational, and where its irrationality is located. Because the agent is committed to it by his unconscious beliefs, it counts as action, and not as nonrational behavior. If it is irrational, it is not because it is habitual and nondeliberate, but because the unconscious beliefs are not well grounded and are inconsistent with other, better-grounded beliefs the subject has.

The idea that beliefs may be unconscious does have its own problems. One can be reasonably sure that a person does have the belief attributed to him if he is able to summon it up into consciousness and report on it, or at least to recognize it as his own. But this is what the psychoanalyst's patient is very often unable to do. Of course, even the testimony of someone off the analyst's couch may be suspect. People can have commitments which override their epistemic action commitments and result in their misreporting their beliefs. The trouble with psychoanalytic attributions of belief is that there is often no evidence independent of the explanandum to support the attribution of the unconscious belief. Just as a very general desire, for example, the desire to act rationally, adds nothing to a Humean explanation of action in the absence of independent evidence that the agent has that desire, so it cannot be sufficient to explain an irrational action that it would appear rational supposing the agent held a certain belief. There have to be independent grounds for believing that he does. The present theory commits one neither to support nor to reject the possibility of unconscious beliefs. But supposing that the Freudian can provide independent evidence for their existence, the theory provides an explanatory framework into which his account would comfortably fit.

## 6. Conclusion

A false theory that has been dominant for a long period may inform many of our intuitions, and it may seem obvious when a better account strikes us as implausible. The aim of this chapter has been to undermine in several ways the false intuitions that the objectionable Humean model has so long sustained. Desires, according to my account, are not primitives in explaining action; the case of the obsessional neurotic strongly suggests that free-floating desires unrelated to more basic beliefs could not provide a foundation for an adequate explanation of action. So far from being primitive, desires are actually reducible to forward-looking, self-related beliefs and the action commitments they imply; in a whole range of instances they are not even necessary to explain action. Even where Humean desires seem most at home, they relate to actions to which we are committed by basic beliefs about enjoyment or painful experience. The existence of the vague desires the Humean summons up to sustain his theory in less favorable cases is usually impossible to establish independently of the action to be explained; by contrast, the beliefs on which I rely as underpinning the paradigmatic Humean desires, such as the belief of the hungry man that he will enjoy food, are hardly open to doubt. And lastly, the theory advanced here as an alternative to the orthodoxy has the further merit that it points towards a unified theory of rational action and belief.

# 3

# Reasons in conflict: Quandaries and consistency

## 1. Preference theory and cognitivism

In this chapter I shall pick up the question, referred to briefly in Chapter 1, whether there are formal conditions for deciding and acting rationally in situations in which an agent's beliefs commit him to actions which are mutually excluding. Can someone act rationally if the courses he perceives as available in a given situation are ranked differently according to whether he considers them in the light of one evaluative belief rather than another?

The difference between principles, values, and such other kinds of evaluative beliefs as there may be, which was a leading topic in Chapter 1, need not concern us much in this chapter. Unless one postulated a lexical ordering of commitments, for example, that the action commitment deriving from any person-oriented evaluative belief necessarily overrode any deriving from, say, an outcome-oriented belief, similar problems would arise whether conflict occurred between two principles, two values, or a principle and a value. If, for example, in the manner of Robert Nozick, rights commitments were thought to be absolute side-constraints on other kinds of action commitment, then the particular form of the commitment would indeed be significant for the way in which conflicts between it and other commitments could be rationally resolved. Even so, since conflicts might still arise between different rights commitments, a theory of practical rationality would still need to offer guidance on the resolution of such conflicts. I do not share Nozick's view that rights always have priority. Nevertheless the formal account of conflict resolution offered below would provide a way of setting out the problem even for an absolutist. It also shows how it could not be resolved on his terms, should there be more than one absolute side-constraint. And that suggests that Nozick's cannot be a theory of practical reason.

The theory of conflict resolution offered in this chapter depends on a notion of a preference function drawn from decision-theoretic models. The cognitivist account of rational action offered in Chapter 2, however, may seem to raise difficulties for such a theory. Preference, choice, and decision, the favored categories of standard decision theory, all have a strongly volitional flavor, volition being taken as different from belief, and related to motivating desires. According to Hobbes, for instance, the will represents the last desire in deliberation; for others it registers the strongest desire, desires being understood as something like mechanical forces. Understood in these terms, a preference would be a relation between desires which would issue, in appropriate situations, in actual choices or decisions, where the agent did what most attracted him or what he most desired. I shall argue, however, that preference, choice, and decision can easily be dissociated from this action model and still be usefully employed in giving an account of rational action within a basically cognitive theory.

## 2. Consistency and conflicts of action commitments

A number of distinguished philosophers have insisted of late that complete consistency cannot be a condition of practical rationality, because some moral conflicts cannot be eliminated. In Bernard Williams's words, "[It] must be a mistake to regard a need to eliminate conflict as a purely rational demand."[1] In Williams's view, there can be no guarantee, the world being as it is, that an agent could not be put in a situation where whatever he did would be wrong – and this due to no defect of rationality but to a wrong embedded in the situation itself that may or may not be the agent's fault. According to Williams, Agamemnon at Aulis, committed by his role as commander-in chief to the horrifying deed of sacrificing his daughter to placate the goddess in order to save his army, was caught in a dilemma of this tragic kind.

Stuart Hampshire characterizes the traditional view that he and Williams are criticizing as follows:

> The tradition is that to know why the moral claims that seem to us intuitively right are really right is to be able to show that they form a coherent system. Then the moral claims have the backing of reason. . . . [Conflicts] between claims are rendered intelligible by . . . [a] theory, which explains why the conflicts must arise and how they are to be solved. . . . [This traditional view] associates rationality in moral judgment with coherence, which in turn implies an absence of irresoluble conflicts between moral claims.[2]

44

But unhappily:

> ... no sufficient reason of any kind is on occasion available to explain a decision made after careful reflection in a situation of moral conflict; ... there is unavoidably a breakdown of clear reasoning in choosing what the future is to be, because the reflective and second-order desires which, coupled with beliefs, guide the choices point to goals which are irreconcilable in the actual world. ... If there is no valid theory to serve as the ground of a choice between irreconcilable dispositions, different choices will tend to be made by different men. ... In the history of an individual the choices that he makes in conflict between duties and reflective inclinations and purposes will constitute his own character as an individual. The causes explaining his choices will not all be found in rational assent to a valid theory.[3]

I suggested in Chapter 1 that the theoretical possibility that at some time the arguments may run out may have to be conceded; then, if different men make different choices, there may be no way of deriving, from an ultimate principle acceptable to any rational being, a demonstration that one choice is rationally cogent and another unacceptable. (I shall say more about objectivity in practical reason in Chapter 4.) But however that may be, there is no necessary connection, of the kind that Hampshire seems to suppose, between the unavailability of a universally cogent argument, and the possibility of coherence in the practical judgments and actions of a given individual. There are certainly decision-theory models that formulate conditions for this internal consistency, and they do not all postulate what Williams calls "a currency," such as pleasure or utility, in terms of which the rational agent is required to maximize. The Hampshire/Williams type of ethical theory is more sensitive, no doubt, to the agony of moral dilemmas than is act-utilitarianism, but it leaves the process by which the rational chooser arrives at action decisions in such cases quite unillumi-nated. Moreover, in asserting the unavoidability of wrong-doing and the consequent appropriateness of remorse, it gives a false account, in my view, of the state of moral consciousness to which the conscientious chooser in such a case must reconcile himself.

The decision theory I shall propose later in this chapter tries, then, to show (1) how the traditional requirement of consistency in practical rationality, which Hampshire believes to be impossible, can nevertheless be met by a rational chooser and (2) that it is consistent for a rational decision maker with a settled scheme of values, principles, and role commitments not merely to make decisions when action commitments conflict, but also to decide in one instance in accordance with the action commitment of one value, principle, or role, in another instance in accordance with another, and in a third to find a compromise that partially satisfies both. Someone for whom a particular value or principle had priority over the whole range of possible situations would indeed be rigid, obsessed, or fanatical; rationality requires consistency of some sort, but not necessarily of that sort.

## 3. Roles as sources of action commitments

For the sake of expository convenience, I shall develop the theory of conflict resolution that follows in terms of role conflict, rather than of general values and principles, such as happiness or truth telling. For the action commitments of roles can often be more sharply contrasted in conflict situations than can those of other kinds of evaluative beliefs. The dilemmas of Orestes, Agamemnon, and (my own favored example) Lucius Junius Brutus, the Roman consul who sentenced his own sons to death for rebellion, are grounded precisely in the commitments of the well-defined and competing roles with which the agents are identified. Each role is informed, as it were, by a characteristic value or principle – filial piety, military duty, civic duty, patriotism, paternal care – and to be virtuous in that role is to be guided in action by this principle or value.

It is a common feature of these stories that, in the situation confronting the hero, he identifies strongly with each of his conflicting roles; that is, he believes not only that each role implies a strong commitment to action, but also that each of those actions would, in the absence of another similarly strong commitment, be the thing for *him* to do. These are not like disaffected conscript soldiers who recognize but dissociate themselves from the commitments of their social role; the heroes' roles are internalized, generating beliefs about their own personal action commitments. We do not need to ask, therefore, whether the hero's view of his commitment would be shared by another member of his society, for we are not using the idea of a role as a sociologist might, to explain an agent's behavior in terms of socially defined expectations. What is important for my present theory is that a rational agent believes himself to be the focus of a coherent set of action commitments deriving from his relations with other people, which he sees as governed by standard rules and expectations he accepts as warranted. It is his own understanding of his roles, not those of other people, that immediately generates his beliefs about the thing to do. An actor playing Hamlet may conform to the stereotypical understanding of the melancholy Dane, but he can also play the role in the light of his own different understanding of the part – perhaps to the disgust and outrage of the theater critics. My account of role commitments would be quite consistent, therefore, with someone's having a highly idiosyncratic idea of what some particular role committed him to do, and even with someone's inventing a new role for himself.

It is also a feature of the classical stories that when roles compete, neither role is peripheral; both are deeply implicated in the problem situation which generates the tragic dilemma. I shall speculate, however, on what such a person as Lucius Junius Brutus might have done in other situations in which, though his roles were the same, their saliences for him were different, or, as we might say, the relative weights he attached to them in those different situations varied. I hope to elicit from these examples, then, a model of consistency in action where conflicts can be resolved, now in accordance with one kind of action commitment, now in accordance with another, and to give some formal account of what it would be like to take a rational decision in cases where each of two or more conflicting commitments seems to possess lexical priority.

## 4. A decision theory for resolving quandaries

The decision-theoretical model of practical rationality postulates a chooser, confronted by options he is capable of ranking, either strongly, in terms of preference, or weakly, in terms of preference and indifference. Behind this notion of "preference" there commonly lurks, however, the further notion that options are ranked according to the degree they are expected to satisfy desires. Given the Humean model of rational action, this is plausible enough. Someone who prefers hard- to soft-centered chocolates simply expects to enjoy them more and, in the absence of any contrary belief, is committed to choosing them as the ones to eat. And this is quite compatible with the cognitive account of desire offered in Chapter 2. The decision-theoretical notion of preference does not have to be taken, however, to interpret every preference in terms of enjoyment prospects, nor should "preferred to . . ." be taken to mean "yielding, or expected to yield, more enjoyment than . . ." All that is required for the formal model is that preferences satisfy the conditions for an ordering, that is, transitivity, completeness, and asymmetry (or symmetry of indifference), and a disposition to decide for what ranks highest. The chooser acts rationally if he acts to attain the most preferred position in this sense; tastes and desires are only some among the great variety of considerations that can generate an ordering of the required kind.

The second idea which is important for the decision-theoretical model is that of the trade-off. If more than one action commitment is relevant to a decision, and the ordering of options is not settled conclusively by a priority rule over the relevant range, there must be a trade-off between them. For this there must be a disposition to surrender one commitment in favor of another in some consistent way. That is not to demand, necessarily, that there be some objectively valid theory from which the correct rate of exchange be derived, if by that is meant that the rational agent must be able to demonstrate conclusively that his is the only reasonable rate. Suppose, however, that someone, a humane gardener, believes that, as a general rule, it is more important not to hurt people than to avoid damaging grass by walking on lawns, but, nevertheless, there are some near-perfect lawns that, in his view, ought to be protected even at the cost of some small hurt to the feelings of someone thoughtlessly trampling on them. The gardener clearly has a trade-off rate between degrees of damage to lawns and hurting human beings, and it is a rate that he might be able to defend, in a rough sort of way, by reference to other beliefs that he has, for example, the relative time it takes to create a perfect lawn and the duration of hurt feelings. If accused of overreacting to the damage, he can find among his other beliefs grounds on which to defend his action as reasonable.

Hampshire recognizes the importance of the trade-off in rational decision making. He writes, of the Aristotelian balance between public and private life, that

> The pressing moral problems within this way of life are problems of priorities, which can equally well be thought of as trade-offs; how do I balance the moral claims of friendship against the duties of public life?[4]

But Hampshire claims that beyond such instances are moral conflicts where there is "no trade-off and no compromise and no striking of a balance." Such were the dilemmas, no doubt, in which, in Hampshire's view, Agamemnon and Orestes found themselves.

Hampshire is mistaken, however, in equating priorities and trade-offs. To trade one value against another one must see them as in a sense substitutable – more of one compensating for less of another. The options open to us meet our competing commitments in varying degrees, and to reach a rational decision – to do the best we can in difficult circumstances – we have to be able to set a rate of substitution between them over the relevant range. Unlike a market price, which is also a rate of substitution, this is, in one sense, a subjective rate, the rate at which I am prepared to trade off commitments of one kind against commitments of another. That can be done without our having to express the force of each in terms of some common currency, such as utility or money; there can be a foreign exchange market without a gold standard.

Of course, one may have reasons for setting one rate rather than another, and one may believe that the rate one hits upon is the only justifiable one. In that sense the rate may not be subjective. Substituting Terry's chocolates for Cadbury's, the consideration governing the rate of substitution will probably be thoroughly subjective, that is, the relative personal enjoyment one gets from one brand against the enjoyment derived from the other. Certainly, the fact that I enjoy Terry's more is an objective truth about me, but because it is about my preferences alone and, unsupported as it is by any reasons for them, is not assessable as an appropriate or reasonable preference that could bear on other people's choosing, it is properly called subjective.

There may be some value or principle, however, which, over some particular range and for some particular chooser at least, is not substitutable for some other. In given market conditions from some fungible resources $P$ one might choose to have $N$ apples or $M$ oranges or some combination in between, substituting at the market rate $N/M$. But if we can start spending from $P$ on neither oranges nor apples unless we have first bought a bag in which to carry them home, there is no personal substitution rate between bags and fruit over the range of one bag, even though there will be a *market* substitution rate (i.e., their relative prices). This is a case of lexical priority, where there can be no trade-off until the minimum condition has been satisfied. The no-compromise situations that Hampshire regards as discontinuous with the trade-off cases probably involve priorities of just this kind. The agony of Agamemnon's situation is that, in choosing a strategy as supreme commander, saving his army and the fleet takes priority absolutely over concern for his daughter Iphigenia. But his role of father commits him to a corresponding priority in reverse. Tragic conflicts are not just conflicts of commitment – that is happening all the time. They are conflicts in which, considered in turn, each of two values appears to have an absolute priority over the other.

## 5. The situational relativity of role commitments

Lucius Junius Brutus is celebrated by Livy in Book II of his history of the Roman Republic as the consul who, out of a sense of civic duty, sentenced his own sons to death for plotting to overthrow the Republic and restore the Tarquins. I shall take his as a paradigmatic case of role conflict and build on it a decision-theoretic model for a rational solution to such problems. Brutus's problem was a conflict between the commitments of consular office and paternal role. We may take it for granted that, austere republican though he was, he had some affection for his sons, too, but the point of the story is not so much the conflict between affection and duty as between the commitments deriving from the private family values and from the public values of the consular office. Throughout the example I leave Brutus's roles constant, changing only the decision situations into which they enter and their relative salience in those situations.

Brutus's first problem is to rank the possible actions open to him in different situations in the light of his two roles. I shall construct three such situations, specifying, to begin with, only the conditions relevant in each case to the role of consul, ignoring all action commitments implied by any other role.

### Situation I
As consul Brutus must deal judicially with two rebels, for whose offence the normal penalty would be death. He can entertain the following possible actions:

    I.1. Sentence them to death.
    I.2. Use his office and political influence to get them off lightly.
    I.3. Connive in their escape.

He ranks them, in terms of their adequacy in fulfilling the commitments of the consular role, in the order given above.

### Situation II
On his way to attending a Senate committee meeting, something occurs of a noncivic nature which would make him late

for the meeting if he stopped to attend to it. He has three options:

II.1. Ignore the distraction and arrive on time.
II.2. Attend to the other matter but first arrange to send a message to the Capitol instructing the committee to proceed without him.
II.3. Miss the meeting and attend to the other matter at once without delaying to send a message.

I suppose that he will rank the options, in terms of their adequacy to the commitments of his consular responsibilities alone, in that order.

### Situation III

Brutus is due to open a charity bazaar on the Martian Fields. As before, something crops up that would delay him if he attended to it. His options are similar to those in Situation II, and he ranks them, as before, in the order III.1, III.2, and III.3.

Suppose, now, that Brutus ranks these options not merely in independent sets, as above, but in a composite ranking, according not only to the success of each option in meeting the commitment of the role in its own particular context (i.e., its measure of role fulfillment) but also taking account of the gravity of that context from the consular point of view (i.e., of the salience of the role in that situation – of the extent to which consular values are implicated in it). Each option would be assessed, in relation to the others, as the product of these two variables. Brutus may consider, for instance, I.1 and III.1 do everything that his office requires of him in their respective situations; nevertheless, III.3, which is a total neglect of III.1, would still be a lesser dereliction than I.3, the corresponding neglect of I.1, because the consular role is less salient in the opening of charity bazaars than in administering justice. One can be a pretty good consul even though one opens few bazaars but would be a pretty bad one if one neglected one's judicial duties. So one would expect Brutus to rank I.1 above III.1, and I.3 below III.3, as ways of being a good consul.

Of course, this may not be so. Brutus may take an ultra-Kantian view, that since his reason for action is that it is a *duty* and not, for instance, a consequentially valuable action, any dereliction would be just as bad as any other: The content of the duty does not affect its status relative to other duties. I.1, II.1, and III.1 would then rank

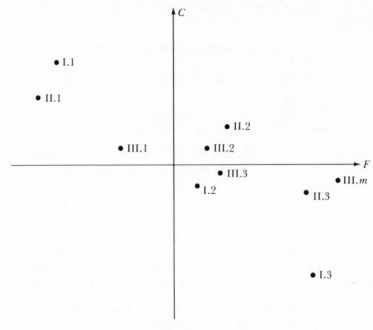

**Figure 1**

as equally satisfactory consular performances, and everything else would be equally unsatisfactory. But this would be an extreme and somewhat austere judgment; I suppose that even Brutus would have preferred to be the sort of consul who cut charity bazaars to being one soft on rebels.

Add to the stories, now, some reasons for Brutus's not fulfilling the commitments of his consular role, specifically reasons arising from his role as father which, in each case, would conflict with those commitments.

**Situation I:** The rebels are his sons.
**Situation II:** His sons (not the rebellious ones) are drowning in the Tiber, and need his assistance.
**Situation III:** He is expected at his son's birthday party.

Suppose that for each situation he now has three options, each of which can be located on a graph (Figure 1). On the $C$ coordinate is measured consular role fulfillment, that is, the product of the degree of success in meeting the role commitment and of its relative

52

salience in the particular situation. Fatherly role fulfillment is measured along the $F$ coordinate. The options in each situation are now as follows:

### Situation I

I.1. Sentence sons to death.
I.2. Use influence for light sentence.
I.3. Connive in sons' escape.

### Situation II

II.1. Arrive at committee on time, leaving sons to drown.
II.2. Find messenger; attempt rescue after delay; arrive late at meeting.
II.3. Rescue sons without delay; send no message; get soaking wet; miss meeting.

### Situation III

III.1. Open bazaar on time; miss party.
III.2. Put in appearance at party; send message to Martian Fields; arrive late for bazaar opening.
III.3. Miss bazaar altogether and go to party.

Observe that when Brutus ranks these performances as fulfilling to a greater or a lesser degree the commitments of a particular role, he does so according to his own evaluative beliefs about the nature of the role. But that is not to say that these beliefs are subjective, in the sense that Brutus's preference for one brand of chocolate over another is subjective. They are implied, in Brutus's judgment, by a complex of beliefs about what it means to be a Roman citizen, what the Republic stands for, the function of the family in Roman social life and the function of the paterfamilias within it, and so on. And these are not facts about Brutus, except in the trivial sense that anyone's believing any proposition $p$ is a fact about the believer. Brutus's beliefs about his roles are about objective facts in the world, what he takes to be the case whatever he or anyone else might think about it. Consequently, when Brutus ranks his options, he does so for anyone who occupies corresponding roles. Nor is it a matter of his *simply* preferring that others share his rankings; he believes that his beliefs about the Republic, the family, the paterfamilias, and so on are true beliefs, that anyone not sharing them is in error, and that they commit anyone who grasps them to the

53

same ranking of the options as the one he has arrived at. Admittedly, someone with a less exalted view of public office might have rather different beliefs about the correct ranking of the options. He and Brutus would then require a great deal of patience, good will, and a belief in the value of agreement rationally arrived at to have any hope of reaching it at all. However, their disagreement may not necessarily be attributable to the subjectivity of their evaluative beliefs, but rather to their incompleteness. The premises at their disposal may be simply insufficient for a determinate conclusion. But that is not to say that their differences are not about what is the fact of the matter.

Brutus has not yet been provided, in the theory, with a way of deciding between options that combine ways of meeting different commitments in varying degrees. It would always be rational for him to decide on some I.$m$ rather than on some I.$n$ if, while both equally satisfied his consular commitment, I.$m$ satisfied the fatherly one to a greater degree (i.e., if I.$m$ dominated I.$n$). But the postulated options are not like that. Brutus needs, then, the equivalent of the decision theorist's indifference curves, indicating at what rate Brutus considers that a failure to meet the commitments of one role would be just compensated for by a better performance in the other.

Pareto regarded the indifference curves of classical utility theory as contours on a hill of pleasure, rising as one moved in a positive direction away from the origin. A corresponding (but nonhedonic) application of that idea in the present analysis would be to say that, among options falling on different curves, any falling on a higher will fulfill the commitments of Brutus's roles, taken together, more satisfactorily than will any falling on a lower (i.e., closer to the origin). Each curve thus forms a boundary between options; any on one side would be more satisfactory than any on the other, just as every spot on one side of a contour line is higher than any on the other. I shall call these curves "commitment fulfillment boundaries." Their shapes and relative slopes will express, graphically and symbolically, the surrender value that Brutus attaches to his two roles, each expressed in terms of the other, and to the principles and values that inform them, when they are implicated in decision situations in varying degrees of salience and over different ranges of involvement. The structure of evaluative beliefs so mapped is a graphic profile of Brutus as a rational chooser.

Figure 2 shows such a structure; within the range depicted, Brutus can always trade off a better performance in one role against a

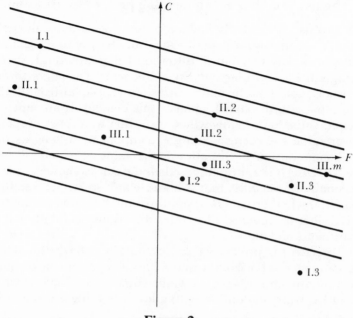

**Figure 2**

poorer in another. His ranking of the options within that range will
then be transitive and complete. Given such a configuration, there
could always be, in principle, some performance of $C$-type commitments which would just compensate for a failure to perform in $F$,
and conversely. I do not mean that some equally satisfactory option will always in fact be available, just that there is nothing
about the structure of Brutus's evaluative beliefs that rules it out
as impossible. An option III.$m$ on the same curve as III.2 would be
as acceptable as III.2; there just doesn't happen to be one – or at
least none that Brutus has thought of yet.

I have now exhibited how it can be rational for Brutus to prefer
I.1, the most thoroughly consular option of Set I, to I.2 and I.3 and
yet prefer II.2 to either II.1 or II.3 and III.2 to either III.1 or III.3.
Rational, that is, given his own understanding of the salience of
each of his role commitments and of the measure of its fulfillment
in each situation, along with his trade-off rate between those commitments. The consistency required by practical rationality is not,
then, a requirement that a given principle or value $C$ should always
take precedence over principle or value $F$.

## 6. The irrationality of intersecting preference thresholds

Livy's Brutus undoubtedly had a stricter sense of civic duty than my profile of him would suggest. One could hardly suppose that he would choose any way out of Situation I that would fall short of carrying out his consular duty in all its rigor. The curve through I.1, in short, could not be downward sloping. The horizontal $AB$ in Figure 3 passing through I.1 makes this evident. It amounts to a threshold value for $C$ below which no option would be acceptable, however large the corresponding $F$ component, so long as there existed some option in Situation I, the value of which fell on or above $AB$. On $AB$ are superimposed all the curves shown as joining it diagonally from *above;* that is because any option located to the right of I.1, whether on $AB$ or above it, must be more acceptable than I.1, since it provides at least the same minimal fulfillment of $C$ commitments and more of $F$.

Because Brutus prefers I.1 to any option lying below $AB$, no curve can cut the horizontal line $AB$: $AB$ represents a boundary separating any option with a $C$ value equal to or greater than the value of I.1, from any option with a lower $C$ value, irrespective of

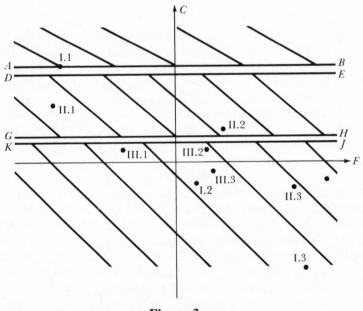

**Figure 3**

the values of $F$. All above $AB$ fulfill Brutus's roles, taken jointly, better than any below. There can be no trade-offs located below $AB$ so long as a point on or above $AB$ is attainable. Consequently, all the curves lying *below* $AB$ will merge into one line $DE$ on which they are all superimposed. Any point short of negative infinity on $AB$ will be preferred to any point on $DE$.

But just as $AB$ represents a threshold, so $DE$ is a ceiling. There will be options, of course, like II.1 and II.2, not in competition with I.1 which can be ordered on the curves subtended by $DE$. Still, there may be yet another threshold value, represented by $GH$, which may limit the trade-offs in this range just as $AB$ did in the higher range. $KJ$ will then constitute another ceiling, corresponding to $DE$. Using the Paretian analogy of "the hill of pleasure," $AB$, $DE$, $GH$, and $KJ$ are cliff faces bounding chasms; the brink of each cliff climbs as one travels east along it, and everything north of a chasm is preferred to everything south of it.

I have portrayed these horizontals as bounding chasms only for the sake of clarity of exposition and illustration. Chasms are not a necessary feature of the theory; indeed, if Brutus's preference structure is to be assumed to be complete, they cannot be permitted. But $AB$ and $DE$ can be concurrent; "contours" would then run off diagonally in both directions, their extensions parallel to the $F$ axis, all superimposed along $AB/DE$. This line would then represent a vertical precipice, the brink and the foot of which would both rise eastward along its entire length. No contour would cut it, despite appearances in two dimensions to the contrary, for the values would be different on each side of $AB/DE$.

Brutus could get along with a role-fulfillment preference structure of this sort; any option could be located, and any two options could be ordered by it. He can run into problems, however, if, in the pertinent range, the structure is either incomplete, so that some options are not determinately located on it, or if the structure manifests threshold values in two dimensions. Figure 4 is a case of an incomplete structure. Suppose the $C$ axis to represent respect for humanity, and the $F$ axis commitment to caring for one's children. $AB$ is a threshold level of respect (or disrespect) for humanity well above cannibalism. Normally we can satisfy our family responsibilities without falling so low. But suppose in a famine the only way to do it (I.$c$ in Figure 4) was to dish up the neighbor's children. With a threshold on $AB$ we simply couldn't do it, and we should leave our own children to starve (I.$x$). But with a corresponding threshold $DE$ for $F$, we couldn't do that either. We "wouldn't

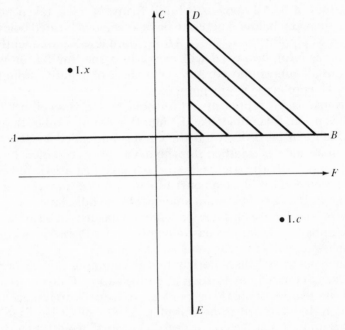

**Figure 4**

know what to do for the best," because we could entertain neither option as a possible course. Such a preference structure rules out a rational choice in such a situation.

Agamemnon's case, in which, according to Williams, whatever he did would be wrong, may be different. Suppose he had a preference structure that had a place for such horrendous possibilities, and was therefore complete; but suppose besides that it manifested thresholds in two dimensions. In Figure 5, $AB$ is the lower threshold of the commander's role ($C$), $RS$ of the father's ($F$). Point 1 on or above $AB$ represents sacrificing Iphigenia, thereby saving the army and the fleet. Point 2, on the right of $RS$, represents sending Iphigenia home to Clytemnestra but also losing the army and the fleet. Points 3, 4, and 5 are other options, such as holding ritual games with an outside chance of propitiating the goddess or trying to get another god on one's side by assiduous prayer. But because the chances of these strategies succeeding are very low, they can't compete with 1 and 2. (Otherwise, since they are ways of ensuring the safety both of his daughter and the troops, they would be fully

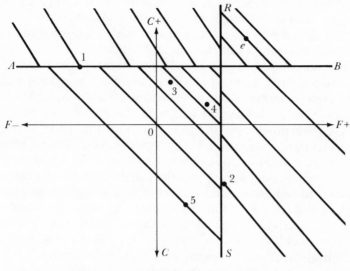

**Figure 5**

compatible with both of Agamemnon's role commitments, and would be located in the region of *e*, above both thresholds.)

We can now see how it is that whatever he does must seem to Agamemnon wrong. Any threshold signifies that he is committed to selecting any option above it rather than any below it. But since 1 and 2 each lie above one threshold but also below another, to choose either in response to one commitment is necessarily inconsistent with the other. Because his ordering of the options fails to satisfy the condition of asymmetry required for rational choice, while at the same time being in no wise a condition of indifference, he has no way of choosing the lesser of two evils, of making the best of a bad job.

## 7. Making the best of a bad job

The stark and dramatic quandaries of Greek mythology highlight the dynamics of moral conflict but seem somewhat removed from the day-to-day experience of the politicians of modern democracies, of whose dilemmas Bernard Williams has written with such percipience. These arise as much within a role as between some value specific to a role, such as concern for military security, and something nonspecific, such as simple honesty. I have developed the theory so far as though each role were informed by one single principle related to its *telos* or point, which supplied the moral structure or coherence of the role. When that is the case, one can say with confidence that in some given situation the role requires this action or that, even when there is no book of rules listing the appropriate responses. But roles are rarely so obligingly simple. Williams rightly claims that a minister's commitment, as a member of a government, simply to get on with the job of governing, can quite often require of him strategies of concealment, breaches of faith, and manipulations that accord ill with his democratic commitment to deal in a straightforward way with the electorate he claims to represent and to which he acknowledges responsibility. His political role is thus a composite of at least two subroles, the representative and the administrative, which can and often do conflict as much as two distinct roles ever conflict or as much as a role commitment and a general moral principle conflict.

Within a total commitment structure, one might identify a particular substructure, that of a person's role as politician, within which trade-offs must be made, as much as between roles. Deceiving his constituents, making trouble for his colleagues by insisting on frankness, offering his resignation, will all be ranked according to the commitments of competing subroles, and located on a two- or multidimensional role-fulfillment map, the general shape of which would constitute his understanding of the total significance of the role. What the role required of him would then emerge from the location of the options on that map, to be set against other role-specific and non-role-specific requirements.

Williams is critical both of moral philosophers and of politicians who take no account of the cost of moral decisions. Politicians who are too readily satisfied with their "morally disagreeable" decisions, who have no sense that they have had to accept a moral cost, are not to be trusted, in his view, even when there are political reasons to justify them. Moreover, the lack of scruple displayed by such people would be supported by utilitarian moral philosophy. And to the extent that utilitarianism is modeled on certain branches of economic theory, the criticism has some force. In the economic theory of production in a capitalist economy, for instance, the combination of factors that yields the highest return for a given outlay is the only one worth considering; since maximizing net return is equivalent to optimization, the entrepreneur has nothing to regret when he turns down all competing strategies. And the same may be true of any theory that employs the notion of a common currency, whether money or utility, which rational action must maximize. One doesn't regret the income one has missed out on by not investing in bonds of one sort if one used the cash to invest in bonds with a higher yield. If all advantages are reduced to a common currency, only suboptimal decisions can have real costs in opportunities missed.

The idea that an opportunity cost can retain its conceptual identity would be more plausible, however, in the theory of consumption. Anyone with limited resources who must choose how to allocate them between competing enjoyments, between apples and oranges, for instance, will have a strong appreciation of opportunity cost, of enjoyment foregone, even when the bargain is believed to be worth the cost. Similarly, if reasons for action figure in a theory of rational action as goods, values, rights, principles, and so on, and are not reformulated in the currency of expected utilities, each retains its conceptual identity; it might be set aside perhaps for some more compelling reason but would not be absorbed into it, as the idea of a $100 profit can be absorbed into the $200 option accepted in preference to it.

The theory of rational action sketched in this chapter makes it a requirement of rationality that a person not have the kind of preference structure depicted by either Figure 4 or Figure 5. Neither Hampshire nor Williams accepts such an account of rationality, precisely because it requires that rational agents be able to reach conclusions consistent with all their evaluative beliefs, which both declare to be impossible.

Williams requires that in the moral quandaries of politics "decent political existence" demands reluctance and hesitation. That, however, presents no problem for my account of rational action. I ask only that a rational politician be able to reach a decision, not that he be able to reach it easily, without reluctance, hesitation, and dismay. The phrase "to reach a decision" is more revealing than "to make a decision" just because it draws attention to the fact that deciding rationally is a process, not an act. The agent casts around for available options, ponders them to create in the imagination a lively sense of the possible world that would be brought into existence if this or that were adopted, and progressively fills in details until, out of the action commitments of this thickening texture of factual and evaluative beliefs, there emerges a conviction about the thing to do. That process, which is one of discovery, is not something different from the one described in my decision-theoretic analysis. It is rather a phenomenological account of what I have hitherto referred to as locating the options on the map. Decision is not something further that occurs afterwards, except when the preference structure is incomplete, symmetrical, or intransitive. Normally it emerges as the options are located: One doesn't require a further effort, for instance, to draw the curves in order to discover the trade-off rate, any more than one needs to draw indifference curves to discover one's relative preference or substitution rate for apples and oranges. The process of locating the options on the map, however, may not be at all simple, for it requires moral sensitivity to identify among the many features of the different options those that are relevant to one's values, principles, and role commitments and, having identified them, to assign to each its salience in the situation and the degree to which its requirements would be met by the action in question.

Agamemnon's problem, as I recounted it, was complicated and agonizing just because, when all the options were located, they still could not be ranked. No choice emerged from a settled preference structure as optimal, or even as minimally bad.

It is not just a fortunate accident that agonizing dilemmas such as Agamemnon's are not features of the daily lives of ordinary people. In Chapter 1 I suggested that our preference structures, which include religious, political, and esthetic rankings, as well as simple enjoyment expectations, are related to the standard situations that confront us in daily life. Technical and social innovation frequently catch us unprepared. We learn to fill out the lacunae in our decision structures, to accommodate the new decisions we have arrived at, as our experience broadens. Because Agamemnon's problems do not often come your way and mine, we do not know what we should do if one day they did confront us. We are fortunate, in witnessing Euripides' *Iphigenia*, that we enjoy the observer's perspective, from which we can appreciate Agamemnon's agonizing quandary, learning a good deal, no doubt, that is theoretical about rational choice and virtue, without being obliged to resolve his problems. But if such decision situations were a feature of our common culture, we should have to come to terms with them, and settle how the values trade-off under comparable conditions. We should then have a role-fulfillment map which, over that range, did not exhibit the lacunae and the incoherences that Agamemnon's did, and we should be able to say with assurance what would be the thing to do.

Confronted, however, by situations that reveal these lacunae, a person has to discover how to extend or connect up his value/ principle/role-fulfillment curves in regions where he has believed hitherto that trade-offs and subthreshold choices would be impossible. That way, indeed, he adds inches to his stature as a rational decision maker, for he is then equipped to deal with further situations he could not have dealt with before. He now knows better what he really believes and in a sense knows better who he is. I do not say that he is necessarily a nicer or even a better man for that; whether being able to think the unthinkable and do the undoable improves the character is an open question. But the man who cannot do it when his vocation or ill luck demands it of him is likely to collapse into neurotic guilt and remorse.

But the choice he is to make is not arbitrary for all his lack of a settled preference structure in the relevant range. I have used the phrase "to discover how to extend or connect up his value/principle/ role-fulfillment curves" to suggest that there are both cues and constraints already within a person's belief structure suggesting how the restructuring is to be done. For such dilemmas never exhaust our moral resources altogether. We draw on other evaluative beliefs in discovering how to deal with them. I do not mean, of course, that we find, in the end, a common currency that settles the relative values of the options. Rather, because every such belief is embedded in an encompassing network of beliefs, abandoning or modifying one will be found to be less disruptive of the total personality than abandoning or modifying another. Orestes discovers that he *can* kill his mother; he *cannot* rest until his father is avenged. He discovers that, of the two men that are his possible futures, it is the matricide, not the impious son, that he can accept, albeit with misgiving and a sense of guilt. That is not to impute a narcissistic motive; it is only to redescribe the process of moral discovery that I have called "extending the curves." It amounts to coming to terms with seemingly intolerable alternatives in decisions that we cannot evade. It is what lies behind the Sartrian doctrine that, confronted by the moral abyss, we make the existential choice which thereafter constitutes our moral personality. But the choice is not, all the same, the totally open one that Sartre would have us believe.

Williams's doctrine that there are situations where anything we can do would be wrong – that there are simply wrong situations – is therefore unacceptable. There are certainly tragic situations where making the best of a bad job involves doing someone – or many people – a wrong, in the sense that it fails to respect their rights and allows no way of compensating them for the loss. But to wrong someone in that sense may not be the wrong thing to do, even though the moral costs are very high.

It is a condition of moral health, however, that we assimilate even the most horrendous of decisions we are forced, just occasionally, into making. We may decide in retrospect, of course, that the decision we made was wrong – not a wrong decision from a selection any of which would have been wrong, but just wrong when another would have been right. But that, too, involves having a coherent and complete preference structure. For to call a decision wrong in that sense is to say that it was not the thing to do, and that is different from saying that there was no *thing to do*. Assimilating such a decision is thus to form a settled moral view; it is consistent with repenting it, with experiencing remorse at having done wrong, but not with spending the rest of one's life seeing oneself as a kind of vessel of wrath or as the victim of circumstances such that whatever one did would unavoidably have been wrong.

# 4

## Values and objectivity

### 1. On valuing

"Value" is a philosopher's abstraction. Though in everyday conversation we commonly talk about "setting a high value upon" or
"giving good value for" something, we rarely have occasion to talk
about "a value" as such, and if we speak of a person's "values," we
are borrowing rather self-consciously from the kind of quasi-
technical vocabulary that philosophers have constructed for talking about problems in moral philosophy, rather than about moral
problems. It is the verb *to value* that seems basic. "He values your
friendship," "She values that picture more than life itself" are
pretty unproblematic. So if the verb is more at home than the
abstract noun in the language of practice, it may be more profitable, even for philosophical purposes, to begin with the verb. This
has the further advantage that we may be less tempted to look
around in the noumenal world for esoteric, "nonnatural" properties to correspond with those abstract "values." J. L. Mackie con-
vincingly argued (for those that needed convincing) that, supposing such properties to be primary qualities of objects, in that
sense "objective" and quite unrelated to the perceptual and cognitive modes of valuers, they would have to be not merely strange
but impossibly elusive.[1]

I take it that to value some $X$ is to prefer any state of affairs $S$ of
which $X$ is a feature, to any state $S'$ in all other respects similar to
$S$, from which, however, $X$ is absent and to prefer $S$ is to rank $S$ over
$S'$ for the purposes of choice, admiration, commendation, and cherishing. There may be instances of valuing, it is true, where not all
of these are to the point. One may admire a sunset, but there is
little one can do to cherish it. Still, if one were positive towards $X$ –
a person, perhaps – in some of these respects and negative in others, the question could well be raised whether one truly valued $X$ or
whether, for instance, one loved him without valuing him, as one
might love an idiot child: One might feel protective and compas-

65

sionate toward him, but one could not admire him. But though one can be strongly disposed to cherish without valuing what one cherishes, cherishing is necessarily part of valuing if the object valued can be cherished at all, and when it cannot, we may experience a kind of regret, as when a flower wilts or a sunset fades, that there is nothing we can do to preserve it. The popularity of photography, and formerly of portrait painting, may have something of this about them: If we cannot preserve what we value by cherishing it, we can still cherish a kind of symbolic representation of it.

There are, however, deviant possibilities. Someone might have an obsessional detestation of something or someone, despising it and wanting to hurt it whenever possible, yet not want to see the world without it, preferring that it should continue to exist as an object on which to vent his spleen, while using what he deemed contemptible about it as his excuse or justification. Considering his preferences among states of the world, one would have to say that this person valued his whipping boy, but the grounds for the valuation would be precisely those qualities that were his reasons for despising him. It would be strangely inconsistent, for instance, for such a person to confess to his preference for his victim's continued existence with faults unchanged, while roundly abusing him for having them. This is not just a case of having some reasons for valuing him and others for not valuing him, as one might say that a movie was visually beautiful but intolerably long-winded in its dialogue and narration. The whipping boy is cherished just because he is despicable, not in spite of it. And that is what makes the case deviant.

So far I have offered an account of valuing as if it were a simple matter of a disposition and state of mind of the valuer, a matter one might say of *mere* preference. And it may seem that some valuing at least is that and nothing more. If, however, we follow Thomas Nagel[2] and Derek Parfit in distinguishing agent-relative and agent-neutral values, we have a way of objectivizing values, in at least one sense of "objectivity."

Health, relief from pain, and the satisfaction of thirst can be appreciated as values irrespective of the particular agent perspective from which they are viewed. One does not have to know something particular about Alan to know that it is better that his thirst be satisfied than not. Or rather, we should have to know something very special about him, that he was under special medical treatment, for example, for this not to be true. Such values are "agent neutral." By contrast, if Alan has set himself the project of

66

playing all Beethoven's piano sonatas from memory, he will value his own success, but there is no evident reason for anyone else to prefer the state of the world in which he brings it off to one in which he does not. Or if there is, it is indirect, depending not on the intrinsic valuing of his achievement, but on the valuing of his hedonic experience of satisfaction in his success. Such a valuing might be quite undermined if the enterprise successfully accomplished was intrinsically evil. Whether there exists a reason more direct than the hedonic one for valuing it will depend on whether the project is substantially (and therefore agent-neutrally) valuable. A talented but unexceptional amateur pianist could hardly commend his success to anyone else as *valuable*, however much he quite properly values it himself. And if Alan's valuing something is not enough to make it valuable, Betty cannot be committed merely by her belief that Alan values $X$, as opposed to her belief that $X$ would delight him, to any action to realize $X$. There are reasons for wanting people to be happy, and for valuing their happiness, but these are not reasons that make their *values* reasons for action for everyone else.

But if the pianist is a Schnabel, with rapidly failing sight, his learning to play Beethoven's sonatas from memory is to be preferred not only by the pianist himself but by his audiences too; and not only because his being able to continue playing would keep him happy. And arguably, if there are reasons for ranking a world in which there are more great performances above one in which there are fewer, his success is to be preferred by anyone, whether the valuer expects to hear them himself or not. That is to say, it is possible to value good performance in an auditor-neutral way, not just as a prospective enjoyer oneself. My thesis requires that to believe something valuable in this way would imply a defeasible action commitment to promote it if one could and to look to others to do the same; a purely agent-relative valuation would imply no such commitment. I shall try to meet a challenge to this part of my thesis in Section 2.

Commending something as "valuable" goes, then, well beyond valuing it. One makes the claim that there are reasons why it is *to be preferred* (ranked superior, that is, for the purposes suggested above), reasons that are, at some level at least, agent neutral. Such judgments of value make a claim to objectivity; they are not *simply* statements of preferences, like "I should enjoy an apple more than an orange," that is, "I rank an apple above an orange from the perspective of my own future enjoyment" (though not necessarily

67

from the nutritional perspective, which is agent neutral). Even the belief that one would enjoy an apple more has, of course, an objective truth value, since it makes a claim about how things are, whether absolutely or conditionally, in the world of which the speaker is a part. It will be false if, after all, it turns out that he enjoys an orange more; when it comes to the test, he may discover for himself that he has misjudged his own preference. A statement of a preference is subjective just in the sense that it declares a state of the subject. But it is also a statement about the subject's preference as one fact in the world and as such may be true or false, independently of some further preference, for example, for the statement's being true or for its being false.

Subjectivists may well concede this account of the objectivity of preference ascriptions. What they would contest is the objectivity of what is *preferable*, or to be preferred. According to some subjectivists, to say that $A$ is preferable or to be preferred to $B$ may be only to make a declaration of a further preference, that is, "$A$ is preferable to $B$" is said to mean "I prefer that $A$ be preferred to $B$." This is implausible. It would not follow from Alan's preferring $A$ to $B$ for an agent-neutral reason $R$ and also preferring that Betty or that people at large should also prefer $A$ to $B$, that Alan's preference must be for their also preferring $A$ for reason $R$. Alan may think, for instance, that if people at large preferred $A$ to $B$ for reason $P$ rather than for $R$ they would be more likely to act to bring $A$ about. So Alan might prefer a socialist state for high moral reasons but believe that the masses would be more likely to bring it about if they preferred it for purely self-interested ones. He would have a reason, therefore, to prefer that they did not share his reason but yet shared his preference.

In judging $A$ *preferable* to $B$ for reason $R$, Alan must be understood to be making the general claim that precisely this reason $R$ makes $A$ the thing to prefer; but this would not in itself imply the subjectivist's claim that Alan has a preference for or an interest in anyone else's sharing his preference for $A$, for whatever reason. He may have an interest, indeed, in their *not* sharing it, if their sharing it raised the market price of $A$ by increasing the demand for it. He is committed to believing only that anyone sharing his grounding belief $R$ would be equally committed to sharing his preference for $A$ over $B$. He is not committed to preferring that anyone should actually do so.[3]

To say that something is preferable, or "to be preferred," then, is to say that there are reasons for preferring it. The question of the objectivity of values thus can be analyzed into three rather more specific questions: (1) whether reasons for preferring refer to properties attributable to the objects, states of affairs, or activities and experiences deemed valuable, (2) whether what constitutes these properties as reasons for valuing is something independent of the preferences of particular valuers or of particular cultures, and (3) (perhaps most contentiously) whether there are criteria for identifying such properties. According to the subjectivist, any reason for deeming such properties values – reasons for preferring their realization in the world – will be agent relative. According to the cultural relativist, they are so only by virtue of the norms extant in particular cultures, and if explanations are offered of how these norms come to be accepted, they are likely to refer to the perceived interests of the particular folk, given their beliefs about their environment and their relations to it.

John Mackie's critique of value objectivism is a subtle variant of moral relativism:

> ... let us suppose that we could make explicit the reasoning that supports some evaluative conclusion, where this conclusion has some action-guiding force that is not contingent upon desires or purposes or chosen ends. Then what I am saying is that somewhere in the input to this argument ... there will be something which cannot be objectively validated – some premise which is not capable of being simply true, or some form of argument which is not valid as a matter of general logic, whose authority or cogency is not objective, but is constituted by our choosing or deciding to think that way.[4]

Mackie concedes that ordinary moral judgments do lay claim to objectivity, and that this assumption has been incorporated in the basic conventional meanings of moral terms, but this claim, according to Mackie, is not self-validating and, if challenged, is found to be incoherent.[5] Our evaluative reasons are related, rather, to what we have *decided* is to be preferred.

Mackie's case against objectivity rests, however, on the supposition that choosing or deciding are somehow antithetical to discovering objective moral principles and values. And this seems to be an error which runs through moral philosophy in the Humean tradition. I argued in Chapters 2 and 3 that reaching practically rational decisions is a process of inferring one's action commitments from one's total belief-structure, which may require the resolving of conflicts and the remedying of incoherences by restructuring the web of belief to achieve greater consistency. Mackie in fact describes just such a procedure:

> ... we might start both with some *prima facie* acceptable general principles, and with the mass of *prima facie* acceptable detailed moral judgements, and where they do not fully agree adjust either or both until the most satisfactory coherent compromise is reached. It is this that John Rawls calls 'a theory of justice'. . . . This is a legitimate form of inquiry, but it must not be confused with the superficially similar but in purpose fundamentally different attempt of thinkers like Sidgwick to advance by way of various 'intuitions' to an objective moral truth, a science of conduct. 'Our sense of justice', whether it is just yours or mine, or that of some much larger group, has no authority over those who dissent from our recommendations or even over us if we are inclined to change our minds. But if there is no objective truth to be discovered, is there nothing left to do but to describe our sense of justice? . . . Morality is not to be discovered, but to be made: we have to decide what moral views to adopt, what moral stands to take.[6]

Mackie's way of alluding to "some *prima facie* acceptable general principles" and "the mass of *prima facie* acceptable detailed moral judgements" suggests that we have them, as it were, by accident, or at least that, unlike science and history, any warrant for asserting them must contain a reference (though possibly a concealed reference) to "a state of the will or a volitional event"[7] and that we achieve coherence by getting our moral beliefs in some sort of order by an appropriate act of invention. Inventing right and wrong is then, for Mackie, a totally different activity from the kind of thing that goes on, say, in history or science.

In the ordinary way of things, of course, we do not need to invent our ethics; we are generally well enough supplied with reasons for doing this rather than that. It is only when reasons appear to run out – when, indeed, we have too many reasons and no immediately apparent rational way to choose between them – that we have a problem, that is, the problem of moral quandaries discussed at length in Chapter 3. But the analogy with history or science holds, thus far at least. Ordinarily the evidence points fairly clearly to this rather than that being the case. But sometimes there are mysteries. There is no evidence, for instance, pointing conclusively to the truth of the hypothesis that Richard III murdered his nephews in the Tower. At least one author thinks as good a case can be made against Henry Tudor. Where the evidence is underdetermining as between available theories, and none of them will in any case account with perfect consistency for every bit of the available evidence, a bold and imaginative historian invents a new one, accounting perhaps for some bits that even the best theories so far in the field could not account for. This is the charm of detective fiction no doubt, but undetermination and the invention of what Karl Popper calls "conjectures" is consistent with there being an objective fact of the matter, even though we do not, and perhaps in the nature of the case cannot, settle conclusively what it is.

Is there a reason for claiming less in practical discourse? It might be argued that in history and science we do at least have an idea of the kind of evidence which, were it available, would be sufficient to determine the correctness of a theory. It is only contingently the case, perhaps, that it is not available. In ethics, however, although there can be reasons within a particular context of argument for accepting *A* rather than *B*, it is always possible, according to the subjectivist, to reject the context. And the kind of rejection the subjectivist has in mind is not the same as when you think you have found reasons for a fundamental reappraisal of some of your central beliefs, a religious conversion or a loss of faith, perhaps; he sees it rather as an act of reasonless will, if such a thing is possible. Then, as Mackie says, *our* sense of justice has lost its authority over the dissenter. Where formerly he shared our moral premises, now he repudiates them; *our* choosing to stand by them carries no weight with him. Still, if that were all, as much might be said of science. Galileo's observations had no authority over the Ptolemaists who refused to put their eyes to his telescope to view the moons of Jupiter. Equally, the Ptolemaists' cosmology had lost its authority over him after he had invented a theory better able to account for the evidence they refused to acknowledge and which he knew very well was there. Their refusal to take it seriously did nothing to impair the objective validity of his theory based upon it. But equally, anyone who takes his own moral perspectives seriously believes that he has good reasons for them, that they are not all agent-relative ones, and that their truth is in no way impaired by the misguided refusal of others to acknowledge it.

David Wiggins has seized on this requirement of seriousness as a central weakness in the subjectivist, noncognitivist position.[8] A subjectivist asks you to take your moral judgments seriously while at the same time holding that they are objectively speaking meaningless or, in Mackie's case, invented, that is, to adopt at one and the same time the inner view, which recognizes the action commit-

71

ments of one's beliefs, and the outer, that there is no reason for holding these beliefs to be true. One or other must be only a pretended believing. If Wiggins is right, the only course open to the subjectivist would be practical nihilism, the acceptance in the inner view that nothing matters.

It is doubtful, however, whether a human being or indeed any being with the physical, sensory, and instinctual, as well as the intellectual, endowments of a human being could adopt such a belief. Could a being experiencing pain or hunger or sexual desire seriously believe that it was absolutely a matter of indifference whether or not he did anything to relieve such a condition, that, if relieving it required as little exertion as Hume's scratching of his little finger, the proper procedure for deciding whether or not to do so would be to toss a coin? Of course, he might just possibly believe that remedying his own pain and hunger was his problem and of no concern to anyone else, but that is different from believing that it is not a problem at all and that, from an inner view, no answer to it is better than any other. It is not the case that what matters only to me doesn't really matter, just because it matters only to me. But if I had invented its value or willfully selected it or just committed myself to it, it really could not matter, since what I have invented I can annihilate, and what I have committed myself to I can renege on, unless some further ground exists – a concern for authenticity, perhaps – for remaining true to such voluntary commitments. But isn't the concern to be authentic itself open to annihilation like the rest?

We are practically rational just as beings adapted to the intelligent manipulation of the world in accordance with their interests; and I mean "interests" to be understood both in the sense of the states of affairs that are of advantage to us and of those significant activities and forms of life that focus and direct what we knowingly and intentionally do. What we call our interests in both senses are already objects of evaluative beliefs. Moreover, because we *know* ourselves as beings with such interests, nihilism runs clean counter to our self-perception. Of course, recognizing our own interests as values does not obviously require that we value anyone else's or, indeed, that we value anything else at all. For that we shall need other arguments. The present point is only that it is extremely doubtful that a program of conceptual revision consisting in the deliberate annihilation of *all* evaluation in our apprehension of our world could succeed or, indeed, be a coherent one, yet the noncognitivist's invitation to exclude valu-

72

VERNON REGIONAL
JUNIOR COLLEGE LIBRARY

ing from the outside view would require us to do just that, supposing ourselves clear-sighted enough to see the implications of such an outside view for an inside view.

Wiggins is not prepared, however, to take cognitivism so far as to say that our moral or practical life is wholly a matter of discovery. He lists five conditions he calls "the truisms of regular truth": the mutual compatibility of all such "regular truths"; their answerability to evidenced argument tending towards convergence on agreement; their independence of our will and of our limited means of recognizing the properties in question; that every regular truth is true by virtue of something; and finally, the complete determinacy of its being (regularly) true.[9] These conditions are characteristically satisfied by historical and geographical judgments, but not by the truths of practical reason. He concedes to the noncognitivist "the absence of the unique solutions and the unique determination of the practical which naive cognitivism would have predicted" and therefore "the need for an organizing focus or meaning or purpose which we ourselves *bring* to life. The mind is not only a receptor: it is a projector."[10] "[We] do not discover a meaning for life; we invent one."[11]

Wiggins resists the "naive cognitivist's" claim that

> ... all the claims of rational concerns ... need to be actually reconcilable. When we judge that this is what we must do now ... or that our life must now take one direction rather than another direction, we are not fitting truths (or even probabilities) into a pattern where any discrepancy proves that we have mistaken a falsehood for a truth. Often we have to make a practical choice which another rational agent might understand through and through, not fault or even disagree with but ... make differently himself; whereas if there is disagreement over what is factually true and two rational men have come to different conclusions, then we think it has to be theoretically possible to uncover some discrepancy in their respective views of the evidence. ... In matters of practice, we are grateful for the existence of alternative answers. The choice between them is then up to us. Here is our freedom.[12]

This is a strange conclusion, for we are certainly not meant to suppose that the choice is reasonless or an existential commitment of the kind which Wiggins rejects in his criticisms of Richard Taylor, earlier in his lecture. And what sort of freedom is it that can be exercised only in the absence of sufficient reasons? In any case, Wiggins does not accept the unreconstructed noncognitivist's conclusion that this leaves only "a limited and low-grade objectivity for the products" of the inventions of practical reason.

Wiggins's argument is fairly obscure, but seems to be that just as in mathematics one invents ways of resolving paradoxes, inventions that are nonetheless constrained by the logical requirements of the system at large, which constitutes the conditions for assertability and therefore of objectivity of the solution, so in practice one invents the way to go on when the reasons seem to have run out. But how is this compatible with the earlier claim that the will "craves objective reasons"?[13]

Perhaps we can do better by going back to Nagel's account of objectivity. For Nagel, as I think for Wiggins, objectivity is essentially an epistemological, not an ontological notion – ". . . a method of understanding. It is beliefs and knowledge that are objective in the primary sense. Only derivatively do we call objective the truths that can be understood in this way."[14] According to Nagel, we acquire a more objective understanding of some aspect of the world by "stepping back from our view of it," by progressively distancing ourselves from the perspective we normally have, replete with particular interests and idiosyncratic concerns.

What account can we give, then, of the "freedom" of choice which, according to Wiggins, is unbounded by universal reasons? Suppose Alan sees Betty making a decision which he himself would not make in her situation but which he thinks she can quite legitimately make. Each may be attending to the interests (in both senses) which constitute his or her own characteristic perspective (formed from their particular experiences, aptitudes, and capacities); they may well go in different directions – choose different projects, careers, even (in one sense) moralities (one heroic, another meek, and so on). Each may even disparage the other from his or her own perspective. But if Alan steps back to a more embracing perspective, both his own and Betty's immediate perspectives may appear as particular instantiations of categories which must be instantiated in *some* form, but variously in all such immediate perspectives. It then becomes possible to see the other's decision as not merely legitimate (if indeed it is), but more, as rationally the thing for that person to choose. Betty's value reasons then become encapsulated, as it were, in the agent-neutral perspective of the objective viewer, who might be Alan, Betty herself, or anyone else. They are then a feature of the world surveyed from that more remote perspective, determining the thing to do for anyone occupying Betty's perspective, but determining it in this encapsulated way for anyone viewing it objectively.

So long as the particularities of Betty's agent perspective had not been filled in, what for her was the thing to do was for others at best legitimate, optional, but not necessary. Now, however, it makes sense to say that the choice is still a choice for reasons which can be acknowledged universally, but not everyone would have the same reasons for choosing just that way for himself. Of course, the detached perspective will not validate every choice; it will still rule out some as illegitimate, whatever the particularity of the standpoint, just because from no standpoint (or from none so far achieved in the process of standing back) could such as these be acceptable.

There is, however, a feature of practical decision making which suggests that this cannot be the whole story and which may provide a way back for Wiggins's "underdetermined" value judgments. I have interpreted evaluation in terms of reasoned preferences for one state of affairs rather than another. One is committed to such a preference by one's relevant attendant beliefs. A reasoned preference for $A$ over $B$ amounts then to an action commitment to select, should occasion arise, $A$ rather than $B$, to admire $A$ above $B$, and so on. But the possibility of preference implies also the possibility of "equivalence," corresponding to what the economist and decision theorist call "indifference," where one comes to the conclusion that *there is nothing to choose* between $A$ and $B$.

Now this may seem to present a difficulty for the cognitivist. I said earlier that a historian may find the evidence at his disposal insufficient to determine what happened to the princes in the Tower. But an objectivist historian would insist that underdetermination does not mean that there was no fact of the matter, only that we have no way of finding it out. But what is the moral objectivist to say in the present case, if the reasons are insufficient to determine whether $A$ or $B$ is the thing to do, and doing $A$ rules out doing $B$? Is there now an objective fact of the matter for the cognitivist to know, as there is an objective historical fact of the matter that the historian would be able to know, if only the evidence was accessible to him?

So far the objectivist is not in trouble. He may say that the reasons for $A$ and $B$ are equally good and better than those for doing anything else, so the thing to do is ($A$ or $B$); what is excluded is (both not-$A$ and not-$B$). In a state of equivalence, the alternative states would possess such properties that neither would be preferable to the other. And this would be as intelligible within a theory that ascribed an ontological reality to values as properties independent of any perceiver, which is Mackie's version of cognitivism, as within one that located them, as Wiggins seems to want, within a system of apperceptions of the world.

The objective truth, in such a case, would be that by virtue of their equivalent properties these possible states of the world could yield no reason for choosing one rather than another. And the rational course then is to toss a coin. Of course, there are situations in which the issues seem so grave that to take a decision in this way would seem very irresponsible. And that may well be because the facts are so uncertain, or one's belief that one has indeed considered everything relevant and assigned it the importance appropriate to it is so hesitant, that to randomize the decision process would seem like abandoning rationality. That mistake was the death of Buridan's ass. The logic of preference commits us to believing that if $A$ is to be preferred to $B$, $B$ is not to be preferred to $A$ and also that if $A$ and $B$ are equivalent, one is not to be preferred to the other, but it does not commit us to believing that one or other (but not both) must always be preferred. So it is consistent with the requirement that practical objective truths be action guiding that there may be occasions when the reasons are tied. The general propositions of principle and value that are the relevant reasons may be true: By virtue of its elegance the vase is to be cherished, by virtue of his honesty the man is to be admired, and so on. But the commitment to action implied by the relevant principles, values, and so forth would then not be underdetermined, in the sense that the reasons available were insufficient to determine the right thing to do; rather they would be sufficient to establish that, within the limits of $A$ and $B$, whatever one does, one does not do wrong.

It may be objected, however, that whereas the practical conclusion "($A$ or $B$) is the thing to do" is tolerable, "($A$ and not-$A$) is the thing to do" is not. If an action is required by one reason but prohibited by another, and there is no further consideration that will settle the matter one way or the other, can a cognitivist give an acceptable account of what, on his theory, looks very much like, not just a conflict of prescriptions, but two contradictory statements about how, morally speaking, things are with the world?

In Chapter 3 I claimed that quandaries of this sort were not irresoluble, or rather that their occurrence was a consequence of irrationality in the agent's belief structure. My case, briefly, was that we arrive at these dilemmas only if we hold incoherent beliefs about the ranking of reasons. Over certain ranges of their application we may attribute to certain principles and values lexical priority over other reasons. Generally this works out all right. It is not all right if the thresholds constituted by two such priority principles intersect, and if the only available options fall below one or the other, or both. Then there can be no consistent resolution without revising such priorities.

Precisely because practical reason has as one of its proper objects the determination of right action, just as epistemic or theoretical reason has as its proper object true belief, a value structure that has these features cannot be rational. In much the same way, one might say that someone with a belief structure that has built-in nonnegotiable beliefs can be rational only so long as there is no possibility that they can yield contradictory entailments. Someone confronted by the contradictory conclusions "$A$ is the thing to do" and "$A$ is the thing not to do" is the victim, then, of a mistaken belief about the moral world. These propositions purport to be conclusive action commitments, not negotiable reasons for action which ground such commitments. And the truth of these conclusions depends on the truth of the claim, not that each of the reasons is as good as the other (which amounts only to equivalence, which yields a permissive or indifferent conclusion), but that each declares the other impermissible. But where no other possible course is permissible either, such conclusions are ruled out by the nature of practical reasons as action guiding, much as logical contradiction is ruled out by the nature of theoretical rationality as oriented to true belief.

It was, of course, horrendously difficult for Agamemnon at Aulis to determine what was the thing to do; nonetheless, one is forced to the conclusion that either (1) the reasons were tied and that either course, whether to sacrifice Iphigenia to save the army or to spare her and abandon the expedition to Troy, would have been permissible in the circumstances, however wrong each would have been had the other not applied, or (2) that the reasons for one were really stronger, that one action commitment (perhaps to sacrificing Iphigenia) really did outrank the other, and that this was the thing to do after all. So it seems to me that Philippa Foot is simply fudging the issue when she says that some conflicting options are "incommensurable, so that we have nothing to say about the overall merits of $a$ and $b$, whether because there is nothing that $we$ can say or because there is no truth of the matter and therefore nothing to $be$

said."[15] Such incommensurability would constitute an intolerable lacuna in practical reason, inconsistent with its object.

Now it may be that when, in a case of true equivalence, one makes a random choice, one is embarking on a branch of historical possibility that will shape one's future valuations quite differently from the way one would have gone had the coin fallen otherwise. After the event, the course that one did not take may appear, by hindsight, less and less eligible. That is not to say that it was ineligible at the time. Suppose that one's quandary were viewed objectively, from an agent-neutral standpoint; suppose, further, that one included, as one must, among the conditions weighed against each other in deliberation, the commitments that would ensue from taking course *A* and course *B*. Deciding to become a doctor, for instance, rather than a lawyer, one would also be deciding between different future persons that one might be, and different action commitments that one would assume. If, now, in the light of such deliberations one could say with truth that which way one went was a matter of indifference because the options were still equivalent, then it would really be the case that the rational choice would be to adopt a nonrational choice procedure. Nevertheless, viewed from the perspective occupied by the agent at a later time, formed as he would be by all the special interests and experiences and accomplishments consequent upon and acquired subsequent to his choosing to be a doctor, that course may begin to appear, from his new particular perspective, the only one that was really eligible at the time the choice was made. How, he might ask, could a person like me choose to be a lawyer if he had the opportunity to be a doctor? But of course, it was the decision that made him the kind of person he now is. His new perspective may be more restrictive than the original more objective one, which contained both possibilities and was not slanted by the special loyalties and commitments since acquired.

The claim I am making for the epistemological objectivity of values has a good deal in common with Ronald Dworkin's account of judicial reasoning. Like Dworkin, I envisage the agent drawing on immense resources for the solving of hard cases and forming "a best theory" of the thing to do; and I would not expect an experienced decider reasonably familiar with his world to find himself very frequently in tied situations any more than Dworkin expects judges to be faced with ties in mature legal systems. Mostly our quandaries arise not from a true equivalence but from epistemic inadequacy; there is so much that we do not know, and the ordering of the reasons – the weighing, as we say, of pros and cons – can be so difficult, that we plump for one course because we do not know how to do better. There may be a better to do nevertheless, and doing worse could still commit us to a course that, in retrospect, we come to regard as better. If that happens we have none the less erred, even though we cannot recognize the fact from the agent-perspective we have by then come to occupy.

I do not know whether this degree of indeterminacy would satisfy the two conditions implicit in Wiggins's account, that is, (1) that "the will craves objective reasons" and often "could not go forward unless it thought it had them"[16] and (2) that at the same time, room be left for the "something extra" which "each man supplies[,] . . . some conception of his own, to make sense of things *for himself*"[17] to leave room for "invention," a kind of moral improvisation. There certainly is room for invention, but in much the same way that there is room in science for conjecture. So someone may invent a stratagem that will meet the requirements of a contingency which seemed irreconcilable, much as a scientist may come up with a theory, such as the general theory of relativity, to meet apparently incoherent evidence. And then one says of the stratagem, "That's the best thing to do," just because it satisfies requirements already presented by one's structure of beliefs, just as we might say of a newly invented theory, "This is the thing to believe," because it fits everything else that we know about the subject. Nevertheless, it is not impossible that each of two or more stratagems could satisfy all the requirements equally well. If that were the case of a scientific theory, we should look for a crucial experiment to determine which was the true one, but in the meantime the scientist is at liberty, rationally speaking, to work with whichever he fancies, for reasons, that is, which might be agent relative. In a practical quandary we should say that, given the knowledge presently available, presuming it an unacceptable option to postpone one's decision indefinitely until enough additional information should provide a reason for one's choice, either course would be permissible; we should say, moreover, that this practical judgment was objectively true.

## 2. On whether to acknowledge something as valuable commits one to valuing it

So far I have taken J. L. Mackie's subjectivism, and his critique of objectivism, as a paradigm statement of the difference between these two positions. According to Mackie, the objectivist mistakenly takes evaluative conclusions to rest on premises distinct from "desires, purposes, or chosen ends." Moral principles themselves, though they may seem to us like facts in the world, are really "to be made," chosen, decided upon, not inferred from any basic truths. The difference between the subjectivist and the objectivist would then be located in their different accounts of what it is for something to be *valuable*.

The rift may develop, however, at quite a different point, at what is involved in *valuing*. According to some subjectivists, while Alan and Betty might agree that some $X$ is valuable, Alan may value it, but Betty may not; yet Betty might be guilty of no defect of reason. Accordingly, while Alan has a reason for action in respect of $X$, Betty has not. A color-blind person might be persuaded that Jackson Pollock's painting "Blue Poles" is valuable as a work of art, but because he lacks the capacity to appreciate a work relying so much on color for its effect, he himself cannot value it. And if he does not value it, so it is said, he has no reason (apart from reasons that might apply to property in general) to take any steps, for instance, to save it from destruction in a fire.[18]

This argument depends on a concept of valuing rather different from the thin concept I have offered in this chapter and in Chapter 1. I take valuing to be a special case of the ranking of a state of affairs $X$ over not-$X$. The *telos* of this ranking is choosing what to cherish, admire, and sustain and deciding which of the two states of affairs it would be appropriate to maintain or bring about if one had the power to make that difference in the way the world was to go. The reasons for a particular ranking might be various, but reasons deriving from the respect owed to persons I have set apart from values, as being reasons of principle or "person-centered." These are not reasons for admiring, cherishing, and so on, but for acting irrespective of the valuable properties of persons. They are unrelated to the bringing about of states of affairs, except in the vacuous sense that any action on principle has the intention of bringing about the state of affairs in which the principle has been acted upon. The crucial difference between the cases is that the reason for the action on principle lies in the action commitments of the principle, not in the ranking of the consequences of the action, or of the enjoyable or other agent-relative characteristic experience of performing it.

Now the kind of subjectivist presently under consideration ties valuing very closely to feelings. The color-blind person lacks the

80

capacity to experience directly what makes "Blue Poles" valuable, just as a person with no sense of humor may know that a story is funny because he has been told so by persons on whose judgment and truthfulness he relies, or because he observes people laughing, and he knows that laughter of this kind is the standard response to something funny. He may even be able to infer, in a theoretical way, what makes one thing funny but not another, by generalizing from the particular instances of laughter-inducing stories. But he will never be able to *see* the funny side of things, any more than the color-blind person can see "Blue Poles" as alive with color.

The color-blind person is, of course, perceptually defective and can be brought to understand that he is. He can then be told about color and can be led to understand, by analogy, perhaps, with musical tones, timbres, chords, and so on, what color can mean to a color-sighted person. And he can be brought to see that something appropriately colorful might be valuable on that account, as music which is harmonically rich might be valuable.

All this, however, the present subjectivist may concede. But he denies that the color-blind person's agreeing that it is valuable – that it is appropriate to be valued by anyone capable of doing so – commits him to action to preserve it, to encourage the painting of pictures which can also be commended on account of their color values, and so on. It is only valuing, knowing the value of something by intimate and direct acquaintance rather than by external knowledge of it, that can commit one to action in respect of it.

Now I can concede that there are things that can be held conditionally valuable. The person who values them may recognize that their being valuable depends on something about the valuer too. Someone who enjoys only hard-centered chocolates has a reason for valuing Terry's Spartan Assortment but not Cadbury's Milk Tray, which contains many soft centers. Assuming that there is nothing about chocolates (such as differential nutritional values) that is capable of grounding a judgment of their value other than that they are enjoyable, and since what is enjoyable is enjoyer relative, someone who likes soft centers has no reason at all to value Terry's, although he recognizes *for someone who likes hard centers* Terry's Spartan Assortment is valuable and therefore to be preferred. But the only ground he might have for saying that they are valuable is that people whose tastes differ from his own enjoy them, and, supposing him to understand benevolence to be valuable, he might treat others' enjoyment as contributing to total well-being, which is valuable in an enjoyer-neutral way. But that aspect of the case aside, he has no reason either to regard them as valuable or to value them himself.

Consumer-relative values form, however, a limited category. Mostly we deem things valuable on account of enjoyer-neutral values, grounded on reasons that generate action commitments for anyone, not just for those capable of enjoying the properties by virtue of which the thing is deemed valuable. So science as an activity is valuable on account of its employing the rational intelligence of human beings and in extending our understanding of the universe; this is not enjoyer relative. One does not need to be a scientist or even a science afficionado to grasp these reasons for valuing it. To say that science is valuable is to say that, in the absence of countervailing reasons, it is not only appropriate to promote scientific inquiry, but also that it is inappropriate to obstruct or neglect such investigation. Moreover, it would be inappropriate not to participate with others in efforts to promote science, if such nonparticipation would amount to obstruction or neglect or if nonparticipation in promoting something we all agreed to be valuable amounted to unfairly leaving others to bear the burden. Failure to support the funding of science from public revenues would be a case of such neglect. Recognizing something as valuable commits one to much the same forms of action, therefore, that one would be committed to by asserting that one valued it – that is, to cherishing, sustaining, protecting, and promoting it.

## 3. On what can count as a value

I said earlier that to value some $X$ is to prefer any state of the world in which $X$ is a feature to any state in all other respects identical with it save that $X$ is absent. We can now hazard an account of what a value might be, namely, whatever it is about $X$ (call it $V$) such that it is by virtue of this that $X$ is preferred in this way. For some philosophers, while there may be any number of things mediately or instrumentally qualifying as $V$, only a quality of human experience could qualify as intrinsically a $V$. "It is in actual consciousness that value resides and in nothing else," wrote Rashdall.[19] This, of course, is fundamental to any kind of utilitarianism, whether the valuable property of experience be happiness, pleasure, the satisfaction of desire, or the experience of beauty, truth, and friendship. Such experiences then count as intrinsic *values*, and other states of the world, things, or activities are valued either as modes of the valuable experience (such as playing a pleasurable game) or instrumentally, as a means to an intrinsic value or an extrinsic one, as one might value a chair for the sake of the comfort that it provides or a carpenter for the sake of the chairs he makes.

This account is not intuitively plausible. It seems to depend on the idea that to value something extrinsically is to value the good feelings to which it gives rise. Of course, one can value good feelings and may, indeed, act quite deliberately to ensure that one has them. Just so might someone, for whom bestowing lavish presents on friends is a source of an inner glow of self-approval, look around for opportunities to give in order to enjoy these feelings. But this does seem to be a rather special case. One could go on valuing an object – a picture, say – even when one knew that one would never be able to contemplate it again. The thought might produce sadness rather than pleasure, but a sadness that arises just because one still does value the object but can no longer expect pleasure from it. Of course, one could know that it still existed, and that knowledge might be a source of pleasure – but again, only because one already valued the object on some other ground. It might be that one valued it for the pleasure one had had from it in the past. But the memory of a pleasurable feeling is not itself a pleasurable feeling; it can be more bitter than sweet.

A more plausible possibility is that the good feelings are necessary signs of value: Whatever in an object is valuable manifests itself by the good feelings it produces in us, just as a story is recognized as being funny by its eliciting laughter in us. It would then be rational to attribute value to something that had provided such feelings, recognizing through them its quality as valuable, even though one would never feel those feelings directly again (as we continue to recognize the story as funny long after familiarity has defused laughter). That would be to objectify the value, in the sense that one located it in properties of an object rather than in one's own experience. It would still raise the question, however, whether those properties could have been said to be valuable but for the propensity of the valuer to experience them in just that way. Would they still be valuable without a valuer? Would a sunset be beautiful in a color-blind world? Suppose in that world someone who had been color-sighted could remember sunsets and know from evidence that there must now be a sunset whose beauty no one could see – would it make no sense to value that sunset for its beauty?

The thought-experiment commonly called the "last-man argument" points up the issue. Suppose a disaster which, while leaving the world's beauty spots, the pictures in all its art galleries, and all the great Gothic cathedrals intact, has destroyed all sentient creatures but one, who is himself about to die. Moved, perhaps, by some obscure rancor, he has rigged up a device which, at the moment of his death, will trigger a nuclear explosion which will totally destroy what is left. Can anyone now contemplating this scenario, and who has the capacity for valuing such things, take the view that because there would in any case be no survivor capable of perceiving those objects as valuable, what would be destroyed would be valueless, and their wanton destruction would not be an act of vandalism? Or should we not say, rather, that our own value perception is not temporally bounded by our own existence as persons, nor do we value axiotima for the sake of our own experiences only, but for the sake of certain properties which are contingently capable of generating such experiences in perceivers like ourselves? Contingently, because we do not value them *for the sake of* that capacity, but for quite other reasons, which may be widely disparate and various, so the contingent fact that no such perceivers might exist does not invalidate the valuing. We can still value a picture in a world become blind; that is, we could value there being such a picture even in an observerless world, since it would still be the picture it is, with the same properties capable of producing the responses that signify its value when viewed by someone with the appropriate receptivity.

## 4. Conclusion

I shall conclude this chapter with two observations, one respecting the incoherence of the quest for an Archimedean point of absolute objectivity, the other suggesting an irremediable plurality of values.

**A.** Suppose that in our last-survivor story the rancorous agent had a deathbed change of heart and relented. After several decades there arrived a race of aliens from outer space with sensory capacities radically different from our own, to whom pictures, cathedrals, and verdant forests meant literally nothing. Suppose them totally incapable of seeing these objects in any of the ways that have led us to say they are beautiful and therefore valuable. They set about clearing what the last man's change of heart had spared. Would these beings be missing a truth that we at this moment can see, or must we say that this truth is available only to us, relative to our particular sensory capacities?

84

I suggested in Chapter 2 that our language cannot be treated as if it were quite unrelated to the kind of beings we are, with the capacities and interests that we are bound to have by virtue of simply being human. To seek a perspective so remote from our particularity that it takes no account of the conditions for our believing and thinking anything at all is to make speech and thought impossible. Our judgments are indeed anthropocentric, not in the sense that we can attend only to the interests of the human species – we need not be species chauvinists – but in the sense that there is no possibility of believing or valuing what cannot be thought in human terms or what a human being could think only by unthinking his humanity. Beyond a certain point the exercise of distancing ourselves from our particular perspective, for the sake of greater objectivity, must break down for lack of concepts in which to formulate a view of the world.

> ... life's having a point [writes Wiggins] may depend as much upon something invented (not necessarily *arbitrarily*), or upon something contributed by the liver of the life, as it depends upon something discovered. Or it may depend upon what the liver of the life brings to the world in order to see the world in such a way as to discover meaning.[20]

As human beings we come with the necessary baggage of our perceptual equipment, our human interests, our evolved generic perspectives. These provide the limits of our objectivity, behind which we cannot go. But if, as I think is the case, they account also for our conception of rationality, they leave no room for a notion of subjectivity that relies on the possibility of an alternative mode of perception so alien that our concept of a reason, for action or belief, could get no purchase on it. So far, therefore, from our being the prisoners of our concept of rationality, there simply could not be a rational being whose reasons were in their essence incomprehensible to us.

**B.** The second observation is that there is little in this account of valuing to encourage a search for a single, ultimate property, the apex of a hierarchy of values, nor even for some small set of properties, such as happiness, preference satisfaction, beauty, truth, or virtue, to which all other valuable properties are reducible. Nor is there any reason to suppose that all axiotima are valuable by virtue of their possessing or manifesting such specifiable properties. I have presented an account of rational *valuings*, of how our beliefs

85

about the world provide reasons for preferring some states of affairs to others, and so commit us to some actions and forbearances, to cherishing, maintaining, and supporting some things and perhaps to eradicating others. There is no reason to suppose that such reasons must always take the form that it is by virtue of a thing's manifesting such-and-such a property that it is to be valued in this way. In any case, value-centered reasons, related teleologically to states of affairs, are not the only kinds of reasons bearing such action commitments; I suggested in Chapter 1 that fidelity to truth and the principles of justice, which I see as reasons of a quite different kind, deriving from what we understand by a person, and by his or her status in a world of persons, provide reasons unrelated to rankings of states of affairs. And between such reasons and value-centered ones there must be trade-offs, just as there must be trade-offs between values. Nevertheless, what I have said about objectivity would apply equally to such principles, and if what is valuable can be the object of knowledge, so also can we have knowledge of what things are properly to be respected, however little reason there may be for admiring or cherishing them as valuable.

# 5

# Natural personality and moral personality

## 1. The principle of noninterference

Imagine Alan sitting on a public beach, a pebble in each hand, splitting one pebble by striking it with the other. Betty, a casual passerby, asks him what he is doing. She can see, of course, that he is splitting pebbles; what she is asking him to do is explain it, to redescribe it as an activity with an intelligible point, something he could have a reason for doing. There is nothing untoward about her question, but Alan is not bound to answer it unless he likes. Suppose, however, that Betty had asked Alan to justify what he was doing or to give an excuse for doing it. Unlike explanations, justifications and excuses presume at least prima facie fault, a charge to be rebutted, and what can be wrong with splitting pebbles on a public beach? Besides, so far as we can tell, Alan is not obliged to account to Betty for his actions. Of course, if Alan were a sentry and Betty his commanding officer, he might indeed be at fault, and she would be entitled to call him to account for neglect of duty. But that is to ascribe special action commitments and liabilities to Alan, and special powers to Betty. Those absent, Alan has no obligation to meet a challenge to justify his performance until there is a charge to answer.

Suppose Betty were to prevent Alan from splitting pebbles by handcuffing him or removing all the pebbles within reach. Alan could now quite properly demand a justification from Betty, and a *tu quoque* reply from her that he, on his side, had not offered her a justification for his splitting pebbles, would not meet the case, for Alan's pebble splitting had done nothing to interfere with Betty's actions. The burden of justification falls on the interferer, not on the person interfered with. So while Alan might properly resent Betty's interference, Betty has no ground of complaint against Alan.

Suppose now that Betty does offer a justification: Alan, she says, is wasting his time – instead of pointlessly splitting pebbles, he

87

could be doing something worthwhile, studying philosophy or working for Oxfam. But Alan doesn't accept this as a justification for interference; even if Betty were right, what has it to do with her? An unfavorable evaluation of someone else's action does not necessarily warrant one's interfering to prevent it.

Further along the beach, Caroline encounters Desmond tearing the legs off crabs, which she believes (whether or not correctly) to be causing pain to the crabs. Consequently, Caroline has good reason to disapprove and perhaps to remonstrate with Desmond. Given her belief, what Desmond is doing is certainly in need of justification. If the pain were being caused by the unfortunate crabs' being accidentally stranded by the receding tide in a rock pool polluted by acid, Caroline would have a sufficient reason to act to prevent them suffering. She may hesitate, nevertheless, to interfere with Desmond. Does she have any right to interfere? Of course, if Desmond were torturing children, or even dogs, Caroline would possibly have fewer doubts; if there were nothing she could do herself, she might at least call a policeman or an officer of one of the voluntary agencies that exist precisely to prevent cruelty to children or animals.

Alan's indignation at Betty's unwarranted interference with his pebble splitting and Caroline's hesitation about interfering with the sadistic Desmond bear witness both to a general principle blocking interference by one person with the freedom of action of another and to this principle's being far from absolute. But even when overridden by stronger reasons, it still locates the initial onus of justification, not with the person interfered with, but with the interferer. Caroline may hesitate to intervene to protect the crabs because she is unsure whether the suffering of crabs is reason enough to satisfy that onus and therefore to meet – as she is bound to do – Desmond's indignant "What has it got to do with you?" If Desmond had been torturing children, Caroline might have felt herself on firmer ground. Unless Desmond is a psychopath, even he can appreciate that his torturing a child is a stronger reason for someone to interfere with his freedom of action than his torturing crabs. Betty may need the special standing of a military command to interfere with Alan's pebble splitting; otherwise, it is no business of hers that he is wasting his time. Caroline, by contrast, may well feel that she is obliged, with no special standing at all, to intervene to protect a child, or even a dog, from Desmond. Protecting a child, at least from hurt above a certain minimum, can be anyone's business.

An interference need not be negative, directed to frustrating a projected action; it may be aimed at procuring the performance of an action that would not be done without it. Of course, there is room for argument about what is to count as an interference, and therefore about what one can reasonably be called upon to justify. Would it be an interference with Alan's freedom to clear the beach of pebbles before he arrived, either with the intention of preventing his splitting them or for some quite different reason, perhaps to tidy it up? Suppose Betty didn't know that Alan was coming down to split pebbles? Or, being herself an accomplished pebble splitter, suppose she beat him to it every time he reached for a pebble? Would it count as an interference with Alan's freedom of action to offer him payment for not splitting pebbles or for studying philosophy instead? Would it make any difference to that question that Alan was very hard up and out of a job? These questions, which are related to the analysis of freedom of action and center on what precisely can count as interference – and therefore on how the principle of noninterference is to be applied – will be considered in Chapter 7. Until I have established a clearer notion of the kind of acting subject that is presupposed by the principle, I shall proceed as though "interference" and "preventing an action" were unproblematic.

Betty does not pretend, of course, that Alan's action is objectionable because it interferes with or frustrates the freedom of action of the pebbles. Not being intentional agents, pebbles neither act nor have freedom to act. Nor do crabs. Their behavior is instinctual, not intentional. They do not project it into the world under some description, embedded in a system of beliefs, as a way of bringing about some intended state of affairs. True, one can describe a crab's behavioral performance as purposive, but in the sense that there is a state which, if attained, would complete the perceived pattern of that performance, bringing the crab to rest. And one can prevent that pattern being completed, thereby frustrating the crab's purpose. To that extent, it is true, a crab can suffer interference.

Suppose that, instead of tearing out their legs, Desmond amused himself by placing his crabs on a board and fencing them around, frustrating their instinctive attempts to conceal themselves or escape to the sea. A sensitive person who quite plausibly interpreted their agitation as distress might object to Desmond's new game. But it would still be an objection to his cruelty, albeit cruelty of another kind, not to his interfering with the crabs' freedom of action. If the crabs showed no distress when confined, but simply gave up digging or moving towards the sea and went to sleep, it would be hard even for someone solicitous of the interests of crabs to say why Desmond should give up his game.

By contrast, someone who protested on Alan's behalf at Betty's interference with his pebble splitting might not be satisfied by her reply that Alan doesn't seem to mind. There is still room to object that Alan has been wronged, whether he minds or not: Alan may be so infatuated with Betty that he positively enjoys being bossed by her. And some people, after all, are too meek to resent being treated like doormats, and are willing to accept more than they should. But though a disposition to turn the other cheek is a standard Christian virtue, it has never been thought to make the wrong, meekly endured, all right. Just because (as I shall argue) the principle of noninterference is not grounded in the evil of the pain of frustration, it is not undermined by the absence of pain. The significant difference between the crabs on the one hand and Alan and Desmond on the other, which is capable of generating a principle blocking interference in their case but not in the crabs', is not that Alan and Desmond are human beings (the relevance of which is not at all apparent), but that they are natural persons.

## 2. Natural persons as causal agents

There is no logical reason why natural personality should be limited to human beings. To understand the importance of the concept of a person in our practical discourse, we need to set aside the biological notion of humanity and attend rather to the phenomenology of what it is to be a person. For it is a standard condition for the attribution of personality that a person conceive of himself as an intentional agent, differentiating himself not merely from inanimate objects like tables and corpses and other animate ones like crabs and chickens, but also from terminally comatose human beings, so-called human vegetables. But equally, our account must explain what it is about personality that leads us to treat persons as capable of generating for other persons reasons for action of a quite different and important kind from any reasons generated by tables, chickens, corpses, and comatose humans. We shall then be able to ask what costs we should have to incur were we to abandon this special way of looking at persons.

To be a natural person is to possess, and to be aware of oneself as possessing, certain causal capacities. It is to distinguish oneself from the *things* in the world which are simply the subjects of happenings, carried along by the tide of events. Things of that kind are held to be causally active only if some performance or property of that thing is a necessary or at least a salient feature of a series of events culminating in the state of affairs which is the effect. If, but for a particular car's skidding, there would have been no traffic accident, we say that that car caused the accident, though the cause was, strictly speaking, its skidding, an event, rather than the car as the subject of that event. But with persons' intentional actions, we really do seem to mean that the subject is the cause of what ensues.

The use of expressions such as "decision making," "making a choice," "forming an intention," suggest a kind of creativity in personal causation, in which the relation between agent and the process initiated by his decision is more like that between a potter and his pot or an architect and his plan, than like the relation between a skidding car and the resulting accident. The agent's intention, not itself an event, gives a special character to the action, the causal event initiating the chain of events that follows. True, there may be a series of events or a process of deliberation before the subject forms his intention. But it would be a mistake to treat deliberation as characteristic of personal causation, for there is frequently no such process; an intentional act may be intended from the very moment that the subject construes a situation as of just that kind to which his ensuing act is an appropriate response. And this recognition may be immediate.

So if one insists that causes are neither things nor persons but events, then the event identified as cause of an intentional action will have to be the change in the subject's beliefs to which that recognition corresponds. Personal causation will then be distinguished from impersonal by the role played in it by changes in the subject's understanding and beliefs which commit him to action, and by his own awareness of such new commitments. It is this consciousness of one's own thought as the prolegomenon to intended action that underlies a person's conviction that he *makes* decisions – that, unlike skids and lightning strikes, they do not just happen to him. Not, of course, that every change that one initiates can be expected to turn out as one has decided; the capacity is all too finite, and one can in any case make mistakes. Nevertheless, a natural person could not be aware of himself as having and exercising a capacity, however limited in practice, to initiate changes in the world by deciding that things should go one way rather than another, unless over a considerable part of his experience his ac-

91

tions did in fact produce the changes that he intended. If cars skidded more often than they responded predictably to turns of the wheel, no one would have the concept of a driver.

A natural person is not bound, however, to disclaim any causal determination of his own actions. Understanding himself as a natural person does not require that he should be, or believe himself to be, quite unlike causal objects or happenings – an uncaused cause. It requires rather that among the elements in the causal sequences necessary to account for his actions as a natural person are included his cognitive appreciations of situations made in the light of preference sets, principles, and evaluations of possible outcomes – his grasp, that is, of the action commitments of his beliefs. A person knows himself as thinking and feeling, and this consciousness of inward processes can itself be the intentional object of thought and feeling; it can be self-monitored, criticized, corrected.

It would not be enough, however, to suppose these intentional processes to be merely epiphenomenal. To be conscious of oneself as a natural person is to believe that one's conscious processes really are causally effective, that what makes the difference to the world is indeed one's deciding, and that some chemical or electronic process unaccompanied by consciousness could not be causally effective in the same way. A being which behaved in all other respects like a person, but was not self-conscious, would be an impersonal automaton, not an unconscious person. Someone who walks in his sleep is not an impersonal automaton because sleepwalking is deviant from his normal or prevailing manner of being. The actions of a person are the effects of his having beliefs and recognizing, even if sometimes inadequately, what they commit him to do. So, though one might say of a nonpersonal entity like the wind that it made a tree fall, one would not mean that the wind had initiated that change by deciding that felling the tree was the thing to do. Its causal agency – its "doing" – would not be of the required kind.

Nevertheless, a natural person may be able to predict with virtual certainty how he will act tomorrow; indeed, he may be able to say with assurance what he would do under conditions that he believes will not arise. And this seems like a capacity to predict his own decisions. Still, this is quite different from saying, as a pessimistic compulsive neurotic might, that he knew what he would do *whatever* he decided. The normal rational agent can often determine what he will, or would, decide to do, because he can infer action commitments from his present beliefs about himself and his world, and believes that he will not (or would not) irrationally act contrary to them. In forming a belief about a future or a hypothetical decision to act, he would, in fact, already have made the decision, for the inferential part of the decision is encapsulated in the process of predicting it. Anyone who knew him well enough could make a similar prediction by taking account of his beliefs, of the actions to which they rationally committed him, and of his capacity to act on those commitments. Believing him to be neither compulsive nor akratic, the observer would suppose that the agent would act on whatever the latter took to be sufficient reasons. Again, because deciding what one is committed to do – or even what one really believes – can expend time and energy, it may be rational to postpone that expenditure. A hard question prematurely decided might be reopened anyway by further information coming to hand or the occasion for decision may never in fact arise. In that case the well-informed observer could correctly predict the action the agent would take if and when the time came, before even the agent himself had deliberated on it – but only by going through a process of inference precisely analogous to the one the agent himself would go through, if and when he came to address himself to the problem. Of course, just because the beliefs from which the observer inferred the action commitments would be the agent's, not his own, he would not necessarily be committed at the end to doing himself what he concludes the agent is committed to doing. He might think some of the agent's beliefs mistaken; others might be agent relative, committing the agent but not himself. For instance, he will not be committed to punishing his neighbor's children just because he believes his neighbor is committed to doing so, nor even, indeed, because he believes that that is the thing for his neighbor to do.

To say, then, that a natural person must be aware of himself as a decision maker or chooser, whose decisions can make a difference to the way the world goes, is not to suggest that there is something essentially unpredictable, arbitrary, or capricious about persons as causal agents. It would be absurd to disregard the phenomenological importance of willing as a central feature of personal experience – of deciding, say, to buy one brand of car rather than another. But it would be just as absurd to suppose that to do justice to this consciousness of freedom required the introduction into the account of action of an element of randomness, of ineffable uncertainty, a special volitional faculty distinct from understanding and feeling, such that until the chooser had actually willed, anything must be deemed possible. The existence of such a faculty no more follows from the actual difficulty of predicting human actions than does the indeterminacy of the weather from the inadequacies of meteorology. Admittedly, there are occasions when the reasons for different courses are so finely balanced, that there appears to be no reason for adopting one rather than another. Then, as I noted in section 1 of Chapter 4, it would be rational to decide randomly, particularly if there is no further time to seek additional reasons. In such a case neither the agent nor the observer can say in advance what will be done. To predict the action he would take might require, for instance, predicting the fall of a coin (which, however, is not unpredictable in principle but only in practice). But the combined conditions of equivalence and urgency are unusual enough not to be taken as paradigmatic and are certainly insufficient to support a belief that rational decision implies an uncaused randomness.

## 3. Natural persons and moral persons

Not every human being is a natural person. Whatever the potentialities for normal development of a newborn infant, its level of consciousness falls far short of that described above. It has to learn, to begin with, to differentiate what is its own – its own body and limbs – from the rest of the world which is other than itself, a level of self-differentiation which some autistic children do not in fact achieve. Without this differentiation it would be conceptually impossible for it to move to the next stage, of discovering that the world can be changed, and that one changes it by behaving in one way rather than another – by screaming, for instance. Only when one learns to scream *in order to* change the world is one equipped to recognize the difference between "world-changing entities" – personal agents – and other things. Only at this stage could the child recognize itself as a world-changing entity and become fully a natural person.

There are some schizophrenic adults who lack the self-awareness of agents, believing themselves to be things moved by external forces. They may have learned the concept of natural personality and believe that there are agents who originate changes in the world by recognizing the action commitments of their beliefs and acting on them, but they do not apply this concept to themselves. A schizophrenic's consciousness, instead, is rather of himself as process or as something to which things happen. In some advanced cases the sufferer may act out this self-conception in catatonic paralysis, becoming for the world, too, the mere object he believes himself to be.[1] In other cases the capacities for conceptualization and ordered inference are radically disrupted, with strange results in the use of language and therefore for intentional action. These sufferers are defective as natural persons. Other defects in rationality, such as paranoia, compulsive neuroses, and psychopathy are not, however, inconsistent with the full self-awareness of a natural person. With such an awareness, one would entertain goals and have the notion of an enterprise or project in terms of which one could be successful or suffer failure, and one would distinguish conditions and events as important or unimportant in the light of these assessments.

Now it is at least conceivable that just as a schizophrenic might have learned the concept of a natural person but not extended it to himself, so a natural person might fail to extend the concept to anyone in the world save himself. If he were to distinguish himself as a person from all the other, impersonal objects in the world, he would certainly have the concept of a person, and he would there-fore be bound to entertain the *possibility* of there being others like himself. But there might be nothing in his experience that would commit him to believing that any other human being really was a person. His uniqueness would be simply a contingent fact about the world.

It has been argued, against such a possibility, that it is only because one comes to understand others as persons that one can come to have the concept to apply to oneself. Following Hegel, John Plamenatz claimed that "self-knowledge in man is not prior to knowledge of other persons, but is acquired in the course of the same practice and process of learning as knowledge of a world that is external to the knower and includes other persons besides him-self."[2] But however this may be as an account of how we come to *have* the concept of a natural person, it does not follow that, having once acquired it, one could not then decide that one was alone in instantiating it. Someone might conclude that he had been mis-taken all along in attributing to other human beings the same personal self-awareness that he has of himself. Perhaps he con-cludes that they are robots left on Earth by alien visitors in the remote past, complex automata whose behavior is in many ways analogous to his own, and that this had misled him into applying to them a concept he had admittedly learned from them, but which truly applied not to them but to himself alone. If he then made the corresponding adjustments to his understanding of himself in the world, he would certainly have purged it of any rational commitment to noninterference in respect of any *actual* being, though not necessarily of a commitment to any possible persons.

Even so, the cost would be enormous. There would be so much behavior to explain away. But more, the consequences of such a cognitive strategy would be rather like those of paranoia. The subject would be forced back into a private world in which he could expect no independent corroboration of his beliefs. Since automata have no motives, he could ascribe to no one but himself the motive of truth in belief formation and would therefore have to treat their "judgments" not as cognitive appreciations of the world from the standpoint of another truth-oriented observer, but as mere inferences from the automated programs with which they happened to be equipped.

Suppose, then, that we ignore such a bizarre possibility, and take for granted that anyone who believes that there are other natural persons like himself in the world, each with enterprises important for him as his own are for himself, has no adequate reason for altering that belief. Such recognition would still be insufficient to commit him to an appreciation of their enterprises as capable of generating reasons for action, as well as for forbearance. For he might have a psychopathic understanding of the world as a Hobbesian state of nature. Each person in such a world could be aware of the others as having distinctive points of view, each with his own beliefs, action commitments, and enterprises, and he would prudently take account of these as facts of life to which he must accommodate his own. Provided each stood to gain and none could simply take possession of another's contribution, they might even contrive to collaborate in a limited sort of way, provided that no one was ever required to commit anything to the enterprise before others had done so too, and provided everyone expected the conditions favoring collaboration to endure until the task was completed and the outcome available for all to enjoy. Mostly, however, they would find themselves wrestling with free-rider problems, unable to ensure continuing cooperation.

In this ruggedly individualist state of consciousness, there could exist only a very rudimentary notion of trust, depending on continuing monitoring of performance. Prudence might dictate sticking to one's undertakings to the end whenever one expected to be involved in collaborative enterprises with the same people in the future. If one knew that a person had no such expectation, it would be imprudent to collaborate with him, but more than that, one would have to explain one's refusal to collaborate by saying, not that one could not trust him, but that one believed that he had no reason to do his part. Trusting a person is more than perceiving how his fulfilling his undertakings could further his own enterprise; it involves recognizing that he has a reason to abide by his undertakings even when they do not promote his goals. And in our supposed Hobbesian world, he would have no reason. Nothing in such a world could sustain a sense of unfair treatment or injury. The impacts of one person upon another might be infuriating and frustrating, but would have to be accepted as natural hazards to be endured.

Between natural persons so related, "reactive feelings and attitudes that belong to involvement or participation with others in interpersonal human relationships"[3] are ruled out because the subjects would be incapable of conceiving of others as the intentional objects of such feelings and attitudes. There could be no love or friendship between them as equals, for each would see the rest of humanity as potentially available instruments for his own purposes. None could acknowledge the goals and values which gave point to the conduct of others as capable of generating any reason for action for himself. Admittedly, a person might come to see the furthering of someone else's well-being or gratification as a constituent of his own enterprise, or the fulfillment of the other's projects might be encapsulated in his own. Someone who does not acknowledge other persons' moral personality is not necessarily lacking in other-regarding concern or benevolence. But such a person would treat others as he treated his pets, enjoying their enjoyment, but seeing them simply as consumers of the enjoyables provided for them. Someone who experienced another's enterprises only in this way could not grasp the importance they had for the other as his own. Just so do possessive parents and lovers, lacking respect for loved ones, smother them with attentions. If the latter show resentment at such treatment, they suffer insult added to injury if they are then reproached with ingratitude. Someone whose concern for the well-being of another person has this self-gratificatory quality can hardly complain of his ingratitude if the subject rejects the offering as unwanted. Gratitude is not owing where there is no respect. In such a situation the one conferring favors is attending to the other not as a subject of enterprises in the face of which he is willing to set his own aside, but altogether as an object of his own benevolent enterprise, in which the other figures as a happy object in his preferred world.

As between lovers, however, neither of whom possessed the notion of mutual respect, the one devoured would hardly know what to complain of. For a complaint – or, indeed, any expression of resentment or indignation, as distinct from mere rage or distress – cannot be formulated unless the complainant already supposes that some respect or consideration is *owed* to him. Resentment and indignation are reserved for persons; one may be indignant if one is obstructed by another driver's selfish parking, but not at a tree across the road, uprooted by the wind. The driver, one believes, ought to know better, as one who from his own experience must understand the problems of parking. Resentment and indignation are reserved for subjects whom we perceive as conceptually equipped to grasp that we too are natural persons like themselves, and who, in their preoccupation with themselves and their own ends disregard what is important to others, to whom they thereby deny the consideration due to persons.

Attitudes like resentment, in short, presuppose, at the very least, the recognition that by virtue of being a natural person one has a minimal right to be considered in a particular way, as possessing a point of view, an appreciation of events and states of affairs not only as a subject of experiences but also as an evaluator, a decision maker and project maker.

Resenting another person's lack of consideration, however, we are already committed to the general principle that every natural person, being conceptually equipped to grasp what it is to have and to value projects of his own, is thereby committed to respecting the standing of every other person as an originator of projects. Seeing ourselves as natural persons, as project makers, in a world with others like ourselves, we have developed a conception of ourselves as *moral persons* too, entitled to a degree of forbearance from any other natural person conceptually capable of grasping that self-perception and of sharing it. Claiming respect – the recognition of our moral personality – on the grounds of our natural personality, we are then committed to extending it to anyone else satisfying the same conditions. Coming to this understanding is the marvelous change that, according to Rousseau, overtakes someone when, entering into the social contract, he substitutes justice for instinct, even benevolent instinct, in his conduct. Moreover, anyone privileged to pursue his own projects in the conditions of the *contrat social* would have every reason for preferring that state to the Hobbesian state of nature, to which he would commit himself were he to reject the conceptual link between natural and moral personality.

According to this account, then, whether it is irrational not to acknowledge a connection between moral and natural personality depends on other constituents of one's way of grasping the world. The small child learns first the concept of natural personality. He has to be taught later that his initial success in gaining others' attention to his wants by demanding it is not a reason for believing that his projects are the sole reasons for actions which other persons can have. Moreover, others' projects can constitute reasons for him to act and to show forbearance. He makes the connection between natural and moral personality only slowly. The experiences of reciprocity and exchange – of gaining benefits in return for benefits conferred – no doubt assists the learning process. A child can be taught the right way to behave (or perhaps how not to behave) towards other people by being encouraged to ask himself, "How would you like to be treated like that?" Once he has succeeded in the imaginative move of putting himself in another's place, he has learned a reason for not treating someone else badly: He would not want to be treated like that himself; no one would want to be treated like that. Now that is quite different from learning not to treat others badly because otherwise they might treat you badly, and it is different, too, from learning that you should not treat anyone badly who does not treat you badly. When one has learned to make the conceptual link between natural and moral personality, one has learned also that one may be bound to show forbearance even when one doesn't expect it in return. A psychopathic criminal who apparently has the kind of self-consciousness that I have described as characteristic of a natural person but who does not make the connection in his own thinking between natural and moral personality, and who cannot be relied upon therefore to act with justice towards others, is not on that account, for someone who does make that connection, fair game, like a dangerous wild beast, to be shot on sight. And just because as a natural person he has the capacity to give or withhold consent, it would not be proper to treat him, like a laboratory guinea pig, as a mere resource.

Most children in our culture are mercifully equipped at last with this conceptual resource. But if someone lacked these concepts, or failed to make the conceptual link between them, it is hard to see how he could be argued into them, provided he live the psychopathic life, free alike of indignation, resentment, gratitude, and trust. But someone who did have a concept of personality that linked the natural and the moral would have the possibility of the forms of life, such as friendship, love, and trustful collaboration, which depend on them, and which he would have reason not to

99

want to abjure. Against a life which included such things, the life of the psychopath would be impoverished and unacceptable. So for someone who understood and valued them, it would be irrational to repudiate an understanding of personality to which they were necessary.

Societies exist, no doubt, in which people do not display this kind of mutual recognition. But they are societies in which the notion of a natural person as an independent project maker is only poorly developed. Spartans might cooperate in suppressing and exploiting helots without conceding much in the way of personality to one another, provided each Spartan identified pretty thoroughly with his civic role and had little in the way of a project of his own. A well-drilled military hierarchy, like the anthill or the beehive, can get along well enough without a conception of respect for persons because it leaves little room for personal initiatives. Hobbes says of ants and bees that "amongst these creatures, the common good differeth not from the private; and being by nature inclined to their private, they procure thereby the common benefit."[4]

But perhaps Hobbes's account is already too individualistic. Ants and bees, so far as we can tell, make no conceptual distinction between private and common; nor with the conceptual equipment supposedly available to a Spartan could it have been easy for him to make it either. And this is true, no doubt, of many contemporary tribal cultures, too. That is not to say that in such cultures the thing to do in every situation is so minutely prescribed by the requirements of one's role that no one can have his own style or way of doing things or that there are *no* enterprises one can make one's own. But these things may not be greatly regarded. One may understand one's nature not as a self-initiated enterprise but primarily as an instantiation of the succession of roles appointed for a life by the culture, as a necessary progression marked perhaps by rites of passage that move from one pattern of action to the next. In such cultures the concept of the natural person as project maker is but weakly elaborated. Conversely, in some religious communities, caring about having one's own way of doing things and caring for a project as one's own may be regarded as wayward and rebellious. There the concept of a natural person is well understood, but the link between it and moral personality is not made. So far from grounding a claim to consideration, the self-consciousness of a natural person would rate as a corrupt consciousness.

Hobbes was right to distinguish the societies of ants and bees from those he knew, whose members had strongly developed con-

100

cepts of personal agency. For men with that kind of self-awareness, social life would be impossible without the mutual forbearance and respect for personal projects (which Hobbes called "complaisance") enjoined by his fifth law of nature.[5] A psychopathic moral solipsist can exist as a deviant in a modern society, but to consider a psychopath's perception of himself and his world as an available option would be to entertain adopting a view of the world which, if standard, would be incompatible with the continued existence of the world it sought to conceptualize. Natural persons who generally perceived one another simply as natural hazards or opportunities, even during their limited alliances and collaborations, could expect no more success in creating a complex modern society or in sustaining its values than can a world of sovereign states in sustaining a stable and confident international order. Amoralism could be canvassed by a natural person as a rational option only if he were prepared to accept in exchange for a social order the war of each against all. Hobbes was surely right to believe that any human being would have good reason to welcome the transition from that to the civil state. However it may be, then, for cultures that lack a substantial notion of natural personality, it is a requirement of practical reason for any that does have it that it make the link with moral personality which grounds the principle of respect for persons.

There is, however, a possible exception to this identification of natural and moral personality. I have argued that not to make this conceptual connection would be to weaken the foundations for friendship, love, and the kind of trusting collaboration that we take for granted in our relations with other persons, and that for a culture that made the connection, it would be irrational to abandon it at the cost of losing these social advantages. But psychopaths are defective precisely in their incapacity to form such relations. Consequently a case could be made out for formulating a conception of moral personality which would be more restrictive than natural personality, so that psychopaths would be excluded from the respectful forbearances due to moral persons. That is, the conditions for moral personality would be stronger than those for natural personality, to include a capacity to form the concept of moral personality and to recognize others besides oneself as being moral persons. For such a strengthening of the qualifying conditions would not involve the loss envisaged in severing the link between natural and moral personality, since one cannot in any case form the beneficial relations that provide at least one *telos* for the conceptual bond with someone who would not qualify. More-

101

over, just as one deals with a threatening tiger by confining it indefinitely behind bars or by killing it, so the society of moral persons need have no compunction in dealing in the same way with a natural person who was also psychopathic.*

I see no way of meeting this argument head on; one can, however, take the Rawlsian course[6] of arguing that the category of psychopath is very uncertainly defined and that it would be morally hazardous to use it to exclude any natural person from the protection afforded by moral personality. By and large, the status of moral persons is better safeguarded without this conceptual revision. Of course, there are value-centered arguments against treating psychopaths cruelly, but these apply with perhaps equal force to tigers.

*Gerald Gaus drew my attention to this loophole in the argument from natural personality from which I had thought it possible to extend a capacity for human rights (the rights of moral persons) to all natural persons. The attempt to save the case owes a lot to his suggestions.

# 6

## The principle of respect for persons

### 1. Persons as subjects of interests

We are now in a position to look more closely at the principle of respect for persons, the grounding of which in the mutual recognition of natural persons was the theme of Chapter 5. Kant believed it to be irrational to treat any human being merely as a means to one's own ends; humanity is to be treated, both in one's own person and in the person of every other, as an end. This latter phrase has since become something of a cliché, but just what it means is not at all obvious. An end is generally taken to be an envisaged state of affairs, to procure which an action is performed or a project, stratagem, or policy pursued, or for which some means, instrument, or tool is employed. It is not at all clear, however, how a human being or even the realization of his humanity in such a being, can be represented as an envisaged state of affairs. The formulation may be, indeed, only an unfortunate residue of an instrumental or consequentialist model of practical rationality, which Kant himself rejected, according to which, if something did not figure in a rational explanation of action as a means, it must figure as an end. In my account of the principle, I focus not so much on the positive injunction to treat persons as ends in themselves, as on the negative prescription, not to treat persons merely as means or tools, or as counters in a strategy or as pieces in a chess game. I interpret this to mean, then, not that persons are ends, but that, however worthy an agent's own ends, his possible reasons for action or forbearance are not necessarily exhausted when he has considered how best to promote them. Not to have regard to the way one's own projects appear to another person affected by them, and to their bearing on his ends and projects, would be to disregard what distinguishes a person from a tool or a beast, namely his awareness of himself as a natural person.

I have adapted Kant's formulation in three central respects. In the first place, because the set of agents possessing the properties that qualify one for respect is not necessarily coterminous with mankind, I have shifted the focus from human beings to persons, and have suggested a view of personality logically separable from humanity. Second, I have argued that the rationality of the principle of respect for persons depends on a particular way of apprehending the world, and (*pace* Kant) that given a somewhat thin understanding of rationality a person might be thought rational who yet did not acknowledge the principle. Third, I have given a sense to "respect" that distinguishes it from concern on the one hand and deference or reverence on the other. It differs from concern in that a person may be treated without the respect due to him as a person even if his well-being is deliberately and solicitously promoted and nothing is done to cause him harm or suffering or deprive him of any advantage which might otherwise have been his. Indeed, one way of treating someone without respect is to impose conditions upon him for his own good, as one might physic a cat, without considering whether it accords with his own view of his good. A complaint still made against some members of the medical profession is that they tell a patient only so much about his condition as they think good for him to know, thereby depriving him of the opportunity to make an informed choice between treatments in the light of probable outcomes.

The respect due to persons, simply as persons, must be distinguished, as well, from "respect" as deference. Deference presupposes hierarchy; it implies acknowledging the person so respected as someone to be looked up to, in some degree better, more worthy, than oneself. It would be shown, for instance, by not contradicting someone whose knowledge of a subject one believed to be in general greater than one's own, even when one felt convinced that on a particular point he must be mistaken. The principle of respect for persons, by contrast, presupposes a certain minimal equality, capable in some measure of overriding established hierarchy. A member of an organization whose seniority, experience, or expertise entitled him to make some contribution to deliberations before its head reached a decision, might fairly complain, if not consulted, that he had not been treated with the respect that was his due – that he had been slighted – even though his superior stood higher than he in the hierarchy and possessed equal experience and expertise. His complaint that he had been slighted, however, would still rest on his special properties or qualifications not shared by the rest of the staff. By contrast, respect is due to all persons alike; it is grounded in the fact that each speaks from his own particular point of view, having perceived interests that no one else can presume to know in advance of inquiry, and which cannot be assumed to be interchangeable with anyone else's. Each, therefore, is a source of claims against, and reasons for, another person, just because the latter's actions and determinations have a different significance when seen, as it were, from the receiving end. Anyone may properly resent the slight of being overlooked as if his point of view was of no account. Respect for persons resembles, in this respect at least, the consideration due to the senior member of the organization, but the ground of the claim to consideration is obviously very different.

Though we have to distinguish respect from both concern and deference, it yet links up with both through the kinds of consideration due to a person's *interests*. This is a slippery notion, but in understanding how at one end of its range interests can elicit concern and at the other end command respect, we learn more about the difference between persons and axiotima as sources of reasons for action. A person's interests are, in one sense, those things which would be to his advantage. We sometimes distinguish his perceived interests, what he believes would make him better off, from his real interests, the conditions under which he really would be better off, whether he believes it or not. Alan's interests in this sense directly provide Betty with reasons for action only to the extent that she is benevolently disposed or is concerned for him – that she values his well-being. If she is unkind, ungenerous, callous, she is no doubt short on virtue, but she is not therefore lacking in respect for him. But if, while truly devoted to his interests, she nevertheless ignored what he perceived them to be, and acted instead on her own perception of them, she would indeed be lacking in respect for him, even though his judgment of his real interests turned out to be mistaken and hers to be correct. To respect someone as a person is thus to treat his own view of himself seriously; a child mature enough to satisfy the conditions for personality offered in Chapter 5 has every reason to resent the indulgent dismissal of its point of view, "Yes, dear, but Mummy knows best," even in the case that Mummy does.

But though the respect due to Alan from Betty may not commit her directly to a concern for his interests, the latter may furnish her indirectly with reasons for action in cases in which she has to decide between Alan's interests and the interests of others, herself included. For his status as a moral person requires of her that, under certain conditions I shall examine more fully later in this chapter, she give his interests equal consideration with theirs. Because the principle of respect requires that no person shall be treated merely as a means, it follows that there can be no class of persons whose interests have a claim to universal priority over others' such that, before the substance of the case for preferring the interests of one to another has been examined, injury to one will be automatically justified by the benefits to be enjoyed by the other. Equality of consideration of the interests of persons is the principle that ensures that anyone recognized as a natural person cannot then be consigned automatically to the back of every queue. It amounts to a repudiation of élitist moralities and discriminatory ideologies which, like racism and patriarchalism, assign an inferior status to whole classes of persons. An élitist might allow, perhaps, that the inferior class had interests deserving of some consideration but would insist that those of the super-men, super-class, super-race, or super-sex would always take precedence, that they simply counted for more. And this would be to maintain that, in some circumstances at least, the interests of one natural person might properly be given no weight at all if they were known to be in competition with those of a superior person, to whose interests the former might therefore be subordinated as a mere means. To respect someone as a person is thus to see him as a subject for a principle of equal consideration of interests, making demands on others for fair and just, and not merely for benevolent, treatment. Aristotle's belief that there were some people who were natural slaves, who could have no ends of their own but were naturally tools for the ends of others, amounted, then, to an assertion that there were human beings who were not properly qualified objects of respect as moral persons because they were not natural persons either. But he provided no criteria, of the sort that I offered in the last chapter, for distinguishing those human beings who were from those that were not so qualified.

So far, however, we have only a very thin sense of "interest" and correspondingly of "respect." For there is another sense in which a person's interests are those forms of activity which provide the foci for his attention and which he perceives as giving point to his actions and his projects. They are those things in which he "takes an interest," such as the welfare of his family, his football team, music, philosophy, or the Freedom from Hunger Campaign.

A person's interests in this sense are not merely objects or objectives to which he as subject addresses himself; they provide the strands of his identity over time, through which he is able to see continuity of meaning and pattern in what he is and does. In what he is today he perceives the residues, the successes and the failures, of yesterday's projects, but equally the interests which inform his present projects reach forward into a future he is still fashioning and which he can understand as also his own just because he can see how its features would express his present interests. For this reason it is quite inadequate to understand his projects merely in terms of the gratification he will enjoy, or how much better it will be for him, if they are successful. His projects are an exteriorization of himself, projections, indeed, of himself into the world; his identity as a person, qualifying for respect not only from others but also from himself, depends on his sense that they are indeed his own, informed by interests which together constitute him an intentional agent with an enduring nature, not simply a stream of experiences, even of remembered and envisaged experiences. The defect of the schizophrenic who conceives of himself not as agent but as thing is not that he does not regard himself as of any value, an object of no concern to anyone (for people can value objects well enough), but that he cannot respect himself as a person because he lacks this sense of himself as a continuing identity of interests.

The respect due between persons is anchored, then, in the recognition of one another as subjects of interests in this sense, making on each the same demand for forbearance and consideration that each makes on other project makers. One may believe the other's project quite worthless in itself. Its claim to respect rests not on its being valuable and worthy of one's concern, or even on one's interest in or benevolent concern for its author but simply on its being a person's project. Betty's interference to prevent Alan wasting his time pebble splitting when he could have been doing something worthwhile like philosophy is impertinent because it disregards Alan's own judgment of the value of pebble splitting and its significance to him and substitutes her own. Her judgment may be correct. Pebble splitting may indeed be a silly, worthless occupation, far inferior to philosophy; nor does the principle of noninterference commit her to refraining from an evaluative judgment of another person's life. If she had regard only for the interests, the possible benefits, that Alan had at stake, that judgment might well commit her to setting his aside. But unless she can claim some special standing, as might be conferred on her by Alan's prior consent or by his being in some special relation of tutelage, by virtue, for instance, of infancy or defect of reason, respect for him requires of her that she acknowledge that his projects are for him, not for her, to choose. But respect for persons requires not only that one consider people fairly as subjects of advantages to be enjoyed and disadvantages to be endured, but also as subjects of interests as the foci of their projects, to be respected by being left to put their own interpretations on their own lives.

For Betty to respect Alan in this sense is to extend the perspective from which her reasons for action can derive. She supplements in deliberation the account she would give of her options, viewed only from her own standpoint, by the account that he would give, from his. And in according him respect she accepts, as properly bearing on her decision, whatever action commitments are generated for her by his account, alongside those generated by her own. So it would be relevant and could be decisive for her that her own plan to clear the beach of pebbles would deny Alan the opportunity to pursue his interest in pebble splitting. Such respect accords well, therefore, with the way we talk of respecting someone's wishes or his privacy or his property. Respecting his wishes may do him no good; he might be benefited more if we disregarded them. But to respect his wishes is to allow one's own judgment of what the situation demands to be shaped, or even overruled, by his; to respect his privacy is to submit to his control of access to himself and perhaps to information about himself, as he sees fit; to respect his property is correspondingly to subordinate one's own intentions in respect of it to his. I do not mean that to act with respect for a person necessarily requires respecting his wishes or his privacy or his property, any more than the consideration due to a senior member of the organization accords him a veto on any decision with which he doesn't agree. That requirement would be too strong. But it requires at least that a person's view be seen to count for something in the calculation, a principle that, institutionalized in one way or another as a form of consultation, sharply distinguishes free from oppressive associations, even though in each there will be decisions taken by some which impose unwelcome constraints on others.

It is now apparent how respect for persons generates the principle of noninterference. We do not feel bound to forbear from using inanimate tools or domestic animals for our own ends because we do not owe them the respect due to persons. To the extent that we conceive of them on the analogy of persons – as some people do of their pet dogs – we do indeed hesitate to *use* them. So if one decided to give up keeping chickens, one might be prepared to sell them without hesitation to a neighbor, or even to slaughter them, treating them simply as a commodity, but one might be uneasy about doing the same to one's pet dog, with which one had built up a relationship that was at least analogous to trust and friendship; notions like desertion and betrayal are not obviously out of place. Whether such beliefs about dogs are reasonable will depend on how far one is willing to ascribe to a dog a point of view, which is to say, how far one believes a dog can satisfy the conditions of natural personality.

## 2. Respect for persons and the best consequences

This way of understanding one's commitments to action in relation to other persons is very different from that of consequentialists according to whom all reasons for action rest ultimately on the values attached to resultant states of affairs, particularly as those states are experienced by sentient beings. A consequentialist policy unconstrained by respect for persons will be indifferent to the status of individuals as persons, attending to them only as receptacles for happiness or, more generally, as vehicles for the realization of some other state of affairs, which, by virtue of the maximization of whatever particular value or ideal utility function is favored, makes the state of the world the best attainable. It would be a matter of indifference for such a policy that some receptacles were fuller than others, provided the aggregate was maximal. Equally, there need be no objection in principle to the total sacrifice of a few sufferers, nor to a system of distribution of valuable experiences that did relegate a class of persons to the back of every queue, as second-class persons – slaves, perhaps – provided the aggregate would not thereby be diminished.

Of course, utilitarians have a variety of hypotheses for meeting such objections. A common move is to show that it is unlikely that the aggregate advantage could in fact be maximized unless individuals were secured against the possibility of suffering discriminatory sacrifices of their interests in the name of the greater good (e.g., by the framing and punishment of innocent suspects to deter others from crime). Bentham argued in just this way for the security of unequal property holdings. Though he believed that, because their marginal possessions yielded less happiness to the rich than to the poor, a more equal distribution would have yielded greater total happiness, he summoned to the defense of his intuition that property rights ought not to be infringed two highly speculative empirical conjectures: (1) The unhappiness of mourn-

ing a loss always exceeds the happiness of welcoming a corresponding gain; (2) the insecurity generated by the fear of subsequent
redistributions would further reduce the increment of happiness
resulting from the initial one. A philosophical theory is hard-
pressed when it needs to rely on such conjectures to meet the objection that it generates counterintuitive action commitments.

There are, of course, very much more complicated kinds of utilitarianism, which modify the simple model by introducing a variety of empirical hypotheses, such as the one that attaining the
ultimately desirable end depends on everyone's actually aiming at
something different, just as in free-market economics achieving the
collective optimum depends on everyone's adopting a strategy to
maximize his private gain. So rule-utilitarians may treat rules as
the criteria for selecting right actions; the consequences of adopting or following various rules are then the criteria for the choice of
a rule. Still, for a consequentialist the best rule must always satisfy
the specification that it coordinates individual actions for the sake
of some ultimate state which is best for people in the aggregate, not
that it coordinates in some optimal fashion what they are all individually attempting to do. What they are attempting is itself a
subordinate consideration and might if necessary be constrained
to the overriding end of an optimal outcome.

Admittedly, there are utilitarians who try to accommodate the
thrust of the principle of respect by accepting as the optimal state
that in which people's preferences are most fully satisfied, conceding therefore that the best strategy is generally to allow a person so
far as possible to do as he chooses. His choice is presumed to express a real preference, either for what he most enjoys doing, or for
an expected outcome preferred by him to any state of affairs which
would result were he denied his choice. The chooser, it is presumed, knows best what will satisfy his preferences most fully. But
this, of course, is just another questionable empirical assumption.
People generally have very complex sets of preferences, and the
attempt to fulfill one subset may well interfere with the fulfillment
of others. It is doubtful whether anyone could work out a wholly
consistent preference set, even among the options likely to present
themselves for decision in the near future, let alone among the
more remote and not easily foreseeable possibilities. A dispassion-
ate and well-informed observer, not confused by the anxiety and
responsibility for actual choice, and able to rationalize and system-
atize the agent's preferences, ensuring that lower-order preferences were consistent with higher-order ones, might very possibly

see more clearly than the agent himself what choice he is really committed to by his structure of preferences. Such an observer would then be justified, if the criterion of optimality were simply the maximum satisfaction of preferences, in interfering whenever possible to substitute his own judgment of what an agent would prefer, for the agent's own.

Someone committed to a doctrine like this might claim, perhaps, to be giving due consideration to the agent's own point of view, and therefore to act consistently with respect for him as a person, since he intervenes only for the sake of the agent's own preference satisfaction. Still lacking, however, is a recognition of the agent's perception of his projects as his own, of their role, and of the interests which inform them, in the agent's awareness of himself as an originator with a continuing identity. The well-informed and benevolent administrator of another person's life may be able to realize states of affairs external to the agent that the latter has it as his object to bring about. But such paternalist management would be a kind of theft, stealing from their author the plans for a world in the making of which he sought the expression and realization of his own nature and identity, leaving him without a part in what he meant to be his own creation. For what the benevolent paternalist is not able to bring about, or only in a very indirect sense, is that the project be realized while yet remaining the author's own.

It is possible, perhaps, that a pertinacious consequentialist would find a way of embracing even this condition of respect for a person as project maker within his formulation of the utility function to be maximized. An all-embracing way of achieving this would be to say, simply, that the maximum fulfillment of the conditions for respect for persons in personal interactions, however these might be enunciated, would be a feature of the best state of affairs. The criterion for action would still be consequential, with the principle encapsulated in the criterion for assessment of consequences. But there would still be one difference between the two theories, though possibly a counterfactual one. If in just one instance acting without respect would have the consequence of maximizing over all cases the observance of the principle of respect, there would still be a reason, within the terms of the pure principle, for observing it even in that instance, since the reason for acting on the principle is to be found in the conceptual connection between natural and moral personality, not in the optimality of the outcome of its being observed. Even so, the reason might not be

111

conclusive. In the consequentialist version, however, there would be a reason for doing so only if the further practical condition were satisfied; that is, optimal results accrue from strictly observing the principle because the monitoring of expected outcomes in particular cases (which would be necessary to establish that a case existed for an exception) would itself impair the beneficent outcome of the principle's being generally observed. It is hard to see why, except in very special cases, that should be so, any more than the optimal benefits ascribed by Bentham to a property system should be impaired by monitoring it with a view to occasional reform.

### 3. Qualifying respect for persons

I have insisted that because the principle of respect for persons is rooted in the way in which natural persons conceptualize themselves and their mutual relations in practical interactions, it furnishes reasons for action which are independent of consequential value considerations. I have not meant to argue, however, that the principle puts an absolute constraint on such considerations, nor that such considerations can never justify overriding the intentions and projects of other persons. The cost of embracing absolute principles in practical philosophy is, as I have argued in an earlier chapter, that when they conflict one must grapple with insoluble quandaries in which one can only do wrong.

Given a principle of noninterference, however, how is one to justify pursuing one's own projects when they interfere with another person's? Can one justifiably interfere with his project, to prevent his interfering with a third person's? If in the pursuit of his projects a person would do harm or damage to something that another believed valuable, would it be consistent with the principle of respect for the latter to prevent it? Would it be consistent with his believing it valuable not to do so? Is an environmentalist's belief in the value of unspoiled wilderness sufficient to justify his attempts to put legal restraints on picnickers in virgin bushland or in blocking the making of roads and dams? And if interference in one or other of these cases could be shown to be justified, but not fully consistent with respect for the other as a moral person and project maker, is anything left of the principle capable of constraining a person otherwise intent on pursuing his own course regardless of what anyone else thinks or wants? Are there reasons for interference that nevertheless acknowledge the special moral status of natural persons?

Betty would not be providing Alan with a reason good enough to justify her interference if she simply said that she disliked his splitting pebbles. To the extent that justification is a public process, its terms cannot be entirely self-reflexive. It cannot succeed unless it is grounded on reasons which are detached from idiosyncrasies, such as the likes and dislikes of the agent, and which anyone to whom the justification is addressed is bound to accept as reasons. But justification is not always public. Private deliberation *in foro interno* is also a kind of justificatory debate. The reasons which ground the principle of noninterference are among Betty's belief and action commitments, which function as objections to her acting simply on her likes and dislikes. If she deliberates rationally she must acknowledge such reasons, and look for justificatory ones that are overriding. Yet in justifying something even to oneself one is both defendant and juryman, and the reasons offered in the former role must be such as one could expect a juryman without one's own particular inclinations to accept. In the role of juryman Betty asks: Can such a defense be acceptable, not just to the defendant Betty, but to someone not in her special position, and more particularly, to Alan, if only he is prepared to look at the matter reasonably, as an impartial juryman might?

If one believes that basic needs provide intelligible value-oriented reasons to anyone, one may believe that an impartial juryman could be relied upon to accept as a reason for stealing food that one is starving. Although one's own hunger is agent relative, it is a particularization of a universal interest; anyone with the basic constitution and dispositions of a human being can appreciate the force of it as a reason. It is embedded in a total nexus of beliefs about the value of life and the conditions for its preservation, the nature of suffering, and so on, that Betty can reasonably see as nonidiosyncratic. But more than that, the location of that particular belief in the nexus will determine the weight to be attached to it, its capacity, that is, for overriding other commitments and withstanding objections. Whether or not some other person actually shares these beliefs or would be persuaded to them in public deliberation, one will accept them oneself as justificatory if it seems reasonable that anyone else should.

But that one simply dislikes what someone else is doing is not a reason of that sort. No one else need acknowledge it as a reason to desist, nor to submit to one's interference, nor even to suffer one's interference without resentment. It is agent relative in the most extreme sense. Only someone who had not progressed beyond the infantile stage of development at which one believes that one's own wants are compelling reasons for action for all others would expect them to commit anyone else to action. For a dislike to be comprehensible as a reason, even to the justifier himself, it must be capable of being presented under some agent-neutral description that anyone else can appreciate as a reason. Or perhaps one should say that one's dislike is no reason at all – that to translate it into a reason for interference one must first ground it on a reason that will make it intelligible to someone else.

Caroline's attitudes to Desmond's tearing legs off crabs illustrate this: Her disgust alone need not bother him. It provides neither Desmond nor anyone arbitrating impartially between him and Caroline with a reason for Desmond either to comply with her preferences or to accept her interference without resentment; her preferences as such commit neither Desmond nor anyone else, and insofar as she succeeds in imposing them on Desmond she does him violence. If she could show that he was causing the crabs pain, and that her concern for pain, even in crabs, was not idiosyncratic but embedded in a structure of evaluative beliefs that made it reasonable, she could properly disregard Desmond's resentment. If Desmond's victims had been children, for instance, Caroline would hardly have hesitated. No reasonable person, she might say, could doubt that children must be protected from torture, and no reasonable person who nevertheless indulged his sadistic tastes could resent interference. Unless Desmond were a psychopath, even he might be expected to see the point of *that* interference.

This way of putting Caroline's perception of her situation suggests one possible solution to the difficulty of reconciling conflicts between the enterprises of natural persons in a manner consistent with mutual respect. For her action to be consistent with her respecting Desmond as a person in the most complete sense, she would have to forbear from interference except by his authority or consent. And this is broadly acceptable for interferences for which the justification offered is wholly in terms of Desmond's own interests. I have given reasons for thinking that in those cases Desmond's stake in his own future is of a kind that may well rule out anyone else's interference except under extraordinary conditions. If, for instance, his reason is so impaired that his intentions can be treated as not really expressing a view of his own interests, or if he suffers from suicidal compulsions that in more lucid moments he disowns, it would be reasonable to claim that restraining him in

114

his own interests would not be disrespectful of his natural personality, just because that personality was itself defective.

Nevertheless an important constraint deriving from respect for Desmond as a person would persist, just so long as it seemed reasonable to go on seeing Desmond under the aspect of natural personality, albeit as a defective instance. Caroline would not be entitled to treat him as a means to just any end of hers. One objective of interference, however, apart perhaps from the protection of other persons who may be threatened by Desmond, would certainly be consistent with this way of looking at his condition, namely, to restore him to a normal capacity as a person; that is, the criteria for paternalist intervention would themselves be supplied by the condition of natural personality. Only if that is impossible would Caroline – or Desmond's psychiatrist – be warranted in adopting as a goal of treatment some other criterion, such as to minimize Desmond's suffering. For it is a residual echo of the principle of respect for persons that as persons ourselves we are reluctant, in determining what should be done to an entity we cannot help seeing under the aspect of personality, to allow that his interests (in the sense of needs and advantages) should be treated as wholly instrumental to the interests of anyone else, even a nondefective person.

With a nondefective person the consent condition which blocks paternalist intervention would be unacceptably restrictive if more widely applied. Caroline cannot reasonably wait for Desmond's consent before she acts to stop him from torturing children. Nevertheless, the departure from the principle of respect for him as a person will be minimized to the extent that she can claim that, whether Desmond agrees or not, her preference for his abstaining from torturing children is grounded in beliefs to which he, and anyone judging between them, is already rationally committed, and which in turn commit him to accepting her interference as justified. Someone who would himself resent being tortured just for fun by another rational and sentient being equipped to grasp that from the victim's point of view torture wasn't fun would have reason not to torture a child. Because Caroline believes that Desmond would resent it, she need not be unduly deterred from intervening to frustrate what he is himself committed not to do; unlike his own victims, Desmond is not himself being made the victim of a project, the minimization of children's pain, for instance, in which, given his own standpoint, he simply could not have a part.

115

To what is Caroline committed, however, by the appeal to the point of view of Desmond's victim? To have a point of view in the required sense, must the victim be qualified as a natural person, or at the very least be able to conceptualize what is happening to it? If the child is a mere infant, it is sentient and suffering, but as yet it has no more a point of view than a chicken or a sheep. Suppose Desmond's projects consist precisely in sadistically inflicting pain on sentient creatures. He may recognize that since he would not willingly suffer pain and would resent it if anyone knowingly inflicted it on him, he is rationally constrained not to inflict it on other persons who would feel about it just as he does. But he may deny that he is committed in the same way not to torture sentient nonpersons. After all, though he would not like to be kicked by a horse, he would not resent it, because horses know no better. He would accept it ruefully as a fact of nature that the behavior of some beings hurts others. Why should a horse's – or a baby's – pain count for him against his torturing it for his own enjoyment, since he looks to a horse or to a baby to be no more considerate of his feelings?

A great deal depends, in this argument, on whether the case can be made out for the rationality of values, on whether there are any evaluative beliefs to which any rational being – or at any rate, any rational human being – is necessarily committed. Is it irrational not to believe that pain (including others' pain) is bad and therefore to be avoided? If it is, then Caroline can maintain that Desmond's inability to grasp the reasons for not torturing infants is a defect of rationality, and that his normal immunity as a person from interference, except for reasons that he could share, is correspondingly weakened. For his inability to share them is due to a defect in him, not to the inadequacy of the reasons. It will still be incumbent on Caroline, of course, to take account of Desmond's own point of view, since his defect of rationality is not sufficient to disqualify him altogether as a natural person. It is not open to her, just because he is unable to see the reasons accessible to a nondefective person which are sufficient to override his own project, to treat him simply as an instrument for hers or anyone else's. It would not warrant, for instance, passing him over for torture to another sadist. But his inability need not – indeed, should not – inhibit her interfering to prevent Desmond's torturing babies.

This argument would not be available to Caroline, however, if she did not accept the rationality of values in the required sense – if she believed, for instance, with Mrs. Foot and others that someone might, without defect of rationality, understand that pain was bad for the sufferer but not see in that fact a reason for action or forbearance for himself except when the pain was his own.[1] Such a person might be held to be insensitive or callous, but those defects of character would not constitute the kind of defects of personality which would weaken the claim to respect. Caroline may yet believe, however, that there are some evils so great that they override the action commitment of her other belief that, as a person, Desmond can properly claim not to be interfered with for the sake of a project, such as minimizing pain in the world, which he cannot see as creating a commitment for him. Believing pain to be generally evil, she would be committed, for instance, to beating off a shark that threatened a child. The same kind of reason would commit her to treating Desmond's torturing of infants like a shark attack, as an objectively bad feature of the world which must be prevented even given that it amounts to imposing upon Desmond the commitments of a point of view which, on the present assumptions, he cannot be shown to be rationally defective in not sharing. If Desmond is incapable of sharing her judgment and acknowledging it as a justification, Caroline is nevertheless committed by it to action. By conceding that his defect is not one of rationality, she admits also that her intervention is not one he is already rationally committed to accept as justified. Nevertheless, given her own structure of evaluative beliefs, a child's pain is a reason which overrides in this instance the principle of noninterference.

## 4. The principle of equal consideration of interests

I have asserted that one can derive from the principle of respect for persons not only the principle of noninterference, but also a principle of equal consideration for the interests of persons. To justify discrimination in the attention accorded to the interests of different persons, one must be able to point to a difference between them relevant to the discrimination being made. This might be formulated negatively as the principle that there cannot be first-class and second-class persons; there is no property a person might possess, nor any relationship that might hold between persons, such that this alone would entitle a person to go without further justification to the head of every queue or another person to place him there. It is now necessary to look rather more closely at this connection, and at the limits of the constraint that it puts on agents' decisions.

117

In elaborating the principle of noninterference, I claimed that Betty's likes and dislikes could not be justification enough for interfering with Alan's activities. One is tempted to make a similar claim for the principle of equal consideration of interests. A judge, for example, is bound to deal impartially between litigants, attending only to those things about them that are legally relevant to the case in hand and setting aside his personal preferences for one rather than another. It is a principle that rules out favoritism, which is why it is associated with ideas of justice and fairness. It would be far too strong, however, as a general constraint on all decisions which differentially affected other persons' interests. It would be pretty implausible if it required, for instance, that one might never buy a friend a drink unless one bought drinks all round, or that since one could not ask every woman to be one's wife, fairness required that one decide by lot among those formally qualified (being of marriageable age, not already married, and so forth), mere liking or personal inclination constituting an unjustifiable favoritism. Favoritism is, after all, an essential requirement of both marriage and friendship.

If the principle really did impose such requirements, it would empty of all significance the first application of the principle of noninterference, that the onus of justification rested on the interferer, not on the agent, who, until a challenge was mounted against his action, might do whatever he liked. For since practically everything one does has effects on others, favorable as well as unfavorable, one would not be able to act at all, even when one conferred only benefits, without being challenged to justify the discriminatory effects of one's actions. This objection is similar to one frequently directed against utilitarianism, that it places on everyone an intolerable burden to justify every act as optimal. The strong principle of equal consideration of interests would make a similar demand, that whatever one did must be shown to be fair. However, this uncomfortable conclusion need not be accepted. It is not that there are situations in which being unfair would be unobjectionable; rather, it is that one is not always bound to assess all the effects on other people of what one does in terms of fairness.

The model of personal interaction I have taken as standard postulates individuals pursuing their own projects, each acting on his own understanding of what it is worthwhile or appropriate to do, given his structure of beliefs and values. Sometimes they compete, sometimes cooperate, but each is committed to abstaining from doing to others what he would consider he had reason to resent

118

their doing to himself. It was not necessary, however, to the condition under which I supposed that the conceptual connection between natural and moral personality would be made that anyone would have a reason to do more than forbear in his relations with others; that condition did not entail a reason for acting positively to promote their interests. If Betty rode roughshod over Alan's enterprises, regardless of their significance for him, ruthlessly pursuing her own, Alan might well come to resent it as lacking in respect and understanding, knowing her to be fully aware of their similarity as self-conscious decision makers. But it is not a necessary presupposition of the moral relationship emerging from the mutual recognition involved in respect that she should have any benevolent concern for Alan. So while her having such concern need not be inconsistent with respect, the withholding of it cannot be a ground of grievance. Correspondingly, if Caroline gives Alan the benefit of her hand in marriage while denying it to Desmond, Desmond is not wronged. Since she has no obligation to be benevolent to either Desmond or Alan, Desmond has no ground for complaint that she favors Alan and not himself. She need favor neither. Nor is she under any obligation to justify her decision, for in this matter she may do as she likes. If Desmond were to claim that in refusing him she had thwarted his project of making her his wife, she has the rejoinder that it is not a project that can be carried through without her cooperation, and though it would be wrong, prima facie, for her to frustrate any project of his that made no demand upon her beyond forbearance, this one required much more of her to carry through. If Desmond denied this, he would be demanding, not that she give equal consideration to his interests with her own, but that her interest be subordinated to his.

Accordingly, Caroline is not called upon to justify her preference for Alan to Desmond or to anyone else. Indeed, the principle of noninterference requires that Caroline should not be called upon to justify anything she does until it has been shown that her decision affects someone else's interests adversely – and that there was, in consequence, a reason for Caroline at least to consider setting aside her own project in favor of Desmond's. Admittedly, Desmond believes that he would have been very much better off had Caroline accepted him rather than Alan. But her not benefiting him does not entail that she has affected his interests adversely; since he had no reasonable ground to expect or require her to give his preferences priority over her own, she could not wrong him by refusing to do so. The idea of a person as the author of her own projects, as

119

engaged in living her life in a way that has creative significance and value to her as her own, must surely rule out the requirement that Caroline must be prepared to defend every one of her decisions against the charge that she has ignored the interests of some person who might have been benefited had she done otherwise.

The principle of equal consideration of interests must operate, therefore, as secondary to the principle of noninterference. The call to justify discriminatory action is in order only after it has been shown that the decision maker had an obligation in this case to deal fairly – to set aside his preferences for the sake of universally acceptable reasons.

Given this restriction on the principle of equal consideration of interests, it is no longer unreasonable to make the claim that, when an agent's pushing ahead with his project would harm another person, or otherwise damage him in a way it would be appropriate for the latter to resent, the agent is bound to give equal consideration to the interests of everyone affected, himself included. That much seems implied by the respect principle that no person can be used simply as a tool or instrument or can be treated as more or less expendable in order to promote the interests of another person.

To apply the principle of equal consideration of interests we require an understanding of harm. We do not harm someone every time we do something different from what would have been optimal for that person. The concept of moral personality that has emerged from this discussion has at its core the idea of a decision maker for whom there is a certain creative elbow room. He is not wholly constrained by the demands others make on him; he has a notion of a life to live, which has somehow to be designed within the constraints set by others doing the same. True, he cannot be an island; there is little he can do without the collaboration of others. Nor are his enterprises fabricated from nothing; he lives off the accumulated resources of his culture. But for all that, he is conscious of himself as fabricating a life and a self as a kind of overarching enterprise, in which he has the most profound interest. For this to be possible it must also be possible that he have room to choose between activities and objectives valued by him from his own point of view; his decisions cannot be wholly controlled by other-regarding considerations. We need, therefore, an understanding of the boundaries of permissible indifference to the effects on others of what we do. The notion of harming another person presupposes standards of interaction which are contestable and culturally variable. In a free-market economy, for instance, it would not count as doing someone harm to compete by undercutting his prices; one has no obligation to competitors beyond observing the rules that define the practice. By contrast, in medieval Europe, where economists' arguments were theologically grounded, the notion of a just price regulated acceptable competition, and to undercut one's competitors and to overcharge one's customers alike counted as doing them an injury. As we shall see in the next chapter, what counts as an interference with freedom of action, and what is acceptable as the legitimate pursuit of one's own enterprise, is subject to interpretations which shift within a wider context of social expectations.

# 7

## Freedom of action[1]

### 1. The complexity of freedom

I maintained in Chapter 2 that no hard line could be drawn between theoretical and practical discourse, and that a proposition that might appear to have no practical implications at all could turn out to carry, at the very least, epistemic action commitments constraining the assertions it would be rational to utter or not to utter, given only that one held a certain proposition to be true. Nevertheless, some forms of discourse are more immediately practical than others. Propositions that directly commend action and others that impute responsibility, justify, blame, or excuse, while not sealed off from descriptive discourse by an is–ought gap or a fact–value distinction, are more immediately practical than, say, the propositions of theoretical physics. The former either directly enjoin what is the thing to do in specific circumstances or are action guiding by implication – an imputation of blame for an action indicates, for instance, that it would not be the thing to do under similar conditions at another time.

Because the concept of a person is profoundly important in such forms of discourse, and because to recognize someone as a person is to incur action commitments of a quite specific type, I devoted the last two chapters to an inquiry into the conditions that an entity must satisfy to be a person. These conditions were not simply stipulated as conditions for a technical term in a theory, nor elicited, in the manner of "ordinary language philosophy," by asking, "What would it be usual to say?" I asked, rather, what conditions a being must satisfy to be a person, if the concept of a person is to be adequate to certain of the linguistic demands made upon it by practical discourse, that is, if it is to be capable of generating the kinds of action commitments implied by principles like respect for persons, noninterference with persons in the pursuit of their projects, equality of consideration of the interests of persons, and, as I mean to show, by the conditions for freedom of action.

122

'Freedom,' of course, is problematic. The range of subjects to which the predicate *free* can be applied is so diverse that one might be excused, perhaps, for treating the word as hopelessly vague. For instance, speech, fall, drinks, acts, states, citizens, choice, can all be termed 'free'; and the range of things a subject can be *free from* – infection, anxiety, undue influence, prejudice, harmful additives, and so on – or what he can be *free to do* – to choose, move, grow, protest – is hardly less diverse. No neat set of necessary and sufficient conditions could be either discovered or even plausibly stipulated for the proper use of 'freedom,' which would embrace such diversity. At the same time, the various senses in which all these things can be free may not be totally unrelated. For this is not a case of homonymy, of the same verbal symbol standing for radically different and unrelated ideas. The ambiguities of 'freedom' are not due to the contingencies of etymology, like the chance similarity in spelling and pronunciation of the two words *tense*, one related to tension, the other to time, which have quite different roots; nor are they like the ambiguities of *bank*, the different senses of which, while deriving from a common root, have developed in quite distinct and semantically unrelated directions. The different senses of 'free' when predicated of the diverse subjects listed above have, despite their diversity, a genuine semantic connection, such that it would be misleading to say that the concept of freedom in "free fall" was quite different from that in "freedom of speech." One comes closer to the semantic reality if one sees 'freedom' as a complex-structured concept, linked internally by a set of beliefs and understandings about, for instance, motion, decision, impediments and interferences, possible goals, interests, and intentions and the conditions for adopting, forming, or pursuing them. Its internal structure is therefore ideological.

What is required, then, is a semantic theory of freedom in which appropriate places can be found for the various ways in which people are held to be capable of freedom and of being denied or deprived of freedom, in which they can be said to be entitled to be free and injured (at least prima facie) if freedom is denied them, in which people are considered the better – or the better off – for being free, and in which the institutions which structure their practices and activities can themselves be characterized as free or unfree, while at the same time serving as vehicles for the freedom of persons or for free activities. Such a theory will be ideological in the sense that it will explain why diverse subjects are characterized as free or unfree in the light of a wider set of beliefs about action, agency, and personality, and about the interactions of persons and their reasonable mutual expectations in their social dealings with one another. That is to say, one will grasp the internal relations of the concept of freedom by understanding its multiple functions in a certain network of beliefs. With a radically different belief structure, the concept would be differently constituted. Or perhaps one should say that a radically different culture would possibly have a complex-structured concept functioning in many ways, like the one we are familiar with but having applications that from time to time might puzzle us, and we might be hard put to it to decide whether it should be termed a concept of freedom at all. It is a central concern of this book to trace the broad outlines of a theory that will exhibit the coherence of a concept of freedom which meshes into a web of beliefs about personality, action, and personal relations with which readers of this book are likely to be familiar, and to which they will find themselves broadly committed by still other beliefs that they hold.

The concept of a person is intimately bound up with agency. A person is one who envisages and initiates actions. I suggested in Chapter 5 that to initiate an action is to have a kind of causal independence that arises out of the subject's having his own understanding of the nature and significance of his behavior, and from that understanding's being causally necessary to the agent's performance. This self-awareness forms, as it were, a loop in the causal chain. Information inputs are processed by the subject's belief structure, the constituent elements of which have practical implications; its conclusions emerge therefore as causally effective commitments to actions. So to be an agent one must have beliefs, including beliefs about one's own feelings, emotions, expected satisfactions and possible disappointments, and so on, which, if one's performances are to count as actions and not simply as behavior episodes, must be not only relevant but causally necessary to them.

There are, however, a number of levels at which a person might be said to possess such causal independence. At a certain basic level lack of it suffices to disqualify a human being from being a person at all. At a slightly less basic level a human being may be defective as a person by virtue of the lack, and therefore qualified as a subject of tutelage, yet still count as a person; at yet another level a person may be fully competent as a person, yet be subject to threats or deprived of information relevant to a decision he has to make, by reason of which he might claim that he could not act freely. And at the highest level one might say that a person,

124

though fully competent and subject to no external pressures, was not causally independent if he was dominated by his own prejudices, blinkered by an unexamined ideology, or a slave to convention. One says of such a person that he is heteronomous; one looks for the causes of his decisions in the opinions and beliefs of other people which his own merely reflect. Yet, as I shall argue in Chapter 8, one wants to distinguish this degree of dependence from the far more radical dependence associated, for instance, with post-hypnotic suggestion or personal domination. The sense in which a person can be said to be acting freely or to be denied freedom of action – what he is free or unfree to do and what it is that might make him unfree to do it – is going to be crucially important in assessing his responsibility for what he does and for what he fails to achieve, for judging his grievances and the legitimacy of his aspirations.

How can agents, who possess causal independence in the basic sense, be said to act sometimes freely and sometimes unfreely? A pendulum can swing freely unless tied back, and lions can roam free unless they are confined by the bars of a cage. Lions and pendulums are not true agents; such things are free if there is nothing to impede their behaving in standard or understood ways, given an appropriate triggering cause, such as the initial moving of the pendulum from its rest position. Yet such impediments can interfere with an agent's freedom of action too: The bars of a cage can interfere with a person's freedom to run a mile. But interferences with freedom of action can be more complicated, just because action involves beliefs and decisions. If one can give an adequate account in terms of impediment of the impairing of freedom by threats, why do beneficial inducements such as offers of trade or paid employment not impair it, except perhaps under the special conditions of exploitation or extortion? If a person possesses the kind of causal independence necessary for freedom of action, the capacity, that is, for decision making in the light of beliefs, under what conditions could his actions count as unfree while yet continuing to count as actions, and not be relegated to that category of behavior – including, for example, tics and metabolic functionings – in the explanation of which beliefs have no part?

## 2. Freedom and power

Freedom, when applied to agents, is a triadic relation: The free agent Alan is free to Φ in relation to some possible frustrating condition *F*. Φ may be regarded as the active term of the relation. Not that Alan's freedom to Φ requires that he actually Φ all the time; indeed, he may never Φ at all, for one may possess the freedom to do something that one never chooses to do. Freedoms belong to the class of modalities like potentialities or capacities, which may exist whether or not they are exercised or manifested in action. The freedom relation between Alan and the type of performance Φ is active in the sense that it looks to the idea of an action rather than to the lack of one, even though Alan's freedom to Φ may require that he also be free not to Φ. If Alan is free to Φ but does not, then, akrasia apart, it is because he decides not to Φ; and that account is in terms of the positive categories of action and decision. *F* on the other hand is the privative condition of freedom in the sense that it is a condition for Alan's performance of Φ that *F* be absent. If Alan is not free from *F*, his failing to Φ is due not to a decision not to Φ, but to the absence of the conditions in which a decision either way would be to the point.

Calling Alan's freedom to Φ a potentiality links 'freedom' with 'power,' at least when relating to agents and action. Or still more generally and abstractly, it relates it to the cluster of concepts suggesting possibility (but not those suggesting probability or likelihood) covered by the Latin verb *potere* and the French *pouvoir*, and to almost all the modalities that in English are rendered by *can* and, of those rendered by *may*, to the ones which have to do with the absence of a normative impediment. It is important, therefore, both to explore just what the links are, and also to distinguish unfreedom from other kinds of impossibility or lack of the power to bring something about. For whereas a person's being unfree to do something usually (though not always) implies that he cannot do it, it is not the case that whenever one is unable to do something one can properly say that one lacks the freedom to do it. For there are incapacitating conditions or conditions that make forms of action impossible that are not also conditions that make one unfree. And because the concept of personal freedom is most at home in the context of complaints, grievances, claims, and justifications, this distinction clarifies when someone's inability to Φ will sustain at most a regret that he cannot do it, and when it can properly be the subject of a complaint that he is unfree to do it.

Power and intention are jointly necessary to explanations of actions. The concept of a personal power, ability, or potentiality does little positive work, however, in explanations of actions actually performed; if a person has in fact Φ-ed, it is otiose to say that he was able to Φ. Admittedly, one may be surprised that he was, in which case one may ask not *whether* but *how* he came to have the power to do it, but to explain why he did it we shall almost certainly focus on his intentions and motives rather than on his powers. If, however, he has not Φ-ed when that might have been expected of him, the answer to the question why he did not may be either that his motive was insufficient to generate the intention to do it or that he lacked the power to Φ. And looking to the future, one needs to know that he has both power and motive before one can be sure that he will Φ. Without one he will not form the intention, and without the other he will not succeed.

Accordingly, before examining freedom of action further, I shall sketch out a conceptual model for ascriptions of power. Consider first the ascription of impersonal power to a motor. It has the power, one may say, to propel a car at 150 km an hour along a highway. Though it doesn't do so all the time, still we say it has the power all the same – the power is latent when not actual or manifest in performance. It is instructive, however, to recognize three kinds of conditions which, any one of which being unsatisfied, will account for the power not being manifest. First, there are enabling conditions which are considered external to the motor itself, such as its being supplied with fuel. A powerful engine will not work unless fuel is in the tank; but because fuel is not part of the engine, it is a condition (unlike its having pistons) for its manifesting its power but not for its having it. Secondly, there are impeding conditions, the absence of which is necessary to the manifestation of the power. An engine will not power a car with the brakes applied. Thirdly, the engine needs to be set in motion by the triggering condition, the turning of the ignition key.

With personal powers one possesses the power to do anything that one would succeed in doing if one tried. Trying is the necessary triggering condition for the exercise of a personal power. Admittedly, one might do something inadvertently, and the doing sufficiently proves one had the power to do it. The best evidence that a powerful but clumsy person possesses the power to cause havoc is that, simply by blundering around, he does so. Had he meant to cause it, one could see it as an exercise of his power, for which he would then be fully responsible. But to describe an event as an exercise of power explains its occurrence as an intentional act, as one the agent meant to perform, which *ex hypothesi* this one is not. In the case of personal powers, therefore, one has to distinguish an exercise from a manifestation of a power. Though one may have a kind of responsibility for what one does inadvertently, it is clearly different from the responsibility for what one does intentionally. The notion of intending an action involves setting oneself to doing it under a description which derives from the beliefs which commit one to it. That action commitment provides what Kant might have called the maxim of the action, as the thing to do. So because what one does inadvertently is not done in accordance with any maxim at all, it cannot possess the intentionality necessary to an exercise of power. Consequently, one's responsibility for doing it under a description different from that under which the action was intended must depend on one's having had the ability to grasp that the action might be so described, whether or not one has given one's attention to it under that description.

The notion of a personal power is not, however, context free. As with engines, a person's intrinsic powers, such as his bodily strength, intellectual capacities, and so on, are distinguished from enabling and impeding conditions and from triggering conditions. The enabling conditions might be the availability of necessary equipment and opportunity, and the absent impediments such things as collapsed bridges that would prevent him from crossing a stream. The triggering condition is the presence of an intention. A person who has the power to $\Phi$, therefore, will actually $\Phi$ if certain standard conditions are satisfied and if he tries.

The conditions for ascribing personal freedom to act are rather different, however, from those for personal powers. For a start, it is incongruous to talk of unfreedom to do things that there could be no point in doing. Not that one would be guilty of logical inconsistency if one said, for instance, that one was unfree to drink nitric acid or, indeed, that one was free to do so if nothing stood in the way of one's drinking it but lack of inclination. But why should anyone want either to drink it or to say that he was free to do so? Or rather, there would be an onus on anyone who did say so to show that a possible intention to do it could be made intelligible. With a power there might be more point. For instance, if one were trying to compel someone to drink nitric acid, which he would not otherwise have any reason to do, it would be very relevant to ask whether, even under compulsion, he would be able to do it, or whether the contact of the acid with his lips might, perhaps, inhibit swallowing. The incongruity of talking about the freedom to do what is pointless or, still more, what there is an overwhelming reason not to do, marks not a logical constraint on the sort of thing that one can be free to do, but rather a constraint deriving from the way in which the concept of freedom of action functions in practical discourse. We might explain someone's not doing something by saying he wasn't free to do it ("Had he been free, he would have done it – he had a reason to"), but what would be the point of claiming that he was not free to do something that no one would have any reason to do? On the other hand, there would be a good deal of point in someone's *complaining* that he was unfree *not* to drink the nitric acid. It is just because the concept of freedom is most at home in formulating complaints and grievances, in claiming rights and demanding consideration of one's interests, that the functional range of the notion of freedom of action is bounded, practically if not logically, by notions of what there can be a reason to form an intention to do.

Consequently, the intelligible bounds of freedom are not immovable. We can discover that we are unfree in certain respects, not only by coming upon restraints that we were hitherto unaware of, but also by discovering an interest in doing something that formerly we had no interest in doing or believed it unreasonable, perhaps, to contemplate except as fantasy and which we only now discover to be a closed option. Even so, not every condition making it impossible for one to do it would count against one's being free to do it; often an impossibility is an impossibility and nothing more. What then is to count against being free to act?

### 3. The impediment theory of free action

One might say, with Thomas Hobbes, that one is free to do anything that there is no external impediment to one's doing:

> Liberty is the absence of all the impediments to action that are not contained in the nature and intrinsical quality of the agent. As for example, the water is said to descend freely, or to have liberty to descend by the channel of the river, because there is no impediment that way, but not across because the banks are impediments. And though the water cannot ascend, yet men never say it wants the *liberty* to ascend, but the *faculty* or *power*, because the impediment is in the nature of the water, and intrinsical.[2]

The point of Hobbes's distinction was to give a meaning to "liberty" consistent with a strictly determinist theory of human action; human beings could act freely in precisely the same sense that water could flow freely; freedom of human action required a hiatus in the causal chain no more than did freedom of material motion.

Yet the cause of water's natural downward motion is not, after all, contained in the nature of water – "intrinsical" – but in its gravitational relation with the earth. If we continue to talk about free flow and free fall, it is because we are presupposing a system of normal or standard conditions, with corresponding normal or natural motions which may, however, be deflected or inhibited by forces external to the system (such as dams and parachutes). Hobbes's distinction between intrinsic and extrinsic causes presupposes, then, a conception of a bounded system operating in a normal and characteristic way under certain standard conditions but liable in other conditions (in outer space, perhaps, beyond the earth's gravitational field) to deviate from this normal behavior. And this is very like the account I gave of the intrinsic powers of an engine. But it applies even more aptly to agents, of whom we can say that they try and decide, would prefer to do *this* but *choose* to do that because conditions make *this* less attractive overall. For though, as I have maintained, we can give a causal account of trying and deciding, we can grasp the thrust of those concepts only by taking account of the causal effectiveness upon action of a belief system, which supplies a kind of independence – a cause "intrinsical" – that neither waterfalls nor motors possess.

Precisely because self-conscious activity is not merely reflective but also reflexive, in that one's thinking about oneself and one's beliefs can cause an alteration in what is thought about, the distinction between intrinsic and extrinsic causal properties can ground a distinction between 'power' and 'freedom' much more significant than Hobbes allowed. There is no possible variation of a motor's behavior that will depend on its self-understanding, and therefore upon an appreciation of the action commitments of its beliefs. When one says, "He did not go to the opera because he wanted an early night," one implies that he could have gone had he wanted, that is, he was free to go. That he did not go was determined by his own decision – a consequence of his own grasp of the actions to which he was committed by his beliefs – not by an external happening like a car breakdown, nor by something internal to him but physical, like a stroke which would paralyze and thwart independently of any belief or understanding of its nature. If an external occurrence, such as a car breakdown, had made it impossible for him to go, there would have been no question of his being either free or not free to go. But if he prudently decided not to go because he believed that he would be arrested as he left the theater, he might reasonably claim not that he was unable to go but that he was not free to go. He might

130

say, it is true, that he had no choice but to give up the idea of going. But he had no choice in a rather different sense from the man paralyzed by a stroke. For the latter, choosing would make no causal difference. But the prudent man did choose. He could have risked being arrested; a truly devoted opera-lover might have taken the risk, free or not. The cause of his not going lies, in part at least, in his appreciation of his situation and in his conclusion that going to the opera is not the thing for him to do. So a question remains to be answered: Under what conditions might someone presented with competing options claim that he has no choice but to accept one and turn the other down?

The analysis of freedom of action in terms of the absence of impediments is unsatisfactory because it would count as free paradigm instances of unfreedom, thereby rendering incoherent the protest against unfreedom which is standard in such situations. Because the actions of an orthodox believer with no inclination to preach heresy would be unaffected by the expectation that anyone who did so would be burned alive, one might want to say that the actions of the orthodox believer were unimpeded and therefore free. But someone else who decides to preach heretical doctrines despite his expecting to be burned for it, an outcome which almost anyone else might regard as a decisive impediment to preaching, would not be impeded either. But being in danger of the stake for preaching heresy is a paradigm case of unfreedom.

Conversely, there is a kind of Stoicism according to which one can achieve freedom by cultivating indifference to everything over which one has less than total control, giving no hostages either to fortune or to other people. Unlike the willing martyr, the Stoic attains greater freedom not by desiring something more, enough to override the impediment, but by learning not to desire it at all, so that the impediment no longer impedes. But this seems a rather overaustere conception of freedom, concentrating more on what one might be free from than on what one is free to do. It might seem a way, indeed, of reconciling oneself to not having grapes by telling oneself that they are sour. It is, in any case, a strategy for decreasing the range of incapacities that will count as unfreedoms rather than for increasing freedom, for it imposes upon unfreedom the condition that one must care for what one is to count as being not free to do. This move may look plausible, perhaps, on account of its similarity to the condition discussed above, that the bounds of unfreedom are set by what it is intelligible to complain that one is not free to do. But schooling oneself not to want to do what

131

others might prevent one's doing is not the same as finding such activities unintelligible.

According to the impediment analysis, only someone (a timid heretic, perhaps) who is inclined to preach but who would be actually deterred from preaching could be counted as unfree. An analysis which makes Alan's freedom to preach depend on whether and how much Alan wants to preach is surely implausible. If one is threatened with a penalty if one $\Phi$s, one does not decrease one's unfreedom to do it by lowering one's inclination to do it, nor does one increase one's freedom to $\Phi$ by increasing one's desire to do it, even though a stronger desire may increase the likelihood that one will do it.

Instead of focusing, then, with Hobbes on impediments and constraints, it may be more useful to begin with choice, and to treat impediments and constraints as limiting freedom only if they restrict options that might otherwise, under standard conditions, be available and eligible. Whether one had an inclination to select an option would then be irrelevant to one's freedom to adopt it. The prudent opera-goer who decided to stay home rather than risk arrest was made unfree, according to the thesis I shall now propose, because the option of going to the opera would have been open to him but for conditions that made that course ineligible. It is in the context of choice, of eligibility and ineligibility rather than of possibility and impossibility, that talk of freedom is most at home. On the other hand, it is not enough for an unfreedom that a course of action can be undertaken only at some cost. For cost is of the essence of choice situations. Without opportunity costs we should have very little work for the concept of freedom, for we should never need to choose; one could always have one's cake and eat it too. Unfreedom arises not from the necessity of bearing costs but from their imposition where they might otherwise not have to be borne.

Admittedly, the question could still be asked why someone, chained by the leg or locked in a cell, who has no choice and no opportunity costs because he has no competing opportunities, is said to be not simply *unable* but also *unfree* to move. Conversely, it is not enough for unfreedom that options otherwise available have been restricted, for that could occur in the course of nature. A landslide makes a road impassable, so that one is unable but not unfree to drive along it. For unfreedom there must be a sense in which not only might the practical impossibility have been otherwise, but the fact that it is not otherwise must be attributable to

132

the action or inaction of persons who can be held answerable for the restriction.

This condition is consequent upon the primary functions of the concept of freedom in practical discourse, as a counter for expressing grievances, claiming rights, and defending interests. Admittedly, the word *free* occurs in strictly descriptive contexts too, and since there is no word "freeness," *freedom* must do duty as an all-purpose abstract noun to refer to all contexts in which the adjective *free* might be used. So one might just possibly need to talk of a pendulum's freedom to swing. But appeals to "freedom" in practical discourse primarily invoke principles with action commitments. In particular they invoke the principle of noninterference, that a constraint on another person's action – on his freedom – calls for justification. For a restriction of options to give rise to a discussion of freedom and unfreedom and not merely of possibility and impossibility, it must make sense to ask, "What justifies that restriction?" But it is pointless to ask for a justification unless one supposes that things might be different from the way they are but for the will or the negligence of a responsible being. One demands justification for an earthquake only if one challenges God: "Why did you make it happen or not intervene to stop it happening?" It follows, then, that freedom in the full sense is about the absence of restriction of the options available to independent agents or choosers, by persons having the capacity for deliberate and intentional interference, who might have made things otherwise had they so decided.

It is a general feature, then, of events or conditions that can be accounted reasons for saying that a person is not free in respect of a certain kind of action that, unlike the tides, they are not natural, unalterable, given, but rather some rational being or beings can be held responsible for them, for bringing them about or permitting them to continue. So by extending the range of restrictive conditions judged capable of alteration, the range of freedom-related contexts can itself be extended. Conditions formerly accepted as necessary may be called progressively into question; the frustrations to which they give rise come to be seen not merely as natural limitations on what is possible, but as restrictions on freedom. For nineteenth-century liberals, for example, economic freedom meant the absence of legal limitations on contracts of employment, pricing, movement of goods, and so on. Market conditions and the rights of property that governed the workers' bargaining power were generally taken to be no more alterable than the weather, the laws of supply and demand no more restrictive of freedom than the laws of gravity. The worker was held to be free in negotiating with his employer because, in terms of all conceivably controllable conditions, there was no restriction on his ability and opportunity to make the best *possible* bargain. Trade unionism and socialist economic theory combined to break down these presuppositions. The workers came to protest not merely against low wages or inequality, but against economic unfreedom – to do and enjoy many things that they now saw as denied to them because the employing class was either unwilling or unable to change economic conditions and property relations that were nonetheless capable of change. This was not just a change in the scientific understanding of society, and therefore an extension of power to manipulate it. An enlargement of technological capabilities can certainly occasion an enlargement of the possibilities of freedom, but there may have to be an ideological change too, a new readiness to call into question the legitimacy of property rights hitherto considered "natural." It was a revolution not simply in technical but in moral possibilities that gave a new reference to "economic freedom."

Of course, someone might concede that the economic system denied certain freedom to workers while yet justifying it on grounds of general utility. But this move must *follow* the admission that the economic and social structure is open to question, a proper subject for moral argument. Agreeing that if some or all of its participants wanted it changed they could change it, he maintains only that they would be wrong to do so. This is very different from the view that it is impossible or the stuff of fantasy that things should be otherwise.

## 4. Freedom, influence, and interference

While restrictions of options interfering with freedom of action require justification, not every case in which one person's action influences or even frustrates another's will count as interfering with his freedom. Influences which affect another person's decisions but do not restrict his options do not require justification as interferences with his freedom. Others, such as the offering of bribes, may require justification, but the charges that they have to answer arise from the contravention of some other principle, such as fairness or honest dealing.

The least problematic influence is a simple request. Suppose Alan asked Betty to lend him $100. It would be out of place for Betty to ask him to justify making the request on some ground of

134

right, as she might had he claimed repayment of a debt, for every-one is at liberty to ask, and everyone is at liberty to refuse. His asking impairs no interest and is no interference with any personal project of hers. She may, if she likes, simply ignore it. Nevertheless, if she agrees to it, the request will have had a causal influence on her actions; she would not have given him the money had he not asked. But that is not enough to make it an interference with her range of choices. For that, the request would have had to be a sufficient and not merely a necessary condition for Betty's agree-ing to it, and there is no ground for saying it was. For she might have refused. A request confronts one with a new option, but unless it alters in some way one's rational capacity to assess it against one's other options, one decides for oneself whether to adopt it or reject it. If, however, Alan had known that Betty felt guilty about being so rich, and deliberately manipulated her feel-ings, he may have been sufficiently skillful to apply a pressure she was unable to resist. And this might well constitute an interfer-ence with her freedom of a type that I shall examine when I come to treat of the subjective conditions for the freedom of agents. But a request exerting pressure, because it calls for justification, is not a simple request.

Alan may influence Betty decisively in other ways without his interfering with her freedom. He may point out to her facts she has overlooked, make clear to her what options are really open and that she is mistaken in thinking she has others; he may offer her disinter-ested advice. In none of these instances would he be called upon to justify his intervention, though he could properly be asked to justify his opinions. Offering advice as such – even bad advice – does not call for justification, at least from the standpoint of freedom, since Betty is at liberty to reject it if she wants; a normal rational person is put under no pressure to act on it merely by reason of its being offered. It may seem to Betty, of course, that options that she for-merly contemplated as available are now closed to her, but then, if they are impossible, they always were, and if Alan's advice has shown them to be only less attractive than she supposed, he has made them no less available to be chosen.

Admittedly, offering uncalled-for advice might be an interfer-ence of another kind, and Alan's intervention might be rejected by Betty as meddling in what was no concern of his. The liberty to offer someone unsolicited advice may be culturally limited to peo-ple standing in some special relation to him, to his parents, close friends, elders of the congregation, priests, and so on. But while this protection of a person from such interventions by all and sundry may be required by some understanding of the notion of respect for persons – by a general right of privacy, perhaps – it is a mistake to confuse it with freedom.

Making an offer of trade or employment is, under standard conditions, another way of influencing a person's actions which enlarges rather than restricts his options, and is not, therefore, open to the call for justification. One may accept the offer or do precisely what one would have done had it not been made. So it cannot make one less free than one was before. The shopkeeper who offers eggs for sale but refuses to give them away for nothing might be said to impede access to eggs for someone who has no money, but it would certainly be odd to say that he interfered with that person's freedom to have eggs, as if the shopkeeper were in the same class as a highwayman who obstructed one's freedom to travel until one had handed over one's wallet. The difference lies in the acceptance of the general framework of property relations as defining the normal conditions of action and therefore the options initially available. Just as the laws of gravitation are represented more plausibly as defining the conditions under which one could fly – if one had an airplane, a glider, or a balloon, but not otherwise – than as impediments to one's flying (as though the ability to fly were the norm), so the institution of property defines the conditions under which I may obtain eggs. Having free eggs, unlike traveling the highway, was an option never open to me anyway. A conditional offer normally creates an opportunity; it erects an impediment only when the condition restricts a range of options formerly or standardly unrestricted.

It is, however, a well-established move in radical argument to claim that property relations do close options otherwise available. Conditions hitherto accepted as necessary initial conditions for freedom are challenged by purporting to show that there is nothing illegitimate, irrational, or absurd in envisaging a social order in which different arrangements would obtain and in which, therefore, forms of action now ruled out as impossible would be eligible options. Short of such a radical revision of freedom, however, to lay down the conditions for enjoying the benefits on offer or to specify the opportunity costs of doing so does not count as making those benefits unavailable, for a world in which they might be enjoyed without those costs is not the environment assumed. Given the property institutions which constitute the standard conditions, offers to trade, so far from restricting the options of the respondent, actually enlarge them and therefore enlarge his freedom of action.

But while many conditional offers are consistent with freedom, some are not. I claimed earlier that to offer a bribe would not be a contravention of freedom; it would need to be justified because it contravened other principles and attacked public interests in impartiality, the honesty of officials, and so on, by giving someone an inducement to betray a trust or neglect a duty. But it makes no one unfree. Yet for someone desperate for money, a bribe may be irresistible. Or so he may plead in excuse.

Or consider exploitation and extortion. Shifting the account of freedom from the absence of impediments to the nonrestriction of options, one can readily distinguish extortion not only from legitimate offers to trade, but also from exploitation, an unjust practice that does not involve unfreedom. Esau, faint unto death after a day's hunting, was in no position to haggle with his brother Jacob over an offer to trade his birthright for a bowl of soup.[3] According to the Authorized Version, "Esau did eat and drink . . . so Esau despised his birthright." This seems a bit unfair; Esau had already given a reasonable enough account of his preference set: "Behold, I am at the point to die: and what profit shall the birthright do to me?" Though he paid a great deal more for his snack than it would have been worth in normal circumstances, his bargaining power was so reduced by his urgent necessity that he could reasonably claim that *he had no choice*, that this was an offer he couldn't refuse. Jacob's deal with Esau is a case of exploitation, of using Esau's exceptionally weak bargaining position to exact a price that was disproportionate to the normal value of the commodity or perhaps to the cost to Jacob of producing it. One does not need to be desperate, however, to be exploited. Ignorance of market alternatives or reckless extravagance makes one vulnerable too.

Nevertheless, though Esau might say that it was impossible for him to refuse Jacob's offer, he acted as he did because there happened to be no alternative course that a reasonable, prudent person could consider eligible, not because Jacob had deprived him of any options. Of course, if one considers that between brothers or between any human beings, one of whom was in great need, the soup should have been available free of charge, then one *is* entertaining an alternative – free soup – that Jacob has deliberately denied him, using his superior bargaining power to extort not only a price but an unreasonably high one.

Exploitation takes advantage of an opportunity for profit which may present itself quite fortuitously; extortion alters a subject's situation so that he becomes vulnerable to exploitation. To use some special bargaining advantage to exact more than a commodity would cost in some normal circumstances, or to offer less for a service (e.g., in wages) than it is worth (given some standard by which to assess it) is always unfair. But it is only when turning the offer down would be inviting deprivation or injury so great that no one would expect a reasonable person to take such a course that one says, "I cannot refuse," or "I have no option but to accept." Exploitation demands both conditions: that there is no reasonably eligible alternative and that the consideration or advantage received is incommensurate with the price paid. One is not exploited if one is offered what one desperately needs at a fair and reasonable price.

Each of these two conditions for exploitation involves a standard. The first assumes a standard determining what would be a reasonable alternative, including the possibility of going without; since one would be free to refuse the offer if such an alternative were available, one would not be unfree if instead one accepted it. But the absence of an alternative would not be sufficient on its own; a monopolist would not be an exploiter if the price he asked were no higher than it would be on an open market, however indispensable the commodity on offer. The second condition for exploitation assumes, then, a price that it would be reasonable to pay for what is on offer. Of course, an outrageously high price would not amount by itself to exploitation but only to bad business if the customers could reasonably choose the option of doing without or of going a reasonable distance along the road to another shop. Extortion, however, goes beyond exploitation, for it requires the satisfaction of a third condition, that the absence of options, which makes the victim vulnerable to exploitation, is the result of some action or failure to act on the part of the extortionist. Extortion is, in this respect, a form of coercion or duress, and the person subjected to it is thereby unfree.

This analysis of duress and extortion helps to explain the difference between the classical economic liberal and the socialist radical for whom low wages are evidence not only of employers' exploitation of workers' necessity and consequent weakness in bargaining power, but also of economic unfreedom. An unemployed worker may be unable to refuse an offer of a poorly paid job when no more favorable opportunity is open to him. For the liberal, unless the

138

employer has arranged things this way (e.g., by blacklisting workers or by excluding competition in the industry), he is acting only appropriately in economic conditions not of his making. He is not responsible for the workers' desperate need; neither is he committing an injustice in offering the market wage. For there is no other standard by which to judge what is fair and reasonable. So, according to the liberal, the worker can complain neither of exploitation nor of unfreedom, but only of misfortune. His opportunities have not been restricted; no one limits his choices or his freedom. The radical, by contrast, insists that the worker's wage can be judged against a standard of need, by the value of his product, by the quantity of labor standardly required to make it, or by what it might be in an economic order differently organized. By such standards the radical finds the prevailing wage exploitative – unreasonable and unjust. Moreover, because the system could be changed, society or its ruling minority can be held responsible for there being no reasonable alternative to the job offered. In the absence of a reasonable alternative, the worker is vulnerable to pressure, and therefore forced to make an unfree decision.

A parallel difference between liberal and radical understandings of freedom underlies what is sometimes called a distinction between "positive" and "negative" freedom. There are situations in which an agent while not intentionally restricted by nonstandard obstacles from selecting an otherwise available option (e.g., there is no law against doing it), would be prevented from selecting it because of the lack of some enabling condition. So it used to be said, ironically, that even the poorest are free to eat in the Ritz Hotel. Freedom of this sort, it is claimed, especially by radical critics of traditional liberalism, is "merely negative," freedom from some constraint which is irrelevant in the absence of the enabling condition. If freedom is valuable, it must include among its constitutive conditions that it can in fact be exercised, that the options are ones that the agent can take advantage of. Only then, it is said, is freedom "positive" – "real freedom" – that is, a freedom which also includes a power to do the thing which is not restricted. Otherwise it merely mocks the impotence of the victims of injustice, like Marie Antoinette's legendary invitation to them to eat cake. Other writers (John Rawls included) would say that this confuses the fact of being free to do something with the value of this freedom to a particular person. The poor do indeed possess the freedom to eat in the Ritz, just as they have the freedom to buy eggs if the price is not extortionate, but the freedom to eat in the Ritz is not very valuable to them in the absence of the enabling condition that they can pay the bill. Indeed, where restaurants are racially segregated, a member of an excluded race might very well value the freedom to eat in restaurants he couldn't afford to eat in, just because exclusion *by race* was an affront, while exclusion by lack of money might not be.

## 5. Freedom and coercion

Earlier in this chapter I offered an account of power in general, but not of interpersonal power. A person's power, most generally, is what he could bring about and therefore would bring about, given that he had appropriate intentions. The power and the intention are jointly sufficient, provided that 'power' is taken to embrace not only intrinsic powers but also opportunities and the absence of any possible impediment.

One way of intentionally bringing things about is to mobilize the power of other people to do whatever is necessary to realize one's own ends. This is the core notion of political power. One can do this in a variety of ways, not all of which impair their freedom. One might enlist their support, for instance, by exhortation, or by reasoned persuasion, demonstrating opportunities and advantages that would accrue to them were they to join freely in a collaborative strategy. But one may also have powers to affect their future life-chances adversely or beneficially, and these powers can be exercised conditionally upon reciprocal performance; that is, they can be used in exchange transactions, in promises to reward compliance or penalize resistance. Political power is often thought of as antithetical to freedom, but this is obviously not necessarily true if, as I suggest, the core notion is the mobilization and deployment of collective effort, rather than the capacity to restrict options. The latter is one source of political power but is arguably parasitic on others if, as Hume claimed, "No man would have any reason to *fear* the fury of a tyrant, if he had no authority over any but from fear."[4] The power of tyrants like Hitler and Stalin are counterinstances, however, to Hume's thesis; the sowing of universal mistrust by fear of betrayal, even among the secret police themselves, inhibits the mobilization of a collective effort to resist the tyrant, whose own power to mobilize his subordinates rests substantially on his power to inspire in each fear of what the others, no less fearful, might do to him at the tyrant's behest.

Nevertheless, a person's power to mobilize the efforts of others by threats and promises depends in part on what the others can do in return. For each has something to offer or deny to the other, even if it is only submissive compliance; each possesses *power against* the other. Even the use of torture to extract a confession might be represented as an offer to trade: In return for your telling what you know, we'll stop hurting you. It is, however, a coercive offer just because the victim's options have been restricted by the torturer to just two: Keep silent and submit to fresh agony, or tell and not be hurt any more. Because (or if) the former is an option he could not reasonably be expected or required to choose, even for the sake of a principle or a cause or loyalty to friends and associates, the latter amounts to "an offer he cannot refuse," or, as we say, "he has no option."

Bargaining is partly a matter of exploring the extent of the other's control over one's own future and of discovering how much importance he attaches to what one can do for or against him, relative to the importance one attaches to what he can do to oneself in return. In comparisons of interpersonal power, each has a determinate power to control the fate of the other, but how effective that power will be as an inducement to action obviously depends on the actual preferences of the persons concerned. If the power that a person possesses against another is measured by the catalogue of consequences he can bring about (such as his ability to destroy his adversary's house), then among the determinants of his bargaining power must also be included the latter's evaluation of those consequences (depending for instance, on whether he is insured against fire, but equally on whether some of his possessions are irreplaceable personal treasures). The bargaining power possessed by each will be a function not merely of their objective situation and capabilities, but also of their preferences. But though a comparison of bargaining powers must take account of these subjective determinants, it will be a matter of objective fact which party has the more bargaining power (or whether, perhaps, they have equal powers). And one party may make poor use of his bargaining power. For example, he may make the high value he sets on what the other can do to (or for) him too apparent, without obtaining corresponding information about the other. Bargaining power influences outcomes, but it does not follow that the party with most power gets the better of the bargain.

For all that subjectivity is a factor in the outcome of bargaining, however, the practices of moral appraisal and of legal judgment do call, as I have already claimed in relation to extortion, for a kind of objective or impersonal assessment of a person's power to accept or refuse an offer, or to resist a threat. In deciding, for instance, whether to accept excuses such as duress, irresistible temptation, and provocation, we necessarily employ standards of what one can reasonably expect of a person. So a claim that one signed a document under duress because one had been threatened with a pinprick would, ordinarily at least, be laughed out of court, even if it were true that but for the threat one would not have signed. Whether one was free to refuse to sign does not depend, therefore, on one's personal disposition to do anything rather than suffer pinpricks; there are standards of relative value employed in such judgments which are attributed to any normal, reasonable person, or which any such person can be held at fault if he does not employ. If someone were to plead irresistible temptation to steal food only three hours after his last meal, one would say that, in the absence of some physiological abnormality or compulsive neurosis, no person's attention to food could be (or should be) so riveted by hunger so soon after eating that temptation could excuse his failure to respect property rights. Three days without food would make a stronger case. Similarly, whether a threat of being deprived of an option otherwise available to him would excuse someone for acting in a way that he would otherwise be blamed for will depend on standard expectations or requirements of just the same kind. And this accounts for an uncertainty in ascriptions of power possessed by one person over another. If Alan has the power adversely to affect Betty's interests and successfully threatens her, he has exercised his power over her. But if the power he has against her is insufficient to support her claim that she acted under duress, her excuse that she was in Alan's power would fail. For when assessing excuses, one looks not only at Betty's preferences but at standards governing the course that she might reasonably be required and expected to choose, whatever her actual preferences.

That one person has power against another does not necessarily have a bearing on the latter's freedom. If he has countervailing power, he need not do what is required of him. It is not sufficient for unfreedom that to secure benefits that another person can provide one may have to bear a cost. For opportunity cost is, as I have already argued, a necessary constituent of free-choice situations. But if there is a wide disparity in what each can do to the other, and if the control that another person might exercise over an agent's fate is such that the latter could not reasonably be expected or required to prefer the imposed consequences of noncompliance to doing what the other wants of him, the first has *power over* the other – the power to make him do what he wants by depriving him of options. So one can never have power over another person unless the power one has against him would be enough successfully to ensure his compliance. And this clearly bears on his freedom. But the mere possession of such power without its being exercised would not be enough to make the other unfree. An option is not restricted by a mere latent capacity to restrict it. For there is a great deal of harm that all sorts of people could do which would give them tremendous power over others if they chose to exercise it to influence their actions but which no one expects them ever to use and which therefore leaves everyone's options unrestricted. Not that expecting a reprisal from a powerful person would alone be sufficient to restrict one's options. A timid or subservient person may anxiously seek to avoid trouble or curry favor by trying to divine the wishes of a powerful superior but get it wrong all the time, producing results not at all in accordance with what the powerful person intended. Indeed, the latter might be totally indifferent to or even dismayed by what the other does, wishing that he would go his own way without bothering to please. One could hardly say that the powerful person had restricted the other's options, for he had done nothing at all to procure or restrain action. The restriction would be purely imaginary, suggested only by the fears and fantasies of the agent himself. For the expectation to bear on the agent's freedom it must be at least well grounded. Nevertheless, if the anxiety of the submissive person is the outcome of past experience of the results of noncompliance, one might plausibly claim that though his freedom of action on this occasion was not restricted because the dominant person's power remained and was likely to remain unexercised, previous exercises had impaired the submissive one's capacity for free choice. I shall examine such conditions in the next chapter.

The most conclusive way to restrict a person's choices is to put him in chains or behind bars. Depriving him of the necessary equipment for an activity, for example, confiscating a mountaineer's ropes, is as effective but is somewhat more specific. Similarly, one can prevent people from reading obscene books by ensuring through censorship that there are none to read. These are ways of impairing someone's freedom to do something by creating nonstandard impediments to his doing it (being shackled is not the standard way of living) or by negating enabling conditions which would standardly be satisfied (we don't expect the ropes we own to be taken from us). These are ways of preventing a person from exercising a power to do

143

something that under standard conditions he would exercise if he chose. This kind of interference, however, has only limited scope. One can prevent a horse from drinking by draining its trough, but there is no corresponding way to make it drink. However, there are other ways to compel people to do intended things. I shall discuss later on some of the more radical ones, ways of manipulating the subjective conditions of choice, changing beliefs or preferences by various forms of conditioning, or more drastically still by hypnosis or brainwashing. My present concern is with interferences that manipulate not the internal condition of the agent but the objective conditions which confront him when he makes his choices. These are the interferences with freedom, by legal constraints, for instance, on freedom of speech, meeting, and worship, with which the liberal political tradition has been most concerned.

The most common of these ways of constraining freedom of action is by threatening penalties for a proscribed action, attaching to it costs which make it significantly less attractive as an option than alternative ones, including the basic one of simply not doing it. However, that would not be enough to sustain a charge, or an excuse, that one has been made unfree to do it. An indirect tax to raise revenue, such as an entertainment tax, may do as much. But to have to pay tax for every visit to the cinema is not like being fined, like Elizabethan Roman Catholics, for every attendance at Mass. One difference lies in the different intentions behind the imposts: A revenue tax, unlike a protective tariff, is not meant to deter people from buying the commodity; it defeats its purpose if it does. But if a penalty is to do its job, it must be set so high that one would not expect the kind of people subject to it to continue to see the proscribed conduct as an available option. Conversely, a fall in money values can make a penalty originally imposed to discourage a certain class of offense so light that the act remains a generally available option, and the payment of the penalty a kind of tax. It is said that before the enactment of the Street Offences Act (1959), London prostitutes treated the forty-shilling fine for soliciting in precisely this way. Penalties and threats of reprisal are typically meant to prevent people from acting, or to compel them to act, in a certain way. Moreover, systems of norms that are supported by threats would not be regarded as restrictive of freedom unless their penalties in general made the proscribed course so unattractive that by accepted standards of interest and prudence it could be considered ineligible – unavailable.

Is it a sufficient condition for unfreedom, however, that an option

144

has been made ineligible in that way, if the agent would not be inclined to it in any case? Or is one unfree if required to act in a certain way, if one would be perfectly ready and eager to act so anyway, as many Welsh mineworkers might pay their union dues irrespective of any sanctions that it might otherwise impose? There is, after all, an evident difference between such a person and one who resents the constraint and would stop paying but for the fear that he might lose his job.

Now if union membership is compulsory, I have no choice but to pay my dues to the union, even supposing that if I had the choice I should still pay. The range of options available to me is not conditional on my own preferences, and the elimination of an option by denying me the possibility of continuing in my job without paying union dues is a restriction of the courses among which I might otherwise choose. Though an agent does *willingly* what he has no option but to do, the fact remains that an external agency has interfered with his conditions of action and has made him unfree to do anything different; he may not resent having to do it, and because he would have done "of his own free will" what he is required to do, one might be inclined to say that he does it freely. But if he is not free to do anything different, what he does cannot in fact be the thing he chooses to do, for he *has* no choice. It is at best what he would have chosen, had the choice been available to him. To abridge an agent's freedom is to abridge the range of his possible choices, not necessarily to act so that he does something that he might otherwise not have done. To say that he willingly or freely acts in the required manner is to say that he acts without resenting the requirement. But whether one is actually free is a function of what options one might have had but for someone else's intervention, or neglect to intervene; it is not a function of the absence of feelings of resentment, of grievance and frustration. If it appears to be so, it is because the concept of freedom of action is doing its most characteristic work in expressing such feelings, and that in their absence one is not prompted to appraise one's situation in those terms. For of course there are many things, such as murdering our friends, that we are quite properly not free to do, and we don't resent at all that that option has been removed from the repertoire of conduct available to us.

But if the range of options available is not conditional upon one's preference, how is it that someone may choose to defy a prohibition which for someone else puts a course of action effectively out of reach? It would be self-contradictory to say that one

145

has done what one was unable to do. Would it be equally inconsistent to say that someone had done what he was not free to do? Is it then the case after all that wanting to do something badly enough makes one freer than someone who wants it less?

Hobbes handled the matter by firmly denying that threats of penalties could make anyone unfree. "All actions," he wrote, "that men do in commonwealths for fear of the law are actions which the doers had liberty to omit." Giving someone an additional motive for action, such as fear of punishment, however severe, to set against whatever motives he might already have, makes him no less free. For he may choose to disobey and take the consequences. Borrowing an illustration from Aristotle,[5] he wrote:

> ... when a man throweth his goods into the sea for *fear* the ship should sink, he doth it nevertheless very willingly, and may refuse to do it if he will. . . . So a man sometimes pays his debt only for *fear* of imprisonment, which because nobody hindered him from detaining, was the action of a man at *liberty*.[6]

But this is too high a price to pay for consistency. Action under the threat of imprisonment is the very paradigm of unfreedom; the incompatibility of freedom and coercion and the problems it poses for political authority and obligation is, after all, what the classical liberal tradition has been about. Hobbes himself acknowledges this tradition in passing when he remarks that "in all kinds of actions by the law praetermitted, men have the liberty, of doing what their own reasons shall suggest, for the most profitable to themselves,"[7] implying that in those things forbidden by the law they do not have that liberty.

It is true, of course, that there is a rule-derived sense in which a person is not at liberty to do anything forbidden by the rule (i.e., not "praetermitted"), irrespective of any threat of penalties, in just the sense that one is not free in chess to move a pawn backwards. A person who makes a promise to another thereby limits the alternatives he is at liberty to choose among. But he has the *power* to break his promise – he is still able to decide not to keep it, and may do so if he has action commitments to the contrary. If, however, a heavy enough penalty is now attached to his breaking faith, he is no longer free to do what he would otherwise like to do, because he cannot do it without attracting a penalty sufficient to make it no longer worth doing.

Hobbes would insist, however, that the agent's freedom is formally unchanged: the only change has been in the objective condi-

146

tions confronting him. He would act as before if that option were still open; but the new circumstance has eliminated that option, substituting a different one which includes the penalty, and this new one is unattractive. Someone else with a different preference structure, like the willing martyr, may decide differently, finding the original action still worthwhile, despite its heavier costs. For Hobbes they are equally free to choose.

It would appear a little incongruous for a conscientious objector in prison for refusing to register for military service to claim that he was not free to refuse, having in fact done so.[8] "Being unfree" comes too close to "being unable" for this to be acceptable. Of course, he was not free to refuse unless he accepted imprisonment as a consequence, but he did refuse. And this seems to support Hobbes's analysis. Someone less steadfast, however, might very well explain in self-justification that once his appeal had been turned down, he was no longer free to refuse: It would be quite unreasonable to expect someone to act in the proscribed way if the consequence was imprisonment. Only someone, he might say, with a disordered set of values or someone of superhuman steadfastness, a saint or a fanatic, would choose such an option. The penalty has made it literally ineligible – one that it would be *inappropriate* for a reasonable, prudent man to choose.

Hobbes's paradoxical insistence that this person is nevertheless free illuminates the action model presupposed by the manner of practical discourse which distinguishes, as I have done, between freedom and personal powers. The model is of a person, possessing the ability to act in a number of possible but mutually exclusive ways, one of which he believes would best accord with his set of preferences were it not for a particular consequence attached by law to his doing it, which leads him to decide it would not be worth doing after all. The freedom he possesses is the freedom of a rational being, a kind of *homo economicus*, making the most prudent choice he can among alternatives with different (if all rather unsatisfactory) utilities. The choice, it is true, may be rigged against him by someone able to allot rewards and penalties (analogous to a monopolistic price fixer) but *given* the conditions, he makes his own choice, he is still his own master. If one accepts that model, the one who submits to the law does so as freely, no more, no less, than the one who defies it.

The forms of practical discourse in which "freedom" and "unfreedom" occur involve evaluations of the conduct of agents themselves deciding evaluatively between possible courses of action.

147

One such form has already emerged: A person whose freedom is restricted by a legally based threat can also be seen as choosing between obedience and disobedience. If he obeys or intends to obey, his own account of his position as unfree invokes an evaluation, that it would be unreasonable to expect anyone in such circumstances not to conform to the law, though admittedly some rash or quite exceptionally resolute individuals might still break it despite the threatened consequences. This would be to offer not only an explanation but a justification or an excuse.

The excuse can be rejected by rejecting the agent's own evaluation and insisting that the threatened penalty did not sufficiently foreclose other alternatives. If in obeying the agent sacrificed some vital principle or betrayed a cause, to insist that he might still have chosen to disobey and to accept the consequences is to insist that he is still responsible for what he did and to blame him for doing it. While the expectation that he would otherwise suffer carried a defeasible action commitment to comply, the principle at stake was so important (it might be said) that it required that the penalty be suffered as the unavoidable but acceptable price that had to be paid. It was not too much to ask that someone with *that* commitment should bear what might otherwise be deemed unbearable. Insisting on the agent's freedom to act thus puts his moral status in question, denying the normal prudential defense, and reasserting his moral responsibility for his action. The agent's counterplea might be to deny that the standard being adopted by his accusers should properly be applied to him. Only a saint, a hero, or a fanatic would have disobeyed; one cannot look for martyrs among ordinary men and women.

A defense of duress against a criminal charge works in a similar way. The accused excuses himself by claiming that he was not free to obey the law on account of some more immediate threat that he could not reasonably have been expected to disregard. This plea can be rebutted either by denying the legitimacy of the interest defended – the need to avoid exposure of one's past crimes will not excuse fraudulent conversion to pay off a blackmailer – or by insisting that, given the importance of the rule that has been broken, obedience to it would not have demanded an excessive sacrifice. So one cannot plead duress as an excuse for killing a third person to avoid being killed oneself. Here as elsewhere in this discussion of actions under conditions in which the consequences are rigged to secure an agent's compliance, excuses, recriminations, and justifications invoke a kind of reasonable rate of exchange between the weight to be attached to an agent's duty and the hurt or damage he might be expected to suffer – even by torture – rather than embrace the prudent option. The defense that he was not free to refuse is acceptable only when the cost to him would exceed that rate.

## 6. Freedom as a contested concept

It has been a recurrent theme in the later sections of this chapter that though a particular action might be said to be possible if one took no account of the way in which an agent might evaluate it, it might nevertheless be ineligible, and that this would be different from saying that the agent himself preferred doing something else. To call it ineligible would be to make a judgment about its standing as an object of rational choice – it would be to mark it as unfit to be chosen by anyone, or at any rate by anyone of the relevant class of agents to which this one belonged. In the depersonalized sense of possibility, one might say that it is not impossible for a loving mother to cut her child's throat, for she has the knife and the necessary physical strength and skill, and one might even stretch the imagination into some horrible situation in which it became a real option. But in almost any imaginable possible world, it would be ineligible, and her perception of it as such would be supported by the whole fabric of her beliefs about the world. The force of her conviction of its ineligibility could be a reason, perhaps, for saying that it was also an impossibility; she could not do it – to try to form the intention might be enough in itself to produce a physical collapse. But we do not need to assume anything like that. Because something ineligible is not to be chosen, it does not rank in the tally of options between which a rational agent may be called upon to decide. Consequently, someone who converts an otherwise eligible course of action into one that would be in this sense ineligible makes one unfree by depriving one of that option.

But what is ineligible in this sense does not always declare itself incontestably. With at least some impossibilities there might appear to be no question of standard-dependence. It is not obviously a matter of standards that it is impossible to swim in treacle. Yet even that could be achieved, by someone doing it for a bet, perhaps, given hot enough treacle and a thermal-insulated suit; but those, of course, are not the standard conditions for the truth of the assertion of impossibility, and one would imagine that the gambler who betted on the impossibility of doing it would not have had such nonstandard conditions in mind. So perhaps impossibilities, other than logical impossibilities, are standard bound too. Indeed, almost any practical assertion of power or of freedom must take for granted a range of conditions held constant, within which one has the power, or is free, to do the act in question. What constraints are there, then, on selecting or dismissing such conditions?

For the purpose of assessments offered in public discourse, in assigning blame, perhaps, making a protest, or declaring a grievance, the conditions taken as given must be ones that anyone to whom the assessment is addressed could give assent to. They cannot be arbitrary, idiosyncratic, or unrelated to a view of the world in which others could share. So the standards by which ascriptions of freedom and unfreedom are governed must be defensible, unless they are already so generally accepted that it occurs to no one to challenge them. For as we have seen, they can be challenged: I have given examples of ideological shifts whereby forms of action formerly held ineligible or impossible have been placed on the political agenda by inducing a change in the standards by which eligibility and possibility are assessed. And such changes are brought about sometimes by analogical arguments, insisting perhaps that what is good for the goose is good for the gander, there being no relevant difference between them, or alternatively, that the differences between geese and ganders are relevant differences that ought to be recognized, given our other practical beliefs which provide grounds for analogous discriminations. Or standards may be changed by challenging the rates of exchange between values. The community's readiness to accept increased costs of production for the sake of industrial safety or public health, installing, for instance, devices in workplaces to monitor levels of noxious substances or phasing out the use of leaded petrol, are instances where the formerly ineligible (because unacceptably costly) course has become, first, a viable option and hence a topic for practical disagreement and, ultimately, an accepted policy.

The standards by which such assessments are made are not merely conventional; the controversies that place them under pressure call on reasoned arguments. Admittedly, the beliefs upon which such arguments rely must themselves be widely held, but that is a condition for their controversial effectiveness, not for their truth. If they are widely accepted, it may be because the general network of beliefs which warrant their assertion and provide their support and justification is either broadly true or at least embedded in ways of looking at the world so fundamentally adapted to the human situation that a human being would find it near impossible to reject.

However this might be, the fact that the application of concepts like 'freedom' and 'unfreedom', 'coercion', 'duress', 'extortion', and 'exploitation' is governed by a variety of standards results in their being contested concepts. Even if arguments can be found adequately to sustain the appropriateness of one standard rather than another, the proof might be long and arduous, and the personal interests that people would have in the results would still account for continuing contestation. But it does not follow that the standards are therefore arbitrary, ultimately relative to particular ideologies, or, in the fashionable jargon, "essentially contested." The kind of discrepancy in standards, which according to the cultural relativists and skeptics is radical and unbridgeable, exists in some measure within cultures too – only the degree is different. And of course, within cultures agreement often does emerge, though sometimes only slowly, as the confidence of more and more people in the old certainties diminishes under the pressure of counterarguments. To the extent that we embark on the task of winning assent by rational argument rather than by mind-bending manipulation, we are committing ourselves to the belief that there is no inherent impossibility about the enterprise, and though agreement may be hard to reach, we can never know that it could not be found by still more patient exploration of the opposition's belief commitments and of our own. To accept the doctrine that concepts like 'freedom' are *essentially* contestable is to abandon the enterprise; argument would then be just one manipulative technique among others, exploiting in bad faith a myth of rationality, by claiming for persuasive moves an authority to command agreement on account of an interpersonal validity, in which, however, the arguer himself had no belief.

151

# 8

# Freedom as autarchy

## 1. The free-choice situation

Chapters 5 and 6 dealt with the principle of noninterference, which, it was claimed, was grounded in our conception of a natural person, and in the conceptual linking of natural and moral personality. From the principle of respect for persons which follows from this linking derives not only the principle of noninterference but also the principle of equal consideration of interests. In Chapter 7 coercion, duress, and extortion were distinguished from other influences on actions, such as counseling, providing an agent with fresh information, or making him offers, which, in standard cases, would not count as the kind of interferences for which justification need be provided, because they do not restrict the options available to a decision maker or a chooser.

Handcuffing Alan, clearing all the pebbles in his vicinity to prevent his engaging in his favorite pastime of splitting pebbles on the beach, imposing penalties on anyone caught splitting pebbles, charging $1,000 for a pebble-splitter's license, or under some conditions demanding exorbitant rates for the right to split pebbles on the only pebbly bit of the beach would be paradigmatic ways of interfering with Alan's freedom to split pebbles. Taken together, these presuppose an agent in a standard choice situation with four components:

(1) The agent has a range of powers and capacities, a determinate set of resources at his disposal, such as pebbles and money, which are the conditions enabling him to act, and a range of possible impediments, such as handcuffs, which are standardly absent.
(2) He is confronted by a set of opportunity costs: If he goes for $x$ he must forgo $y$.
(3) He has a set of beliefs about (1) and (2), for example, about the extent of his resources, their substitutability, their usefulness as means to his ends, and so forth.

152

(4) There are certain activities which he believes are worth engaging in and certain states of affairs to be approved and admired or disapproved and deplored; these form an ordered set of ends and principles, a set of preferences which, in combination with (3), generate his intentions and practical decisions.

I shall refer to (1) and (2), which are states of the world independent of the agent's beliefs, as the *objective choice conditions*. Conditions (3) and (4) I call *subjective choice conditions* because they are states of the agent's beliefs about both himself and the world at large. Whether or not they correspond to the objective conditions, to the extent that the agent is practically rational they will shape his intentions, and someone capable of manipulating them will be interfering with his freedom of action. The physical conditions affecting the agent's mobility, the size of his muscles as well as the shackles on his wrists, count as objective conditions just because his physical capacities and the various restraints which can deprive him of them exist independently of his beliefs about them. Hamlet "bounded in a nut-shell" would have only a very little room in which to move, objectively speaking, however he might count himself "king of infinite space."

Standard cases of one person's making another unfree to act involve actual or possible interferences affecting one or more of these conditions. This may be done by an interference that changes the conditions (e.g., by threatening penalties) or by a failure to alter them on the part of an agent, such as a jailer, who is both able to alter them and, in the absence of overriding reasons justifying constraint, could reasonably be expected or required to alter them to remove the impediment to action. A jailer who was liable to be punished for letting his prisoner go free would himself be unfree to release the prisoner even if he wanted to. The responsibility for the prisoner's unfreedom would then lie with the authorities who have restricted the options of both; for, given the threatened punishment, the jailer cannot do otherwise. That, at least, would be one way of excusing himself when the prisoner begs him to let him go. "It's more than my job – or my life – is worth," he might say.

A coercive or deterrent threat makes a course of action, otherwise attractive to the agent, relatively unattractive to the point of ineligibility, by attaching to it costly consequences that it would not have but for the intention of the threatener. This

153

amounts to an interference that rigs the opportunity costs, as in (2). Or someone can be rendered unfree to leave an island by depriving him of his boat, a case of altering the resources at his disposal, as in (1).

Freedom of action can be interfered with, however, by altering the subjective choice conditions as well as by altering the objective ones. Because a person's practical decisions depend on his beliefs, his actions can be determined by someone else if the latter can shape those beliefs. A person can be misled by false information about the resources at his disposal into believing that he is unable to do what he can in fact do; or he may be wrongly informed about the environment which provides and constrains his opportunities. Censorship may deny him access to information that would otherwise correct his false beliefs and make him aware of options and opportunities which already exist. Or his preferences may be manipulated, for example by media exploitation, advertising techniques, or religious and political ritual practices, such as mass rallies and revivalist meetings, which make him vulnerable to nonrational suggestion. With his beliefs and preferences so managed, his actions can be controlled with no alteration to his objective choice conditions, effectively depriving him of the freedom to do what he nevertheless has the power or capacity to do.[1]

In treating such management as interference with freedom of action, we accept as the model of a free decision-making agent, one who possesses at least a certain minimal kind of rationality. A person is acting under duress if and only if (1) he believes that some of the costs of adopting a certain option he would otherwise favor would be so heavy as to make that course ineligible and (2) those costs would not have had to be borne but for someone's making it ineligible or for someone's not acting in some expected way to remove the conditions that make it ineligible, precisely for the purpose of influencing the subject to decide against his otherwise preferred option. To threaten him with those costs would be pointless if he were incapable of assessing possible courses of action in terms of their outcomes, weighing costs against benefits, and of arriving at a decision on the basis of an ordered set of preferences. Similarly, deception and censorship would be pointless if the subjects were not expected to form their beliefs on evidence and to suit their actions to their beliefs. A necessary constituent of the model decision situation is, accordingly, a decision-making subject satisfying certain minimal conditions of both cognitive and practical rationality.

154

## 2. Autarchy and autonomy

The condition of a decision maker who satisfies these minimum rationality conditions I call *autarchic* – self-directing. I distinguish it both from conditions which fall short of it, which I shall call *impulsions,* and from an ideal that transcends it, which I shall call *autonomy.* Most writers make no distinction between autarchy and autonomy, using "autonomy" to cover both concepts. I have coined the term "autarchy" (which, though to be found in the *Oxford English Dictionary,* is not generally used in quite my way) because, without a way of distinguishing autarchy from autonomy, one cannot make clear that the two states generate reasons for action of quite distinct kinds. Furthermore, despite the need for the neologistic usage, the concept is not itself an innovation, but is deeply embedded in our moral thinking; its isolation is a necessary step in understanding our beliefs about persons and what they commit a person to in his dealings with others.

Autarchy is a condition of human normality, both in the statistical sense, that the overwhelming majority of human beings satisfy it, and in the further sense that anyone who does not satisfy it falls short in some degree as a human being. This is because the standard instance of an autarchic agent is a human person. We need the notion primarily for thinking about entities who are also human, and the conception of autarchy has been formed, along with the concept of rationality, in the experience that human beings have had in dealing with one another, rather than from their dealings with cows and sheep. But it does not follow that autarchy is an exclusively human property; it is at least logically possible that some nonhuman beings might be autarchic – angels, perhaps, or appropriately equipped aliens from outer space or dolphins. Neither does it follow from the closeness of the tie between rationality and humanity that every human being is autarchic. Some with defects of rationality fall short of it.

Autonomy goes beyond autarchy. It is an excellence of character for which an autarchic person may strive, but which persons achieve in varying degrees, some hardly at all. It is an ideal, not a normal condition. A human being is not defective either as human or as a person because he falls short of it, any more than he would be defective as a human person for the lack of the wisdom of a sage or the creativity of Mozart. To be autonomous is to live (in Rousseau's phrase) "according to a law that one prescribes to oneself."

155

But to understand what that might mean and why it should be seen as an ideal must be left until we have a better grasp of autarchy. If, however, we do have reason to value autonomy, and to admire people who possess it, it can, as an ideal, generate reasons for action – to foster it, for instance, by educational practices which encourage independence of mind rather than an unquestioning acceptance of authority or to combat attitudes and institutions, such as race or sex discriminations, which discourage autonomy by fostering self-depreciation and deference.

But because a person may fall very short of autonomy and yet qualify as autarchic, and someone defective in autarchy may nevertheless qualify as a person, neither autonomy nor autarchy is a necessary condition for the application of the principle of noninterference. That principle, however, does not proscribe interference; it only places a burden of justification on the interferer and puts certain constraints on what can serve as a justification. So defective autarchy may justify interferences that would not otherwise be acceptable, interferences in particular that override the agent's own judgment of his own interests. Correspondingly, it may be held to diminish an agent's responsibility for his actions. The respect that is owed to a person may generate different rights and immunities where the person is nonautarchic. What remains unchanged, however, is the condition that the person shall not be used merely as the means to another person's ends. Where paternalist interference is justifiable on grounds of defective autarchy, it must be exercised as a trust in the interest of the beneficial subject, not of the trustee, or for the sake of whatever projects the latter might deem valuable. Defective autarchy is not a justification, for instance, for treating a person as an available experimental object, as one might a fruit-fly.

## 3. Nonautarchic persons: impulsion

No term in common use corresponds precisely to the concept of autarchy, perhaps because we rarely need it. For ordinary practical purposes we know well enough what a normal person is like and an unqualified reference to someone as a person licenses the assumption that that person is autarchic. Lord Bowen's celebrated reference to "the man on the Clapham omnibus"[2] was a way of glossing "the reasonable man," the autarchic person's counterpart in the law of negligence. And just as the man on the Clapham omnibus "has not the courage of Achilles, the wisdom of Ulysses, or the strength of

Hercules,"[3] so autarchy may fall short of the ideal autonomy. For practical, nontechnical purposes, we are more likely to be in need of precise ways of identifying and differentiating deviations from the norm rather than of an accurate formulation of its criteria. Nevertheless, such a formulation was sought in 1843, when the English judges, being called upon to state the conditions under which an accused person might plead insanity as a defense in criminal law, committed themselves in the M'Naghten Rules to minimal criteria for criminal responsibility, which attempted to codify conditions of normality, and therefore for punishability. They relied, however, as much on a specification of the defects that would rebut the presumption of sanity as on a precise characterization of the conditions sufficient for it.

Correspondingly, if autarchy is the norm for human beings, one way to grasp its requirements is to consider what neurotic and psychotic states are deemed to qualify, in whole or in part, someone's responsibility and his entitlement, under the principle of respect for persons, to exercise independent judgment. These states, if severe, might be grounds, for instance, not only for deeming him not liable to blame or punishment for his actions, but for declaring someone incompetent to manage his own affairs, or for putting him under preventive constraint to protect either himself or others from the harm he might inflict on them. They are defects broadly of three kinds: of epistemic rationality, practical rationality, and psychic continuity.

## A. Defects of epistemic rationality

Paranoia is a form of epistemic irrationality; its defect lies not in the failure of the agent to act on the action commitments of his beliefs, but on his being afflicted with a radically disordered belief structure. His practical decisions are between fantasy-options presented by a conception of the world fabricated of a central core of unassailable beliefs defended against counterevidence by a limitless series of ingenious ad hoc hypotheses. Given the agent's view of reality, his actions may seem rational enough; secretiveness, for instance, would not be irrational in a world in which anyone at all might be an enemy agent.

It may be objected that this description of paranoia does not distinguish someone of defective rationality from someone whose ideology or belief structure we just happen to disagree with. What it is rational to believe may depend, immediately at any rate, on the structure of preexistent beliefs to which new evidence has to be assimilated. Precisely how to evaluate developments in Middle Eastern politics will no doubt depend on whether they are set in a context of Marxist, Zionist, or Shi'ite fundamentalist beliefs. Each provides basic theses which, like the paranoid's conviction that he is the victim of persecution, constitute canons of interpretation for each new item of evidence. That is not to say that there is no independent ground from which to judge the relative adequacy of systems. Some belief systems possess greater consistency than others; some have greater coherence, are more embracing, and require less ad hoc ingenuity to accommodate deviant instances, or are both more determinate and more successful in predicting future events. Even so, a paranoid belief system may fare little worse according to these criteria than some more officially recognized ones.

The paranoid system has one major defect, however, from which such ideologies are by pragmatic necessity free. Precisely because they are belief systems capable of generating action commitments for large numbers of people, each makes possible an interpersonal assessment of evidence at least within that ideological system, and to that extent each system remains a public world in which the conceptual distinction between reality and fantasy retains its meaning. By contrast, the world of the paranoiac is essentially private. He allows no one's testimony to count as evidence against his strange beliefs, even if that forces him to impugn the reliability of everyone he meets and to believe that all are in league against him. So he is committed to withdrawal into a private world, to an ideology in which it is impossible to test his perceptions and inferences against *anyone* else's. Disagreement on the point at issue would always count as a sufficient reason for dismissing the other's testimony, on that point at least, as inauthentic, and his motives as almost certainly sinister. Prompted by his anxieties, the paranoiac adopts cognitive strategies that isolate him from counterevidence and so deprives himself of the distinction between fantasy and reality necessary to epistemic, and therefore to practical, rationality.

It is a mistake to think of the paranoiac as if he were like a scientist who doggedly persisted with a theory despite counterinstances because it would be irrational to abandon even a faulty theory that was still fruitful while no better one was in sight. Admittedly, consistency can be bought at too high a price. Someone who undertook a radical overhaul of his entire belief structure for every item of dissonant evidence would indeed be irrational. A

158

rational credent must be prepared to hazard a few unsupported suppositions to account for apparent inconsistencies, rather than allow his world picture to come tumbling down at the first hint of a counterinstance. Suppose an experiment works ninety-nine times out of a hundred, and the alternative to an ad hoc hypothesis that on the hundredth time the equipment was faulty is to have no theory at all. To eschew such a saving hypothesis would be to purchase an unimpeachable consistency at the cost of a belief structure consisting only of discrete, unrelated, particular beliefs. But because it lacked theoretical coherence, such a structure would be quite useless for guiding action because it would have no predictive capacity. So it would be hardly rational to relinquish, on account of occasional minor inconsistencies, the coherence provided by even a faulty theory in favor of no theory of all.

The essential defect of the paranoiac is that, though his theory does provide him with a map of the world, and is action guiding, it is not truth oriented. Even assuming a Freudian-type theory which would rationalize the paranoiac's fantasies as strategies for accommodating painful unconscious tensions, the *telos* of his theories is not to extend his grasp of reality but rather to make his life tolerable to him. It is therefore of no consequence to him that his explanatory procedures cut him off from collaborative inquiry, in which evidence and hypotheses are open to public scrutiny. Yet his anxiety state, so far from being relieved by this epistemic strategy, is generally made more acute, and the subject more miserable. Moreover, his very ingenuity in rationalizing his fears stands in the way of his overhauling his total conception of the world to render it genuinely rational. And without that there can be no relief; because he cannot trust anyone, he cannot seek help from counselors, psychiatrists, or analysts. The paranoid psychotic is nonautarchic because his goals and his beliefs are alike generated by his anxieties in a self-reinforcing circle, in which belief is oriented towards the protection of delusion rather than to truth.

## B. Defects of practical rationality

Nonepistemic defects of practical rationality include various kinds of compulsive neurosis marked by a pronounced incoherence of belief and action. Kleptomaniacs, for instance, have no beliefs – at least at the conscious level – that commit them to steal, nor do they decide to steal; indeed, they may decide not to but steal all the same. And one cannot persuade a compulsive handwasher that, having washed his hands only minutes before, it is pointless now to wash them again, because he has had no opportunity meanwhile to make them dirty. Because he recognizes the dissonance between his beliefs and his behavioral disposition, he may well seek desperately for reasons that would account for what he has to do anyway, but the connection between these alleged reasons and the encompassing network of his beliefs may be extremely tenuous, precisely because his "reasons" are posterior to the neurotic impulse to action, instead of being the action commitments of prior beliefs.

## C. Defects of psychic continuity

Defects of psychic continuity are more radical, because they call into question the very existence of an agent identifiable as even potentially autarchic. In certain schizophrenic conditions the subject lacks the self-awareness of an agent. Although he may possess the concept of agency, of a person originating changes in the world by recognizing the action commitments of his beliefs and acting on them, he does not apply it to himself. Instead, his consciousness is rather of himself as process or as something to which things happen. In advanced cases he may act out this self-conception in catatonic paralysis, becoming for the world too the mere object he believes himself to be.

Equally disqualifying from autarchy is the condition of dissociation, where facets of the subject's personality split in multiple consciousness. According to the psychoanalytic view, this can be an unconscious strategy enabling the subject, through the surrender of his awareness of a continuous self, to evade responsibility not only for what he feels driven to do but also for what he guiltily believes. One persona evades feelings of guilt by blaming another. With the more protean of such subjects, it is hard to know how to ascribe all the behavior attributed to one physical body to a single sustained personal agent. The agent himself may talk as though there were different persons inhabiting and quarreling over his body. In one persona he may claim to know about another, but as someone else whose thoughts he can read. But as the latter he may exhibit total ignorance of the existence of the first.

### Psychopathy

The case of the psychopath is more problematic; there is no view generally accepted by philosophers, psychiatrists, lawyers, and

160

moralists about the proper characterization of psychopathy. It can be presented as a defect of practical rationality, of epistemic rationality, of psychic continuity, or of all three – and to some it is not a defect of autarchy at all but a case of wickedness, that is, of a wholly autarchic person with wholly corrupt beliefs about what can count as a reason for action.

One aspect of psychopathy, however, is an incapacity to treat any but the most immediate consequences of action as relevant considerations for decision making, and a consequent incapacity to formulate and carry through projects requiring deferment of gratification. This is not because the psychopath cannot foresee longer-term consequences or because he rationally discounts for uncertainties. In appreciating the nature of the alternative courses open to him, a psychopath may exhibit a high degree of epistemic rationality, but he will prefer solely for the sake of its immediate rewards a course which he can see will very probably be disastrous in the long run. This is not because he is indifferent to disaster. When it catches up with him, he will not comfort himself by thinking that the pleasures he has enjoyed make it all worthwhile; he will probably display self-pity, regret his decision, and even resolve with apparent sincerity to avoid trouble in the future. But the resolution is strictly theoretical: It is a belief about the thing to do when the time comes, which, when it comes, does not result in the appropriate action. Faced with the same immediately attractive option, he turns to it as before with no kind of struggle. Unlike the weak-willed or akratic person, the psychopath does not perceive the attractive option as a temptation but simply as the course to choose. One is not tempted unless one can recognize that course as *not* the course to choose, that is, unless one has some disposition, however feeble, to act on the prudent (or otherwise overriding) action commitment, rather than to go along with whatever immediately gratifying outcome dominates one's attention. The psychopath has no such disposition. So it is more accurate to describe the psychopath as impelled or drawn by the prospect of immediate enjoyment, rather than deciding between the competing action commitments of his beliefs. All the same, his actions are intentional; he does them under a description which is not fanciful, and they are not automatic reflexes. His irrationality arises from his incapacity to distance himself from his own enjoyments, here and now, even though his beliefs provide him with sufficient and readily accessible grounds for doing differently.

It is arguable nevertheless that in his pathological imprudence, in his inability to perceive his own future states as providing him with reasons for action, the psychopath exhibits a kind of psychic discontinuity. For though he is in one sense self-centered, showing no concern for the happiness or suffering of others, he is also indifferent to his future self too. Living in and for the moment, he fails to grasp that the being whose enjoyments so command his present attention is the same being that will be commanding his attention in a week's time and that whatever reason he has for avoiding suffering now is a reason for avoiding its affecting him then. Only by dissociating himself from that future being, as from someone with whom he has no connection, can he consistently adopt the imprudent stance that he does.

Objection is sometimes made to the inclusion of prudence among the conditions of rationality, that this is a peculiarly culture-bound condition arising in capitalist economies, which depend on the deferment of gratification for capital accumulation. In less affluent cultures living for the moment is far more readily accepted. But if this is true, it could still be accommodated within the condition that future gratifications may appropriately be discounted for uncertainty. People in Western industrial economies enjoy, on the whole, more stable expectations for the future and are less vulnerable to unpredictable and uncontrollable disasters. It might indeed be rational for the Calcutta street dweller to enjoy at once whatever scrap of wealth fortune puts in his way; where could he keep it so that he could be sure it would be there to be spent tomorrow? Tomorrow's cholera or flood could sweep him away without warning, anyway. By contrast, it is a moot point whether the rationality of an agrarian community would demand prudent saving of seed for next year's crop or whether, given the uncertainties of flood, drought, locusts, and crop diseases, it would sanction enjoying what there was while it was there. But in none of these cases is there any difficulty in principle in distinguishing the rational time-preference of the insecure from that of the psychopath, the insecurity of whose future may be due only to his own imprudence.

### Requirements for autarchy; inner-impelled personalities

The personality defects just considered need not be as totally crippling as the account given so far might suggest. A compulsive neurosis or an addiction may affect only a segment of a person's behavior; outside of that, his capacity for rational decision may be unimpaired. Conversely, someone may be temporarily deprived of autarchy by unusually taxing conditions: Someone starving or sexually tormented may be so driven as to lose control. Pleas of "irresistible temptation" and "provocation" amount to pleas of temporary loss of autarchy. Such pleas are not always justified, of course. Whether a temptation or a provocation is irresistible depends not just on what the subject managed and did not manage to resist, but also on what, by certain objective standards, he might reasonably have been required and expected to resist. And his capacity to resist may well depend on how readily he has succumbed to temptations in the past. Acting without further reflection on the most salient of one's action commitments – salient, perhaps, because physical sensations bring immediately and urgently to one's attention beliefs about what one would enjoy or what would relieve one's present tensions – can be a habit one can break; and not to have cultivated more reflective habits is insufficient to support the plea in mitigation that one was impelled to what one has done.

The following requirements for autarchy emerge from this discussion of disqualifying conditions:

(1) It must be possible to identify a single person, displaying continuity over time, and corresponding to a single physically acting subject. These conditions are not met in extreme cases of schizophrenia and perhaps of psychopathy.

(2) Whatever the subject's other aims and objectives directing his inquiries and the forming of his beliefs, they must be subject to concern for truth as an idea regulating the canons employed to select the propositions, hypotheses, and theories it is appropriate to believe; objectives such as the relief of his anxieties or the preservation of self-esteem are inappropriate as regulative epistemic principles. This condition is not met by the paranoid psychotic.

(3) The subject must have, and generally exercise, the capacity to recognize the action commitments of his beliefs and be disposed to govern his action in accordance with the commitments he acknowledges. This third condition is not met by compulsives.

(4) Changes in his beliefs must therefore be capable of effecting changes in his practical decisions and policies, a condition not regularly met by compulsives and psychopaths.

(5) The subject's belief structure must yield a ranking of action commitments, and, aside from discounting for the uncertainty of future outcomes (which in troubled times could

reasonably lead to a policy of living for the moment), the immediacy of an expected gratification must not be sufficient, as with the psychopath, to confer lexical priority. The psychic-continuity condition underpins the rationality of giving consideration to future gratifications which might outweigh present ones. The subject must have the capacity, therefore, to defer expected gratification.

(6) The subject must be capable of formulating a project or a policy, of forming now an intention to act for the sake of a preferred future state and of acting on that intention, now or later.

Notice that (4), (5), and (6) specify capacities. A merely akratic person is held to be capable of rational action but to fail; a compulsive, or someone impelled in various other ways, is not capable of acting rationally in the relevant behavior field. The borderline is not, of course, well defined, and forensic psychiatrists differ profoundly in their testimony in given cases.

Someone incapacitated in respect of any of the six conditions mentioned I shall call *inner-impelled*, because he behaves in some degree like an automaton or a sophisticated robot rather than as a decision maker or a chooser. In severe instances his behavior will often be better described as a cybernetic response to cues, rather than as action in which he acknowledges, implicitly or explicitly, that to which his beliefs commit him. So his responses often tend to be more programmed performances, only very roughly adapted to situations, than actions corrected or adjusted to his changing perceptions of reality.

## 4. Nonautarchic persons: heterarchy

I distinguish someone who is inner-impelled from the other-impelled, or *heterarchic* subject, who is no more a decision maker than the compulsive or paranoid but whose program has been implanted, whether deliberately or otherwise, by someone else. The extreme case is a subject under deep hypnosis. But no less clear is the case of someone responding to a posthypnotic suggestion, having all the appearance of full consciousness, yet casting around for reasons that will commit him to doing what he was commanded. Like the paranoid, his beliefs are not oriented to truth; like the compulsive, an attempt to dissuade him from the programmed performance will create acute anxiety. And like the compulsive, he will

defend the action with reasons amounting to reconstructions of perceived reality which, while possibly extremely bizarre, meet his
criterion of acceptability for belief: namely, that they will yield
action commitments corresponding to what he is programmed to do
anyway.

The submissiveness of a weaker to a stronger dominant personality is a more everyday kind of heterarchy. The two sisters in
Katherine Mansfield's story, "The Daughters of the Late Colonel,"
have been terrorized and totally subdued by an authoritarian parent whose influence has paralyzed their capacity to take any decision without automatically resorting to the algorithmic procedure,
"what would father want us to do?" Their actions are governed by
one overriding commitment, to do what father commands; but this
is grounded in no overall belief system capable of being amended
in the face of counterevidence. Their behavior is quite different
from action under duress or coerced by threats, in which compliance is achieved by rigging the agent's beliefs about the opportunity costs of action; a threat works precisely because the subject is
autarchic, and can make rational decisions on the basis of his beliefs and preferences. Remove the threat and he recognizes that
options formerly ineligible are now available to him. People who
are dominated do not make such calculations. Katherine Mansfield's characters feel faint stirrings ·of freedom when their father
dies, but recoil from it, hopelessly disabled, continuing to obey not
from fear or because they are committed to it by a wider set of
beliefs, but because their capacity to form new projects has been
inhibited by a lifetime of terrified submission. Such people may
grasp the possibility of independent judgment in a theoretical way,
as something that other people, perhaps, might exercise, but it is
not for them.

Such domination can be achieved by crude terror. But terror is
unreliable, since it may deprive the subject of all capacity for consistent action, engendering a pitch of anxiety which inhibits the
formation of any firm intention, even a heterarchic one. Instead,
the subject may oscillate wildly between conjectured courses
which he desperately hopes would appease the persecutor but
which may be quite unrelated to any intention that the terrorizer
actually has. Or as with the *Muselmänner*, victims of the S.S. concentration camps described by Bruno Bettelheim,[4] the terrorized
subject may lapse into a psychotic apathy as a refuge from a reality
too painful and too frightening to support.

But domination can also be more subtly achieved. A victim's need for approval and love may be used as a lever to undermine or prevent the development of independence. Obedient and submissive children and spouses frequently bear the marks of such conditioning. We sometimes characterize people like Olive Chancellor in Henry James's novel *The Bostonians* as moral blackmailers, though moral extortionists might be a better characterization: They try to exact submission by threatening to deprive their victims of love or by inducing in them irrational feelings of guilt should they resist their demands. The pressure they bring to bear differs radically from ordinary extortion or blackmail, however, which requires only that the victim believe in the blackmailer's ability and conditional intent to rig the external consequences should he refuse compliance; the preference set that makes the victim vulnerable to the pressure is not necessarily of the blackmailer's creation. The power of the moral blackmailer, by contrast, relies on his victim's having been made emotionally dependent on his persecutor, whether by the blackmailer or by someone else. It is arguable, indeed, that the love that the blackmailer threatens to deny is necessarily spurious, since it is inconsistent with the nature of the genuine love which the victim craves in that it is used as a manipulative resource. And the moral blackmailer who uses his own prospective suffering as a weapon with which to threaten the victim with guilt is generally exploiting a state of dependence which he has carefully, if not fully consciously, fostered. It is a measure of the victim's heterarchy that he fails to grasp this or, if he does grasp it, to act or react in the way to which such an awareness would rationally commit him. His emotional dependence inhibits a realistic understanding of their relationship; instead, he will probably block out critical and resentful thoughts as disloyal, unworthy, shameful. The renunciation of the relationship, which would be the response appropriate to such thoughts, is thus correspondingly blocked.

Terror and moral blackmail can be combined in a potent mix designed to heighten the victim's suggestibility, to provide compliance without psychotic collapse into impulsion. From the Inquisition to the "mental hospitals" of the Soviet Union, there has been no lack of study of methods of producing heterarchy by what is now broadly termed "brainwashing."

The victims of such domination have had their capacity to function as choosers or decision makers impaired or crippled to a greater or a lesser degree by another person, or, in the case of children reared in corresponding ways, their parents or guardians have inhibited the normal development of autarchy. This kind of

166

treatment of one person by another represents itself to us as a major affront, and is often regarded as a deprivation of freedom. Yet it is very different from, though no more acceptable than, the deprivations of freedom arising from interference with the objective features of the choice situation we examined above. The interferences that were there in question all presupposed an autarchic agent, a chooser or a decision maker making rational choices in the light of beliefs, preferences, and opportunity costs, which, while they may have been rigged, still governed a rational choice made by an independent chooser. Domination is an intrusion of a quite different kind. For it is possible that the *actions* of a heterarchic person may not be interfered with at all; he may have been too well programmed for that to be necessary. Though in one sense he has been deprived of his freedom, the wrong that has been done to him is quite different from that done by making him a prisoner, a bondsman, or by blackmailing him with a threat of public exposure.

Heterarchy is a condition, then, in which a person's preferences, his beliefs, or his capacity to act on his belief commitments have been rigged or impaired by methods that intentionally circumvent or block his rational decision-making capacity. The attempt to question implanted beliefs or to act on the commitments of beliefs that run counter to those so entrenched results in acute anxiety, so that the victim will more readily look for ways of altering the dissonant belief than contemplate any farther the possibility of having to act on it. The principle invoked in protesting against domination is *the principle of respect for autarchy*. Like the principle of noninterference, it derives from the principle of respect for persons. Suppose that someone with the self-consciousness of a natural person should come to believe that he was not a decision maker after all, but a heterarchic person, the states of affairs he valued and the principles for the sake of which he acted having been implanted by someone else. Suppose too that the manner of implantation had ensured that any attempt to examine them critically and independently occasioned him such acute anxiety and distress that he was unable to contemplate any alternatives. His new belief concerning the genesis of his beliefs would undermine all his beliefs, by exhibiting them as oriented to ends other than truth. Nevertheless, his behavior would continue to be oriented to the same ends as before, since *ex hypothesi* he cannot substitute others. So instead of perceiving himself as a natural person originating action, he now sees himself only as behaving in ways apt to bring about determinable outcomes. What he formerly understood

167

as the importance of goals meshed in a web of beliefs that constituted his own identity would now appear only as a kind of mechanical force attracting him to the realization of certain preset states of
affairs. Action would no longer be the manifestation of his own
creative agency.

To find that one's decisions were the outcome of such manipulation would amount to finding that one was not the kind of being
one had thought. To be a decision maker one must have an ordered
preference set; one must believe some things to be important. But
to discover oneself heterarchic is to mistrust all one's beliefs and
therefore to lose one's bearings entirely, since the things one believed important cannot be independently vindicated; every *point
d'appui* turns out to be equally alien. So though he retains dispositions to behave in determinate ways, since the stress of departing
from the ordained program would be too much to bear, the heterarchic victim can no longer hold these as directed to aims and
objectives of his own. He would experience, then, a collapse of
identity, a sense, perhaps, of being possessed by an alien self.
Mistrusting the inclinations that moved him, he would have a
dissociated, schizoid view of himself, as from the outside – always
determined, never determining. And this amounts to the erosion
of natural pesonality. But to manipulate another person so that
the conditions for natural personality would be undermined
should he discover the truth about himself is incompatible with
respecting him as a person.

Objections may be raised to the strength of the conditions suggested for impulsion and heterarchy. In the first place, it might be
argued that the distinction between inner-impulsion and heterarchy is very uncertain. Its importance for my analysis of freedom
lies in the moral difference between attributing a person's defects
as a decision maker simply to his personal incapacities, and to
attributing those incapacities to the actions of others which have
impaired what might otherwise have been a normal autarchic capacity. In the first case a person has been unfortunate; in the second he has been wronged. Since "freedom" is often used to mean
autarchy, someone so incapacitated might be said not to be free.
But the heterarchic person seems to be unfree in a way that the
other is not; for he has been deprived of or denied his autarchy. He
is a victim, who might properly express a grievance, if only he
could recognize the nature and source of his condition. The metaphor of enslavement is not misplaced in the case of the dominated
person; in the case of the compulsive it depends on a misleading

model of the inner politics of the soul. Yet according to many psychiatrists, the distinction might be hard to draw. Paranoia is not like the submissiveness of the Daughters of the Late Colonel. It might appear to be just something amiss with the person's cognitive faculties. And there are psychiatrists who regard it as a physiological phenomenon, susceptible to allopathic treatment. Others, however, will look for early influences on the patient's psyche, implanting programs that cripple normal critical development of the cognitive faculties. Such disagreements do not touch my distinctions, though they may affect the way in which particular cases are classified. If it turns out to be the case that Alan's paranoia is indeed the outcome of the pressures to which he has been subjected by Betty, so that but for her he would have been a normal autarchic chooser, then he has indeed been wronged by her. Respect for autarchy demands that people should not treat one another like that, precisely because it impairs their capacity for freedom. But if Alan's defect is sufficiently accounted for by his genetic equipment or biochemical imbalance, his incapacity for freedom is not due to his having been denied it.

A second possible objection is that my conditions for heterarchy are so weak that we all satisfy them. Since every normal human person is the product of a socialization process, are we not all equipped with implanted principles and values? Can any of us call his beliefs his own? But this objection overlooks the condition that the manner of heterarchic implantation generates such acute anxiety whenever the subject is tempted to call the implanted beliefs, values, or principles into question, or attempts to act contrary to them, that one can reasonably say he cannot do it. And this source of unfreedom is much more like being handcuffed than it is like being put under duress; for the heterarchic victim *has no choice* in the sense, not that the options remaining to him are ineligible, but that choosing itself has become impossible. Such judgments are of course matters of degree, and so are autarchy, impulsion, and heterarchy. My suggested characterizations of these conditions are of ideal types, to which real persons more or less approximate. How far their grievances, excuses, and justifications are to be accepted, how far their imputations or denials of responsibility endorsed, will depend not on whether but on how fully they satisfy conditions for autarchy.

# 9

## Autonomy and positive freedom

### 1. Positive freedom as autonomy

Chapter 7 dealt with what has often been termed "negative free-dom." The analysis centered on an unimpaired chooser deciding between options presented to him under the constraints of nature and those under social constraints, which are taken in context to be as invariable and inevitable as any purely natural impediment to action but not subject to interference by other persons. In the absence of imposed constraints or of interferences with his naturally endowed rational capacities, the person making a choice is taken to be free. Freedom is negative insofar as it amounts to the standardly available options remaining unrestricted by other persons in ways canvassed in Chapter 8, and the capacities for rational decision and the initiation of action that a normal autarchic person would possess remaining unimpaired by the actions of others.

There is, however, an ancient tradition that requires for personal freedom not only that the agent have the capacity for rational decision but also that in general he should use that capacity, that he should actually be motivated by the action commitments of his beliefs, and that these motivating reasons be of a certain sort. This is the account of freedom as positive. It is not, however, the account discussed in Chapter 7, according to which an agent lacks the positive freedom to do something if, even in the absence of imposed restrictions making the option unavailable or ineligible, he is still prevented from doing it because the enabling conditions for doing it are not satisfied. That account takes the agent's preferences for granted, focusing on the objective conditions that might frustrate his acting on them. This other notion of positive freedom looks critically at the subjective conditions governing the agent's choices.

There are varying accounts of just what sort of motivation is necessary for positive freedom. According to one important tradition, freedom consists in acting in accordance with reason, rather

170

than being the slave of one's passions. This view presents problems for moralists and philosophers committed, like Hume, to a philosophical psychology in which any action needs to be motivated by some sort of passion or desire. "Reason," Hume insisted, "is, and ought only to be the slave of the passions, and can never pretend to any other office but to serve and obey them."[1] But no such problems arise for the theory of rational action presented in Chapter 2. Practical rationality, we saw, requires that actions accord with belief commitments. In the absence of contrary commitments, if one believes that one will enjoy getting drunk, one will be both committed and disposed to getting drunk and will do one's best to do so, just because a belief in future enjoyment is always a reason for action, albeit not a conclusive reason. Moralists who regard getting drunk as becoming the slave of one's passions, and therefore contrary to positive freedom, generally reject the supposition that the drunk has no contrary commitments; they would claim that one always does have beliefs committing one not to act for the sake of such an enjoyment, and that these will always override the commitment to get drunk. Their problem then is not merely to sustain that claim by exhibiting the beliefs grounding these overriding commitments (which for the most part they may very possibly succeed in doing), but also to account for the misguidedness of those who don't accept the claim, or the akrasia of those who do, but get drunk all the same. Mistaken beliefs are not hard to explain: Our rational capacities are imperfect, and so even when we have information adequate for inference to true conclusions, we don't always get them right. Akrasia is more difficult. It was suggested in Chapter 2 that akrasia is a case of misdirected attention. The urgency of present sensual experience or the expectation of some corresponding but more subtle form of gratification, such as fame or popularity, or perhaps the acuteness of one's fear of painful experience distracts attention from beliefs with contrary and overriding commitments that one nevertheless holds. For St. Paul it is the law of God at war with the law of the flesh:

> ... What I do is not what I want to do, but what I detest. ... But if what I do is against my will, it means that I agree with the law and hold it to be admirable. ... [It] is no longer I who perform the action but sin that lodges in me. ... In my inmost self I delight in the law of God, but I perceive that there is in my bodily members a different law, fighting against the law that my reason approves and making me a prisoner under the law that is in my members, the law of

171

sin. . . . I myself, subject to God's law as a rational being, am yet, in my unspiritual nature, a slave to the law of sin.[2]

For Paul, without the Spirit of God our rational preference for the law of God is insufficient to redeem us from the sin which dazzles us, so that we lose sight of the truth we know. Without grace we are autarchic but akratic.

Acknowledging a law as binding does not necessarily constitute unfreedom. Indeed, for those who see freedom as positive, that acknowledgment is a necessary condition for freedom. But the law must be the appropriate one. Paul's antithesis between the two laws, obedience to only one of which is bondage, is matched in Rousseau's *Social Contract* by the doctrine that "the mere impulse of appetite is slavery, while obedience to the law which we prescribe to ourselves is liberty." But in Rousseau, the tension between the requirement of freedom that the agent be self-determining, making his own decisions, and that these decisions should in fact accord with his rational belief commitments, issues in a strange paradox. Entering the civil state, man, "who so far had considered only himself, find[s] that he is forced to act on different principles, and to consult his reason before listening to his inclinations. . . . [T]he voice of duty takes the place of physical impulses and right [law?] of appetite."[3] According to Rousseau, the content of the law that we prescribe to ourselves is given by the General Will, in conforming to which the citizen wills what he must rationally will, the good of the whole body politic, on which his own well-being depends. His proper concern for his own good rationally commits him to the good of the whole, which in a well-ordered state will be the object of a collectively adopted law. And if, irrationally, he refuses to obey the law, he will "be compelled to do so by the whole body. . . . [He] will be forced to be free."[4] Admittedly, if the citizens address themselves to sectional rather than to common interests, the will of the assembly, while still the will of all (in that everyone has participated in its expression) is nevertheless not an expression of collective reason. Obedience to that misguided will is not, presumably, the way of freedom. The law the citizen must obey to be free must have the right objects as well as the right source.

Kant relied on a more abstract, a universalized and formalized, version of Rousseau's antithesis of the general and the sectional or private will, of the antithesis between the "law which we prescribe to ourselves" and "the mere impulse of appetite." Kant's antithesis was between practical reason and mere inclination, located in the individual person abstracted from society. So long as we act only for the sake of our desires, we are not self-governing; as in Hobbes's mechanistic theory of man, we are merely attracted and repelled by things external to us, determined to action, not freely determining. Freedom – autonomy – is to be found in obedience to the moral law, to which reason gives us access. But because each person achieves autonomy by exercising his own critical, rational faculty, the moral law, though constraining, is not imposed, as Rousseau had envisaged the civil law imposed (even though by a democratic assembly in which everyone participated), but adopted as one adopts beliefs for which one sees sufficient reasons. It is, in a more direct sense than Rousseau could make it, one's own.

Kant's critics complained, however, that the criteria that Kant offered for determining the moral law were, in the end, purely formal, and the prescription for autonomy empty. Accordingly, Hegel, like Rousseau, turned for content to the community of which the individual was a member – but not to the expressed will of a general assembly. By virtue of his being a member of a community the individual, according to Hegel, already had access to a concrete morality, its *Sittlichkeit*, not as an external imposition but as an essential constituent of his social nature. So his moral obligations were self-imposed, as Kant required, not by rational contemplation from the austere detachment of an Archimedean point beyond all particular moralities, but rather by the individual's recognition of the rationality of the social and cultural reality. This was a system of moral beliefs and institutions which he did not simply belong to, as a grain of sand belongs to a particular heap, but which informed his individual nature, which therefore manifested and instantiated it. Recognizing that *Sittlichkeit* as his own, he satisfies Rousseau's condition that "each, while uniting himself with all, may still obey himself alone, and remain as free as before."[5]

Common to all philosophers in this tradition is the suggestion that someone who is unencumbered by external impediments but acts unreflectingly in response to the desire of the moment is still unfree because he is in bondage to internal pressures he cannot control but which control him. Self-control, or what the Stoics called *autarkeia*, requires the imposition upon unruly passions of the governance of some overriding law, or some principle of harmony which one's free actions can then be seen to instantiate, which will have the independent authority that only God or, in His absence, reason can bestow.

One objection to this kind of moral psychology is that it requires a kind of split in the self; there is an appetitive self and a rational self, yet *the self* is held to be in control and the person free only when the latter is dominating the former. Some romantic critics of rationalist ethics are inclined to turn the theory on its head, preferring "the native hue of resolution" when it is not "sicklied o'er with the pale cast of thought," and locating freedom in action even upon impulse rather than in deliberation.

Another objection is that it becomes hard to distinguish a normal autarchic decision maker who is indolent, corrupt, or self-indulgent from the compulsive who is truly at the mercy of nonrational drives. Equally, it provides no way of distinguishing someone who is dominated by another person from someone who is merely conventional, acting unreflectingly in accordance with prevailing custom or fashion. Kant provides a distinction between the autonomous rational man who obeys the moral law because he sees the rational point of it, and the heteronomous man who, while acting perhaps in precisely the same ways, is merely keeping up with the Joneses. But Kant does not bridge the gap between formal conditions for practical rationality and the concrete practicality of the thing to do, here and now. Hegel, by contrast, sure on the whole that the thing to do here and now is what the prevailing *Sittlichkeit* demands of you, fudges the distinction between autonomy and heteronomy, leaving little space for the radical critic of convention.

The tradition which attaches value to positive freedom needs to be able to make all these distinctions. The true compulsive lacks freedom in a profounder sense than the akratic person; the former is not accountable for his compulsive acts; the latter is fully accountable for his self-indulgent ones. Again, the person who possesses the capacity for rational decision making is a free agent but is not necessarily admirable on account of that; he may exercise his capacities in despicable ways or not at all. Nevertheless, as I have argued in preceding chapters, he is the subject of a fundamental moral principle, the principle of respect for autarchy, and the respect owed to him as an autarchic person demands that his own judgment of his own interest be not overridden by someone else's claim to know better. As a person he is a proper subject for considerations of principle; he may claim justice and the fair consideration of his interests. As an autarchic person, he may not be deliberately lied to, deceived and utilized as another person's tool or plaything, humored or indulged like an infant, or manipulated as one might manipulate a logically programmed computer, even in his own interest.

But in none of these ways does the autarchic person necessarily

174

come up to the standards set for him by Kant and by the moralists of the nineteenth century, such as Kierkegaard, Nietzsche, and J. S. Mill, who in their very different ways held up for admiration the courage and independence of mind of the person who did not passively accept convention but could claim to be the author of the law by which he lived. The problem is to find a sense more direct than Rousseau's, less metaphysical than Hegel's, Kierkegaard's, or Nietzsche's, and less paradoxical than any of them, in which autonomy can be accepted as a personality ideal, without so desocializing independence of mind that the autonomous person is endowed with a capacity to live according to a law he prescribes to himself but bereft of any resources with which to fabricate such a law. Hegel acknowledged the problem in a passage in which he refers to Socrates and the Stoics as instances of

> ... the tendency to look deeper into oneself and to know and determine from within oneself what is right and good [which] appears in ages when what is recognized as right and good in contemporary manners cannot satisfy the will of better men. When the existing world of freedom has become faithless to the will of better men, that will fails to find itself in the duties there recognized and must try to find in the ideal world of the inner life alone the harmony which actuality has lost.[6]

But this is pretty hazardous; to rely on the individual conscience is in Hegel's view at least as likely to elevate "the self-will of private particularity" into a principle of action, which is evil, as to make "the absolutely universal its principle," an achievement which, however admirable, would, according to Hegel's own epistemology, be very mysterious indeed.[7] Hegel can't help admiring truly autonomous men, but he is unable to give an account of how they can be that way, given their social essence. Which is why he fudges the question.

## 2. The characterization of autonomy as an ideal

The principles of action that I have associated with autarchy do not depend on anyone's valuing the autarchic person, in the sense of "valuing" which commits the valuer to admiring, cherishing, or seeking to sustain the valued object in that state and with those properties which are the ground for its being held valuable. Some autarchic people are contemptible and corrupt; their continued existence may give no one satisfaction, not even, perhaps, themselves. Nevertheless, the principles of respect for persons, noninterference, and respect for autarchy, with their derivative principles of fidelity and truth telling, all generate for other persons reasons for action and forbearance in their dealings with them. And the worthlessness (or worse) of the bearer of these immunities makes the principles no less cogent as reasons.

Autonomy, by contrast, is an excellence, to which people can approximate in varying degrees, and the perfection of which is a rarely realized ideal. Persons are admirable according to the degree of autonomy they attain. Not that autonomy is an all-embracing excellence; a less autonomous person may be on balance more admirable, by reason, perhaps, of his exceptional kindliness or some brilliant artistic gifts, than someone more autonomous. But the measure of his autonomy is one measure of his value, and it varies from person to person.

The difference between autonomy and autarchy lies first in the addition of the idea of a *nomos* to the characterization of the decision maker. The *nomos* corresponds to the positive freedom theorist's notion of a law, which confers on the life of the autonomous person a consistency and a coherence deriving from the consistency and coherence that he can achieve in the network of beliefs by which his actions are governed. To the extent that a person lacks that coherence, he is *anomic*, acting on impulse or on whim, not because he is impelled or compulsive, but because he acknowledges nothing as a reason for doing otherwise. Caring for nothing, the inclination of the moment is his only source of action commitments. He is autarchic in that he does not lack the capacity to order his preferences according to a coherent set of beliefs and to act on them; it is only that he possesses no principles that could structure such an ordering. In an extreme case it would be hard to tell someone who was autarchic but anomic from a psychopath. But whereas psychopaths are thought to be defective in the capacity to order their lives differently, so that they could not be taught to live by principles or ordered values instead of by responding to the immediacy of an expected gratification, anomic persons are thought to have a capacity to grasp a more considered way of living but have simply never learned how to do it or to value anything which living by a *nomos* could offer in return for the postponement of gratification.

A heteronomous person also possesses the capacity to order his life according to a *nomos*, and, unlike the anomic one, he really does so; his life may be as coherent, indeed, as that of the autonomous person. The heteronomous person, however, receives his

176

*nomos* ready-made, as a well-trained, well-drilled soldier may live punctiliously according to the *Manual of Military Law* and battalion orders. His actions can be quite properly seen as appropriate responses to the world as he apprehends it, but that apprehension is structured by beliefs he has simply introjected uncritically and unexamined from his social milieu, from parents, teachers, workmates, bosses, his priest, or the sergeant-major. It is not that he is incapacitated from independent judgment; he is not like the heterarchic person, whose attempt at critical appraisal of key beliefs would be blocked by acute anxiety. This one governs himself, but by a *nomos* simply borrowed from others, which he has done nothing to make his own. Of course, there are soldiers whose training has been so thorough as to deprive them of autarchy, but these belong to the pathologies of military discipline; heterarchic soldiers are not good at responding flexibly and with initiative to emergency situations in battle, however well they may perform on the barrack square. Good soldiers are heteronomous rather than heterarchic. Autonomy is not a disqualification, but it may not be good for discipline.

Fundamental to a person's autarchy is his consciousness of himself as the author of intentional changes in the world. Admittedly, the person who has a place on an assembly line, so far as concerns that role alone, is not likely to see himself as an originator. The total product is remote from his performance, and his sense of personal responsibility for its creation is likely to be weak. But of course his whole life need not be like that; if he fries an egg for his breakfast, he can recognize this at least as his own work and can judge whether he has done it well or ill. Admittedly, if the greater part of his waking hours is spent in mindless repetitive routines he perceives rather as molding him than as ways in which he molds the world, the remaining activities in which he perceives himself as able to make a difference to how they are done may be so insignificant that he loses his grip on autarchy in a kind of schizoid consciousness. But though radical critics have pointed to this as an aspect of that pathology of industrialism they call "alienation," it is obviously an exaggeration to treat this as the standard mode of self-perception, even among the people whose work comes closest to this paradigm.

The life of someone capable of an autarchic appreciation of his own activities can be represented as a process of *self*-creation, even though the person himself may not be aware of it under that description. When a potter judges the pots made by a colleague, his

177

judgment necessarily goes beyond the pots to the potter himself, who will be deemed not merely to have done well or badly, but to be a good or bad potter, to be improving, going stale, and so on. But in judging his own pots, knowing them to be his own, there is a practical dimension about the judging that is inescapably absent from any judgment he makes of someone else's pots and of their creator, even if the standards by which he judges them are no different. If being a potter is an important constituent of his way of life, he will earn his own respect according to his skill and integrity in the creation of pots. So his judgment goes beyond assessing the pots, not merely to an assessment of himself as potter but to an assessment of his life as a person, for being a potter is a central element in his being the person he is. Moreover, his appraisal is necessarily practical, too, associated with resolutions, hopes, and projects for future creations. For he possesses a control over his future work that he has over the work of no one else. The very dissatisfaction that he feels in spotting imperfections and mistakes in his pots can motivate him to try harder and do better, or to give up and do something else, just because his dissatisfaction is also with himself as the responsible agent.

This characterization of personal agency applies not only to the artist and the craftsman. It is as true for one's performances as banker, revolutionary, father, or friend. For every role description there is a set of standards by which a person will assess his performance, and therefore himself, unless the role is one which, imposed on him like the role of soldier on the unwilling and alienated conscript, plays no part in his conception of what and who he is. Failing in such a role may leave him unmoved because good soldiers are not for him admirable. But he cannot be similarly indifferent to his own bad opinion of his performance in a role he accepts as part of his own characterization as a person. A heteronomous person accepts the role if and only if others do so too. And his judgment of how well he performs in it may be formed in the light of criteria for the role accepted, again, from those around him. But heteronomous or autonomous, in assessing his performance in a role he accepts, a person by implication assesses himself, and in making the judgment he commits himself to some further development of his life project.

What distinguishes the autonomous from the heteronomous in their pursuit of such a project? True, the heteronomous person accepts the criteria for assessment that people around him accept, but it is not a necessary condition for autonomy that one be eccentric or unorthodox. One might say that to be autonomous a person's *nomos* must be his own, not merely one picked up from *heterotes*, from others about him. But how can anyone be the author of his own *nomos*? Surely everyone is governed by the basic presuppositions of the culture which has furnished the very conceptual structure of his world, the traditions into which he has been inducted, the demands of roles he has internalized? The very canons of rationality that he employs when he thinks himself most independent in his judgment have been learned as part of his cultural heritage. One's range of options, both in belief and action, is as much circumscribed by such mental furniture as the highest speed at which one can travel is governed by the prevailing technology.

The distinction between autonomy and heteronomy, however, is not affected by this truism; it is a distinction between character types, all of which are subject to these conditions. It is certainly necessary to a person's autonomy that he be capable of rational choice, and for that he needs criteria, rules of inference, and a conceptual scheme for grasping the options from which the choice is to be made. To be autonomous one must have reasons for acting and be capable of second thoughts in the light of new reasons. It is not to have a capacity for acting without reasons or for conjuring action commitments out of nowhere. And for reasons one must have a system of beliefs from which action commitments derive and into which new evidence can be assimilated, yielding new commitments. How could anyone come by these bits of basic equipment except by learning them in the first instance from parents, teachers, friends, and colleagues? Someone who had escaped such a socialization process would not be free, unconstrained, able to make *anything* of himself that he chose; he would be able to make nothing of himself, being hardly a person at all.

Within this conception of a socialized individual, however, there is still room to distinguish as autonomous a person who is committed to a critical, creative, and conscious search for coherence within his system of beliefs. He rests neither on the unexamined shibboleths and conventions of a traditional culture nor on the fashionably outrageous heresies of a radical one when they lead him into palpable inconsistencies. The resources on which he will rely for this critical exploration must lie, necessarily, within the culture itself, supplemented, perhaps, by those elements of alien cultures with which he has become acquainted. But such elements, too, have to be assimilated into the network of his own cultural beliefs, to be located in and related to the overall framework of his

179

intelligible world, before they can be accessible to him. Within this complex web – perhaps "tangle" would be more appropriate – he will try to create his own consistent pattern, appraising one aspect of it by critical canons derived from another. As an artist or a scientist must draw on the resources of an existing tradition to contribute creatively to its development, so an autarchical man must construe it for himself to become autonomous.

At certain critical junctures in our lives a novel situation can reveal that certain principles or evaluative beliefs that we had taken to be constitutive of our characters, because at the core of our belief system, and which make certain kinds of action "unthinkable," commit us nevertheless to radically conflicting actions or attitudes. Such beliefs may have had hitherto a kind of compartmentalized application in our lives, insulated from one another, their inconsistency obscured. Or beliefs long accepted as obviously true while no occasion pressed us to look at them critically may be eroded under pressure by other, incompatible yet unimpeachably grounded, beliefs, and to abandon the latter may be even more disruptive of our sense of who we are – and of the proper *telos* of belief – than to recognize the inadequacy of the old self-image. We discover experientially what considerations we cannot override without losing our grasp of reality and of our own identity. Members of western Communist parties went through such experiences in 1956, when Soviet troops suppressed the Hungarian government of Imre Nagy. The Vietnam war was a correspondingly revelatory experience for many Americans. A person is, or is capable of becoming, autonomous to the extent that he is capable of making such discoveries and of reforming his belief structure to resolve such incoherences. The heteronomous person looks in his uncertainty to others for cues, to point a way to resolve his dilemma, or, too timid to recast his idea of himself or too vulnerable to social pressure to conform, he clings to the habitual self-image and suppresses the intrusive ideas, denying to himself that they are or ever were his. Like the akratic person, he suffers from a defect of attention, distracted from dissonant beliefs by the expectation that to contemplate them squarely would be painful or create an anxiety he does not know how to cope with.

It is not a condition for autonomy, of course, that a person make a conscious decision before every action. Someone who did that would be an existentialist gone mad or be suffering from a neurotic anxiety that he might do the wrong thing. Most of the autonomous person's actions would be appropriate but nondeliberate responses to situations falling into fairly standard, recognizable categories. Living according to a *nomos* does not demand continuous ratiocination. Though in perplexity we may need to articulate principles, in order to ponder what we really stand for, their mode of existence is much more commonly as ways of identifying a situation as *this* rather than *that*, grasping its relevant features and intimating the action to which such an understanding commits one. People in tribal societies know well enough what is to be done in a given situation but rarely need to refer to principles. In their deliberations they are far more likely to canvass alternative descriptions of a situation with different action commitments, to decide which is the most appropriate one, without articulating the rule or norm that makes it so. Equally, in courts of Common Law it is unusual, except in hard cases, for the judge to articulate in abstract universal form the principles of law underlying the precedents he will cite in support of his judgment or those from which he will distinguish the present case. Nevertheless, previous decisions are constituted precedents relevant to the present judgment, and are reasons capable of justifying it, only because they instantiate a principle common to both, which could be isolated and stated generally without reference to the facts of particular cases. In hard cases judges may well be forced into doing so, albeit reluctantly, and with a sense that a formal statement of principles, which otherwise exist as modes of reasoning to be intuited rather then enunciated, deprives them of the subtlety and flexibility which has enabled the Common Law to adapt itself to some seven centuries of social change. True Common Lawyers have little taste for the strict categories of statutory pronouncements.

Because the concept of autonomy has been formulated in terms of criticism *within* a culture or a tradition, it does not presuppose that there be ultimate and objectively valid principles or evaluative truths in terms of which received beliefs are to be assessed. Suppose it were a logical truth that someone reared in a tradition that took little account of some very general principle, such as respect for persons, or some value, such as the value of human life, could not be persuaded by reasoned argument into adopting it as a practical belief, because his culture (or language) lacked essential concepts for the formulation of such principles. He might have no way of questioning, for instance, his own indifference to the claims of other persons to be told the truth or not to be treated as means to his own ends, even though he understood that other people held such beliefs which he, however, could see no point in. His inability to question his belief that lying was unobjectionable would not then be inconsistent with his being autonomous, but only because *ex hypothesi* to question it would be logically impossible. This is quite different from being incapacitated from questioning beliefs by a socialization process which, by instilling guilty feelings, has inhibited questioning he might otherwise have freely undertaken. If he held beliefs that were logically impregnable, which differed from corresponding beliefs held by others, they would have to be regarded as defining elements of his character – he would be a species of person who held such beliefs, and there would be other species which held different ones. There could be sociological explanations of these differences, but they would not entail that all these people were necessarily heteronomous. For the autonomous person is not necessarily one who can give reasons for *all* his beliefs; it is required only that he be alive to, and disposed to resolve by rational reflection and decision, incoherences in the complex tradition that he has internalized. Such criticism would always be internal; the reasons on which he could draw would always be, in that sense, within himself. Though he is open to persuasion, it can succeed only by invoking principles and beliefs to which he is already committed at least as firmly as to the ones under attack. For rationally persuading someone to abandon a belief requires that he be shown that to continue to hold the belief would be inconsistent with believing something else it would be still more difficult for him not to believe.

It appears, then, that autonomy is an ideal available only within a plural tradition, for it requires that two conditions be satisfied. In the first place, it requires that the subject's beliefs be coherent and consistent; secondly, their coherence must be the outcome of a continuing process of critical adjustment within a system of beliefs in which it is possible to appraise one sector by canons drawn from another. A monolithic system, in which, for instance, social and environmental conditions had remained virtually unchanging for centuries, and in which ways of acting had been routinized by a kind of natural selection process for all the major eventualities, and which encountered no alien cultures, would simply lack the incoherences which leave space for autonomous development. Where there is no work to be done, none can claim credit for doing it. Autonomy has become a conscious ideal in modern Europe since the Renaissance and the Reformation displayed great rifts in its culture, demanding that men and women define what they believed, without being able to rely upon unshaken and unshakeable authority. Fifth-century Athens, with its cosmopolitan commercial culture, was in many ways similar, and produced Socrates, who condemned the unreflective life. And the decay of Hellenic civilization and later of the Roman Republic, with the influx of strange and challenging ideas from Asia, each produced its own brand of Stoicism, demanding of the individual that he put his own intellectual and moral house in order.

Autonomy is an ideal for troubled times. When a rapidly changing and receptive culture invites inputs from strange sources which it admits faster than it can readily absorb, men and women feel the need either to discover what matters to them (or more objectively, what really matters), or to seek certainty by short cuts, submitting to some authority which will reinforce guilt and peer-group opinion in the repression of disturbing ideas. But it is not a comfortable certainty; the measure of its precariousness is the high emotional charge, the feverish persecution of nonconformity, required to preserve it from intrusive doubt. For these people, the alternative to heteronomy that they fear is not autonomy, which they lack the strength and confidence to aspire to, but an intolerable anomie – a moral lawlessness, in which there is no freedom, but only a total lack of orientation.

# 10

## Autonomy, integration, and self-development

### 1. The Freudian "ego" – Repression and rationality

I shall begin this chapter by exploring the Freudian model of the natural person, a very different one from my own. But I shall show that as the Freudians' interest expanded from psychopathology to embrace normal psychology, many of them developed models of "ego-autonomy" corresponding quite closely to my own model of the autarchic chooser. In ego-autonomy they found too the germs of personality ideals like integration, self-determination, and self-realization, ideals which are a good deal older than psychoanalysis. I consider these ideals further in Chapter 11 in order to examine more fully the relation between the notions of the ego and of the self which they presuppose. In this chapter I look at the relation between autonomy and two other ideals with which it is easily confused, particularly since the term "autonomy" is often used in connection with them.

In my discussion of "positive freedom" in Chapter 9, I referred to various traditional accounts of the relation between reason and passion, of how a person might be liberated from enslavement to "the mere impulse of appetite" by obedience to a *nomos* and of freedom as conformity to the law of reason. I elicited from a critique of this tradition the distinction between autarchy and autonomy, the latter a creative disposition to strive for coherence and the elimination of conflicts and inconsistencies latent in one's hitherto unexamined belief structure, as they are forced on one's attention by new and unfamiliar situations. Autonomy is, besides, a disposition to act on commitments grounded in that structure, which, in the process of rational reconstruction, one has made into a *nomos* that one can call one's own. A person is autonomous to the degree that his striving for such consistency in belief and action is successful and that the disposition continues to govern his life. The requirements of autarchy are less demanding. Autarchy is the normal state of the natural person, possessing a capacity for deciding for reasons between perceived options. Impelled and heterarchic states, though compatible with natural personality, are nevertheless defective just insofar as they fail to satisfy one or other of the conditions for autarchy.

Impelled and heterarchic states, rather than the conditions for normality, provided the starting point for Freud's analysis of the psyche. As a clinical psychologist, treating abnormal and neurotic behavior, he was disposed to see his patients as driven rather than deciding; he thus adopted, at least in his early work, a mechanistic explanatory model, according to which the subject was impelled by inner drives – the *id* – which threatened to destroy him unless they could be restrained. But whereas rationalists such as Plato and Spinoza had postulated an independent rational faculty as the regulative force within the soul, Freud allowed himself no source of controlling energy that was not itself contained within or derived from the very id it was its function to control. In infancy, he supposed, the person is, in a primitive sense, free – all id – seeking immediate gratification of every impulse, an undiluted expression of the pleasure principle. Experience of external reality, however, develops a secondary organization within the person, the conscious 'I', the self, or ego, which becomes invested with a psychic energy of its own, able to frustrate immediate gratification and to divert the organism from courses that would be painful or destructive. The authority of the ego is not something independent of the pleasure principle but derives from it, a detour or loop leading the libidinous energy, which is otherwise directly released in the immediate gratification of impulses, into channels that will really yield gratification rather than frustration. The ego is thus a principle of prudence constraining the id, but from within it.

At the Oedipal stage, the child embraces within the ego the *superego*, the introjection into the ego of the feared and loved father, paternal prohibitions and prescriptions being adopted as part of the child's self. Impulses that would offend it, ideas and memories that would excite its anger, are now repressed by the ego into the unconscious, preserving the subject from the pain of recognizing them as his own. "The theory of repression," Freud wrote, "is the cornerstone on which the whole structure of psycho-analysis rests."[1]

Repression, however, is not a successful method of dealing with the conflicts of the psyche because it results, under stress, in mental illness. It is inefficient because it produces at worst a generalized neurotic incapacity to deal with the world and at the best a

185

debilitating absorption of energy devoted to controlling the threatening impulse. Freud conceives of the instinctual drives as constant inner forces, needing the equally constant expenditure of psychic energy to keep them under.[2]

Other defensive techniques are available, however. Less debilitating than repression but almost equally unsatisfactory is inhibition, both the inhibition of feeling, the stifling of impulse before it develops sufficiently to constitute a threat, and the inhibition of action (ego-restriction), the refusal to participate in any activity, to go anywhere or do anything that might awaken the impulses that generate anxiety. In both cases the personality is impoverished.

Freud suggested two other methods of dealing with the threatening drives which call for little or no frustrating expenditure of energy. The sexual libido, he believed, could be sublimated into desexualized channels, becoming thereby the source of man's highest cultural achievements. But the capacity for sublimation was limited; few people could find such creative outlets, and even these people could displace only a part of the libido in this way.

In the 1915 essay on repression, however, Freud refers in a puzzlingly offhanded way to "a good method to adopt against an instinctual impulse," namely, "a rejection based on judgment (*condemnation*)."[3] Rejection, unlike repression, "occurs with the full knowledge of the ego," and the impulse then loses its force, but continues to exist in the memory; whereas in the case of repression, the reverse is the case – the memory is repressed but the energy remains.[4] In 1936 he referred again to "the normal method of warding off what is painful or unbearable, by means of recognising it, making a judgment upon it and taking appropriate action about it."[5] A therapeutic analysis is successful if it enables the neurotic patient to deal with repressed material in precisely this fashion.

Freud characterizes such rejection as "a process of decision" to reject an impulse "seeking to convert itself into action." His account, it is true, is cast in mechanistic terms: A small amount of energy is expended in envisaging, in imagining, what it would be like to adopt the attractive course of action; this causes an experience of pain and a consequent repulsion which, instead of triggering an energy release in bodily action, as would be the case had the imagined experience been pleasurable, has the effect instead of defusing the impulse.[6] But such metaphors can be abandoned without significantly altering the account: Finding a course of action at first sight attractive, a rational man will take the trouble to consider what it would be like, all things considered, to adopt it – what it would cost in discomfort, inconvenience, in the abandonment of principles, to indulge the desire – and will decide whether the gratification would be worth the cost. If not, he would give it up without repining. Or, using decision-theory metaphors, one might say that the decision involves appreciation of the net expected utility of a course of action in relation to available alternatives. The rational person then acts to maximize expected utility. According to Freud's account, "the automatic mechanism of the pleasure–pain principle is brought into play and carries through repression of the dangerous impulse." But the impulse, now squarely faced, is defused, and the repression is of the impulse, not of the beliefs and memories that generated it. The neurotic, by contrast, continues to yearn for what, realistically, he recognizes he cannot have, the opportunity cost being excessive, but represses into the unconscious what one might call his reasons for wanting it.

Freud's account of the unconscious strategies employed by the neurotic to mitigate or adapt to the pain of such a denial made sense of a good deal of otherwise inexplicable behavior. It is significant, however, that his method employs explanations modeled on rational action; the frequently bizarre performances of neurotic and psychotic subjects are rationalized by imputing to them belief structures which would make their actions appropriate, what they would indeed be committed to, were those beliefs true. But it is a kind of rationality imputed to a shadow-agent, the Unconscious, to explain the irrationality of the agent's conscious performances. Success in psychoanalysis consists in the subject's coming to understand the repressed irrationality and to deal with it rationally in consciousness.

## 2. "Ego-autonomy" and freedom

In 1939 Heinz Hartmann pleaded for attention to "the problems of autonomous ego development," a major element of which is the functioning of intelligence, which yields, on the one side, a better mastery of the environment but also "what is particularly important, . . . a better control of one's own person." "It is crucial for the ego that it can use rational regulations, while it simultaneously takes into account the irrationality of other mental achievements. The rational plan must include the irrational [i.e., the id] as a fact."[7]

The model of personality employed by the ego-psychologists, among whom are counted Hartmann himself, David Rapaport,

Bruno Bettelheim, and Eric Erikson, is that of an embattled ego, subject to the insurrectionary pressure of repressed id impulses but beleaguered equally by pressures from external reality which, as we shall see, can under conditions of great stress, such as the concentration camp environment, combine with certain id drives to overthrow the ego. The interest of the ego-psychologists focused, therefore, on the conditions for building up a consistent and reliable personality, capable of sustaining such pressures. This presented, however, a theoretical problem. According to Freud, the ego originated in repression, and the therapeutic process of psychoanalysis operated by bringing repressions into consciousness and thereby depriving them of their psychic energy. If the ego was to be seen as a source of stability, it must be assigned an autonomous existence capable of surviving the exposure to consciousness in analysis of the conditions of its formation. For instance, though an aversion from cruelty might originate in a reaction-formation from anal sadistic impulses, it can become, nevertheless, a sustainable feature of the autonomous ego. "[What] came about as a result of conflict sooner or later may become independent of the conflict, may become relatively autonomous." So altruism can become an independent "motivating value," even though "it arose as a reaction formation." The ego is thus an emergent entity, a system with rules and relationships amenable to independent investigation.[8]

A motivating factor in the ego-psychologists' focus on ego-autonomy has been their dissatisfaction with rather negative and conformist characterizations of the goals of psychoanalysis, such as "adaptation," "adjustment," and the reduction of tension or anxiety. The model of a relatively autonomous agency in the psyche, conferring on the agent a measure of independence alike from stimulation from within the id and from the external world, suggests an affinity between the psychoanalytic ideal and the ancient tradition in moral psychology which defined human freedom in terms of self-determination.

Stuart Hampshire drew attention in his British Academy Lecture of 1960 to this affinity with Spinoza's conception of human freedom.[9] For Spinoza every particular thing in the natural order, human beings included, has an inner drive, or *conatus*, to preserve its own character or organizational principle, its own particular stability and identity in relation to its environment. Though a person's actions are determined, like everything else, by ascertainable causes, he is free to the degree that the causes are ascribable to his own thinking nature, and are not merely re-

188

sponses to external stimuli which excite the passions. For the Freudians, however, threats to ego-autonomy come from two directions: both from the id and from external stimuli. The id exerts constant pressure, which must either be neutralized for good by repudiation or repressed by a constant expenditure of psychic energy. External stimuli can be avoided by flight or avoidance. By contrast, Spinoza, like Hobbes, considers the human being as a subject of passive powers (*passions*), which are dispositions to be activated by active powers, which are attractive or repellent external forces. But unlike Hobbes, Spinoza believed that these passions and the forces that stimulate them can be defused by understanding them, engaging the *conatus,* a kind of proto-Freudian libidinal drive to self-preservation, in defense against them. So for Spinoza, as indeed for Freud, rational self-understanding is the key to self-determination – to ego-autonomy.

The recognition of libidinous drives as self-generating pressures even in the absence of external stimuli creates for Freud a theoretical and a practical problem that Spinoza did not have to solve. Practically, the ego must discover how to discharge tension in a way that will not endanger the stability of the person; passions demand action and cannot be treated, as Spinoza treated them, simply as latent potentialities. According to Spinoza, the kind of activity in which man delights – the activity in which his *conatus,* his essence, is manifest as self-preserving and self-determined – is the understanding of his own nature. This understanding provides, as it were, the psychic energy required to prevent his reacting mindlessly to the external stimuli to his passions, defending by prudent regulation the integrity of the self. The Freudian self-determining ego, on the other hand, must be more than a *conatus* to preserve the organism by self-understanding. Freud's libido – the general source of energy – is primarily a sexual drive, albeit capable, if need be, of desexualization by sublimation. Bodily desires, however, will not be assuaged merely by rational understanding of their nature; psychic health requires that they be satisfied.

## 3. Ego-autonomy, identity, and the integrated personality

It is not only against the instinctual drives and environmental stimuli, however, that the ego must defend itself; its autonomy is threatened, too, by the superego, which Freud saw as part of itself, its own creation. In some cases of neurosis the ego is afflicted with severe guilt; in Freud's terminology, it enlists the aggressive drives to pun-

189

ish itself at the behest of the stern parent it has introjected. Here again the ego-psychologists have seen the problem as one of building up the autonomy of the ego, of strengthening it against the authority of the superego. For this it must attain what Eric Erikson called "a sense of inner identity" or "ego-identity," a term which characterizes the subject's self-awareness.[10] It is not merely that the subject needs to differentiate himself from the not-self. So much is an early childhood achievement which begins when the infant discovers that the gratification of only some of its impulses lies within its control. "Ego-identity" is rather the awareness of "a self-sameness and continuity to the ego's synthesizing methods, *the style of one's individuality.*"[11] This sense of continuity embraces not merely the past – what the adolescent has come to be during long years of childhood – but also a projection into an anticipated future.

Erikson's account of the development of a sense of identity stresses the relation between how the individual sees himself and how he sees others as seeing him. In childhood, his security and gratifications depend on the love and approval of a small circle of others on whom he models himself and who may, indeed, impose their own models upon him. What he is for himself is what he believes himself to be for them. Later, he encounters a peer group that offers him different roles and has other expectations of him. As his interpersonal relations multiply, so too do his possible roles and self-identifications. The so-called identity crisis arises from this complexity of personae; seeing himself mirrored in other people's ideas of himself, the adolescent is troubled to know which is the real he, which the distortions. Which opinions can he disregard, which matter so much that he cannot but share their approval and disapproval?

> The search for a new and yet reliable identity can perhaps best be seen in the persistent adolescent endeavours to define, over-define, and redefine themselves and each other in often ruthless comparison, while a search for reliable alignments can be recognized in the restless testing of the newest in possibilities and the oldest in values. When the resulting self-definition . . . becomes too difficult, a *sense of role confusion* results: the young person counterpoints rather than synthesizes his sexual, ethnic, occupational, and typological alternatives.[12]

For some the strain is too great: Preferring even a negatively valued identity to a bundle of contradictions, they become delinquents and dropouts, investing "pride, as well as need for total orientation in becoming exactly what the careless community ex-

190

pects [them] to become." Others, "driven to decide definitely and totally for one side or the other," embrace a totalitarian movement. Despairing of finding a "whole" identity, a coherent conception of themselves which will integrate the partial and disparate residues, they prefer to submerge themselves totally in a single role commitment. For Erikson this amounts to defeat: "To have the courage of one's diversity is a sign of wholeness in individuals and in civilizations."[13]

Ego-identity is closely related to self-respect and self-esteem. Someone engaged in discovering who he is, in welding the images of himself into a coherent whole, must believe in his own worth and must have a degree of confidence in his own right to have a view of his own about himself. Erikson puts the origin of self-esteem very early in childhood, at the anal stage, when the child is learning self-control. In the control of bowel movements, in determining if and when events shall occur, the child gains its first experience of itself as agent, as author and originator of changes in its environment, and as having choices about the changes to originate. Furthermore, this experience is associated not with the instinctual indulgence of the primary impulse, but with the discovery of the capacity for *self-control*. The frustration of this stage of development or parental overinsistence on performance to order might plausibly impair the child's appreciation of this fundamental fact about personality and the development of its self-consciousness and self-respect as a chooser.

There is a significant connection, then, between decision making and self-control. Someone who acts only upon impulse because he lacks the consciousness of alternative possibilities between which he can decide, or lacks the sense that the way the world goes is open, that he can make it go one way or the other, is defective as a chooser. The concept of the free agent, of natural personality, presupposes then the concept of self-government: Not to know what it is to govern one's impulses is not to know what it is to decide.

The development of a firm ego-identity, an autonomous ego, depends, however, on something more. The child must have a sense of trust, an assurance that his "faith in himself and in the world will not be jeopardized by the violent wish to have his own choice"; he relies on parental firmness to protect him from disastrous errors yet needs to be backed up in his attempts to stand on his own feet. But he needs especially to be protected against the sense of having exposed himself prematurely and foolishly, which we call shame, and "that 'double take,' which we call doubt –

191

doubt in himself and doubt in the firmness and perspicacity of his trainers." Without the formation of self-confidence and self-esteem the later struggle against the superego will issue in "the irrational repudiation, the total prejudice against themselves which characterize severe neurotics and psychotics."[14]

In the course of this discussion of ego-autonomy the notion of 'the self', and related notions of 'self-control', 'self-esteem', and 'self-determination' have become increasingly evident. The last three do not necessarily presuppose, of course, the existence of some entity, the self, which does the controlling, esteeming, or determining of some other not-self; indeed, the reflexivity of these expressions requires the contrary; subject and object are the same. But an analytical schema which populates the psyche with an id and a superego, as well as an ego, and asserts the possible but not necessary autonomy of the last of these, raises the question how the reflexivity is to be understood. Is self-determination, for instance, the same as the autonomy of the ego, the control of the primitive impulses and the introjected superego by the rational reality principle? That is, do we simply translate reflexivity at the macropersonal level into the politics of the psychic faculties? And is the hypostatization of 'the self' simply a category mistake?

There are reasons for resisting this interpretation. To possess ego-autonomy is indeed to be autarchic rather than impelled. But the conceptions of personality implied by the ego-psychologists' notion of ego-autonomy seem to go beyond autarchy. They seem to require that one be aware of oneself, not merely as having the capacity to initiate changes in the world in the light of one's beliefs and preferences, but to be aware of oneself too as possessing a determinate character, an identity, and further that one be able to appraise one's actions as consistent with it or as being out of character, and that such appraisals constitute grounds of decision. A self-determining agent must be able, then, to govern his responses to situations in accordance with general principles and be able and disposed to reject an impulse to act as inappropriate. A self-determining person has his own standards of consistency for himself which are more than the mere regularities of behavior he observes in other people and in things. Someone who lacks such standards, or cannot act in accordance with them, feels "pushed around" – a victim of circumstances or of his own impulses. Or he seeks anxiously for cues, to resolve the indecision that springs from the lack of criteria by which to decide what it is appropriate to do. So the concept of the self as agent is intimately connected with the idea of self-government as the capacity to set aside impulse and immediate gratification for the sake of policy or principle.

The ego-psychologists mentioned above were concerned particularly with the conditions under which such a capacity not only would develop, but could be strong enough to withstand stress. Bettelheim's moving record of his experiences and observations in the S.S. camps at Dachau and Buchenwald, *The Informed Heart*,[15] is a study in part of the conditions under which ego-autonomy will break down and of the features of the personality which give it strength to survive. These seem to be very closely related to the ones explored by Erikson and might be termed the conditions for *integration*. The integrated person has the capacity to remain autarchic under conditions in which mounting anxieties threaten to overwhelm the capacity to judge whether the responses one is disposed, under stress, to make to one's environment are really appropriate to it.

A person has an integrated personality if he manifests a strong sense of his own identity, a firm grasp of his own values and principles, an image of himself as a certain kind of person and as author, shaping, or at least interpreting, the world in the light of that self-characterization. Without it a person will yield to environmental pressure. If, as in the case of the concentration camp victims, virtually no space remains for actions that the person can feel himself significantly to originate, it is still something if he remains aware of himself as a perceiver with an independent point of view. As Bettelheim describes it, part of the S.S. technique for breaking down personality consisted in making it dangerous even to show that one was noticing what was happening about one, so that the instinct to protect himself tempted the victim to give up the observation that was necessary to forming an independent view of his environment. Again, though to survive one might have to limit one's acts to total compliance, however detestable, and nothing besides, it was still something if one could retain the power to make that independent appraisal of detestation. If one complied out of a policy for survival, one could still perceive oneself as making a choice, for one could still see the act as falling within limits beyond which one could not and would not go without totally surrendering one's identity or self-perception. The breakdown of a personality came when obedience was granted as a capitulation, when there was no description that the agent could give of his action such that it remained his own decision, albeit one among horrendous alternatives. With capitula-

193

tion came defenses such as identification with the masters and the adoption of their values.

The effect of coercive terror, according to Bettelheim's account, is a reversion to a childlike dependence. The subject's anxiety, his very drive to preserve his life, could force him "to relinquish what [was] ultimately his best chance for survival: his ability to react appropriately and to make decisions."[16] The external stimulus to the primary instinct of self-preservation may be so great that the fabric of the ego – the rational reality principle – simply breaks down, and the victim responds not with a decision but by setting up defenses, in some cases by internalizing the values of the oppressors but in extreme cases by becoming mere reactors to external pressures. The so-called Mohammedans, the walking corpses in the camps, unlike real Moslems, who "made an act of decision and submitted to fate out of free will," gave "the environment total power over them . . . when they gave up trying to exercise any further influence over their life or environment," obeying commands automatically, initiating nothing and registering neither feeling nor comprehension.[17] In psychoanalytic terms, the environmental pressures began by enlisting the inner drives by evoking terror. But the outcome was a total dissociation of external behavior from the drives and a defensive inhibition of all emotional response. Then behavior requires no motivational explanation, only an account of triggering causes. This constitutes the extreme case of what I have termed heterarchy, or other-impulsion.

In the final stages of breakdown, the victims were incapable, despite extreme hunger, of responding even to offers of food made to them by fellow prisoners. The collapse of the ego was then quickly followed by death.

"However restrictive or oppressive the environment may be," wrote Bettelheim, "even then the individual still retains freedom to evaluate it. On the basis of this evaluation, he is also free to decide on his inner approval or resistance to what is forced on him." But this is a pretty exiguous employment for the decision-making capacity (or ego). "A sense of autonomy depends everywhere on the conviction that one can make important decisions, and can do it where it counts most."[18] The faculty of decision making is liable to atrophy without employment: If nothing one does or even thinks can make a difference except to one's own view of oneself, and where even to make it apparent that one still has that much independence is perilous, there is every temptation to surrender. Those who survived were, on the whole, those I have called "integrated personalities."

194

Bettelheim calls these integrated personalities "autonomous," and this is right enough, given his notion of ego-autonomy. But this terminology obscures important differences. Among the survivors were some who were ideologically most strictly disciplined, the least flexible and critical, members of strict religious sects, such as Jehovah's Witnesses, and of disciplined political groups, including members of the Communist party. Their integral strength lay precisely in the narrowness of their ideological commitment; knowing with certainty where they stood, their standpoint of judgment never wavered. These were David Riesman's "inner-directed" personality types. Most vulnerable were the other-directed ones, whom Rousseau describes in the *Discourse on the Origin of Inequality* as setting "a value on the opinion of the rest of the world; who can be made happy and satisfied with themselves rather on the testimony of other people than on their own." Such a person "knows how to live only in the opinion of others, so that he seems to receive the consciousness of his own existence merely from the judgment of others concerning him."[19] Such people I have called heteronomous. Having no firm grasp of their own identities, they were accustomed to rely for cues for both action and judgment on others in their social peer groups, and depended for self-esteem on the esteem of their neighbors. Deprived of these accustomed supports, they became anomic, disoriented, and ultimately heterarchic or psychotic. Of both groups, the inner- and the other-directed, one can say that they entered the camps as autarchic persons; but neither would satisfy the conditions for autonomy in the sense that implies that the *nomos* by which they lived and survived was their own, made so by the critical appraisal and rational elaboration of their beliefs and principles of judgment. The ideologues survived on account of a firm core to the ego – a strong sense of identity built on a more or less coherent world view to which, however, they were quite uncritically committed. New situations would be readily and unambiguously assimilated to a relatively few well-formed paradigms, minimizing conflict and anxiety. Whether reared in the faith or possessing the unshakable commitment of the convert, such a person is heteronomous, not autonomous, if for instance he is prepared to use the Holy Scriptures or the works of Lenin to ground his belief and action commitments but is not prepared to recognize or even to contemplate the findings of geological and biological science or the evidence of history as challenges needing to be met by reasoned counterarguments, at least as rigorous as those he would deploy in disputes *within* the framework of the system he accepts.

So, unlike Rousseau's character who seeks only to keep up with the Joneses, the integrated ideologue does not rely for cues on contingent others; he determines his actions by reasons, not by promptings. But the *nomos* within, which generates the reasons, is not fully his own, because adopted without critical examination, untested by the resources of a wider tradition available to him. Like the Freudian superego, it has been absorbed into the ego, yet it is still an alien authority. Nevertheless, it is capable of providing the ego with the strength and integration that the heteronomous but nonintegrated person lacks. If conflicts arise which might touch his received faith, he is disposed to resort to defenses rather than to reasons, but he is not incapable of appreciating criticisms, should his defenses fail. Were one so incapable, one would be not just heteronomous but in some measure heterarchic (or psychotic like the paranoid), an impelled man.

The inner-directed heteronomous type was not, however, the only kind of person who survived the stresses of the camps. Bettelheim survived, too, with what was very evidently quite a different orientation, that of a critical, scientific, and detached observer. This was the identity he already recognized as his own before entering the camps. On his own account, preserving and cultivating it became for him a deliberate policy. So Bettelheim himself would qualify as autonomous not only in his own but also in my more exacting sense. He lived by critical values, the point of which was apparent to him; indeed, in the early pages of *The Informed Heart* we are told of his early critical exploration of the Freudian and Marxist ideologies that formed his cultural milieu in Vienna in the 1920s. He moved in the direction of Freud and away from Marx for reasons, and in a way, that did not make them objection-proof. Nevertheless his orientation, like that of the heteronomous Jehovah's Witnesses, was firm and coherent enough to provide him with the integral strength to resist.

Bettelheim wrote *The Informed Heart* not primarily as a study of concentration camp psychology, but rather as a tract for the times, a study of the strains that affluence and abundance put on ego-autonomy in a world of rapidly changing values. This was not a new theme; Durkheim, who coined the term *anomie*, criticized modern industrial society in very similar terms, and Alastair MacIntyre's recent book *After Virtue* is similarly concerned for the doubts and anxieties of a culture without moral certainties. Technical progress, says Bettelheim, has created many more opportunities between which modern men and women are called upon to decide. But the very rate of change in our plural culture and the weakening of parental authority has resulted in ambiguous and uncertain value structures. One is often unable to recognize any conclusive reasons for choosing one thing or one way rather than another, so that

> the psychic energy spent in reaching a decision is wasted, and the individual feels drained of energy without purpose. Basically, reaching a decision . . . depends on a man's ability to eliminate, first, all solutions clearly not in line with his values and personality. Then very few solutions remain possible and to choose the correct one is relatively simple. A person who is not well integrated, who does not follow a consistent set of values, cannot . . . cut the problem down to size . . . [and] feels overpowered by any new need for decision.[20]

Modern mass society, Bettelheim claims, fosters a sense of restricted autonomy, rather than a sense of freedom, by overwhelming us with choices we cannot handle, because our value structures are too weak to make the kind of initial sifting which is necessary to rational decision. Unable to decide, we look elsewhere for cues and accept heteronomy. The integrated person, by contrast, could deal readily enough with multiple options; he would be able to eliminate those that were quite inconsistent with his values, and if there remained a number that were equally attractive, he would have no hesitation in making a random choice. But the source of his strength is not that he has strong preferences, as Bettelheim seems to suggest. For a Stoic indifference is also a kind of integration, and a Stoic is no less free to choose because he has weak preferences. The personality disorder that Bettelheim exposes is that when confronted by multiple options we may be too uncertain of our preference structure, too anomic, to trust our judgment that there is nothing to choose between the options, that we really are indifferent about them. Not to know whether you have a preference is by no means the same as assured indifference, and it is the former that is the source of the anxiety that we may be choosing wrongly, though we can see no ground for saying which choice would be right. Someone with firm principles and tastes, however rigid, pig-headed, and prejudiced, nevertheless knows how to choose. The criteria governing his choices are well-defined and his options well-ordered. Of course, they may be rather nasty criteria, and he may be criticized as prejudiced; personality integration may not be everything. But a personality ideal that has no place for it must, according to the accounts not only of Bettelheim but of others who have studied survival under stress situations, be seriously defective.

# 11

# Self-realization, instinctual freedom, and autonomy

## 1. Self-realization

Many writers influenced by the neo-Freudian ideas of ego-autonomy discussed in Chapter 10 have looked to the notion of "self-realization" for a personality ideal somewhat more substantial and more specific than integration. The idea that the personality has some kind of essence, struggling for realization or free expression – that positive freedom consists in actualizing this ideal self – is a recurrent theme in moral and social philosophy. It was central to T.H. Green's concept of moral freedom, a man's reconciliation "to 'the law of his being' which . . . prevents him from finding satisfaction in the objects in which he ordinarily seeks it, or anywhere but in the realisation in himself of an idea of perfection."[1] As a subject of rational will, all his action is, in an ideal sense, oriented to "self-perfection," though he may be mistaken in seeking it where it is not to be found. But the "law of his being," which is reason, is also the moral law. Reason and will are "expressions of one self-realising principle." If all men are seeking the same rational self-realization, the conditions for its achievement tend, albeit imperfectly, to a concrete expression in what Green, following Hegel, took to be the historical manifestation of reason in the conventional moral code and in traditional institutions.

Neo-Freudian self-realization theorists, such as Erich Fromm and Karen Horney, would certainly reject the identification, even in principle, of the real and the ideal. Indeed, modern man's opportunity for self-realization is seen as coming precisely from the weakening of traditional authority. But this alone leaves him isolated, powerless, alienated and confused, a prey to "the fear of freedom," anomic, and vulnerable to neurotic breakdown. The "full realization of the individual's potentialities, together with his ability to live actively and spontaneously"[2] requires something more than the lifting of authoritative constraints.

199

For Fromm, in contrast to Freud, other-regarding needs and desires, love, hatred, and tenderness, are not the secondary outcomes of frustrations or satisfactions of instinctive needs, but fundamental psychological phenomena which, however, can develop only when primary needs have been satisfied. Culture is not grounded in the sublimation of erotic impulses, but arises from these fundamental creative needs which, however, are manifest only in conditions of abundance. So (bringing Freud and Marx together) Fromm contends that the forms of culture, the manifestation of creative needs and desires, depend on traits of social character which are shaped in their turn by productive forces. So the problem is to realize the possibility of a society in which these manifestations will be generally amiable rather than the reverse.[3]

Fromm is operating, if somewhat vaguely, with a conception of self-realization which depends on potentialities, planted rather like seeds in the soil of personality, awaiting favorable conditions to sprout. But as any gardener knows, the sprouting of some seeds is not at all to be encouraged. Like Rousseau, however, Fromm's reply to the objection that a man's potentialities may be aggressive and antisocial is that

> . . . man is neither good nor bad; that life has an inherent tendency to grow, to expand, to express potentialities; that if life is thwarted, if the individual is isolated and overcome by doubt or a feeling of aloneness and powerlessness, then he is driven to destructiveness and craving for power or submission. . . . [If] man can realize his self fully and uncompromisingly, the fundamental cause for his social [*sic:* antisocial?] drives will have disappeared and only a sick and abnormal individual will be dangerous.[4]

Still, there will always be, as T.S. Eliot remarked,

> . . . *the passage which we did not take*
> *Towards the door we never opened*
> *Into the rose garden.*

Man's very status as a chooser condemns him to the denial of some of his potentialities, and the greater his opportunities, the more of his potentialities he will be forced, in choosing, to deny. Every decision, as the economists say, has its opportunity costs. The crucial questions are not how far a person realizes his potentialities, but whether the ones that he does realize are worthwhile, whether they are the ones that are most significant for him and whether the

200

constraints on his choices could have been set wider, allowing the realization of others too.

Christian Bay looks harder than does Fromm at the notion of "the self" to be realized (or in Bay's terms "expressed"), characterizing it, for the most part, in terms not of potentialities but of the notion that a person has of his own identity. He explores, for instance, the relation between "the self" and "the ego," endorsing a passage from Solomon Asch:

> The self, being a phenomenal representation, does not include all that belongs to the ego and at times apprehends the ego wrongly. The ego is prior to the self and far wider than it. The self is not the mirror image of the ego; there is between them the same kind of relation as between the physical object and its psychological representation. There can be grave differences between the person as he is, as science would describe him, and as he would view himself.[5]

"Self-knowledge" would then be the conscious and preconscious knowledge the person has of his own ego, and since the ego is not fully open to consciousness (since, according to Freud, it includes whatever exercises repression of material into the unconscious), it may be incomplete knowledge. It may also be mistaken, for it may simply misconceive the ego. The self, then, seems equivalent to the person's ego-image. (Bay calls it, somewhat confusingly, a "self-image"; this must surely be wrong, implying as it does that the self is an image of an image.) The ego then becomes the agent as noumenon, the self a phenomenon, the agent as he appears to himself in acting or what he believes himself to be.

Now while I do not think that this corresponds to the way we commonly talk of "the self" (and I do not think that we talk about it often – in ordinary usage, *self-* and *-self* are simply reflexive affixes so that we speak freely of "myself," but only very rarely of "my self"[6]), Bay's proposal does suggest a useful analytical concept. It permits us, for instance, to give a fairly strict account of what it means to be honest with oneself, to act authentically. A person can now be said to act authentically when the conception he has of his own action – his conception of the self in action – corresponds to the real ego in action. The motives he imputes to himself are then genuinely his own; that is, a psychoanalytical account would not treat them as rationalizations. For though the ego may repress real motives, allowing only rationalizations of them into consciousness, still, as the repressive agent, it must be in touch with the unconscious motives. "The boundaries of the self," says Bay, "are drawn

201

by the process of repression or dissociation. The self is the individual's awareness of acceptable characteristics of his own personality."[7] Successful psychoanalysis extends the patient's self not only by making him aware of painful experiences and motives (what Bay confusingly calls "unflattering self-insights" – confusingly because they are insights into the ego) but by making them acceptable to him. "Psychological freedom is measured by [a person's] capacity to accept and act upon a realistic image of his self and of other people."[8]

We act authentically, then, when we acknowledge the real motives of our acts and accept these acts as consistent with our ego-image, the self.

Bay makes an explicit connection between this notion of the self and "self-esteem." If the self is an image of one's own qualities, it includes

> . . . an appraisal of one's own record and competence in all one's important roles or social relationships. . . . [Each] role is important to the extent that the individual's self-esteem is enhanced when he is performing the role well or diminished when he is feeling he is doing poorly in it.[9]

So one may judge whether a role enters into the self by the degree of satisfaction or dismay occasioned by success or failure in it. The completely alienated worker or the disaffected conscript soldier takes no pride in his achievements in the role or accepts with equanimity the criticisms of his superiors because the role means nothing to him. Or if he resents their criticisms, it is because he resents being judged by criteria which are constituents of the role he so grudgingly bears. But when a role is truly a part of the self, what the person makes of it affects his consciousness of his identity; having the role is a necessary part of being the person that he is, and his performance counts for him as a stage in self-creation.

Apart from a somewhat cursory consideration of "psychological freedom" as a goal for psychoanalysis, Bay does not explore the possibilities of this notion of the self for the ideal of self-realization. In an illustrative example he defines psychological freedom for a patient as

> . . . a maximum understanding of and interaction with herself – a realistic awareness of what her basic needs and potentialities are and the ability and enduring effort to develop this self in the direction of an equally realistic ego-ideal.[10]

Now this suggests a notion of self-realization more viable than Fromm's, for it requires not the full realization of potentialities but only "a realistic awareness" of them. It is obviously important for the enterprise of self-creation that one should know what is possible – both the extent and the limits of the available options. If one adopts a totally unrealistic ego-ideal, the outcome, as Karen Horney insists,[11] will be a neurotic self-hatred. The self to be realized must be what Horney calls the real, not the idealized, self – not an image that demands too much. More accurately, the ego-ideal to be realized must be one that it is possible for that person to become, not one beyond his reach.

Self-realization, understood in this way, is very different from the ideal of self-assertion that attracted the wilder romantic spirits of a century ago. There is no virtue here in insisting on one's uniqueness, on the idiosyncratic; neither is the notion of self-realization necessarily individualistic, if by that is meant that in striving for self-realization one has regard only to oneself or that one makes the state of one's own psyche the pivot of one's life. The idea of the self is the idea of the set of one's beliefs, one's own values and principles and ideals, by which one governs one's practice. Self-realization is a process of becoming what those beliefs commit one to become. One's reasons are not narcissistic, as is the ideal of self-assertion; one acts not because the beliefs are peculiarly one's own but because one holds such beliefs to be true, whether they are widely shared or idiosyncratic, and because the action is what they require one to do. But one's self-esteem is necessarily dependent on the degree to which one can meet these requirements.

In a meritocratic society, people are under pressure to set their standards high. The forms of life to which we commit ourselves as being worthwhile are seen as challenges to excellence or at least to distinction. Equal opportunity in education generally means an equal chance, so far as external conditions are concerned, to try for very unequal esteem. Social democracy has generated more general and fiercer competitiveness, not less. The child encouraged to set his sights high finds it hard to live peacefully with his failures, judging his actual achievements harshly by too glorious an ego-ideal. Protestant and Kantian ethics are no kinder in their moral demands, no less severe on failure, and consequently damaging to self-esteem. Self-hatred so induced may take the form of a neurotic self-abasement, a refusal to try, or an equally neurotic defensive self-glorification, whistling in the dark.

203

None of these conditions is likely to foster an autonomous reassessment of one's real capacities and a proper esteem for what it is truly within one's powers to achieve. In a competitive society, only someone with a self-esteem firmly grounded on an experience of consistent regard and affection – demonstrably proof against failures – can be expected to survive his disappointments with his own performances without self-hatred. And since in such a society everyone not only decides to a considerable degree his own goals, but is encouraged to aim high, so nearly everyone will have to face up to the fact at some time that he is not quite as good as he believed, that his true potentialities fall short of the ideal he has created for himself. So a viable ideal of self-realization must *provide* for failure, as necessary to learning by experience; the ego-image guiding the choice between potentialities to be realized must be subject to correction and modification, in the light alike of failure and easy success. Ideal and achievement thus function as parts of an experimental process to discover which, of those ideals a person can esteem, he can realistically aspire to realize. And this is true as much of worldly or vainglorious goals as of high-minded, ascetic, or devotional ones.

This conception of self-realization now comes close to my ideal of autonomy, and goes well beyond the concepts of ego-autonomy and of an integrated personality. Or rather, it goes beyond them, and approximates to autonomy, given the kind of plural moral experience that prompts Erikson's "identity crisis." For in narrowly circumscribed societies, where there is considerable homogeneity and stability of standards, values, and roles, there is little room for role ambiguity. The ego-image of an individual who identifies himself by his place in a unique progression of socially sanctioned roles will correspond at virtually all points with the image that others have of him; the esteem in which they hold him and in which he holds himself will be a function of his roles and his performance in them. Such a person will not lack integration, nor could he be said to fail to realize the self, since that self is given unambiguously by his social location, and in passing through the life-succession of roles, he realizes himself. Should he leave the society, its unambiguous injunctions can still support him so long as nothing happens to shake his identification with it, nor the introjected structure of his beliefs, and so long as his range of new experiences can be assimilated to the ones for which his culture provides. Within his society, he satisfies the condition that he has a realistic awareness of his potentialities, socially limited and defined as they are, and he strives, living the life of his limited society, to realize a realistic ego-ideal. Where he falls short of the ideal of autonomy is in the lack of the critical appraisal of the belief-structure that grounds his performances, and this for the good reason that in the hypothesized homogeneous, coherent, and stable environment there would be no standard by which to exercise criticism and no judgment that was not already his own.

This conception of the complete introjection of socially generated beliefs and ideals is, of course, an ideal type; no actual society would ever fully satisfy such rigorous conditions. There are societies, nevertheless, in which firmly integrated personalities realize their "selves" inasmuch as they fulfill the expectations they have of themselves according to the *nomos* they acknowledge – but a *nomos* which can be called their own only if one sees them, as one might see the members of a beehive, as manifestations of an organic social personality whose collective requirements are so homogeneous and so unshakably introjected that the individual would not know how to set about making the *nomos* his own by working through it critically and creatively.

Traditional tribal societies are usually taken to exemplify such cultures. Bruno Bettelheim's study of kibbutz-reared children[12] suggests, however, that modern societies can also approximate to this ideal type. According to Bettelheim's account, the kibbutz provides the child with tremendous group support; from his earliest infancy he identifies, not with parents, but with an age peer group with whom he shares all his most important experiences. Together they form a collective superego which each introjects, yet each being a constituent part of it, this collective consciousness is his self. For this reason the kibbutz child suffers no crisis of identity such as occurs in American or Australian children, when the paternal image is challenged by competing roles thrust upon them by peer group, teachers, and so on. The outcome, according to Bettelheim, is a personality type which is immensely confident so long as it feels the peer group morality behind it but which is utterly incapable of challenging it.* This is not simply because the individual fears peer-group disapproval (though of course he does), but because he has no

---

*It should be said that Bettelheim's study was confessedly impressionistic – not a study supported by statistical surveys and such instruments. Moreover, Bettelheim was handicapped by the fact that he spoke no Hebrew. Many Israeli social psychologists repudiate his conclusions. Nevertheless, the study is immensely persuasive. My concern, in any case, is with the critical structure, rather than with the truth of the empirical conclusions of the study.

alternative moral resources on which to rely in mounting the challenge. For the kibbutz is himself, and there is no part of him which is nonkibbutz, not even an idiosyncratic parent-image.

The kibbutz child has both strengths and weaknesses. On the one hand, a massive integration: a capacity to withstand battle strain and a loyalty which is not the submissive self-hating devotion of a totalitarian personal surrender, but related to the solid self-esteem of a full member of a fraternity. On the opposite side, however, a certain poverty of emotional experience, arising precisely from the fact that the most meaningful relationships have been with a group, and that the individual has never had the experience of exploring another's personality in conditions of privacy and intimacy. And without that, he has little experience of exploring his own. So his emotional life tends to be shallow and his capacity to enter into another person's experience somewhat restricted. But above all he has no experience of wrestling with moral issues: The way is always plain, his role and duty clear, and everyone whose opinion matters to him is in agreement. Outside the kibbutz he may "feel out of place and awkward," but he feels "still inwardly superior because he is convinced of the moral superiority of his way of life."[13]

For those like Bettelheim who are deeply conscious of the disintegrating stresses of modern society, there is inevitably a tension between the ideals of autonomy and integration. This is not because the autonomous person cannot be an integrated person; indeed, the reverse is the case. Because the autonomous person has tested the coherence of his moral beliefs and is conscious of having made them his own by exploring the point of them and of having worked to resolve conflicts and ambiguities, he has a strong sense of the kind of person he is and of the kind of life to which he is committed by his view of the world. He is in little danger of falling into anomie under conditions of stress and change. But the conditions for becoming this sort of person do carry the risk of anomie for those who fail in the task. The autonomous person works his way through the Erikson "crisis of identity," precipitated by the fluid, ambiguous, plural tradition out of which emerge the conflicts which set the task, but there are people for whom the crisis is too great a test. In the traditional tribal culture and in the kibbutz there is no crisis; everyone knows exactly the kind of person he is and what must be done to satisfy what others require of him and what he requires of himself, possessing therefore the integration born of assured esteem and unchallenged moral certainties. In the extreme case of such a normatively integrated society, there would be few neurotics; but equally there would be few with the moral and psychological insights of a Freud, an Einstein, or indeed of a Bettelheim. But just because the heteronomy of a member of such a society is that of an integrated personality who identifies fully with the *nomos* which governs his actions, it differs profoundly from the heteronomy of the middle-class professionals and businessmen who succumbed to anomie in Dachau and Buchenwald. For these the *nomos* was imposed from outside rather than introjected, a tangle of conventional requirements out of which the subjects made nothing coherent. So instead of being able to infer their commitments from a *nomos* that was comprehensible to them, albeit one to which they had made little individual critical contribution, they had to look to others for cues to what action was appropriate in given circumstances.

## 2. Autonomy and "spontaneity"

With the doubtful exceptions of Fromm and Horney, the writers mentioned in the past two chapters have belonged to that ancient moral tradition that associates freedom with autonomy and autonomy with self-mastery, with the control by a rational faculty of instinctual impulses and passions responding to external stimuli. This faculty provides the *nomos* which is necessary to freedom, not antithetic to it. And their integrative ideal is of a person who can go on governing himself by a *nomos* even under conditions of strain and rapid culture change.

In the cases of Fromm and Horney there is the further notion of something in the person striving to express itself:

> . . . inherent in man are evolutionary constructive forces which urge him to realize his given potentialities. . . . [Man] by his very nature . . . strives towards self-realization. . . . [With] such a belief in an autonomous striving towards self-realization, we do not need an inner strait-jacket with which to shackle our spontaneity.[14]

Or consider Abraham Maslow: "Self-actualization is intrinsic growth of what is already in the organism, or more accurately of what *is* the organism itself."[15]

Writers in this style are made uneasy by an ideal which seems to lay great weight on the control of emotions, believing that this fails to recognize the value of the uncalculated, immediate, instinctive response to other human beings and to the environment in general.

Maslow's élite of "self-actualizers" manifest, among their other virtues (many of which seem to coincide with the integrative and autonomous ideals), the capacity to be spontaneous on appropriate occasions. But this is clearly a governed spontaneity rather than a total surrender to the impulse of any moment.

Maslow's notion of spontaneity is closely tied to his distinction between "motivated" and "expressive" behavior. Motivated behavior is goal-oriented, the rational means to a determined goal. "Expressive behavior . . . simply mirrors, reflects, signifies or expresses some state of the organism." So "the most desirable way to dance . . . is to be spontaneous, fluid, automatically responsive to the rhythm of the music . . . a passive instrument fashioned by the music and played upon by it." But few dancers can achieve this spontaneity; most "will be directed, self-controlled, and purposeful, will listen carefully to the rhythm . . . and by a conscious act of choice fall in with it." These will be poor dancers, for "they will never enjoy dancing as a profound experience of self-forgetfulness, and voluntary renunciation of control unless they finally transcend trying and become spontaneous." Spontaneity of this kind can nevertheless be learned; one can learn to "drop inhibitions, self-consciousness, will, control, acculturation, and dignity."[16]

Such spontaneity can be a deep source of enjoyment, and the person who has imposed upon himself so unbending a rule that he is incapable of it is clearly missing something. But it is evidently something one must be able to choose to indulge only under appropriate conditions. "[The] healthy person is not only expressive. He must be able to let himself go. . . . But equally he must have the ability to control himself."[17]

Spontaneity in this sense cannot be a way of life, since it must be subject to a general monitoring in accordance with beliefs that determine whether the occasion is indeed appropriate for it. The dancer's spontaneity is, after all, confined to the occasion of the dance. If it spilled over into a sexual assault on his partner, its appropriateness would be at least questionable. Nor is it a style which could be a feature of every kind of activity. What would it be like to do philosophy or mathematics spontaneously? But in those areas in which one can act spontaneously, to behave so is not inconsistent with autonomy as I understand it, provided that one behave with spontaneity subject to monitoring of this kind.

One of the features of Maslow's conception of spontaneity is not, however, this capacity for self-forgetfulness in free emotional expression, but rather the capacity to act in accordance with the commitments of one's beliefs without the need for deliberation. But this, of course, is very different from acting on impulse or in a way that is simply expressive of one's feelings. To hold a belief and to recognize and act upon its commitments does not require that one rehearse it before acting, any more than one needs to rehearse the rules of the road before stopping at a red light. And much of the time this is indeed how we meet the contingencies of our daily lives. But someone who acts spontaneously in more problematic situations, in the sense of acting to express feelings or emotions, is at least as likely to act wrongly as rightly, and the spontaneity of the action will not then redeem it. In the film *Lady Caroline Lamb* (1972), Caroline, horrified by the poverty of the beggars in the Colosseum in Rome, throws a jeweled bracelet into the crowd, with the result that the man who catches it is killed by the others in the scramble to wrench it from him. The *thoughtlessness* of the action is precisely what we find wrong with it, and it is hardly redeemed by its being the spontaneous expression of benevolence.

The attractiveness of spontaneity as a character trait is best understood by what it is taken to negate. The self-actualizers' spontaneity, according to Maslow, is manifest in a lack of artificiality or a straining for effect. They are not motivated by the desire to put on an act, either to impress others or to prove something to themselves. They are "problem centered rather than ego centered. They generally are not problems for themselves and are not generally much concerned about themselves."[18] Their spontaneity, that is, consists in the absence of second-order motivation; they act for the sake of the problem in hand, rather than for the sake of their view of themselves or the view that others might have of them in their dealing with the problem in hand. Consequently, spontaneity is opposed to a timidity in the expression of emotions for fear of what others might think. Equally, spontaneity might be thought of as the antithesis of hypocrisy. The nonspontaneous agent might be one who deliberated before action in order to find a reason for not doing what he believed he ought to do but would prefer not to have to do. Or he might be cautious in the expression of emotions for fear of what he might be committed to. Spontaneity in these senses comes close to authenticity, the antithesis of action in bad faith.

Spontaneity in any of the senses here considered would be consistent with autonomy, though not required by it in all senses,

209

provided that nondeliberative spontaneity is subject to the kind of rational monitoring for appropriateness considered above. A cautious person who pauses before making a decision to be sure that he has not overlooked any relevant consideration would be lacking in spontaneity but might well be autonomous. On the other hand, someone unable ever to act without deliberation would probably be a neurotic subject; a rational economy of effort and time requires that we acquire and develop the capacity for recognizing the salient features of a situation and for responding appropriately to them without further thought.

### 3. "Self-realization" and "instinctual freedom"

The account of self-realization given by the Freudian revisionists is criticized in the last chapters of Herbert Marcuse's *Eros and Civilization* for reasons quite different from any that I suggested above. His criticisms deserve some attention because they point to some genuine problems inherent in the ideal, and because they are linked to what seems at first sight a total repudiation of the ideal of self-mastery.

Marcuse claims that the goal of therapy that he attributes to "Fromm and the other revisionists," namely " 'the optimal development of a person's potentialities and the realization of his individuality' "[19] is unattainable, not through any limitations on the techniques of analysis, but because a repressive reality principle limits the potentialities of a person who is the product of a repressive culture. To cure such a person, one would have to define his "personality" in terms of its "possibilities *within* the established form of civilization"; that is, one would have to be content with a merely adjusted personality. Or one would have to "cure" the patient to become a rebel or a martyr.

Marcuse's point might be made less tendentiously by arguing that potentialities to be realized are culture relative. A person's potentialities $p$, $q$, and $r$ are what he might make of himself under a given range of conditions, which constitute his opportunities, and the one who optimizes is the one who makes the best of them, who is therefore best adjusted to reality. Envisage a set of different conditions altogether and the range of potentialities changes. So the range open to serious consideration – as distinct from fantasy – is culturally given. Christian Bay's account of "self-expression" hinged on a person's "realistic awareness" of his basic needs and potentialities and on his having a realistic ego-ideal. Marcuse could properly argue that what is a realistic view of one's potentialities depends on what conditions are considered open to change. After all, someone's intellectual potentialities would be vastly enlarged if grafts of additional brain tissue were counted among the possible variables. Being realistic, Marcuse might say, generally means accepting the range of possible variants sanctioned by the existing culture. So Marcuse would insist that the psychotherapy that aims to get the patient to accept this reality, to come to terms with his capacity for gratification within the constraints it imposes, simply subjects him to the repressions it sustains. Because the repressive society rules out certain states as utopian fantasies or immoral indulgences, certainly not realistic possibilities, a person is inhibited from adopting them as constituents of a realistic ego-ideal.

Marcuse is right thus far: Possibilities are "real" assuming certain attendant conditions. We are realistic in our goals to the extent that we can control the conditions for attaining them or that those we can't control are likely to go the way we want. But surely *some* limits *must* be recognized, else we claim to be God; what then must a society take to be beyond its power? There may be forms of self-realization that would be attainable if only people had the awareness of their social situation necessary to their changing it. Whether we regard these potentialities for self-realization as realistic or dismiss them as fantasies depends on how seriously we take the possibility that people might achieve the alternative vision.

Freud's reality principle forces us to distinguish between our aims and our fantasies; the question is where the dividing line must fall. To a radical like Marcuse it is repressive insofar as it identifies the current society with what is possible. Marcuse insists that the kind of society we currently know need not be accepted as the context that sets limits to human potentialities. Envisage a society without domination – what might men be then! And once the radical descends again into the Cave, to accept the culturally dominant view of the bounds of the possible is, for him, tamely to adjust to a repressive reality: He has seen potentialities far beyond these, which the unliberated conservative scorns as castles in the air.

The concept of a potentiality is thus contested, like the concepts of freedom and unfreedom, coercion, duress, and exploitation discussed in Chapter 7. Views about a person's potentialities are not absolutely right or wrong, but are reasonable or unreasonable, according to the scale of change in the enabling conditions one is

211

prepared to entertain as not beyond the bounds of the feasible. Step beyond those bounds – and there is no way to determine beyond dispute where they properly lie – and one enters the realm of fantasy, where the intellect may play but a seriously intended critique of reality is pointless, except in the allegorical manner of *Gulliver's Travels,* More's *Utopia,* or, antithetically, *Animal Farm.*

# 12

## Autonomy, association, and community

### 1. Communitarian critiques of liberal individualism

Autonomy as understood in the liberal individualist tradition has
come under fire in recent years from critics who denounce the
entire tradition as dehumanizing and the kind of society that it
informs as alienating. It rests, they say, on a model of man that is
descriptively inadequate and morally defective, and the quasi-
contractual theories of human association that derive from it are
invalidated by their faulty foundation. In Chapter 10 of *Politics and
Vision*, Sheldon Wolin brings together a variety of such criticisms
to illustrate "one of the dominant themes of modern thought, the
revival of social solidarity." Sociology and psychology, he claims,
"have agreed that modern man is desperately in need of 'integration.' " His need to "belong" and to experience satisfying relations
with others can be fulfilled if he is able to identify himself with an
adequate group, one which will provide him with membership, a
defined role and assured expectations. Ours is "an organizational
age which longs for community."[1]

Human beings, it is said, have a need for mutually supportive
relations, a need the liberal theory of man and society ignores.
Consequently, the account I have given of respect for persons, of
the relations of forbearance between autarchic persons who recognize in each other a common moral personality, might be taken,
perhaps, as legitimizing cold indifference, a standoff between individuals who care nothing for one another. And so it does, as far as it
goes, for it is an account of a minimal condition for moral relations
between persons – it is not an ideal. It leaves altogether open
whether the projects it imputes to people should be prompted by
*concern* for other human beings. Respect has to do with rights and
the moral status of the other – with what he is entitled to – and is
therefore indeed a standoffish consideration; *concern* has to do
with well-being, with needs and sympathy, and therefore with entering with understanding into the experience of the other. The

virtue associated with the first is justice, with the second benevolence. One can respect an enemy while wishing him ill; if one has a concern for someone, one wishes him well – his necessities and his sufferings strike one as reasons for acting to alleviate them if one can.

Liberal individualism, according to its critics, takes no account of the "species-being" of human beings. The proper object of human action is human well-being, as much of others as of oneself; man remains alienated from his true nature until a concern for others informs all his projects. However autonomous the autarchic person might be, he would be falling short of the ideal for man if the ends of his enterprise did not include human well-being – or perhaps consist wholly in human well-being. Man's species-being is not merely social but sociable, realized in closely integrating communitarian relations, characterized by mutual concern and caring.

Few of these critics would reject, however, the ideals of self-determination and self-development which, in the age of J.S. Mill, T.H. Green, L.T. Hobhouse, and Thomas Dewey, of Gladstone and Lloyd George, were accepted as the heart of "the new liberalism." Bourgeois society is found wanting by many of its critics precisely because they believe that it frustrates these ideals. Judson Jerome says of the "communalist" ideal that it is "of a mode of association which combines maximum self-actualization and individuality with maximum cooperation and commitment to the welfare of others, in which selfishness is transmuted into self-fulfillment and dependency into love."[2]

My object in this chapter is not to defend bourgeois society from its critics, nor, indeed, to provide a different description or interpretation of it from theirs. Neither do I intend to describe actual communitarian alternatives to it, save by way of illustration; the reader may challenge any particular description without shaking the argument. The chapter is concerned more with models, ideal types, or paradigms in terms of which people conceptualize their own societies and possible ideal alternatives. These models rest on certain propositions about the nature of man and are informed by certain values and principles.

If a liberal were to be rationally persuaded by a communitarian that his models of man and society were defective in the way the communitarian says they are, he might be conceding either that his was already only a partial or qualified liberalism or that the liberalism he professed was to that extent incoherent; for the communitar-

214

ian's reasons could get no purchase on him unless they invoked beliefs, principles or criteria of relevance that the liberal already acknowledged. On the other hand, it might be the case that the core of his liberalism could accommodate without serious disruption the communitarian criticisms which invoke the social nature of man. My object in this chapter is to discover how much of the communitarian ideal the liberal could be brought to accept while yet remaining uncompromisingly true to the core liberal commitments to respect persons and autarchy and to value autonomy. Equally, I shall distinguish the kinds of communitarian ideals that liberals must find unacceptable because incapable of accommodation to those core commitments. I shall take it for granted that, having already constructed so great a part of the theory of freedom, we need no further inquiry into the credentials of these core commitments.

## 2. Individualist models of social collaboration

Society for the liberal is compounded of natural persons, each a self-governing chooser, responsible for what he does to others and for what he makes of himself. Locke attributed to him natural rights, which might be interpreted as normative capacities that a person possesses by virtue of his natural capacity as a chooser, and on account of his commitment to making his own way, pursuing his own enterprise, in a fluid and contractual society. The classical economists employed a basically similar model of a rational agent already equipped with individually conceived goals, selecting from a range of available strategies the one which would do best, that is, which would maximize utility or satisfaction from the standpoint of those goals.

Such agents, associated in a market economy, would both collaborate and compete. When the outcome of a collaborative strategy would provide everyone with more of whatever he happened to want than he could hope for by going it alone, everyone would have a reason for collaboration. Collaboration does not depend, then, on the parties' valuing collaboration for itself or for anything intrinsic to the collaborative activity, but only for what each believes he can get out of it (of course, this includes any enjoyment of his own part in the activity, as a footballer might enjoy running and kicking or the glory of being one of the winning team). He would have no reason for collaborating if he could find no positive answer to the question: What is there in it for me?

The surplus earned by collaborative over noncollaborative action could be shared out in various ways, so long as each one's share amounted to more, in terms of his individually conceived ends and values, than he could get by staying out of the coalition. So, beyond the collaborative there is also a competitive element in the association, in which each seeks to maximize his own gains at the expense of the others'.[3] This may be true, of course, even in a team game: a Man of the Match award encourages players to compete while requiring that they collaborate to win.

Hobbes supplied a theory of political association to match the competitive–collaborative model. What made political association possible was the fundamental equality of men; no one had power enough alone to secure himself against the rest. By credible threats of punishment governments could provide everyone with a selective incentive to practice forbearance in his relations with everyone else, establishing thereby the minimal conditions for collaboration.

In Kant's moral philosophy there are certain analogies with Hobbes's model of man, even though their doctrines differ in other respects quite fundamentally. Each supposes a self-contained individual chooser; each issues in a kind of standoff relation between persons. For Hobbes the fundamental feature of civil and moral association leading to standoff is equality of power; for Kant it is the recognition by each person of every other as being of equal moral standing, as a potentially free and rational will, a member of the kingdom of ends, with the rational capacity to apprehend and embrace the moral law as his *nomos*. Between such persons relations are ordered by the principle of respect. "Respect," says Kant, "is properly the conception of a worth which thwarts my self-love"; that is, it amounts to recognizing in the other the subject of a morally significant enterprise that counts as a reason for not treating him as an instrument of or an obstacle to one's own inclinations, as if he had no view of his own that warranted consideration.

Whereas for Kant autonomy was a logical consequence of a person's rationality, however little he actualized it in his practice, for J.S. Mill it was an ideal character trait to be developed, by virtue of possessing which a person is admirable. Mill was far too sensible, of course, to believe glibly in the kind of austere romantic hero who was master of his fate and captain of his soul, but he was very conscious, too, of social pressures to conform and believed that nobility of character demanded firm convictions and moral courage, a bold, independent, and inquiring intellect never closed to argument

216

and experiment. Such a person would be self-determining, self-developing, and autonomous.

The association of "economic liberalism" with business ethics and with free-market economics has tended to muddy the popular understanding, particularly in the United States, of the human ideal that the liberal tradition has cherished. Business corporations (so goes the argument) stand for unrestrained commercial practices and small government, and these are tenets of economic liberalism. Corporate business awards its prizes to conformist organization men; therefore (the argument concludes), liberalism favors a heteronomous conformity to the business ethic. But even were the premises true, the conclusion would not follow. An alternative conclusion is that business, while adopting (if somewhat selectively) some of the economic tenets of classical liberalism, has very little else in common with that tradition, least of all its human ideal.

Nevertheless, the individualist model of man and society outlined so far might quite properly be criticized as lacking in humanity. In its earliest versions, indeed, the model had very little satisfactory to say about the concern people have, or ought to have, for one another. Before the Reformation, care for the sick and the needy had been seen as a religious duty, organized by religious orders, and sustained by charitable offerings. Post-Reformation England, deprived of its monasteries, was forced into some secular provision. But it was scanty and grudging. A society that had learned to respect persons as independent and responsible for themselves expected them to be provident too and hardly knew what to make of the unfortunate, the misfits, and the dropouts. Concern for others was properly structured within the family – or at the most within a rural community. Otherwise it was to be expressed in more or less formal religious observances.

If nineteenth-century industrialism generated the tough-minded individualism of the 1834 Poor Law commissioners, it awoke too the humanitarianism of reformers like Lord Shaftesbury and prompted numerous private and secular charity organizations, as well as societies for the education of poor children and for the provision of hospitals for needy patients. The competitive–collaborative model clearly did not fit these developments any more than the monasteries of the Middle Ages. Certainly, the members of such organizations collaborated, but to benefit others, not themselves, and competition between members, perhaps for public esteem for their good

217

works, would have been accidental, not something required by the nature of the enterprise. And though their clients may have competed for the handouts, they were neither members of the organization nor in any associative relation amongst themselves.

## 3. Transcendent collective enterprises

The welfare organization is best treated, perhaps, as a special case of a form of association I call a *transcendent collective enterprise,* which arises from a common concern for some valued endeavor or worthwhile activity which must be pursued collectively. I have in mind organizations like orchestras, scientific research institutes, religious orders, and revolutionary parties, where the *telos* of the association is either the activity itself, like music making, or some ideal state of affairs to which it is directed, such as a communist society or ecological stability, rather than the well-being of the members of the enterprise, whether considered individually, reciprocally, or as a group whole. Before saying more about welfare organizations, therefore, I shall inquire whether the liberal model can satisfactorily accommodate, in general, association in collective enterprises, the *telé* of which transcend the well-being of the members.

Every member of an orchestra may have an interest in music, in the sense that they all have a concern for it; music making gives a consistent direction to their activities, as love of God gives direction to the activities of the monks. But to say that one has an *interest in* music making is not to say that music making is *in one's interest,* that is, conducive to one's well-being. Though we should commonly think ourselves better off for being able to do what we are interested in doing, there is no absurdity in saying of someone that he sacrificed himself for a cause in which he was interested, that he put the cause before his own well-being. So in a transcendent collective enterprise each participant's concern alike for his own well-being and for the well-being of each of the others, is subordinate to a concern for the activity, or for an ideal to which it is directed, which is the *telos* of the association.

I mean by the *telos* of the association whatever it is about it that for those involved in it makes it worthwhile to sustain it; I do not mean to imply that the association has been devised consciously and deliberately as an instrument for some premeditated purpose or even, where it was so devised, that its present *telos* is necessarily the same as that original purpose. The religious purposes that the

218

medieval founders of colleges in the universities of Oxford and Cambridge had in mind were very different from what the present members of those institutions would understand as their *telé*. The *telé* of an institution are those purposes or activities which its present members or participants believe it should be engaged in, for which its structure and organization are appropriate, and which accord with principles and values of a developing tradition of which it is a part.

Now though the classical liberal individualist theories of society took little account of transcendent collective enterprises, those theories can be extended to cover those enterprises without distorting their core values. The relations between participants are consistent with mutual respect, and though a collective enterprise transcends the private ends of any individual, freely associating participants will see it as realizing, not as overriding, their own enterprises. Consequently, they need not surrender autonomy to participate in it. An autonomous musician need not be a soloist. If he adopts as an enterprise the making of music in orchestras, he accepts collaboration as a necessary condition for doing so. He sees that his own role must fit the total conception and accepts ability to collaborate as a criterion of proficiency and success in the activity. He may autonomously subordinate himself, too, to the authority of the conductor, disagreeing perhaps with his interpretation, but freely conforming all the same to the role of second flute as the conductor understands it, for that is the nature of collaborative orchestral performance. Something similar can be said of a scientific research establishment. Of all activities we are inclined to regard science as the one that most depends on the right of independent judgment. Yet it is surely rational for someone participating in team research to accept leadership from a research director who allocates particular research projects, decides which theories to follow up as likely to be the most fruitful, and so on. Of course, the autonomous flautist or research scientist does not surrender judgment unconditionally. Because his commitments to the organization derive from his primary commitment to the *telos* of the activity, he cannot avoid monitoring the former in the light of the latter without loss of autonomy. If he finds the conductor's interpretations always boring or the research director's hunches perverse or his attachment to theories merely obstinate, he will look for another orchestra to join or for a job in a different laboratory.

These examples highlight the distinction between autonomous and heteronomous participation in such enterprises. A heterono-

219

mous person's commitment will follow where the rest of the orchestra or the laboratory leads, whereas the autonomous scientist's or instrumentalist's commitment to a particular laboratory or orchestra will always be conditional, deriving from his own standards of what constitutes worthwhile performance. There may be room, of course, for heteronomous participants. A proportion of heteronomous workers in a laboratory who will be content to work assiduously at the tasks assigned to them, accepting direction without looking critically at the point of their tasks, may not impair and may even accelerate progress in the enterprise. But if all were like that, the laboratory would be pretty unproductive, and the music made by a wholly heteronomous orchestra might well be pretty dull. Transcendent collective enterprises need at least some autonomous participants if they are not to grow stale, but it is not a necessary condition for their productivity and high performance that all the participants should be so. Indeed, the contrary might be the case.

I may be taken to task, perhaps, for introducing into an account of a liberal view of autonomous activity an alien reference to traditions of behavior as constituting the *telos* of the institution in which the autonomous subject participates. Liberals are prone to think of traditionalists as heteronomous. The notion of action in a tradition, however, so far from being inconsistent with liberalism, is logically necessary to it. I argued in Chapter 9 that the truism, what we are and can become, is circumscribed by the cultural influences that furnish us with our conceptual equipment, does not affect the distinction between autonomy and heteronomy. Of course, people don't join orchestras or science labs because, by a process of independent creative imagination, they come up with science or music as spontaneously conceived ends. They are traditions into which people are inducted from childhood; science is a culturally formulated and traditionally transmitted end. But this strikes at nothing that the individualist cannot readily give up.

While insisting that the rational person was his own moral legislator, Kant also resisted the idea that he imposed the moral law on himself, precisely because he thought it out of place to speak of the moral law being *imposed* at all, since there were *reasons* for deciding to live by it. Analogously, just because the tradition that values autonomy is also a rationalist tradition, it cannot require that the autonomous person conjure his *nomos* out of thin air, adopting it by a kind of random fancy, kicking aside the *nomoi* of his culture, its traditions, as so much clutter. One's reasons for engaging in an activity as worthwhile, for accepting the principles and standards that regulate it as constraining one's own performances, must already be built into one's conception of the world, which one must have received initially from those about one, as conceptual resources made available by the cluster of subcultures that combine to make one what one is – or rather that provide the materials for what one can become. One can receive from alien cultures only what one can assimilate to what one already has. Autonomy is not so much an end-state as a disposition to sustain a certain sort of process for which an initial condition is a conflict or incoherence. An autonomous person labors to resolve such incoherences as seems appropriate to him, thereby making himself – but not *ex nihilo*. Unlike the heteronomous person, however, he is not merely an instantiation of a cultural mold or form. The difference between them lies in their manner of dealing with their cultural inheritance, not in whether they possess one or whether they draw on its resources. So in a scientific or a musical culture, there will be people whose grasp of the activity is rooted in the traditions of that culture, who appreciate that it makes collaborative demands, and who are prepared for the sake of the activity itself to accept the constraints which that puts on their merely willful or fanciful creativity. But they may also be capable of creatively extending and enlarging the tradition, drawing on resources which are also available to their collaborators, innovating therefore in ways that can be significant to them too.

### 4. Welfare organizations as transcendent collective enterprises

The peculiarity of welfare organizations is that their *telos* lies not in the practice of an activity, such as science, which is valued irrespective of the welfare of persons, but precisely in promoting welfare. But because the beneficiaries of the organization are not at the same time members of it, the concern for well-being is either curiously impersonal, quite different from the concern that members of a family might feel for one another, or it is a patronizing concern, a one-way flow. One of the criticisms made, indeed, of charitable organizations by pioneers of the welfare state was that they denied to the client the respect due to him as a person and consequently deprived him of self-respect, fostering dependence and heteronomy. Sir William Beveridge, a self-professed liberal, produced in 1942 the famous report which launched the modern

221

British welfare state, legislatively realized by a Labour government, and claimed as a socialist innovation. It largely superseded
both benevolent societies and friendly societies, replacing them
with a national, state-organized scheme which would make welfare administration largely impersonal. The merit of the change, in
the view both of Beveridge and of the Labour government, was that
the needy person could now demand social security payments as a
matter of right and social justice, without the need to cringe or to
rely on anyone's benevolence or concern for him in particular.

In meeting the criticism that it showed too little concern for the
well-being of persons, liberalism, now committed to a notion of
"positive freedom" congenial enough to Fabian socialists though
not to Marxists, steered firmly away from communitarian ideals.
For though in the welfare state the recipients can claim to be members and not just the clients they were of charitable organizations,
nevertheless their well-being is provided for bureaucratically[4]:
They are qualified members of a beneficiary class, receiving appropriate assistance from others in the differentiated role of official
helpers. The helpers might on another occasion themselves be
qualified beneficiaries, but this would represent a change of role; it
would not be as fellow participants with other helpers that they
would benefit from the organization.

In a sense, membership of the association, the state, is still not a
logically necessary condition for qualifying as an object of concern.
At one time, for instance, the British National Health Service was
open on the same terms to foreign visitors as to citizens; now it is
not. But its essential character has not been altered by the change.
And this betokens a difference between this and communitarian
relationships, for, as will shortly emerge, it is essential to the ideal
of community that differences between the treatment of a member
and a nonmember, and differences in the attitudes of members to
one another and to nonmembers, are substantively related to the
criteria of membership. They could not be changed by an arbitrary
ruling that this or that person shall now be considered qualified;
nor can the qualifying conditions themselves be easily changed by
administrative fiat.

Welfare organizations, then, whether charitable or state, are transcendent collective enterprises of a special kind, rather than instances of community, because, in the first place, relations between
the helpers and the helped are not reciprocal. The *telos* of the organization is not in the *relations* between members, but in the promoting
of a general principle, of welfare or social justice, such as "Everyone

222

has the right to the satisfaction of basic needs." The social worker's involvement with his clients is thus impersonal, in the sense that each client's deprivation is relevant only as an instantiation of a general evil that the organization exists to remove. This is different, not merely from the standoff of competitive – collaborative relations, but also from the sympathetic bonds and the personal involvement with the needs and sufferings of one another to which communitarian critics of individualism attach such great importance. The dedication of the professional social worker is much more like the dedication of the musician to a *telos* transcending his own personal attachments. I do not mean that welfare workers are never humane, nor that they all treat their clients as "cases," if that means that they treat them with no respect for them as persons. But in another sense clients must always be cases, instances of a generally defined role. For the relationship lacks reciprocity – there is no presumption that the roles might be reversed, that the concern evoked by the client's plight might be evoked in the client himself in precisely the same way by the plight, if not of this "other" then of some other equally entitled to call upon it.

## 5. The variety of communitarian ideals

Communitarian ideals, then, require more than a concern for well-being, for that too can be impersonal. They call for *sympathetic* concern, a caring for the other "as if it were oneself," for some measure of identification with the fate of the other. Though one cannot literally feel his sorrows, his sorrows can give occasion for sorrowing that he sorrows; the injuries he suffers excite indignation and resentment on his behalf; one rejoices in his triumphs and preens oneself vicariously on account of them.

Knowing that others feel for them in these ways is part at least of the mutual support that members of a community are said to give to one another. But this support may be a great deal more. Knowing for instance that one's opinions and judgments are shared by others, one feels that the responsibility for holding them is shared too. Someone, who is alone in holding an opinion, is likely to find his confidence in it oozing away. But if an opinion is shared, even if it is proved wrong there will be comfort in knowing that it was on account of nothing singularly defective about one's judgment. It may be easier to stand by one's standards against the mass if one has the support of others that one trusts.

It would be a mistake, however, to assume that community nec-

223

essarily strengthens autonomy. Someone leaning on community for support may have found for himself a ready-made group *nomos* that he can embrace as a substitute for making a *nomos* of his own. Admittedly, for someone lacking full personal integration, struggling painfully towards autonomy, support of this kind may be essential if he is not to disintegrate into anomie or worse. The greater the achievement, however, the smaller the need: Much as Socrates valued community, he needed support from no one in confronting his accusers.

The kind of mutual concern I have just sketched is arrived at and mediated only through a pretty complete commitment to the whole group. In a very illuminating study of utopian communes, R.M. Kanter finds in the notion of commitment the core of the communitarian ideal.[5] For Kanter commitment to a community is

> ... a reciprocal relation, in which both what is given to the group and what is received from it are seen by the person as expressing his true nature and as supporting his concept of self. . . . A person is committed to a group or to a relationship when he himself is fully invested in it, so that the maintenance of his own internal being requires behaviour that supports the social order. A committed person . . . has a sense of belonging, a feeling that the group is an extension of himself and he is an extension of the group.
>
> Commitment thus refers to the willingness of people to do what will help to maintain the group because it provides what they need. . . . A person is committed to a relationship or to a group to the extent that he sees it as expressing or fulfilling some fundamental part of himself . . . that he perceives no conflict between its requirements and his own needs.[6]

In Chapter 2 I drew attention to the ambiguity of *commitment*, distinguishing an active sense and a passive sense. In the active sense, one *makes* a commitment, as one makes a promise, by voluntarily assuming a set of special responsibilities and obligations. It is in this active sense that one is *committed to* a group. A person actively commits himself to the community in joining it, undertaking special obligations and responsibilities towards the group, both as a whole and individually. But Kanter's account of the motives that one might have for making such a commitment draws on the notion of a person's perception of his own self, and the belief that the community expresses a fundamental part of it. Having these beliefs, he is committed in the passive sense to perceiving membership of the community as the way to go and to giving the community the support required of him by his membership of it. Committing himself to it is thus the carrying out of the action commitment of his beliefs about himself and the nature of the community to which he decides to belong.

It is, then, by virtue of such a commitment that the "significant others" evoke a special concern from each committed member: By virtue of their common commitment to sustaining the pattern of relations constituting the community, they know one another as comrades, as brothers and sisters. Mutual support, sympathy, and understanding flow to those who are known not merely to value the common enterprise (an outsider might do that) but to have invested their personalities in the same venture.

Liberal individualists shy away from this kind of thing when it is offered to them in the context of political theory. Yet it is by no means antithetical to moral and social attitudes that many liberals would freely acknowledge in respect of friendship, marriage, and family relations. A good deal depends, however, on how one understands the commitment to the community, on what one takes to be its purpose, and on what one takes oneself to be committed to do, and on whether the commitment is regarded as conditional or absolute; for the answers to these questions will be reflected in the pattern of relations regarded as ideal.

I shall distinguish three communitarian models. One, the *total community*, has had a good deal of influence on political thought; it must surely be unacceptable as an ideal to anyone unwilling to surrender the values of individuality and autonomy that I have taken to be central to the liberal tradition. The second, which I call *mutuality*, so far from repudiating these values, is unattainable except by people who take them very seriously indeed; it is, however, largely irrelevant to political organization. The third, which I call *comradeship*, is something of a halfway house between the other two. But I suggest that any instance of it large enough to be politically relevant would be inherently unstable, liable to move either towards total community or to break down into competitive – collaborative association.

## A. *Total community*

Charles Horton Cooley thus defines the idealized relationship between individual and community:

> In so far as one identifies himself with a whole, loyalty to that whole is loyalty to himself; it is self-realization. . . . One is never more human,

225

and as a rule happier, than when he is sacrificing his narrow and merely private interest to the higher call of the congenial group.[7]

The city of Rousseau's *Social Contract*, modeled on ancient Sparta, is a paradigm of the kind of community founded on this identification. The peasant communes of Mao's China and the nineteenth-century Perfectionist commune Oneida, founded in 1848 by John Humphrey Noyes, seem to have been informed by the same idea. The solidarity of the group is the touchstone by which all other claims are to be judged. Just as Rousseau deplored the existence of "partial general wills," so in Oneida social arrangements, such as a very complex set of mating regulations, were designed, for much the same reason as Plato's in Book V of *The Republic*, to discourage any special, personal attachments, whether sexual or parental, that might estrange the member from the central love in the community.

The total community borders on the transcendental collective enterprise in that its *telos* is the sustaining of a set of idealized attitudes and relations, almost a depersonalization of the members, despite the heavy stress laid on their mutual sympathy, concern, and support. For the individual is required to surrender his idiosyncratic self-image for the sake of the love he earns by becoming a loyal and committed participant. A person making a commitment to the community, says Kanter,

> . . . should see himself as carrying out the dictates of a higher system, which orders and gives meaning to his life. He internalizes community standards and values and accepts its control, because it provides him with something transcendent. This commitment requires, first, that the person reformulate and re-evaluate his identity in terms of meeting the ideals set by the community.[8]

So the community requires of him self-criticism in the light of its own standards and the ordeals of public criticism and also what Kanter calls "mortification" – "the submission of private states to social control, the exchanging of a former identity for one defined and formulated by the community."[9] Each, as Rousseau says, gives himself entirely to the community.[10]

Communitarians are critical of the liberal individualist because, they say, he assumes that the only way in which an individual can take a communal end as his own is to see it either as instrumental to his private ends or by making the satisfactions of other people the objects of his own private satisfaction. Communitarians claim that one can be aware of oneself in a quite different way, not just as a constituent of a community, but rather as a manifestation or instantiation of the community as a universal idea, so that one's personal ends would be directed to the collective good and to the promoting of the ideal ends of the whole community just because one's self is a communal self. This accounts for the importance, in communitarian ideology, that Kanter ascribes to "identification" with the community. When one says, "As an American, I am committed to . . . ," one's being an American is then taken not as a contingent role that one can assume or not as one chooses or even as appears appropriate for the time being, but as a constitutive fact about oneself. And it requires, further, that the interests of America and Americans be given special consideration and weight, that one takes pride in American achievements and feels vicarious shame when Americans – or American statesmen – behave in shameful ways.

This comes close to the Hegelian account of the state as a concrete universal. But it does not commit one necessarily to total communitarianism, as is evidenced by the fact that liberal-minded neo-Hegelians such as T.H. Green, Bernard Bosanquet, and F.H. Bradley all thought roughly along these lines. But these liberals laid stress, as communitarians do not, on the importance of the citizens' rights, which, while deriving precisely from the overall community purpose and the common good, nevertheless concede to the individual the critical opportunities that the total communitarian denies. While the neo-Hegelians saw these rights not as natural but as community-endowed, they opened the way, nevertheless, to a conception of autonomy which in moral terms is individualist, but is grounded in an organicist moral epistemology, in which the rational judgment of the individual would necessarily instantiate the moral sentiment of the social whole.

Total community is totally incompatible with autonomy, as I have defined it. The condition for "healthy" membership, as specified by such a community's own standard of health, is a heteronomous and unconditional commitment to the commune's standards and a willing reliance on its support. Independence of judgment in the face of public criticism within the community is not for a total communitarian a virtue, but a defect to be censured by the withdrawal of the community's loving concern.

If one attends only to the form of autonomous decision making, there would appear to be nothing against autonomously adopting any procedure whatever for the taking of future decisions. The hero of Luke Reinhart's novel *The Dice-man* pursued freedom in personal plurality rather than in integration, by committing himself to decide on the throw of the dice between all the options that at any moment appealed to the disparate sides of his personality, giving each its chance of expression in action. The Dice-man, too, might claim to live according to a law he had prescribed to himself, and to have had reasons for making the commitment. But observe the pluperfect tense: An absolute commitment to such a procedure, whether to the dice, to the priest, or to the total community, involves the distancing of oneself thereafter from the considerations that intitialy led one to it. For if the commitment is to be absolute, the question whether there really were, and still are, good enough reasons for making it is not to be reopened. Though the rule is genetically one's own, in the sense that one originally prescribed it to oneself, both the rule and the prescriptions proceeding from it now confront one from outside; the rule is now as much an alienation of the self as is the brute externality of a stone idol that one might carve to venerate. Continuing self-prescription has been abjured by the absoluteness of the procedural enactment; one is not to ask whether to go on with the procedure itself. Contrast this with a conditional commitment, which one must continuously monitor to assess whether the considerations originally thought to warrant it still do so in the light of longer and broader experience. If this monitoring can go on, the self-prescription can be held to be continuously renewed, but if the commitment is to giving it up, the apparently autonomous adoption of the community's *nomos* – or of the rule of the dice – amounts to a surrender of autonomy to an alien determinant.

No one makes an alien rule his own by merely *deciding* to be guided by it. It must be an authentic expression of his system of beliefs, a principle he comes to understand as already informing and giving coherence to his beliefs, attitudes, and judgments. Or if he has beliefs that do not cohere with it, he has to explore his beliefs and the conception of himself which corresponds to them, to know whether to disown the rule after all, and stick by the deviant commitments that follow from his beliefs. The rule may seem compelling, as in a case of conversion, yet the agent may still find himself unable to surrender some deviant commitments without totally disrupting his whole belief system, or at least without gravely prejudicing his core beliefs. So he must at the very least go on exploring ways to define the new rule so that it will accommodate what he cannot authentically abandon.

Self-knowledge, the congruence of action and belief, and a concern that these features be maintained by a vigilant critical moral consciousness – all these are necessary for autonomy. Someone who chose to surrender this concern would be surrendering autonomy, something an autonomous person could consistently do only if he had an overriding reason, committing him to the pursuit of some other ideal. This would be to invest, however, a degree of confidence in the *final* autonomous abdication of autonomy which is out of keeping with the autonomous person's critical nature, for the surrender entails abjuring the practice of criticism and any further review of the rightness of the total commitment. It *could* be done – "absolute autonomous commitment to the surrender of autonomy" is not logically incoherent. It is pragmatically incoherent, however, unless the stakes that warrant the gamble are very high indeed. Someone who believed that the salvation of his immortal soul depended on it might accept the gamble, but one would need to look hard at the rationality of the premise before accepting this as an autonomous choice.

There is one sense, however, in which an absolute abdication of the autonomous judgment is impossible. However one might try to commit oneself to a nonrational decision procedure, it is always logically possible for an autarchic person to change his mind. As a proposition in normative logic, this is true, just as it may be true that a sovereign legislature can do anything except abridge its own sovereignty. But as a matter of fact, someone making the act of abdication may thereafter school himself to obedience, constantly reinforcing the psychological barriers in the way of autonomous recantation. One might imagine such a person moving through heteronomy to a state of heterarchy, where the very thought of critically appraising the community to which he had committed himself generated a degree of anxiety that made rational criticism impossible for him.

It is remarkable that commitments of this kind should so often be referred to in the communitarian literature as "liberating," and conducive to personal growth. Perhaps, for a near-anomic person, acceptance of the community's rule provides a kind of integration, and therefore a sense of purpose and effectiveness in action which he formerly lacked, even though the integration is in pursuance of a *nomos* uncritically received. But as I argued in Chapter 10 in the context of concentration camp survival, integration is not necessarily autonomy; one can be inner-directed but heteronomous. Similarly, the security and friendship, the firm identification with the group, may liberate the natural springs of trust and affection

229

which had been formerly blocked by anxiety and mistrust or could find no fitting and safe object. But while this may be a happier and even perhaps a healthier condition than neurosis or anomie, it is not autonomy, and only in the sense that feelings are more spontaneously expressed and the person less inhibited can it be called "liberated." Such liberation of the feelings, ungoverned by reason, is nevertheless governed by the introjected constraints of the community, which may, of course, permit greater spontaneity of emotional expression than more individualist environments.

## B. Mutuality

There is, however, a second kind of relationship, resembling total community in that it calls just as much for deep active commitment, but which depends on a high degree of autonomy for its full realization. Such a relationship may be found in some friendships, marriages, even in some families. The *telos* of this relationship is to be found, as in the other, in the quality of the relation itself and not in some goal extrinsic to it. But unlike the other, the relation is seen to be in process of creation and development, and the participants are somewhat like artists working on the material of their own mutual perception and their mutual concern.

It is of the essence of this relation that it is fully participatory. Each respects and values the other as a full partner, and exerts his own effort in the expectation and trust that the other will do likewise. If one of the partners adopts a heteronomous role, seeking cues from others rather than exercising an independent perception and judgment of the relation, the enterprise would be to that extent a failure. For its particular nature is its mutuality, the extent to which each is sensitive to the others' response to his own effort, is prepared to monitor his own attitudes to his partners severally and to the partnership as a whole, and to adjust to changes in the interests, tastes, values, and personalities of the others.

Unlike the total community, the object here is not to preserve an ideal pattern of unchanging relations; on the contrary, the enterprise is to keep the partnership moving, to make it a vehicle through which the personalities of the partners can develop autonomously, without destroying it. This is their joint enterprise, as authors collaborating to write a book find their ideas changing and developing as a direct outcome of the collaboration. But the difference is that the authors need have no concern for each other except in relation to their specific and specialized enterprise,

230

whereas mutual concern for the other as a person is an inelimi-
nable element of mutuality. The authors collaborate in a transcendent collective enterprise for the sake of an end beyond their
personal well-being. It is no more necessary to good authorial collaboration than to a research establishment that all the authors be
autonomous, though a participant who had no independent ideas
in the relevant area but merely accepted and enlarged on those put
forward by the others would be something of a passenger. But a
mutuality is a collaboration over the broadest spectrum of the
partners' concerns and will therefore flourish the more autonomous the partners are. There are friendships and marriages, of
course, where one partner dominates and another responds to
cues. But theirs is an enterprise with a somewhat different *telos*,
less ambitious and less demanding, though for some people it may
be happy enough. In such a relationship, however, the heteronomous partner is parasitic, and the one will be liable to fall into a
pattern of treating the other like a pet, with small respect, though
possibly with the greatest concern and affection.

I have pitched the requirements of mutuality pretty high, so
high indeed that it could hardly be attained except in intimate
face-to-face relations where knowledge of others can be pretty complete and the monitoring of relations pretty continuous. Some of
the numerous small communes with anything from a half-dozen to
a dozen and a half members which sprang up in great numbers in
the 1970s but are rather less fashionable in the more dour and
individualistic 1980s seem to have entertained some ideal such as
this, however short of it they fell in practice. The larger the group,
the more difficult it is for each partner to process all the relevant
information about the others, to remain sensitive to the nuances in
their responses to his initiatives, and to make the effort to sustain
the personalized concern for each. That is why it is an inappropriate model for political organization. Yet I suspect that the total
community ideal is often found attractive because it is confounded
with this one. Of course, a political system may structure a society
which includes mutualities, just as many national states structure
societies which are comprised largely of nuclear families. But an
association of mutualities would not be a mutuality writ large, any
more than the nineteenth-century British state was a Victorian
family writ large.

Martin Buber's *Paths in Utopia*, which had a very considerable
influence on the growth of utopian communalism, seems to fall
into just this error. The book is concerned with "restructuring"

231

society "through a renewal of its cell-tissue."[11] Stressing the value of close personal relations in community, Buber concludes that "a Nation is a community to the degree that it is a community of communities."[12] But the model of contractual association can be extended in this way, as a federal association of associations, only because the first-order association can be treated, for organizational and institutional purposes, as a bearer of roles, rights, and obligations in the greater association analogous to the natural person in the lesser. Community, however, is not a matter of roles and powers alone, though the information which each member has to process will necessarily include the roles, powers, and obligations of the others; it must extend, also, to reciprocal sympathies and concerns which *people*, not institutions, can feel for one another. A federation of communities may be a transcendent collective enterprise or a collaborative association; it cannot be a mutuality, nor can it simulate the attractive intimate qualities that constitute a mutuality an ideal relationship.

## C. Comradeship

Comradeship demands a sufficient degree of interpersonal concern to qualify (as the welfare organization does not) as a community. It leaves more room for personal autonomy than the total community, while yet demanding less as a creative endeavor than relations of mutuality. Each participant has a concern for every other which is different in quality and in degree from the concern he has for nonparticipants, and different just because that person *is* a participant. The relation is not personalized, however, in the way that reciprocal concern is personalized in the mutuality. For in the mutuality there is a sense in which partners are strictly speaking irreplaceable. The gap left by the death of a spouse or a friend cannot be filled by recruiting a similar and fully qualified replacement. Each departure impoverishes the enterprise, and though a new recruit may enrich it, it will be by making of it something different and *sui generis*. This is because mutualities have a necessarily historical dimension; each set is therefore unique. What the partnership has been so far shapes the partners' perception of what it is now, and so it enters essentially into its present character. No newcomer could share it fully. The history of its growth is a defining part of the relationship, not a merely genetic and contingent fact about it.

But in a comradely community – say, a moderately large kib-butz, an extended family, or even a regiment – there can be recognition of concern for anyone fulfilling the qualifying conditions for membership, which may include, for instance, someone who has recently enlisted or has married into it. This concern would extend beyond the welfare administrator's concern for the qualified benefi-ciaries. Being a member and recognizing another as a comrade, one is led to care "as if it were oneself" for his vicissitudes. This is not a generalized altruism which would extend to anyone, partici-pant or otherwise. What makes comradeship a kind of community is that the criteria for membership are also criteria for sharing a common fate. Something of the same sort may exist between com-patriots, at least in times of crisis: Certainly, the awareness of sharing a common fate in 1940 had a great deal to do with British solidarity and with the readiness of people to supplement their more usual standoffish attitudes of minimal respect with a concern for and involvement with others' well-being.

The problem with a community of this kind is to sustain the sense among its members that being a member is a centrally impor-tant feature of their lives. Religious communities or ideological ones like kibbutzim cohere because the ideology assigns overriding importance to being a member, and it is through this conscious-ness of self and others that mutual concern is mediated. Similarly, patriotism, a far looser and generally weaker group awareness, becomes an effective cement when, as in total war, the criteria for membership of the nation are patently also qualifying conditions for a common fate. But sustaining so heightened an awareness of belonging demands in ordinary times an insistence on ideological conformity that consorts ill with autonomy.

## 6. The size of communities

A crucial factor in the compatibility of community and autonomy may well be size. I suggested earlier that the sheer impossibility for each individual of processing the amount of information necessary to keep a mutuality flourishing beyond a mere handful of people makes this a politically inappropriate model. As the group in-creases in size, there comes a choice between aiming *either* to keep all its members involved with one another in all their interests and concerns, at the cost of their being committed to a more intense ideological consensus, *or* to relax the demand for completeness, looking for mutual trust, support, involvement, and concern for members in only a restricted range of their activities. So members of a profession may exhibit reciprocal concern in matters that touch their common professional culture but be relatively indifferent to one another outside that area.

One's membership of a mutuality is consistent with, indeed demands, autonomy because one is immediately active and self-determining in creating the partnership. So there is no occasion to demand that the member submit to the group. As the group expands, however, its coherence comes to depend increasingly on individuals' readiness to submit to standards that for any given person have an objective existence independent of his own. Increasingly the group insists on the difference between itself and the world beyond, and therefore on the importance of ideological purity. And so it moves in the direction of total community.[13] Otherwise, it must contract its scope, conceding that in some aspects of their lives its members must look outside for significant relations, condoning their adoption of some values at any rate that other members will not share. So a member may form deep and far-reaching attachments to the Labour Party, to a university, or to the Catholic Church – or to all at once. None of these, not even the church, makes, in reality, demands as total and exclusive as, for instance, Oneida or the Hare Krishna sect. But if the members of a comradely community came severally to form diverse attachments of this kind outside it, it is hard to see what bonds would continue to hold it together. A mutuality, with its close personal involvements and mutual respect for persons, might be able to absorb such diversities. Each member could have a vicarious interest and concern for the spiritual progress of every other, even in directions in which he could not directly follow. But the looser and more impersonal texture of comradeship seems to have no corresponding way of accommodating outward-looking diversity without dissolving into competitive collaboration.

I have not considered the retreat communes that flourished in the 1970s. People withdrew to them from the world of imposed roles, living simply, relaxed and undemandingly together, everyone let be to "do his own thing." I doubt whether these are, properly speaking, instances of communitarianism, since the survival of such arrangements generally depends on participants' willingness *not* to become involved with one another, except perhaps at the most superficial level of sharing domestic chores. Even so, the mortality rate of such communities is generally very high; participants move in and out very freely, often moving on from one to another, making no commitment of any sort. This is not a prescription for autonomy but rather for anomie. It is living without direction or purpose, with no *nomos*. At best, such retreats may provide an unharassed breathing space for people needing time to decide what to do with their lives. They do not add another to the already available options between which the person has to decide.

# 13

## Human rights and moral personality

### 1. Rights as reasons for action or forbearance

A person's duties are reasons for him to act or to forbear, whether he wants to or not. A person's rights, on the other hand, are reasons for someone else to act or forbear. So too, however, are a person's needs, his pain, his deserts, and possibly his merits. These too can give rise to duties which rest on other persons, but do not necessarily establish rights against those persons. What then distinguishes rights from other reasons for action and, in particular, from reasons constituted by the welfare needs, not of human beings alone but of other valuable objects (axiotima) as well – hens, works of art, or rain forests?

To say of someone that he has a right to Φ is paradigmatically to say that by virtue of a set of normative relations that hold between him and some particular respondent or people at large, there are certain demands such that his making them would be a reason for the respondent's acceding to them and would put the latter in the wrong if, without some overriding reason, he did not accede to them. H.L.A. Hart, in an influential article, points to the power of waiver as a distinguishing characteristic of a right. "If common usage sanctions talk of the rights of animals or babies," Hart wrote, "it makes an idle use of the expression 'a right,' which will confuse the situation with other different moral situations where the expression 'a right' has specific force."[1] Talk about the rights of animals and babies can be replaced by phrases like "It would be wrong to treat them like that," or "One ought to treat them like this." What characterizes ascriptions of rights is that, in the standard moral cases at any rate, the holder of the right is thereby in a position either to require performance of what is owed or to waive the claim, as he chooses. If Alan has a right to be paid $100 by Betty, Betty has a reason (moral or legal or both) to pay Alan $100, unless Alan eliminates that reason by waiving his right. And that is for him to decide. By contrast, if a baby or an animal *needs* food,

236

that is a reason for supplying it, whether or not the subject chooses that you should or is capable of choosing that you should. A right is thus a normative resource,[2] a capacity to constitute a reason for action for other persons, as it suits one's own interests and projects. A liberty, a form of right somewhat weaker than the power to exact specific performance from another person, amounts to a ground for rejecting considerations advanced by someone else as reasons for desisting from a project. "All the same," one might say, "I am at liberty to do it." Rights are therefore at least freedom constituting, at most opportunity creating. To ascribe moral rights to subjects incapable of freedom or of grasping an opportunity is to debase the linguistic currency.

There is no problem, however, in ascribing *legal* rights to a subject, such as an infant, incapable of natural choice; one simply empowers someone else, a trustee or a guardian *ad litem* to make appropriate choices on the principal's behalf. And if infants can have legal rights, why jib at conferring them, as some environmentalists would like, on environmental objects, such as forests or rivers, which could be made beneficiaries of protective trusts just as infants can? For there is no difficulty in ascribing benefits to axiotima. But notice the difference between the position of a trustee or guardian and of a natural person exercising his rights on his own behalf. The discretion of the trustee or guardian is constrained by the condition that the power of choice be exercised only for the advantage or in the interest of the beneficiary. No such constraint limits a principal's exercise of his own rights. For those are related to his interests, not in the sense of what would be to his advantage, but of the kind of interests that give a consistent direction to his activities, whether these are to his advantage or not. His rights are resources for controlling the behavior of others, for manipulating his social environment for his own ends, whatever they may be. Having rights enables him to pursue what *he is interested in,* and this may be very different from what is *in his interests.*

But of course rights are also restrictions on the freedom of the person or persons for whom the right constitutes a reason for action or forbearance. And so rights need to be justified, both in general principle and in their specific exercise. For there may be reasons sufficient to make the exercise of one's right or liberty the wrong thing to do; possessing a right does not guarantee that one is morally justified in insisting that the corresponding duty be carried out. It might be, for instance, ungenerous or inhumane to do so. But that does not alter the fact that, given one has a right, the

237

person on whom it bears has a reason (though not necessarily a conclusive reason) for complying with one's demands.

So to fail in one's duty *in respect of* someone or something is to be morally or legally delinquent, but it is not always to do that person a wrong, since one can have duties in respect of someone that are not also duties *to* him. What one does or what one neglects to do may be harmful to someone, but it may not be an injury (*injuria*) in a strict sense, that is, a denial of a right (*jus*). The man who fell among thieves was worse off than he would have been if either the priest or the Levite had done his Good Samaritan duty and helped him, but though they failed to help him, they did him no wrong. Good Samaritan duties carry no corresponding rights. The reasons they had to help him were not on account of any right he had against them, but rather on account of his need for their help. One may have a duty to act generously towards one's business rivals, but it is not a duty that one owes *to* them; they have no ground for grievance if, using only fair business practices, their competitors drive them into bankruptcy. The duty to be generous is indeed a reason for action or forbearance, but not of a kind that the bankrupt could manipulate as a normative resource, to secure the cooperation of others in getting him out of his difficulties, as he might a contractual right to the payment of outstanding debts. It is a mistake then to think that for every duty there is a corresponding right.

Of course, the man who fell among thieves would have no less justification than generations of Christians since his misadventure for condemning the priest and the Levite for their failure in charity. But though it was he who suffered from it most directly and acutely, no special kind of reproach was available to him that was not equally available to anyone else; though the prime sufferer from their callousness, this gave him no special standing, different from that of any other moral critic of their actions. All rational persons stand in the same position to condemn inhumanity, whoever is the victim. By contrast, someone whose rights are infringed has in addition a justifiable grievance and grounds for resentment that onlookers do not have. For a wrong, an injury, constitutes a failure in justice, not in mercy or benevolence; it is a failure to render what is due, and not just a failure to do what it would be good to do for the sake of the best consequences. Onlookers may condemn injustice in general, from the outside, as it were, but the particular individual denied his right is in a special position to complain. If one has a right, then whoever has a corresponding duty has a reason to act, aside from the consequences. Injury or wrong, in this strict sense, has to do with fairness and fidelity, which in turn are related to respect for persons. One way in which a person acquires rights is through another's promise; if Alan enters into an undertaking with Betty to Φ, he gives her a reason to expect and require from him a certain performance, on the basis of which she arranges her own projects. She is wronged if he fails her, however better the outcome of his doing so than if he had fulfilled his promise.

Equally, Alan suffers a wrong if Betty treats him unfairly by discriminating on irrelevant criteria in her treatment of him and others. (See the discussion of the principle of equal consideration of interests, and the limits on its application, in Chapter 5, section 4.) In part, the principle of equal consideration is a matter of formal rationality. It is irrational, or at best nonrational, to treat like objects differently. For instance, because there are the same reasons for keeping two equally fine paintings in an air-conditioned room, or for feeding all one's battery hens the same laying pellets, it would be irrational, other things being equal, to favor this one and to neglect that. True, if the paintings were one's own property and one enjoyed looking at one and not the other, one's preference could then count as a reason for choosing one and neglecting the other. If the paintings were masterpieces, however, one might believe that, though one's own, they were also part of the cultural heritage of mankind, and that one's position was rather like that of a national gallery curator, whose purely personal preferences ought not count as reasons for discrimination in the treatment of the pictures in his charge. There is nothing weird, in this case, in saying that the pictures, as axiotima, have needs related to their continued well-being which constitute for the owner as curator reasons for action, and that if they are of equal value then the reasons are equally cogent.

Nevertheless, it would be weird to ascribe rights to the pictures. Considerations of welfare are insufficient on their own to create a right. If one gave some of one's hens no food at all, one would be not merely irrational but morally delinquent too, because to starve chickens is cruel. And there are laws to protect animals from cruelty and neglect. But the offense punished is not that one acts unjustly but that one acts cruelly.

The principle of equal consideration of the interests of persons adds to the purely formal requirements of rationality the substantive requirement that in considering the treatment of persons one look to their interests, and from this derives a right to fair treatment and a reason for grievance and resentment if one does not get it. So if the social decision processes work so that Alan gets too little food and Betty too much, we may be inclined to say not merely that the system is irrational or bad, like a picture gallery whose curator neglects its pictures, or cruel, like a careless poultry farmer, but that it is unjust; Alan is not merely harmed but wronged or injured by it. That is not just because human beings are to be valued more highly than hens or pictures, so that the consequences are more to be deplored if they get less than they need to keep them in good condition; there is an additional delinquency of a totally different kind. Neglecting the well-being of hens can raise questions of moral goodness; neglecting that of human beings can raise those questions too, as in the case of the priest and the Levite, but it can raise the further questions of justice and right. What is the relevant difference between hens and pictures on the one hand and human beings on the other, that questions of right and justice apply to the latter but not to the former?

## 2. Human rights as the rights of natural persons

It is a mistake to make the distinction rest on the difference between *human* beings and others. It is not their being human, which is a simple biological feature, that makes the moral difference. In Chapters 5 and 6 I elaborated an account of natural personality and of its relation to moral personality and the principle of respect for persons. It is the fact of natural personality, not of humanity, which makes the crucial difference between right bearers and other objects. From the basic deontological notion of respect for persons, which has nothing to do with valuing them, derive the principles of noninterference, respect for autarchy, and equal consideration of interests, the set of general principles discussed in Chapters 6, 7, and 8. All of these principles generate rights. At a slightly less abstract level, if a legal order is to exist to regulate relations between persons, no natural person can be denied a capacity for legal rights, since the *telos* of legal right is to provide natural persons with institutional normative resources safeguarding their capacities for selecting and pursuing their own projects.

To these three classical Kantian principles I add a fourth. Because Alan has a conception of himself and is not *only* an object of perception by others, for Betty to observe him, report on him, participate in his activities for her own purposes, without considering what significance such observation, reporting, and so on would have for him as the subject of action and experience is to wrong him, just because it is to treat him without the respect due to a person. This *principle of privacy*, which I shall treat more fully in the next chapter, shifts an onus of justification from Alan to Betty. The principle of noninterference leaves Betty at liberty to observe and report on anything whatsoever, unless Alan can provide a reason to justify interfering with that liberty; the principle of privacy, however, puts the onus on Betty to justify actions which, but for that principle, she might do without having to justify anything at all. Without a shift in onus, it would be for Alan to provide special reasons why Betty should not treat him, with or without his agreement, as an object of amusement like a performing flea, as an object of curiosity, like a geophysicist's bit of moonrock, or as an object to be appreciated, as a connoisseur might regard a painting. None of these observer attitudes is consistent with the respect due from one person to another.

These principles are so broad that they hardly qualify as rights; they are rather rules of procedure in justificatory discourse. For that very reason one can claim for them universal and unqualified application to everyone who counts as a person. Nevertheless, they do yield some more substantive principles that can properly be expressed as human rights. For instance, though there is nothing in these principles to prohibit the punishment of crimes, the principle of respect for persons grounds a right not to be punished under retroactive laws, to be the victim of unexpectedly severe "exemplary" penalties for the sake of deterring others, or to be taken hostage to put pressure on others. These practices are unfair and fail in respect, since in the first case the victim is penalized for pursuing projects which at the relevant date there was no lawful reason for him not to pursue, and in the second and third cases, the victim is singled out as a lever for manipulating the behavior of others, regardless of his standing as a natural person with a point of view deserving of consideration and with projects claiming the forbearance of other persons.

In the standard instance of a criminal penalty, the offender is punished for what he has chosen to do, from among options which he knows are weighted to make some less attractive than others. Such weighting is of course a constraint upon freedom and therefore in need of justification (see Chapter 7), but whether we see it as infringing a human right depends on the nature of the option penalized; for the principle of noninterference is not an absolute license to do whatever one likes, but a liberty to do whatever there is not a good reason for one's being prevented from doing. And any reason for interfering which the subject himself is rationally capable of seeing as such, and would indeed see as such if he looked at the matter independently of his personal involvement, would be a good reason for interference. If the reason is good enough, the person suffering a just punishment is rationally committed to acknowledging that (1) he has knowingly made a choice the unacceptable consequences of which, though deliberately imposed by an authority, he has brought upon himself, and (2) these consequences are not an arbitrary infringement of his prima facie right (the right not to be interfered with) to the range of options otherwise available but can be rationally justified as a way of preventing bad actions. By contrast, retroactive punishment and the inflicting of unexpectedly severe exemplary penalties penalize the victim for having made a choice among a set of options quite different from the set that would have been presented to him had he been making his choice at the time of his being penalized.

## 3.  Human rights – defeasible or absolute?

A "human right" is what H.L.A. Hart has called a "general right," attributable to "all men capable of choice . . . in the absence of those special conditions which give rise to special rights," that is, rights which arise from special transactions or relationships.[3] As with the older notion of natural rights, human rights are attributable (if at all) to every person, prior to any undertaking into which he may have entered. Though by subsequent deals he may agree to waive his rights, a person enjoys them in the first place independently of his consenting to any contract or covenant, actual or imputed, from which limiting constituent conditions might otherwise be inferred. Human rights are enjoyed by all people simply as people, not as participants in some agreed practices. Like John Rawls's "natural duties,"[4] they are those that contracting parties in the original position would have reason to acknowledge, but they are not constituted by the contract. That is not to say that some social practices may not be conditions for the implementation of such a right. Someone claiming the right to marry as a human right[5] might say that though it can have practical application only in a society with marital institutions, it is not membership in such a society that confers the right; no society, once having instituted marital practices, could legitimately confine the right to members

242

of that society, nor could it require that they satisfy any special conditions – say of race, nationality, or religion (and some nowadays would add sex) – not constitutive of the practice as such.*

But could any right be *that* unconditional and universal? All the familiar qualifications – of general welfare, public security, health, and so on – suggest that Alan's human right $R$ is the right of any human being *except under some condition C*. But in that case it would evidently not be a sufficient condition for the right that Alan is human, or, more precisely, a natural person. A familiar response to this objection is the admission that human rights are only prima facie rights. A prima facie right is not, however, like a prima facie case – a case which, on closer inspection, could turn out to be groundless, and so not really a case at all. A prima facie right really is a right, a genuine reason for moral or legal action. It is prima facie only in the sense that it is not necessarily a conclusive reason. In particular circumstances it is capable of being defeated or overridden by stronger reasons.

One of the attractions for liberal individualists of the consensual theory of political authority is that it offers a legitimation of those restrictions of general rights that seem practically unavoidable. If Alan's natural right $R$ is overridden by public safety condition $C$, one can comfort oneself that anyone consenting to government waives $R$ in any $C$, and assuming that the power of waiver is in any case a constituent of any human right, and therefore of $R$, $C$ is not really a defeating or overriding condition but one that activates that very power. When Alan says to Betty, "Don't bother to pay me the $100 you owe me," his right to $100 is indeed extinguished, but by the exercise of a power that is a constituent of the rights relationship. For if Alan were obliged to accept Betty's $100, it might seem more appropriate to say that, like a tax collector, he had a power and a duty to exact it, rather than a right to it. Correspondingly, consensualists are disposed to regard political authority as the outcome of a waiver of human rights to act on one's own initiative, free of coercive interference.

Such arguments from consent are, however, generally unsatisfactory. If they are intended to legitimize actual political and legal restrictions on natural or human rights, they have to show that the

---

*Note, however, that Art. 12 of the *European Convention for the Protection of Human Rights and Fundamental Freedoms* (1950) qualifies the right of "men and women of marriageable age" to marry "according to the national laws governing the exercise of this right." This right would be consistent with the South African apartheid marriage laws which prohibited mixed race marriages.

individuals concerned really have agreed to such restrictions. If, more radically, they maintain that individuals have not agreed, the consequences might be acceptable to an anarchist but to no one else. If, however, the consensual theory is offered only as a model of what it would be rational for individuals to agree to under conditions which present them with a problem of coordinating their projects, it cannot be assumed that actual individuals, who may never have been in such a position, or who may be less than rational, have indeed waived the rights in question. Human rights are not conditional on their *rational* exercise. A model is, in any case, an "as if" device – it may be heuristically apt, but unless in a particular situation its postulates can be shown to be satisfied in the essential respects, it can neither explain nor justify. It is not enough that the model generate results corresponding closely to the *explananda* or *justificanda*. The consensual model will explain and justify restrictions on human rights only on the assumption that the essential respect in which the actual situation corresponds to the model is not the given consent of the subject, but that in such a position any rational person would consent – that there is sufficient reason for Alan to waive his right, whether or not he actually acknowledges the reason and does waive the right.

The point of human rights doctrine has not been, in any case, to provide legitimation for political authority but for claims against tyrannical or exploitative regimes. If the doctrine is to keep its cutting edge, it must permit us to say that human rights *survive* political association, rather than that political association extinguishes such of them as are necessary to its purposes.

A partial solution is that a right defeated or overridden is not necessarily a right lost. The practice of compensation when private property is compulsorily acquired by public authorities is a recognition that, though considerations of public interest may override a person's right to decide how to dispose of his property, they do not thereby extinguish his rights in the matter. The right of which he is deprived must be made up to him in some other way, else he suffers injustice. But of course the imprisonment or the killing of criminals is not like that. The right to life or liberty is held forfeit, not just overridden by a stronger consideration.

The classic declarations of human rights, issuing generally from compromise between a vision of a free and just future and a sharp awareness of the political hazards of an unstable present, have hedged their bold affirmations of right with cautious escape clauses.

244

Consider Article 8 of the *European Convention for the Protection of Human Rights and Fundamental Freedoms:*

1. Everyone has the right to respect for his private and family life, his home and his correspondence.
2. There shall be no interference by a public authority with the exercise of this right except such as is in accordance with the law and is necessary in a democratic society in the interests of national security, public safety or the economic well-being of the country, for the prevention of disorder or crime, for the protection of health or morals, or for the protection of the rights and freedom of others.

The qualifying form of words in the second paragraph suggests that while the right is not extinguished (for what is envisaged is only interference with the exercise of the right), it may properly be overridden by certain weightier but very broadly specified considerations. Similar phrases occur in Articles 9, 10, and 11, qualifying the rights of freedom of thought, conscience and religion, freedom of expression, of peaceful assembly and association, including the right to join trade unions. Even so fundamental a right as the right to life (Article 2) is qualified to permit capital punishment imposed lawfully by a court as a penalty for a crime. Yet why, if such rights are *human rights*, should someone's being guilty of a crime deny him enjoyment of them? Do people enjoy such rights as persons or only as well-behaved persons, as judges enjoy security of tenure *quamdiu se bene gesserint?* If criminal behavior can extinguish any human right, does it extinguish all? And how serious must the crime be for this to happen? And if not all rights are extinguished, how do we decide which survive? This is not a purely theoretical question; it is forcefully posed by proposals for compulsory psychosurgery and conditioning therapy for criminals, including the castration of sexual offenders. People who object to such treatment as invading the criminal's human rights would not always object on the same grounds to imprisoning him, possibly for a long period.

## 4. The *telé* of human rights

A possible way to maintain the universality of human rights is to try to specify with some precision what conditions would defeat a claim to a human right, or, to put it more accurately, so to define

245

the right that what belongs absolutely to any person is the right only to have or to do whatever is not excluded by such conditions. The right to have or to do anything that is excluded would not then be overridden, since it would never have existed. Article 5 of the *European Convention*, dealing with the right to liberty and security of persons, proceeds rather in this way: Having stated the general principle, it enumerates six fairly precise conditions (the lawful detention of a person to prevent the spread of infectious disease is one instance) which nullify the right. The framers of such declarations could never be sure, however, that all the appropriate excluding conditions had been specified. Defeasibility is open-ended.[6] So they fall back on generalities and catchall phrases that blunt a declaration's cutting edge. For unless some systematic and intelligible principle can be elicited from the exclusions already accepted, what is to count as a reason for admitting further excluding conditions? And to say of such a principle that it was "intelligible" would be to say that there is a reason why someone, simply as a person, should not enjoy such a right under the excluded condition.

It may be more promising, however, instead of stipulating that human beings have a given right, and then trying to draw up lists of ad hoc excluding conditions, to ask why the given right is to be attributed to them at all. For then we may be able to reconcile the right with some at least of the excluding conditions, on the grounds that these limitations do not interfere with the *telos* or point of the right. I mean by "the *telos* of a right" whatever it is for the sake of which the right exists, that gives point to ascribing it. I prefer not to speak of the "purpose" or "end" for which it exists, for that smacks too exclusively of consequentialism. Some rights may be ascribed because the consequences are generally good; but some may have a different sort of point, having to do, for instance, with the respect owed to persons.

Carl Wellman, following the lead suggested in analytical jurisprudence by Wesley Hohfeld, Albert Kocourek, and others, has drawn attention to the structural complexity of human rights.[7] Each complex right, he says, clusters around a core right which identifies the nature and contents of the set; it is this one that all the others – powers, privileges, claims, and immunities – are really all about. I doubt, however, whether selecting one from the complex set of rights is the best way of comprehending their structural unity. We can talk of a particular complex as, for instance, *the* right to privacy, because there is a *telos* or a group of related *telé* that explains why this power and this liberty must be included in the

246

right, while some other need not be. The right to privacy is a particularly good example to work with because, as a relative newcomer, it is still not very well defined and in order to make its way
it has to thrust aside other well-established rights, such as the
rights of free enquiry and free reporting. In doing so, it compels us
to examine not only the importance of privacy, but also the point of
the rights it challenges. In the next two chapters I shall ask just
what interests a human right to privacy would protect and what
claims to privacy can be set aside without prejudicing the idea of
human personality to which, I believe, the notion primarily relates. Conversely, in assessing media claims to inquire and report
freely, it makes good sense to ask what the *telos* of this right may
be; to what extent would it be impaired, for instance, were the
right to publish details of someone's illness restricted so that the
patient could not be easily identified? And if exceptions to such a
restriction were allowed in respect, say, of persons who occupied
or were candidates for high public office, would the right to privacy be lost if the subject could continue to enjoy it by resigning or
withdrawing his candidacy? And just as slander is an abuse of free
speech, because giving people the opportunity to defame one another is not what the right is about, so privacy to batter one's
spouse or child is not what the privacy of the home is about. It is
not so much that the rights of the victim override the right to
privacy of the batterer; it is rather that the batterer's claim to
privacy is parasitic on a valid claim based on a genuine human
interest in cultivating personal family relations. Bashing spouse or
child is not a way to do that. So the right to immunity from interference to bash them in the privacy of one's own home is undermined
by a fuller account of the interests claiming protection.

There are three fundamental moral propositions on which a
schema for rationalizing human rights can be erected, which
would show us where to look for their *telé* and suggest a way of
testing whether a given claim that such a right existed could be
justified:

    (i)   Natural persons ought to be respected as moral persons.
    (ii)  Human beings are objects of value (axiotima).
    (iii) Certain directions of human development are desirable, and
          certain qualities are human excellences.

These propositions are not all of the same type. The first is deontological; the second two are axiological. Since the notion of a right
belongs, according to the theory elaborated above, to deontological

247

rather than axiological ethics, it will be necessary to show how the latter can generate rights at all.

## 5. Human beings as valuable objects

I have used the term axiotimon to refer to something it is appropriate to value or esteem, distinguishing it from the notion of a person, properly an object of respect and forbearance. It would be irrational, other things being equal, to believe that there were reasons for regarding something as an axiotimon but not care whether it existed, flourished, or decayed. To all axiotima, therefore, can be ascribed needs – conditions necessary if the object is to remain that by virtue of which it is valued, as a racehorse would cease to be valued as a corpse. I have claimed that while the word *welfare* is generally reserved for human beings or, at the broadest, for the higher mammals, the concept is applicable without any incoherence to inanimate objects like pictures or to environmental objects like ecosystems, which need to be protected and cared for and for which concern can properly be felt and displayed. Moreover, insofar as any object is an axiotimon its welfare needs constitute reasons for action or forbearance for anyone in a position to attend to them, just as one would consider the needs of a child to be reasons to attend to it.

Human beings, no less than pictures, racehorses, or trees, are *axiotima*. This is the second of the propositions enunciated in section 4. In particular instances this may not be true. The world would have been better had Hitler, Himmler, and Heydrich, for instance, never walked the earth. There is, nevertheless, a prima facie case for believing that human beings are to be cherished: They are the most immediate objects for the sentiments of love, friendship, sympathy, and pity, which we regard as among the characteristics of a good human being and the reciprocal experience of which we value. But a prima facie case can turn out to be wrong; such sentiments might be extinguished as we survey the more monstrous instantiations of the species. Nevertheless, by and large there are reasons for believing that most human beings are properly to be valued. The conditions without which human beings could not live or retain the features by virtue of which we perceive them as axiotima are their basic needs. Where these are not otherwise supplied, they constitute for anyone reasons for action. Failing to act on such a reason is a failure of charity and benevolence. But should it also be seen as a denial of a right, and if so, why?

Recent declarations of human rights include social and economic rights, such as "the right to a standard of living adequate for the health and well-being" of a person and his family, "including food, clothing, housing and medical care." The change that has occurred since the earliest Declaration of the Rights of Man is that what was then seen only as the material of duties of benevolence – to care for the poor and the unfortunate, according to what one could reasonably spare from one's own more extensive needs, for instance – is now the material content of the rights of the poor, that is, welfare rights.

It is not completely clear where the correlative duty lies. Some people would say that we all have a duty to one another; others would say that it rests with the State. This is not, however, a very satisfactory account. On the one hand, if, for instance, everyone was getting a perfectly satisfactory education from religious bodies and voluntary organizations or from an open educational market, would the State be failing in a duty to meet the human right to education? On the other hand, if despite the efforts of a given State to meet its people's basic needs, they still starved, so that its duty to provide for them remained unfulfilled, and if people elsewhere ate to excess, would it be altogether absurd to say that this was unjust, and that the human rights of the needy were being neglected or denied, but the State was not at fault?

The change in outlook which has generated the notion of a welfare right is to be accounted for as a convergence of axiological and deontological considerations. If human beings were *only* objects of value, the moral language of benevolence would be adequate to account for the duties we have in respect to one another. This was sufficient for medieval Christian theology. The new development is the individualism of seventeenth-century England and its American colonies – epitomized in Leveller Colonel Rainborough's "the poorest he that is in England hath a life to live as the greatest he," and the corollary, that anyone who was "to live under a government ought first by his own consent to put himself under that government; and ... the poorest man in England is not at all bound in a strict sense to that government that he hath not had a voice to put himself under." This is an assertion of the moral personality of every English natural person, and a political inference that the rights to equal consideration of interests and of noninterference demanded political representation.

The second stage was the growth of public responsibility for welfare services in the economically developed nations of the West.

Public assistance in earlier centuries, whether administered by monasteries or the parish vestry, could still be seen as a way in which the wealthier classes' duty of benevolence was conveniently institutionalized. Where everyone now, as a moral person, had a right to vote, and economic management and income distribution became a regular and recognized feature of State policy, everyone's need became a subject of claims on State consideration, and this as a matter of just distribution, not simply a natural consequence of social laws, like the laws of supply and demand, the rigors of which were to be mitigated by charitable giving. If it was within the power of a government to treat its gross national product as a pool from which resources could be allocated to provide public goods like defense and roads and to meet social needs like education, the poor were getting less than their due if at the very least their basic needs were not being met. For, to echo Colonel Rainborough, they were as much persons as the rich and therefore entitled to equal consideration. Though it might be shown that equal distribution of the whole pool might have disincentive effects on production and so reduce the net amount available for distribution, nevertheless, unless there was at least equality in distribution to meet basic needs before anything was made available for luxuries, the poor, as *persons*, could legitimately complain that they were receiving less consideration than others, that their interests were being given less consideration than those of other similar *persons* distinguishable from them in no relevant way.

Notice that in the above exposition, "needs" have given way to "interests." Nonpersonal axiotima have needs but not interests. Human welfare rights arise, not directly from a right that one's needs, even one's basic needs, be satisfied, but rather from a right to fair treatment, to the equal consideration of one's interests, along with those of every other beneficiary in the social distribution of goods. If there are to be institutions allocating resources which can take account of needs in the distributive process, then no one's needs for the less basic goods should be satisfied before everyone's need for the most basic; as subjects of interests, all alike engaged in the pursuit of self-chosen projects, we have grounds for resentment at being deprived of the basic requirements for being a project maker at all, when others do very much better. True, as axiotima, some people are more valuable than others; some perform work of great value, whether extrinsically, in that others benefit from what they do or, as with artists, that the work they do is intrinsically valuable; others are rightly valued simply as persons

250

with excellent characters and virtues, to be admired and cherished for themselves. Still others have nothing at all about them to admire and much to despise. Under the aspect of axiotima, therefore, a claim to equal consideration of the interests of human beings would fail. Accordingly, while the equal consideration of the basic interests of persons as choosers has lexical priority over considerations of value in respect of the needs of human beings as axiotima, differential attention to their further needs in the light of the value of the person and his projects becomes justifiable as resources become available to go beyond the meeting only of basic needs. Distribution might be varied too on something like John Rawls's difference principle, that Alan might be allocated more than Betty, who fares least well in the distributive practice, if the upshot is that there is more to distribute and that Betty benefits too from the difference in treatment.

From a doctrine imposing a duty on each State to satisfy the welfare rights of its citizens, as a matter of social justice, it has been a short step to holding mankind corporately responsible for human rights everywhere and to asserting the rights of poorer states to the help of the wealthier so that the needs of their poorer citizens can be met. International aid began as benevolence; it is increasingly being claimed as a right.

## 6. Rights to the conditions for autonomy

So far I have not extended the notion of need beyond the conditions necessary to preserve axiotima, and particularly human beings. Unlike pictures, however, human beings have a capacity for development. One can assign value to them, therefore, not only as biological objects but as beings achieving various degrees of excellence and admirable in proportion to their achievements. If we focus on the degrees of value, we shall be led away from human rights, as was Nietzsche, to the special claims of the superman as an axiotimon whose excellence exceeded that of ordinary human beings. But if we focus instead on the many and varied forms of excellence towards which human beings aspire, and in particular on autonomy as an excellence peculiar to a moral person, and in principle accessible to all, the argument for a human right to basic needs can develop into a right to the conditions for the attaining of whatever degree and kind of excellence of which a person is capable. The rights to such conditions would presumably include the *Universal Declaration* rights to education, to leisure, and to partici-

251

pate in the cultural life of the community, interests common to all autarchic persons.[8]

The ideal of autonomy is one of the *telé* of that set of human rights which have to do with freedom, especially freedom of thought and expression, and of that nexus of rights aimed against unreasonable detention, interference with free movement, and forms of political repression generally. Autonomy requires conditions in which criticism can flourish, in which a person can discover, from the open confrontation of the ideals cherished in his society, where he stands, what he believes, and what he is. From a deep exploration of the concept of autonomy, we can derive, perhaps, a more coherent understanding of such rights, of their extent, and of any limiting conditions set by their *telé*. It is important to know, for instance, whether there are conditions that a *nomos* will have to satisfy if a person acknowledging it as his own can do so rationally. Such conditions would then constitute logical limitation on the freedoms which can qualify as human rights, without their universality being compromised by vague notions like the "weighing" or "balancing" of considerations.

## 7. The rights of children and of the dead

The distinction I have made between needs and rights rests on the distinction between axiotima and persons, and on the condition which applies to persons but not to axiotima that they are capable of making choices relating to their projects and their interests. This rules out infants, as Hart observed, as subjects of rights. Small children, from, say, the age of two or three, begin to have projects and interests of their own, and may be considered bearers of rights. But because they cannot be regarded as fully rational, the rights they possess will be qualified, as the rights of people defective in autarchy – compulsives and paranoids, for instance – are qualified. Paternalism is justified and overrides rights of self-determination to the extent that it is exercised for the advantage of the child. Compulsory education is warranted, therefore, by the consideration that a young child does not possess a minimal prudence and a capacity to judge its interest in being educated.

There is, however, a further objection that might be made to my account of rights. Suppose a child deprived in infancy by his parents or guardians of basic welfare conditions, resulting in the stunting of his growth and poor health in adulthood. Does the grown child have grounds for resentment against the parents for what was done to him as an infant? And if he has, must one say that even before he qualified as a person he had welfare rights by virtue of the person he would subsequently become? Rights would then be ascribed to him not as an actual but as a potential person.

This road is uncongenial to those who defend a woman's right to an abortion. The claim that infants, as potential persons, have rights, though they do not satisfy the qualifying condition of natural personality, can obviously be extended to fetuses and even zygotes, which also have the potentiality for development into persons. Some people claim a right to life for the fetus but concede that, in a case where a choice is forced between the life of the fetus and that of the mother, the mother's right prevails. Leaving aside theological questions such as the date of ensoulment, to assign this priority seems to acknowledge that a fetus does not have the same ontological status and that it is not the equal in moral dignity to a mature person. The physical fact of the merger of sperm and ovum, or even its implantation in the womb, is not an impressive ground for consideration of the resulting piece of jelly as a subject of interests in the required sense. As the fetus comes to resemble a child, the ascription to it of rights appears more plausible. On the other hand, if any distinction in treatment is to be made between a fetus at $x$ and at $x + n$ weeks from conception, we need a form of argument more flexible than can be gotten from the notion of a potential person's right to life.

It seems more reasonable to stick to the distinction between persons as right holders, by virtue of their capacities for projects and rational choice, and axiotima as proper objects of benevolent concern, while adding a further reason of a derivative kind. It is a feature of axiotima that we do not lose all sense of their status when they are so damaged that they lose irreparably the characteristic property that led to our valuing them in their perfect state. We value human beings as axiotima, so when they die we treat their corpses with a kind of respect – but not of the same kind with which we treat living persons. We are not bound, for instance, by a principle of noninterference or equality of consideration, because dead persons no longer possess the relevant powers that ground those principles. It is rather that we accord the corpse a kind of dignity, by virtue of what it has been. We see it, as it were, under the aspect of humanity, not under the aspect of meat, or garbage, suitably food for pigs. The form of humanity still provides the corpse with human significance, albeit defectively. To see it as a dead human being is to characterize it not merely in terms of what

253

it is, as if it had no history, but also in terms of what it was. Similarly, one would not use an irreparably defaced masterpiece to wrap up the fish, saying breezily, "It's not much use now as a painting, so let's make *some* use of it." Or if one did, one would be open to the criticism that one was insensitive or could never really have valued the painting if one can use it so now. To accord something dignity because one sees it in the light of an axiotimon is to ascribe to it a kind of shadow value. Many people would be shocked and disgusted by the treatment of corpses by medical students in the dissecting room, as lacking in the kind of reverence appropriate to the object which, having once been a human being, must still be understood in the light of that description. Similarly, jokes by archaeologists about the mummified corpses they exhume from tombs even thousands of years old seem to lose sight of the connection between the mummy and the axiotimon from which its significance for us derives, as a former human being who lived and worked and strove as a person, albeit in a society long dead.

Perhaps there is a corresponding shadow respect. We give weight to the wishes of dead people although, since they are no longer persons, there is no longer someone there to whom respect can properly be accorded. It makes no sense, given the understanding of rights that I have defended, to accord rights to the dead, since there is nothing dead people can do with them. We do not injure a dead person by ignoring his wishes. Yet we may well believe that there is a reason to respect even now the wishes that a person now dead had when he was still alive, because he survives for us as an idea, and we see his wishes in the light of that idea, even though it is no longer instantiated in the live, deciding, project-making person. But because we apprehended him as a person when he was alive, we can think of his known wishes as extensions of the form or idea in terms of which we grasped what he was then, his essential nature. This may even be true of wishes imputed to him: "Jesus as we knew him would not have wanted us to behave like this." Mortality is not wholly fatal to personality so long as such an idea of the dead person remains in the awareness of the living, any more than the destruction of particular recordings – perhaps all recordings – of the Beethoven String Quartet op. 135 would be fatal to its survival as an idea. The idea requires, it is true, material equipment for its present realization, just as one might say that to survive physical mortality the idea of this or that person requires accommodation in the mind of a living person to be fully realized.

Understood in this way, however, the known wishes of a person now dead can still constitute reasons for action for the living. Admittedly, such reasons would commit us to action now to no greater degree than they would have done when he was alive. Given that a live person's wishes do not automatically create reasons for action for other people, neither do the wishes of the dead. While someone who dismissed all thought of the dead as sources of reasons would be not only insensitive but, if the general lines of this argument be accepted, irrational too, the according of a special weight or sanctity to deathbed wishes that the wishes of the living do not have seems either sentimental or superstitious.

Somewhat analogously, the child which is yet to become a person can be understood in the light of that potentiality. Later on in life when he has become a person, he can claim that his treatment in his early months or years had not been appropriate to an entity which should have been grasped in the light of what, in normal circumstances, it would become. But because this kind of reason, like that invoking respect for the wishes of the dead, depends on a kind of projection, forward or backward, to a different state of being, to what the infant will be or to what the corpse was, the extent to which the subject of the quasi-right actually approximates to the fully personal nature or essence in terms of which its present nature is grasped, is going to qualify the extent to which respect is accorded. The zygote is so remote from actual personhood that it is hard to see it even in the light of this rather attenuated principle as a proper subject for respect. The neonate is much more like a person, though it is certainly not an actual one, but if it is neglected and grows up stunted in consequence, the adult has genuine grounds for complaint that the treatment early accorded to him had ignored his nature as a person-to-be.

## 8. Human rights and community

Chapter 12 was concerned with the compatibility of autonomy and community as complementary or competing ideals. I shall examine in this part of this chapter the compatibility of an idea of human rights with the claims of communitarianism.

John Kleinig has suggested that "Where people do love and care for each other, there is no need for recourse to rights-talk, since what is due to the other will be encompassed within the loving or caring relationship." Appeals to rights, it is suggested, are in place only when "the primary moral relations of love, care, and concern

255

have broken down."[9] Now it is an open question whether love, care, and concern are indeed the primary moral relations. According to my account, the respect for persons is at least as fundamental. Love and care can be stifling and crippling unless they are associated with respect and the recognition that the loved object is also a person who has projects of his own which demand forbearance. The most benevolent paternalism puts the father's purpose for the child above that of the child for himself, no matter how loving the father's purpose may be. If there is indeed no need for rights *talk* where love and respect are conjoined, it is because respectful love acknowledges the loved one's rights, forbearing as well as cherishing. This is the condition of mutuality, defined in Chapter 12. Here there is indeed no need for expressions of claims, grievances, and resentment, the characteristic context of rights talk. But the absence of talk, even of a consciousness of rights in need of defense, should not be taken to show that rights are irrelevant or unimportant to such relations or that they are not acknowledged and respected. On the contrary, the reflective beloved may well perceive with gratitude that his lover is sensitively alert to make such protests unnecessary. In a community of this kind, each remains secure in his freedom, freely conceding to the other or others what is due to them as persons, confident that they will joyfully do the same for him, as an expression of love conjoined with respect.[10]

A more fundamental challenge to my theory of rights comes from people who accept a more organicist view of society than mine, in which, to use Michael Sandel's expression, a person is not prior to community but constituted by it.

> Deontology insists that we view ourselves as independent selves, independent in the sense that our identity is never tied to our aims and attachments. . . . But we cannot regard ourselves as independent in this way without great cost to those loyalties and convictions whose moral force consists partly in the fact that living by them is inseparable from understanding ourselves as the particular persons we are – as members of this family or community or nation or people, as bearers of this history. . . . To imagine a person incapable of constitutive attachments such as these is not to conceive an ideally free and rational agent, but to imagine a person wholly without character, without moral depth.[11]

An individualist might claim that there was nothing in this that need seriously disturb him. It is the individual *ready-supplied* with goals and values, not an amorphous potentiality for decision making without decision-making resources, who is the subject of human rights. The self-governing chooser of the individualist model must choose, in fact, according to criteria that his society supplies. But how he came by them and the part, if any, that he has played in making them his own, need not affect the claim that individuals, *as they are*, stand in a relation of moral equality to one another. And this prohibits, prima facie, the subordination of one man or woman's purposes to those of another, and requires that his or her interests be given equal consideration with others', and that his or her projects be accorded equal respect, so long at least as they do not interfere with those of others.

Dismissing the genesis of a person's projects as irrelevant, however, overlooks the possibility that in equipping individuals with their goals and values the society may generate precisely the kind of subordination that the theory rules out. A woman socialized into role expectations subordinate and subservient to those of some man, will conceive all her projects within that framework. An account of her human rights that accepts those projects and expectations as data, as constitutive of herself, as Sandel might put it, will seem very inadequate to critics who see the socialization process as institutionalized exploitation. And corresponding cases can be argued, of course, with reference to class or race. A theory of human rights, those critics would say, must be capable of exposing such manipulative exploitation, but it cannot do that if, by rejecting the genesis of an individual's values as irrelevant, it denies itself the opportunity to expose some projects as merely factitious.

If a theory is to remain individualist and a theory of freedom, while yet being able to go behind the goals individuals actually set themselves, it must go beyond an account of human beings as merely choosers, as such choice may well be exercised within exploitive constraints. It must recognize humans as realizing their natures only when they achieve the stature of *autonomous* choosers, who by a process of rational criticism of received values examine and revise their goals as incoherences manifest themselves, so that what they choose can be seen as issuing from their own rational natures, and not simply as socially given. And this in turn must have important implications, for instance, for the kind of child rearing and education that a society supports.

Consider just one area in which these considerations might raise difficulties both for the classical view of human rights and for Sandel's communitarianism. To what extent can a society committed to the promotion and support of human rights accept without

257

protest the continued existence within it of social structures that, like traditional Middle Eastern and Balkan families, generate female personality types that are predisposed by upbringing to embrace subservient goals? These women are no doubt "constituted" by their community allegiances, but are the results acceptable? The family has been commonly regarded as the collective beneficiary of the individualist theory of human rights. Article 6 of the Constitution of the Federal Republic of Germany declares:

> (1) Marriage and the family are under the special protection of the state. (2) The care and upbringing of children are the natural rights of parents and their duty incumbent upon them primarily. The state watches over their performance [of this duty].

Article 41 of the Irish constitution of 1937 asserts:

> The State recognizes the Family as the natural primary and fundamental unit group of Society, and as a moral institution possessing inalienable and imprescriptable rights, antecedent and superior to all positive law.

Sections 2 and 3 of Article 26 of the *Universal Declaration of Human Rights* announce, as though there were no problem of declaring these rights in harness:

> Education shall be directed to the full development of human personality and to the strengthening of respect for human rights and fundamental freedoms.

> Parents have a prior right to choose the kind of education that shall be given to their children.

A new dimension to the theory of human rights is added by introducing the notion of "the full development of the human personality" (a notion already examined in Chapters 10 and 11) as part of the reason for attributing rights to human beings, a reason over and beyond their merely being able to pursue whatever enterprises, worthy or unworthy, they happen to have. This provides, as we shall see, a bridge from the individualist theory of human rights into what I shall refer to as "the species theory."

A criticism of the individualist theory more radical than those I have considered so far is that it accepts the stunted, alienated individual of bourgeois society as an expression of man's nature. So Marx wrote that "the so-called *rights of man*, as distinct from the *rights of the citizen*, are quite simply the rights of the *members*

258

*of civil society,* i.e., of egoistic man, of man separated from other men and from the community. . . . The liberty we are here dealing with is that of man as an isolated monad who is withdrawn into himself."[12] By contrast, "the essence of *man* is the *true community* of man"; the "real, conscious and authentic existence" of his "species-activity" and "species-spirit" "consists in *social* activity and *social enjoyment.*"[13]

Now these notions, though not pellucid, are clearly meant to go beyond the view that man's nature is social in the sense that the projects of individuals, living in proximity to one another, are bound to interact, that there will be advantages for each in coopera- tion, and that their projects depend on socially learned values. A possible view, more Hegelian perhaps than Marxist, is that the ful- fillment of an individual's intellectual and spiritual nature requires participation in activities that no man can originate and sustain on his own. We are species-beings in the sense that our enterprises are necessarily embedded in some continuing tradition, in terms of which we discover what is worth doing. However solitary our lives in terms of personal human contacts, we cannot conceive that any- thing we do is worthwhile except as we see it as responding and adding to some collective activity of the species, be it literature, science, or yoga. But as a matter of fact, very few activities can be pursued solitarily; we realize or fulfill our natures in participating with others directly, performing in orchestras or laboratories, work- ing in production teams or football teams. So we participate not only in collective activities but in collective enterprises. To this extent, then, an individual's rights, if understood as conditions for self-realization, would have to include rights not only to access to such activities and enterprises, but also to the kind of preparation and education that makes participation possible.

But many would go much further. According to Cardinal Woj- tyla (now Pope John Paul II), "Man as a person fulfills himself through 'I–you' interpersonal relations and through the relation to the common good, which permit him to exist and act together with others as 'we.' " His "personal subjectivity" "does not close man within himself and make of him an impermeable monad; quite the contrary, it opens him toward others in a manner that is distinc- tive of a person."[14] Alienation occurs when

> . . . in the social dimension the presence of alienating factors is re- vealed in the fact that the plurality of human subjects, of which each is a definite 'I,' cannot develop correctly in the direction of an authen-

tic 'we'. . . . The social life is, so to speak, beyond him; it is not only against him, but even 'at his expense.' Existing and acting 'together with others,' he does not fulfill himself, either because he alone has alienated himself, or because the society, owing to some faulty structures, does not give him the necessary basis for self-fulfillment or even refuses to grant the rights he possessed before.[15]

A society that displays such "faulty structures" might be said, then, to be refusing the individual his human rights, by confining him to the egoistic level of being that Hegel and Marx identified as "civil society" and by denying him the opportunity to participate with others in living a community life. Cardinal Wojtyla does not particularize the conditions for persons to "develop correctly in the direction of an authentic 'we,' " but they could well be very different from those required by the individualist's objective, the autonomous chooser. The virtues of a member of a fraternal order are more conformist than critical; the qualities of character disposing him to find fulfillment in a common good, affirming "the essential homogeneity of the personal subject and of the human community," give little support to the individualist model of the self-creative person, making his own kind of coherence out of the tensions of a plural and conflicting tradition. So one would expect the kind of human rights that are important for the one to be far less significant for the other. If the fulfillment of an individual's nature requires participation in a community, much will depend on the kind of community and the terms it lays down for participation. If the socialization of the individual's nature into a particular community is what counts, as Sandel and Wojtyla seem to suggest, then the individualist does him no service in encouraging him to look critically at the community, asserting the rights of conscience against its social certainties, and alienating himself from the very social matrix necessary for his self-fulfillment. The Middle Eastern girl would then *need* her family upbringing, and the Aborigine his tribe. Without them, or encouraged to stand outside them, they are, according to this account, not liberated but deprived.

Observe that within this species mode of conceptualizing human beings there is still room for human-rights talk, and the rights are still those of individuals, though the content of the ascribed rights might be somewhat different from the individualist's. An individual denied acceptance or rendered unacceptable to his proper community group would be wronged, not just miserable and unfortunate. There is a kind of complementarity between individual self-realization and the common good, such that the individual has a right to the fulfillment which comes when he contributes his share to that good, as the violinist at the fourth desk in the orchestra contributes and is fulfilled as a person in the collective realization of a symphony. Nor is the present theory *necessarily* hostile to the traditional liberal rights of conscience. A theory of human nature very close to the species view was advanced by liberal writers like L.T. Hobhouse and Ernest Barker in the early decades of this century.[16] They salvaged liberal values and rights from the threat of an absorbing common good by insisting that everyone would be worse off if the autonomous development of individuals were impaired, and that a truly autonomous person would will the common good anyway. So the common good itself demanded the recognition of human rights, and a community which made it a condition for acceptance that individuals forfeit their independence of mind would be impoverishing itself. All conflicts, according to this optimistic view, can be harmoniously resolved.

The liberalized species theory has the saving grace that it does not abandon the principle of respect for persons, but writes it into the notion of the common good. Other types of species theory, however, do not acknowledge that principle. The socialization of the Middle Eastern girl is into a culture that denies her the respect due to a person and therefore denies to her also the human rights that derive from that principle. An arranged marriage, promoting family alliances and accompanied by payment of dowries, makes her into a commodity or a resource, taking no account of her own view of herself and of her capacity as a source of independent projects in the world. Her conception of herself and her possibilities for action does not include the possibility that she might choose a husband for herself, but this does not invalidate the criticism that, in other respects a fully competent and self-conscious chooser, she has been so treated that her autarchy has been impaired in important respects.

The species theory has this attraction, however, as against the individualist theory: It can make room fairly readily for the notion of group rights, not in the sense of rights to affirmative action or positive discrimination in favor of individual members of underprivileged groups, but in the sense in which we talk in Australia of "aboriginal land rights" – rights that members of groups enjoy collectively. For if human beings realize their natures only in communities, and the nature of a particular individual bears the differentiating marks of the group or groups into which he has been fully socialized, the existence and quality of life within that group be-

261

comes a condition for the fulfillment of any individual member of it. Any such group represents a vehicle to be cherished for the sake of those who, by nature members of it, have a claim in fairness to the conditions for its vigor and survival, alongside the better-endowed cultural vehicles in the society. But the argument from the common good of the community would then derive its moral force from the rights of individuals to enjoy that good; it would not be an independent, even less an overriding, consideration.

## 9. Rights and the common good

The idea of a common good is evidently a potential rival to a theory of individual rights. For the strict individualist, it is at best a misleading way of referring to an aggregate of individual goods, the outcome of a cost–benefit calculation, or some lexically modified version of the same, assigning certain priorities.

But the conflict between private right and the common good (or the public interest) is not just a matter of numbers but one of types of reasons for action. Individualist theories admit that aggregative welfare considerations can be reasons for action but would almost always be "trumped" (the metaphor is Ronald Dworkin's) by an important individual right. By and large, the only reasons that prevail against rights are other rights. And if we accept the individualist's aggregative account of society, the benefits accruing even to millions of people no more justify *wronging* one person by denying him his due than would the benefits accruing to just one other person. For the individualist theory of rights rests on the postulate that every individual stands on the same footing, a corollary of the principle of respect for persons, which implies that no one can properly be sacrificed for the benefit of another. For that would be to treat one merely as a means to the benefit of another or, in Dworkin's terms, to treat him "as less than a man, or as less worthy of concern than other men."[17] And if not for one other, why for several millions?

The kind of species theory that I associated with Hobhouse and Barker comes down on the whole in favor of rights, but for the sake of a view of community good which depends on individuals' being subject to minimal legal restraints and able, subject to safeguards for the weaker bargainers, to settle their collaborative arrangements by free negotiation. But the more one fills out the conception of the community good, not as a harmony of individual goods but rather as a transcendent ideal which informs and gives meaning to the experience of participant individuals, the more abstract the notion of an individual right becomes, and the more cogent the claim of the community good to prescribe guidelines for individual rights.

At the limit, the notion of individual right disappears, and we encounter a different theory, in which the collective good of the community, state, nation, race, or working class becomes a preeminent goal making overriding demands. The moral standing of individuals is then quite different from their standing in any of the theories discussed so far. As elements in the greater whole, they have duties to serve its good. As being properly beneficiaries of its well-being, their own welfare will admittedly figure in the assessment of what counts as the community good: They may be objects of concern, though concern for the good of the whole will not merely aggregate the concern felt for individuals. But failure to consider them as persons or to allow their individual interests weight against considerations of policy will not *wrong* them – for when the common good becomes a transcendent ideal, means-end policy calculations are the *only* ones that have independent standing.

Justice, fairness, and rights get no grip – or only a derivative grip – in such a theory, for they are notions that depend on every right-holder's having an independent moral standing. Individual rights cannot be means to a collective end; or if they are, they are bound to be provisional, rule-of-thumb principles, on which little reliance can be put. Admittedly, individuals participating in a practice, valued and supported because it is believed to promote the common good, may be assigned a quasi-independent standing as holders of rights so long as the practice endures. But if the rights depend on the practice, they fail as soon as the common good requires a different practice. And the case for maintaining the rights in order to sustain the practice – as a collectivist revolutionary regime might sustain the practice of private commerce by maintaining property and contractual rights during a period of transition – loses validity the moment some other practice promises better results. Then it is not just a matter of rights being overridden. That happens all the time, even in regimes informed by individualist theories (*pace* Ronald Dworkin). But when rights are overridden, they are held nonetheless to be perfectly valid rights, and the person deprived of them will be held to be wronged unless he is compensated for his loss. In the revolutionary situation, because changing the practice would not override but would extinguish the right, talk of compensation would be an ideological solecism.

263

# 14

## The principle of privacy

### 1. The semantics of privacy

#### A. *The categories of privacy*

I remarked in Chapter 13 that the rights of privacy were relative newcomers to the human rights scene and for that reason were still in need of precise definition and needed to make a place for themselves by elbowing out of the way some applications of other, well-established rights, such as the freedom to observe, to report, and to inquire. I hope to show in this chapter and in the one following how, by considering their *telé*, one can go quite a long way in delineating the bounds of particular human rights where they appear to conflict with others. But it will greatly assist the inquiry if we can first clarify some confusions in the use of *privacy*.

Though many of the scholars and official committees who have ventured into this perplexing area have thought that deciding on a definition of 'privacy' was indispensable as a preliminary to reviewing the principles which should govern attempts to protect it, others have despaired of constructing such a definition. Though paradigm cases of invasions of privacy are recognized readily enough, they are so disparate that there seems little chance of framing a comprehensive but determinate definition on which an enforceable legal right might be grounded. Paradigm instances are already covered indirectly by principles of equity, laws of defamation, and so on; beyond other piecemeal legislation, the courts might be relied upon, they say, to assimilate other related problems to these established paradigms as they arise.

Others, reluctant to leave to the courts a margin of discretion so wide as to be legislative rather than judicial, have offered a variety of definitions, some stressing the exclusion of publicity, others the protection of areas of personal activity from interference and intrusion, still others the psychological isolation of the subject in his privacy, and more besides. More remarkable than this, however, is

264

the failure of such writers to agree on the category to which privacy belongs. Some, like Warren and Brandeis, appear to *define* it as a right.[1] This tends to load, if not entirely to beg, the question whether anyone ought to have the power to deny access to any information, places, or activity called "private"; alternatively, the very definition of privacy would have to include or take into account the reasons why some matters but not others should enjoy the protection of such a power. Definition and justification then become inextricably confused.

A.F. Westin, the author of a major work on privacy, is not helpful. He says in one sentence that privacy is "a claim" and in the next that it is a "voluntary . . . withdrawal of a person from the general society . . . either in a state of solitude . . . or in a condition of anonymity or reserve"; that is, privacy is a state or even an act of withdrawal.[2] Lusky calls it "a condition enjoyed by one who can control the communication of information about himself,"[3] and W.L. Morison follows him in part, though the "condition" that he favors is that "of an individual when he is free from interference with his intimate personal affairs by others."[4]

On the very same page that Lusky defines "privacy" as a controlling condition, however, he also declares that we "ought to avoid welding together the descriptive and legal aspects of the concept. . . . Our basic term should refer to the interest whose protection is under consideration."[5] Yet to refer to privacy as "an interest" itself presupposes that it is something people would be better (or believe they would be better) for having, and that already amounts to an evaluative presupposition in favor of privacy. Nor is there any reason for thinking that there is anything logically primitive about privacy considered as an interest; there could be opportunities for privacy which would benefit no one, in which no one could conceivably have an interest. Indeed, some lonely people might find the notion of an interest in privacy almost unintelligible. Nor is there anything pleonastic in attributing to someone an interest in privacy, as there would be if privacy were necessarily an interest. I shall suggest later that the interests people do have in privacy and its protection are very diverse, deriving in many cases from other interests, some personal, some commercial, some political. We need to understand then how the different privacy categories – claims, states, interests, and rights – are related. That will clear the way to the more substantive question, whether there are reasons for saying that persons, natural and corporate, have a right to it.

**a. Privacy as a state.** I take the logically most primitive notion of privacy to be that of the simple state of being private, that is, of not sharing an experience, a place, or knowledge with anyone else. A more complex variant notion is of a state in which either there is no sharing or there is sharing only because the subjects want to share; so a group of persons are conversing privately if all are there by agreement and are not observed or overheard by anyone not of their party.

**b. Privacy as a power.** Privacy as a state shared by agreement leads naturally enough to the conception of privacy as an ability or power to control access by others to a private object (to a private place, to information, or to an activity). This is the ability to maintain the state of being private or to relax it as, and to the degree that, and to whom, one chooses.

**c. Privacy as an interest.** Someone has an interest in privacy in the sense that it would be *in his interest* to have it, if he would be better off for being in a private state or for having the power to control access to it. Whether he would really be better off for it might be more contentious than either whether he is actually in the state or whether he has the power, since whether he is better off on account of his being private is an evaluative matter, even when it is what he desires; we certainly cannot take it for granted that giving a person what he wants is necessarily in his interest. Adults as well as children can be made worse off by giving them what they want. (That may not be a sufficient reason, of course, for refusing them, if they have a right to it. Respect for persons requires that ordinarily one does not substitute one's own judgment for that of the person whose well-being is in question. He has a right to make his own mistakes.)

**d. Privacy as a right.** A person enjoys privacy as of right if he possesses the normative capacity to decide whether to maintain or relax the state of being private. A normative order provides Alan with a normative capacity if Betty's status within the order will be changed or will remain unchanged, according to whether Alan decides to give or to relieve her from some reason for acting or for forbearing. So by inviting her into his house, where she would otherwise have a reason not to be, he relieves her of that reason for forbearance. Once invited in, she no longer has a reason not to be there, unless Alan, as the right-holder, subsequently asks her to leave; that would create for her a new reason for action. So if someone has a legal right to privacy, he also has a way of controlling others' access to and participation in his private states; for when the courts put their authority, and ultimately the police power, behind a person's claims, they supply other people with a motive for respecting them, whether they already had one or not.

Moral rights do not motivate in the same way. Nevertheless, anyone who, in exercising a moral right, sustains or creates a reason for action for other people may in fact motivate them, if they are rational. For to have a reason is to have an action commitment, and not to act on it in the absence of any contrary commitment is to be irrational. Though our conversation in a secluded spot in a public park may not be protected by law, someone overhearing it may acknowledge that in asking him to move away we invoke a moral right to privacy, supplying him thereby with a reason for going. Of course, someone who does not acknowledge the right, at least under these conditions, recognizes no reason for going. Or he may acknowledge the reason but still refuse to go. But not to be motivated by a reason that one acknowledges to be a reason is one of the ways of being irrational.

**e. Private objects.** "Private rooms," "private affairs," and "private correspondence" belong to the category of privacy rights. There are legal, moral, or conventional norms that constitute reasons not to try to share or participate in such objects without the permission of the specified holder of the privacy right.

The use of *private* in such a context invokes a norm; it only indirectly describes a state of affairs. Rather, it signals the sort of behavior which is appropriate to the object. So it is not misapplied in a given instance just because some people pry or gatecrash. If, however, it became the practice to enter some particular room marked "Private" without waiting for permission, one would be inclined to say that the room was no longer private. But that would be not simply a description of a new situation in which the occupant's *ability* to control access had broken down, but rather a recognition that the signal was now misapplied, that the occupant's right to exclude having lapsed, it was now *appropriate* to enter uninvited.

## B. Privacy, secrecy, and confidentiality

Both individuals and corporate persons, including governments, may be able to control access to information and to places like military establishments which are described as "secret" rather than "private." Secrecy overlaps with privacy; for instance, a person confiding private information to a friend may ask him to "keep his secret." But for a matter to be private it is not sufficient that it be kept secret and consequently not publicized. It must not be public in the further sense that the person in question is not liable, in principle, to answer for it in terms of principles, procedures, or standards held to promote a wider "public interest."[6] No one, not even a politician, has to justify painting his dining room table yellow before a court of law, nor to answer for it to his electorate; it is not something for which he has a public responsibility. He acts, we say, not in his official role, but as a private citizen. A private citizen, unlike a public official, has no special duties for which he is publicly answerable. Again, the directors of a private business, while subject to the ground rules of private-business games, can do as they like within those rules, without having to answer to anyone outside the business, but only to their shareholders, who are participants in the corporate person to which the relevant privacy attaches.

This conception of privacy is closely bound to the liberal ideal. The totalitarian claims that everything a person is and does has significance for society at large. He sees the state as the self-conscious organization of civil society, existing for society's well-being. The public or political universe is all-inclusive: *all* roles are public, and every function, whether political, economic, scholarly, or artistic, can be interpreted as creating a public responsibility for and in its performance.

The liberal cannot give absolute specifications, however, for what is private and what is not, because privacy is context-relative. I do not mean that standards differ between cultures. That is also true, but it is a different kind of relativity. *Within the one culture* the same matter may count as private or not, relative to the social nexus in which it is embedded. The rest of the politician's family may call him to account for painting the dining room table, just as the firm's shareholders may call its directors to account. He may do what he chooses with his bedroom, but others besides himself (his family may say) have a legitimate interest which he is not entitled to disregard in the furnishings in the dining room. What is private in this sense is not a matter of what I am *able* to control, but what I am at liberty to deal with simply according to my own taste or discretion, without regard to anyone's interests but my own, and that will depend on rules of law, morals, or conventions, according to context. That is not to say that the private area is confined to what does not *affect* others' interests – to what J.S. Mill called "self-regarding" actions. I may be at liberty to disregard the way some act of mine affects the interests of others, as when I cut my prices in a free market. What I charge may well be my own private affair, even though it affects other sellers. Conversely, if one believed that in deciding whether to Φ Alan ought to have regard to the public interest, then, even though no procedure existed in practice for calling him publicly to account for his decision whether to Φ, one would resist his claim that whether he should Φ was his private affair.

*Private* and *secret* are alike Janus-headed; they can be used either purely descriptively or in a way that invokes norms, standards, or principles. A secret code is one that is not understood, and is intended not to be understood, except by a group of initiates. When the enemy secretly breaks it, it is no longer secret. But the official key to the code marked "Secret" is like letters marked "private": The mark invokes a rule that objects so marked should not be "shared in" except by those who are appropriately authorized according to the rule. Invoking the rule is itself, of course, a way of implementing de facto control if there are sanctions that operate against those who disregard it.

Nevertheless, though the extensions of *private* and *secret* overlap, they are not interchangeable concepts. Much that is properly called "secret" (military plans, details of security organizations, and so on) is not also private just because these are matters of public interest, even though they are not, and ought not to be, publicized. Equally, information considered private, in the sense that it is of a kind that ought to be within the control of the person it concerns, may nevertheless be made public de facto by, for instance, a press report, without its normative status being affected.

A further complication arises from the association of privacy with confidentiality, which is to be found on both sides of the public/private divide. A confidential relationship is one in which it is understood that communications are *not to be shared* with nonauthorized outsiders. The phrase points to an unambiguously normative relationship. One could not define confidentiality except with reference to the complex of obligations laid on a recipient of information within a particular norm-governed role relationship, such as that between solicitor or bank manager and client. Confidentiality operates as a norm-based protection both of what is private and what is public but secret.

269

## C. Corporate privacy

The sense in which a corporation's affairs can be private requires a somewhat more complex analysis, for the range of persons having free access to private places, information, and so forth will depend on formal rules defining membership of the corporation, and specifying which of its role bearers are to have free access to what. A shop foreman, though a member of the organization, might still be refused access to the books, on the ground that they were private, and this would be quite different from refusing him a peep at the letters the manager received from his wife. Any person can count both as insider and as outsider. As insider, he does not require permission or invitation respecting matters to which his role entitles him to free access; however, as an outsider – one whose role does not entitle him to access – he will require it.

Any part of the corporation's operations for which it was answerable as an official agency would not be among its private affairs. A public corporation like British Rail or the Australian Broadcasting Corporation does not have private affairs, though some of its business may be secret or confidential. And within the total frame of reference of the corporation, some matters, rooms, cupboards, even correspondence, may be called private because the role-bearer entitled to control them has very wide discretion in what he does with them, even though the corporation might ultimately be held externally accountable for it.

Secret government defense contracts of a private firm would hardly count among its private affairs. For a start, it would have obligations, not rights, of secrecy, obligations owed to the public at large, or to the public's authorized representatives, the government. It is not a player with a free hand in the ordinary game of competitive business.

## 2. The ethics of privacy

There is an important distinction to be made between privacy claims grounded on intimate and personal interests, and those necessary for the success of social practices valued on other grounds. Privacy claims inevitably compete with other interests, such as freedom of scientific inquiry, news reporting, business and administrative data collection, and so on. In trying to strike a proper balance between them, we need to take careful account of the different kinds of interests that privacy control serves to protect. Inti-

270

mate and personal affairs are one kind to which our culture in particular attaches importance; but there is no reason to think that when we come to assign priorities, especially for legislation, privacy will always stand in the same relation to competing interests, no matter what types of interest a privacy right would defend. The best way, then, to set about deciding how much importance to give to privacy will be to prepare a typology of privacy interests, of the different ways in which people might be better off for being able to control access. We may then be in a better position, instead of confusing practical issues with appeals to omnibus rights of privacy, to decide, with reasons, what weight to give to each, or rather, to decide their priorities (I shall say something later about attaching "weights" to arguments). All this, however, must wait until the next chapter. In this one, I shall provide a justification for a widespread concern for privacy that is not necessarily related to any interest at all.

## A. Respect for persons, noninterference, and the principle of privacy

"Why," asks little (or not-so-little) Johnny, "mustn't I peep at people through cracks in their curtains? Why do they get cross with me when they catch me at it? What harm does it do?" The last question is a trap: Many (but not all) people resent being spied on, stared at, gossiped about, or clinically exhibited as interesting specimens, even when no harm is either done or intended. Their reason for resentment may on occasion be overridden by legitimate, not to say important, interests in free inquiry; we may then be content to treat peeping as just a breach of good taste or good manners, better not regulated by law. Nevertheless, claims to privacy rights will be seen in sharper perspective if we grasp what underlies the resentment.

There is nothing intrinsically objectionable in observing the world, including its inhabitants, and in sharing one's discoveries with anyone who finds them interesting, and this is not on account of any special claims on behalf of, for instance, scientific inquiry or a public interest in the discovery of truth. For I take as a fundamental principle in morals a general liberty to do whatever one chooses unless someone else has good grounds to interfere to prevent it, grounds that would appeal to any rational person. The onus of justification, in brief, lies with the advocate of restraint, not on the person restrained. In Chapter 5 I derived this principle of noninter-

271

ference from the principle of respect for persons. Is there any principle that can reverse this onus in favor of a prima facie claim that Alan should not observe and report on Betty unless Betty agrees to it, *whatever* Betty is about? Is there a principle of privacy extending prima facie immunity to inquiry to all human activities, or is it rather that there is general freedom to inquire, observe, and report on human affairs, as on other things, unless a special case can be made out for denying it with respect to certain activities that are specifically private?

The first possibility may appear at first sight extravagant, even as a prima facie claim. Anyone, it might be said, who wants to remain unobserved and unidentified should stay at home or go out only in disguise. Yet there is a difference between happening to be seen and having someone closely observe and perhaps record and report on what one is doing, even in a public place. Nor is the resentment that some people feel at being watched necessarily connected with fears of damaging disclosures in the Sunday papers or in graduate theses in social science. How reasonable is it, then, for a person to resent being treated as a redstart might be treated by a birdwatcher?[7]

I have postulated a kind of intrusion which does no obvious damage. It is not like publishing details of someone's sex life and ruining his career. That would affect his interests, and I am trying to isolate for the moment reasons for immunity to observation, reporting, and so on that do not depend on interests but on the principle of privacy deriving from respect for persons.

What is resented is not simply being watched, but being watched without leave. If observation were intrinsically or consequentially damaging, it might be objectionable even if done with consent. In the present instance, consent would remove all grounds for objection. Observation of this sort is not evidently a breach of the principle of noninterference, or if it is, the interference is of a very indirect kind. Threatening a man with penalties or taking away his stick are both direct interferences that would prevent a man from beating his donkey. But if he stops simply because he is being watched, the interference is of a quite different kind. He could continue if he chose; being observed affects his action only by changing his own perception of it. The observer makes the action impossible only in the sense that the agent now sees it in a different light, through the eyes, as it were, of the observer. The intrusion is not therefore obviously objectionable as an interference with the agent's freedom. There are, it is true, kinds of action, such as ones that depend on surprise, that could be made objectively impossible merely by some-one's watching and reporting on them. But my present purpose is to inquire whether a general case, not depending on special conditions of that sort, can be made out against such intrusions.

Of course, there is always a danger that information may be used to harm someone. Tyrannical governments or unscrupulous indi-viduals may misuse information amassed about people to their dis-advantage. The more one knows about an individual, the greater one's power to damage him. A utilitarian might say that fears of this kind are the only reasonable ground for objecting in general to being watched. Eliza Doolittle resents Professor Higgins's recording her speech in Covent Garden because she believes that a girl of her class subject to so close a scrutiny must be in danger of police persecu-tion: "You dunno what it means to me. Theyll take away my char-acter and drive me on the streets for speaking to gentlemen." But the resentment of the bystanders is excited, not by some possible disad-vantageous consequence of the phonetician's ability to spot their origins by their accents, but by something else which is intrinsic to Higgins's performance. "See here," one says, "what call have you to know about people what never offered to meddle with you? . . . You take us for dirt under your feet, dont you? Catch you taking liberties with a gentleman!"[8] What this man resents is surely that Higgins is failing in respect for persons; he is treating people like objects or specimens – like "dirt" – and not like subjects with sensibilities and aspirations of their own, capable, as mere specimens are not, of reciprocal relations with the observer. This failure is, of course, precisely what Eliza, in her later incarnation – the ladylike crea-tion of Pygmalion-Higgins's artistry – complains of too.

Finding oneself an object of scrutiny, as the focus of someone else's attention, brings one to a new consciousness of oneself, as something seen through another's eyes. Indeed, according to Sar-tre, it is a necessary condition for knowing oneself *as* anything at all that one should conceive oneself as an object of scrutiny.[9] It is only through the regard of another that the observed becomes aware of himself as an object, knowable, having a determinate character, in principle predictable. His consciousness as subject of pure freedom, as originator and chooser, is at once assailed by it: He is fixed *as something*, with limited probabilities rather than infinite, indeterminate possibilities. Sartre's account of human re-lations is of an obsessional need to master an unbearable alien freedom that undermines one's belief in one's own freedom; for Ego is aware of Alter not only as a fact, an object in his world, but also as the subject of a quite independent world of Alter's own, wherein Ego himself figures as a mere object. The relationship between them is therefore essentially hostile. Each, doubting his own freedom, is driven to assert the primacy of his own subjectivity and to demand its acknowledgment by the other. But the struggle is self-frustrating: Alter's reassurance would be worthless to Ego unless it were freely given, for if it were not it would be just another fact of Ego's own subjective world, yet the freedom to give the reassurance would at once refute it, for Alter's freedom entails the *objective* appearance of Ego, as something determined, in Alter's world.

What Sartre conceived as a phenomenologically necessary dilemma reappears in R.D. Laing's *The Divided Self* [10] as a characteristically schizoid perception of the world, the response of a personality denied free development, trying to preserve itself from domination by hiding away a "real self" where it cannot be absorbed or overwhelmed. The schizoid cannot believe fully in his own existence as a person. He may need to be observed in order to be convinced that he exists, if only in someone else's world. Yet, resenting the necessity to be what the other perceives him to be, he may try at the same time to hide, often in irrationality. His predicament, like Sartre's, may seem to him not to arise from the *manner* of his being observed, but to be implicit in the very relation of observer to observed.

Sartre, however, does not show why the awareness of others as subjects must evoke so hostile a response. Even if it were true that my consciousness of my own infinite freedom is shaken by my being made aware that in the eyes of another I have only limited possibilities, still if I am not free, it is not his regard that confines me; his regard only draws my attention to a truth I was able formerly to disregard. And if I am free after all, then his regard makes no difference. And if there is really a dilemma here, may I not infer from it that the other sees me too, not only as object, but as possessing the same subjectivity as he does himself, and therefore has the same problem as I? Could this not be as much a bond between us as a source of resentment, each according the other the same dignity as at least a subject from his own point of view?

It is because the schizoid cannot believe in himself as a person that he cannot form such a bond, or accept the respectful regard of another. So every glance is a threat or an insult. Still, even for the nonschizoid, there are ways of looking at a person that do diminish him, that provide cause for offense as real as any physical assault.

274

Women complain of such looks as forms of sexual harassment. But that cannot be a sufficient reason, of course, either for the victim to go into hiding or for others to go around with their eyes shut. It does suggest, however, that if, as a doctor, one has occasion to make someone an object of scrutiny and study or, as a clinician, the topic for a lecture, the patient will have grounds for resentment if the doctor appears insensible to the fact that he is examining a person, to whom being observed makes a difference, and who will also have an independent view and evaluation of what is discovered or demonstrated by the examination.

It is a mistake to think that the only objection to such an examination is that an incautious examiner could cause damage to a sensitive patient's mental state, for that might sometimes be avoided by watching the patient secretly. To treat someone without respect is not to harm him – it is more like insulting him. Nor is it scrutiny as such that is offensive, but only the fact that the scrutiny is unlicensed.

The principle of privacy provides reasons, then, which restrict Alan's freedom of action in certain respects on account of the need for Betty's agreement. It is not the case, of course, that Betty's having a certain attitude toward *anything* that Alan proposes to do would alone be sufficient for her wishes to be a relevant consideration. She will certainly have attitudes and wishes about some actions of Alan's that do not affect her own enterprise at all; if she dislikes cruelty to animals and would be pleased if Alan stopped beating his donkey, that would not itself be a reason for Alan to stop. It is the conception of Betty as chooser, as engaged in a creative enterprise, that grounds reasons for others. So her preferences are considerations for Alan only if what Alan does makes a difference to the conditions under which she makes her choices, denying an option or changing the significance for her of acts which remain open. Betty may disapprove of Alan's watching Caroline or overhearing her conversation with Desmond, but Betty's own conditions for action remain unaffected. On the other hand, if Caroline knows that Alan is listening, his intrusion alters Caroline's consciousness of herself and of her experiences in relation to her world. Formerly self-forgetful, she may now be conscious of her opinions as candidates for Alan's approval or contempt. But even without self-consciousness of this kind, her immediate enterprise – her conversation with Desmond – may be changed for her merely by Alan's presence. I am not supposing a private conversation about Caroline's personal affairs. What is at issue is the change in the way Caroline apprehends

275

her own performance, whatever the topic. Alan's uninvited intrusion is an impertinence because he treats it as of no consequence that he may have effected a change in Caroline's perception of herself. Of course, no damage may have been done; Caroline may actually enjoy performing before an enlarged audience. But her wishes in the matter are always a relevant consideration, as Betty's are not, and in the absence of some overriding reason, if Caroline is inclined to object, she has legitimate grounds. True, there are situations, as in university common rooms, where there is a kind of conventional license to join ongoing conversations. A railway compartment offers a similar license in Italy but not in England. In such situations, if one does not wish to be overheard, one must either whisper or stay silent. Equally, there are conditions in which it would be rude to engage in a private conversation; polite guests do not whisper to each other at a dinner party. Conventions create public occasions where rights of privacy are overridden.

The underpinning of a claim not to be watched or listened to without leave will be more general if it can be grounded in this way on the principle of respect for persons, rather than on a utilitarian duty to avoid inflicting damage. Respect for persons will sustain an objection to secret watching that may do no actual harm to anyone. Covert observation – spying – is objectionable because it deliberately deceives a person about his world: It thwarts, on the basis of reasons that are not his own, the agent's attempts to make rational choices. The objection, then, is not that observing Alan would hurt his feelings. To protect his feelings by keeping him in ignorance of what was happening, so far from eliminating the injury to Alan, would exacerbate it by the further insult of deliberately falsifying his self-perception: Thinking himself master of his private world, he would behave the more intriguingly for his manipulator's ends. One cannot respect someone as engaged on an enterprise worthy of consideration if one knowingly and deliberately alters his conditions of action while concealing the fact from him.

The offense is different in this case from Alan's open intrusion on Caroline's conversation. There, Alan's attentions were liable to frustrate Caroline's attempt to communicate privately with Desmond, or, even if she had no such intention, it would be liable to affect her conversational enterprise by changing her perception of it, altering it by virtue only of her knowing that Alan was listening. In the case of covert observation, Caroline is unaware of Alan, yet she is wronged because Alan is deliberately "making a fool of her," by falsifying her beliefs about what she is about. Suppose her to be in a situation in which she might be observed but in which she chooses to act privately; for anyone to watch without her knowledge is to show disrespect not only for the privacy she has chosen, but for her as a chooser, since it implies a disregard for the way she chooses to present herself to the world. A policeman may treat suspected wrongdoers like this only if there are good grounds for believing in a need to frustrate what they are about, overriding their rights as persons to privacy. Psychiatrists may be justified in treating the insane in the same way, but only to the extent that the insane are incapable of rational choice and in need of tutelage, and that the goal of secret surveillance is the subject's own welfare. Insanity does not legitimize turning people into exhibits for public entertainment, however, as was the practice in former times.

The close connection between the general principle of privacy and the principle of respect for persons may account for much of the resentment evoked by the idea of a central data bank collating all that is known about an individual from his past contacts with government agencies or his past use of credit-granting facilities. Much has been made, of course, of the dangers of computerized data banks. The information supplied to and by them may be false or, if true, may still put a person in a false light by drawing attention, for instance, to delinquencies of a distant past now lived down. A good deal of legislative ingenuity has been exercised, accordingly, to devise appropriate safeguards against the use of information power. Yet for some objectors it altogether misses the point: It is resented that anyone, even a most trustworthy official, should be able at will to satisfy any curiosity, to possess himself of a composite picture which, even though accurate in detail, still permits him to interpret it in a way the subject finds humiliating, and is powerless to influence, because it is done without his knowledge, let alone his consent. One may feel humiliated when one regards the image of oneself that another sees as despicable, and whether or not one believes it to be just, one may be unable not to identify with it. Since what others know about him can radically affect a person's view of himself, to treat the collation of personal information about him as a purely technical problem of safeguards is to disregard his claim to consideration as a person to whom respect is due.

I have argued as if the principle of respect clearly defined the boundaries of the person. But this is not altogether clear. If someone stares at my face, I cannot help seeing his gaze as focused on me. I am no less self-conscious if I catch him scrutinizing the clothes I am wearing. But should I resent scrutiny of the clothes I am not wearing – a suit, perhaps, that I have given to a charity? Or of my car, in the street outside my home or in the service station? What counts for this purpose as *me*? It is not enough that I do not *want* something to be observed; for the principle of respect to be relevant, it must be something about my own person that is in question, otherwise any mere wish of mine would be a prima facie reason for everyone to refrain from observing and reporting on anything at all. And though prima facie reasons are not conclusive, this one seems no reason at all. For I do not make something a part of my person by having feelings about it. The principle of privacy proposed is that a person who desires that he himself should not be an object of scrutiny has a reasonable prima facie claim to immunity. But the ground is not in his desiring but in the relation between himself as an object of scrutiny and as a conscious, experiencing subject and agent. And it is clearly not enough for someone simply to say that something pertains to him as a person and therefore shares his immunity; he needs a reason for saying so.

The intimate connection between the concept of the self and one's body would seem to put that beyond question (though a schizoid perception of the world suggests that dissociation even of these closely linked concepts is not beyond the bounds of possibility). Beyond that point, cultural norms cannot be disregarded. In a possessive individualist culture in which a person's property is seen as an extension of his personality, an index to his social standing, a measure of his achievement, or an expression of his taste, to look critically at his clothes or his car is to look critically at him. In other cultures the standards might well be different. The notion each person has of his own extension, of the boundaries of his personality – what can count for him as an occasion for personal pride or shame – is unquestionably culture-variant. Consequently, the application even of a quite general principle of privacy will be affected by culturally variant norms, regarding, for instance, family or property.

## B. *The force of the general principle of privacy*

The principle amounts only to a prima facie ground for limiting the freedom of others to observe and report, placing upon them a burden of justification but not overriding any special reasons for observing and reporting. Unsupported by special reasons, it may

278

be quite insufficient to sustain a case for legal restraints; the protection of privacy in general may be less important, perhaps, than the danger to political freedom from legal restrictions on reporting. An obligation to show a reasonable public interest in every instance of reporting would result in an overtimorous press. The courts have been properly wary of recognizing rights that might discourage if not disable the press from publicizing what *ought* to be exposed.

General principles are reasons, but not conclusive reasons. They point to what needs to be justified, where the onus lies, and what can count as justification. Consider the difficult case of the privacy of celebrities. According to a learned American judge, the law "recognizes a legitimate public curiosity about the personality of celebrities, and about a great deal of otherwise private and personal information about them."[11] But is all curiosity equally legitimate, or might there be something about the kind of celebrity that legitimizes curiosity about some aspects of the person but not about others? Is there no difference, say, between a serious historian's curiosity about what (and who) prompted President Johnson's decision not to run for office a second time and the curiosity to which the Sunday gossip columnists appeal? If the person is in the public eye for some performance he intends to be public or which is in its nature public, such as conducting an orchestra, this may make "human interest" stories about him more entertaining and exciting than stories about an unknown. But the fact that many people enjoy that kind of entertainment is not a reason for overriding the principle of privacy; for though there is a presumptive liberty to do whatever there is not a reason not to do, the claim to have whatever one enjoys is rationally restricted. To treat even an entertainer's life simply as material for entertainment is to pay no more regard to him as a person than to an animal in a menagerie. Of course, anyone who courts publicity, as many entertainers do, can hardly complain if he is understood to be offering a general license. But merely to be a celebrity – even a willing celebrity – does not disable someone from claiming the consideration due to a person. Admittedly, it opens up a range of special claims to information about him, to override his general claim to privacy. Candidates for appointment to the United States Supreme Court must expect to be quizzed about their business integrity. Or to take a rather different case, because an eminent conductor participates in a public activity with a public tradition, anyone choosing conducting as a profession must expect his musical experience – where he was trained, who has influenced his interpretations – to be matters of legitimate interest to others concerned as he is with music. But this is not a warrant for prying into other facts about him that have nothing at all to do with his music: his taste in wines, perhaps, or in women. The principle of privacy will properly give way in one area, but would stand in any other to which the special overriding grounds were irrelevant. For the principle is not limited in its application; it is a prima facie reason for immunity from publication in respect of *anything* a person does.

# 15

## Interests in privacy

### 1. Private affairs

To claim immunity on the ground that an inquiry is an intrusion into one's *private affairs* is to make an argumentative move of quite a different kind from an appeal to the general principle of privacy. For the concept of private affairs entrenches the privacy of certain special areas far more strongly than the mere presumptive immunity of the general principle. To justify an intrusion into these areas, one must have not merely a reason, but one strong enough to override special reasons for *not* intruding. So while the interests of phonetic science might justify Professor Higgins's impertinence in Covent Garden, they would not be good enough reasons for bugging Eliza's bedroom.

One's private affairs relate not to the principle of privacy but to the interests that people have in privacy. The activities and experiences commonly thought to fall within the special area of private affairs are diverse and in some cases at least culture dependent. Some seem to have no rational ground at all for being private. Why should the bodily functions which in our culture are appropriately performed in solitude include defecation but not eating? Of course, so long as some acts are assigned to this category anyone who has internalized the social norms will be painfully embarrassed if seen doing them. Embarrassment is indeed the culturally appropriate response in a society with the concept of *pudenda;* anyone not displaying it may be censured as brazen or insensitive. But while it would be rational to care about privacy in these conditions to avoid painful embarrassment, the rationale would depend on a conventional norm that may itself have no rationale.

Not all privacy interests are like this, however. I promised in the previous chapter to produce a typology of privacy interests. These fall broadly into three categories, the personal and intimate, the proprietorial-commercial, and the freedom based.

## A. *The privacy of personal relations*

The claim to privacy in respect of personal affairs is partly grounded in the conception of a person as a responsible chooser and partly in the related excellences of integration and autonomy. I discussed in Chapter 10 the problem of personal identity which confronts people in a culture with plural traditions, undergoing rapid technological change and subject to unprecedented social and geographical mobility. The problem is to recognize or create in oneself a coherent set of beliefs, to locate oneself among the diverse range of competing possibilities available in such a society, adjusting to external pressures and accommodating oneself to unforeseen alterations in one's expectations for the future. Managing such an internal economy is complicated by the need to assume a variety of roles, to project a set of self-images or personae onto the world. In his role of father a person projects a different image or persona from his other roles as bank clerk or club secretary. These varying projections are not necessarily false or inauthentic; one manifests lack of integrity or inauthenticity only when, in shifting roles, one shifts as well the values and principles that inform them. One's roles may together constitute a reasonably coherent and consistent whole – a personality.

Consistency, however, is something we may aim at but only imperfectly achieve. The management of so complex a set of relations and the self-assessments and revisions implicit in it, would be quite impossible if one could not insulate one life-sector from another, if one could not choose what of oneself to reveal here, what there. One underpinning of privacy claims, then, is the interest a person has in establishing, sustaining, and developing a personality. Taken off his guard, discovered in one role while projecting the persona of another, a person is embarrassed because he has lost control of his personae in an ambiguous situation and is at a loss to know what response is appropriate in terms of the complex notion he has of himself.

While, on the one side, we have an interest in protecting our privacy for the sake of the management of our individual personalities, we have an interest, on the other, in protecting the privacy of our personal relations. By "personal relations" I mean relations between persons which are considered valuable and important at least as much because of the quality of each person's attitude to another as for what each does to, or for, the other. All characteristically human relations – as distinct from relations that might

exist between stones or wombats – involve some element, however small, of role expectancy. We structure our relations with
other people according to an understanding of *what* they are and
what accordingly is due to and from them. That may exhaust the
relation. If the railway booking clerk gives me the correct ticket in
exchange for my fare, he has fulfilled his function. The point of
the relation calls for no more than this. The grating which sepa-
rates us, with just enough space to push through a ticket or a
coin, appropriately symbolizes the impersonality of the relation.
One cannot be indifferent to the booking clerk's performance, but
one need not attend to his personality.

The relation between mother and son or husband and wife is
necessarily more than this, or if it is not, that instance is defective.
Here too there are role expectancies, but each person will fulfill
them differently. There is room to be a father in this or that way.
But more than that, only a part of what it is to be a father has been
met when the specific duties of the role have been fulfilled. Beyond
that the value of the relation depends on a personal understanding
between the parties and on whether and how they care about each
other. Father and son may be meticulous in the performance of
their roles, but if they are quite indifferent to each other, the relationship misses much of its point. Relationships between friends or
lovers are still less role-structured than family relations, though
even here there are conventional patterns – gifts on ritual occasions, forms of wooing, and so on. But they are primarily symbols:
Their point is to communicate a feeling or an attitude, to reassure,
perhaps, or to make a proposal. And though they could be gone
through even if the feeling did not exist, the performance would be
a pretense or a deception, parasitic on its principal point.

Personal relations can be of public concern; children may need
protection, for instance, from certain kinds of corrupting relations
with adults. But while it may be possible and desirable to prevent
such relations altogether, there is little that third parties can do to
regulate or reshape them. By inducing the booking clerk to do his
job more efficiently, or passengers to state their destinations more
clearly, the railway staff controller can improve the relations between them. But this is because he can keep them up to the mark;
they are all interested exclusively in role performance, and each
has a clear notion of the standard that the other's performance
should reach. But friends can be kept up to the mark only by one
another. There is no adequate mark that an outsider could use to
assess them, for friendship is not confined by role requirements.[1]

To intrude on personal relations of this kind may be much worse than useless. People do take their troubles, of course, to friends or marriage guidance counselors, but this is to invite the counselor to become, albeit in a restricted way, a party to the relationship. Or rather, the parties enter into a relationship with the counselor, the success of which depends on the latter's resolve to keep it a purely second-order relation, demanding of him, however, a sensitive and reticent understanding of the first. Personal relations are exploratory and creative; they flourish with care and attention, requiring continuous adjustment as the personalities of the parties are modified by experience, both of one another and of the relationship's environment. Such relations could not exist without conditions that excluded intruders. One cannot have a personal relationship with all comers, nor carry on a personal conversation under the conditions of an open seminar.

Charles Fried has argued that a necessary feature of love and friendship is a "sharing of information about one's actions, beliefs, or emotions which one does not share with all, and which one has the right not to share with anyone. By conferring this right, privacy creates the moral capital which we spend in friendship and love."[2] I confess that I do not know how culture-bound these notions are. Other cultures tolerate much higher levels of publicity in personal relations and a degree of curiosity about everyone that would be indecent in middle-class America, Britain, or Australia. They seem, nevertheless, to manifest love and friendship. It is arguable, however, that the type of personal relationship which is valued as intimate in our own culture simply does not exist in more open cultures. The closed bourgeois nuclear family promotes a small group introversion, an intensive mutual exploration of a few personalities and a preoccupation with their interrelations. This produces a personality type that looks for similar explorations in its friendships and conjugal relations. The novel, an art form characteristic of modern European culture, reflects such preoccupations; sagas, epics, medieval romances, and classical dramas do so to a much smaller degree. Beyond this, within the privacy of the closed group, mutualities can evolve marked by reciprocal concern, a deep commitment to the development of the relationship itself as a common enterprise.

Though personal relations need some freedom from interference, different kinds of interference affect them differently. An extreme kind is the attempt to participate – to turn, for instance, a relation *à deux* into one *à trois*. The attentions of observer and

284

reporter are not necessarily always so objectionable. A strong-minded couple might pursue their own course undisturbed under the eyes of a reasonably tactful and self-effacing paying guest. Of course, the uncommitted observer makes most of us self-conscious and inhibits spontaneity in personal relations. I do not know whether this is a psychologically necessary fact about human beings or only a culturally conditioned one. Certainly, personal relations are not impossible in places where people live perforce on top of one another. But they call for a good deal of tact and goodwill from the bystanders; there is some evidence that in such conditions, people develop psychological avoidance arrangements – a capacity for not noticing and a corresponding confidence that one will not be noticed – that substitute for physical seclusion.[3]

There is, of course, a darker side. In the privacy of the small group, the strong may cruelly exploit the submissiveness of the economically or emotionally dependent whose sufferings are decently veiled from the world outside. Contemporary communal life-styles and the encounter-group movement, which encourages complete self-disclosure to a more or less random collection of strangers as a way of freeing oneself from guilt and shame, are partly reactions to these darker sides of the privacy of the nuclear family. According to Bruno Bettelheim,[4] the kibbutz movement in Israel was in origin a rejection, especially by young Jewish women, of the stifling introversion of the east and central European Jewish family of the turn of the century, a turning outward to a larger group which would make fewer intense emotional demands.

Other writers have criticized preoccupations with privacy, particularly the privacy of family relations, as part of the pathology of post-Renaissance bourgeois society. Consider Edmund Leach's strictures:

> In the past, kinsfolk and neighbours gave the individual continuous moral support throughout his life. Today the domestic household is isolated. The family looks inward upon itself; there is an intensification of emotional stress between husband and wife, and parents and children. The strain is greater than most of us can bear. Far from being the basis of the good society, the family, with its narrow privacy and tawdry secrets, is the source of all our discontents.[5]

Paul Halmos, too, speaks of "a hypertrophied family devotion and family insularity" arising from the attempt by contemporary man "to transcend his solitude. . . ."

[He] may finally negate his apartness in an obsessional affirmation of family ties. . . . Friendship and companionship, when manifestly present in the marital couple, is regarded as an instance of great virtue even when it is equally manifestly absent in all other relationships. Furthermore, the nepotistic solidarity of the family is another symptom of the contemporary attitude according to which the world is hostile and dangerous and the family is the only solid rock which is to be protected against all comers.[6]

To concede this diagnosis need not weaken the argument for the right to exclude, for it may imply only that in modern societies we seek personal relations with too few people, the ones we form being consequently overtaxed by the emotional weight they are forced to bear. On the other hand, I argued in Chapter 12 that mutualities, the closest kind of personal relations, were necessarily limited to a few people because more would entail an information overload.

The importance of personal relations suggests a limit to what can be done by antidiscrimination laws. Whatever the justification for interference with the freedom to discriminate in, for instance, hiring workers, there are some kinds of choice where a person's reasons for his preferences and antipathies are less important than the fact that he has them. If domestic personal relations are valued, constituent members of the family must be left to decide who can be accepted into it, for example, as a lodger or, even more, as an adopted child. Club membership may be different. True, we join clubs to cultivate personal relations, such as friendships, but we do not expect to form such relations with every member. The mere presence in the clubroom of people whom one would not invite to join one's circle of intimates need not endanger the relations within that circle. Nevertheless, if the club's members are in general antipathetic to a particular group, to deny the right to exclude may create tensions which defeat the otherwise acceptable end for which the club exists.

Of course, merely having prejudices gives no one the right to discriminate unfairly and irrationally in all his relations at whatever cost to the personal dignity of an outsider. Insofar as the relations can be specified in terms of role performances, it is reasonable to demand that discriminations be based on relevant differences. But to the degree that the point of the relationship has built into it a quality of life depending on reciprocal caring, it qualifies as an area of privacy and is therefore immune from regulation. In times of racial tension there may be overriding reasons, of course,

286

for discouraging the forming of exclusive clubs whose rules can only seem inflammatory. But this is to invoke reasons which in the special conditions override the reasons for privacy based on personal relations.

I observed in Chapter 11 that Bruno Bettelheim formed the impression from his observation of kibbutz-reared youngsters that they exhibited a more superficial sensitivity and a lesser capacity for deep emotional attachments and human understanding than do children reared in Western nuclear families. On the other hand, they were less liable to neurosis, had a much surer grasp of their identity and a corresponding capacity for coping with stress. There are certainly communitarian societies in which de facto privacy is very small indeed, but whose members would not consider this a defect. They would claim that their members neither valued nor needed privacy – that for them it was not an interest in any sense, since they were better people for the lack of it.

It is possible no doubt to debate whether the introverts of Western bourgeois society are more admirable human beings than the extroverts of more open societies. We might ponder whether, if we had the planning of a society from scratch, we should do well to equip it with cultural ideals like the cultivation of individuality, autonomy, and mutuality at the cost of a relatively high incidence of neurosis. Perhaps it would be better to encourage the uninhibited extroversion of communal living where veiling is indecent, even at the cost of acceptance of less refined sensitivities and greater conformity of life-styles. Social prophets may see themselves making such God-like choices. For most of us, however, it is more urgent to find ways of living better within the values and the societies we know. We are largely what our social inheritance has made us, and while we can look critically at some of our values, there is no rational way of criticizing all at once. The judgments we make about our privacy arrangements must take the rest of our cultural ideals largely as we find them. Individuals like ourselves in our kind of culture, then, do have an interest in privacy in the management of the internal economy of their own personalities and of their personal relations with others.

From the primary interests that people have in the privacy of personal relations derive specific interests in privacy (a) of personal place, (b) of personal information, (c) of personal attention.

**a. Privacies of personal place.** I mean by this the ability to restrict entry to the places – mainly of course to homes, but also to hotel bedrooms, private clubs, gardens, and so on – in which people rely on individual seclusion or on being together in groups of their choice. Intruders in such personal places deny us release from Mr. Prufrock's need to "prepare a face to meet the faces that we meet." They constrain the easy intercourse of friends that depends so much on the unspoken understandings and the stock of common but excluding experiences, and they impede the intimacies of lovers, who seem to need seclusion even in cultures where privacy in general is not easily found or particularly highly regarded.[7]

**b. Privacies of personal information.** By this I mean the ability to prevent unauthorized access to facts about oneself that "give one away" – that if freely available would impair one's capacity to manage the complex system of appearances with which one confronts the world. I include, too, information about one's intimate relations with others, which may also need delicacy in management, and publication of which would tend to fix them as public, objective facts. When we are made to see ourselves as others see us, we do not necessarily see ourselves more truly. Sartre describes in *Saint Genet* how the boy, Jean Genet, caught out in petty theft, is *called* a thief. The propertyless foundling's innocent way of dealing with a sense of personal inadequacy in a propertied world by making some small thing his own suddenly becomes for him a total characterization. The public image of himself as thief imposes itself upon him as a reality he cannot evade. So he becomes a thief. Similarly, the eye of the *voyeur* can impose its soiled vision on the self-consciousness of its object, to affront and spoil what it sees. The dislike of data-banks referred to earlier might in part be accounted for in this way.

**c. Privacies of attention.** Such privacies concern the ability to exclude intrusions that force one to direct attention to themselves rather than to matters of one's own choosing. Clamorous noises, unpleasant smells, and importunate solicitations, in person or by telephone, can be a nuisance anywhere at any time. They are additionally objectionable as invasions of privacy when they penetrate into private places or intrude upon one's attention at times one calls one's own. Interference by the boss with one's daydreams in the office is not such an intrusion because at that time and place one is not at liberty to attend to matters of one's own choosing.

Part at least, then, of what is meant by "private affairs" is the range of intimate, personal interests, and if the extensions of "intimate" and "personal" are clear in a given society, however they may vary between societies, we may be able to give a reasonably precise account of the extent of private affairs for *that* society. The trouble begins when divergent standards develop within a society. References to "intimate personal interests" are not as informative for the United States, Australia, or Great Britain in 1986 as they would have been a half-century earlier, before the sexual revolution.

## B. *Proprietorial/commercial interests in privacy*

Between activities that are public, in the sense that the agent carries them out in the course of official duties or is answerable for them in terms of the public interest, and those that are intimate and personal lies a class of private activities which very evidently affect the well-being of others but in which individuals exercise their discretion without public responsibility. The organization of private property, and the market economy resting upon it (what economists refer to as "the private sector") may be regarded as a particular kind of practice or game or a set of interlocking games; provided only that they abide by the ground rules, individuals and groups are allowed to make their own moves according to their judgment of their best interests, without being called upon to justify their actions to a wider public.

This conception of privacy is close to the core of the liberal tradition. The totalitarian claims that everything a person does and is has significance for the society at large. He sees the state as the self-conscious organization of society for the well-being of society; the social significance of our actions and relations overrides any other. Consequently, the public or political universe is all-inclusive, *all* roles are public, and every function, whether political, economic, artistic, or religious, can be interpreted as involving a public responsibility. The liberal, by contrast, claims not merely a private capacity, in which he is not responsible to the state for what he does, subject to respect for the minimal rights of others; he claims besides that the private is the residual category, that the onus of justification is on anyone who claims that he is accountable.

From these primary interests derive each player's proprietorial/commercial interests in privacy, such as the exclusion of restraints

289

and inquiries by public authorities, but also his interest that competing players be restrained from using practices that give them an unfair advantage over him, or permit them to use his assets to their own advantage without his consent. Much of this area is already protected by legal rights of property, prohibiting trespass on private premises, domestic and commercial alike, the stealing of documents, infringement of copyright, and so on. But industrial espionage involving neither trespass nor theft is not at present prohibited, for there is no copyright in ideas as such.

The distinction between personal and proprietorial/commercial interests in privacy is brought out sharply by the following cases.

A recording company was restrained from publishing a record cover bearing, without their consent, photographs of a pair of ballroom dancers named Henderson; it was held that the record cover would have falsely represented them as being associated with the company.[8] Morison comments that the tort of passing off, which provided the Hendersons with their remedy, cannot be invoked except where there is a misrepresentation and cannot apply where the statement is true. Since a person has an "interest in preventing unauthorised use of his name, likeness and life history" even when there is no misrepresentation, the remedy is by implication inadequate.

The nature of this alleged interest is, however, worth examination. William John Sidis,[9] who had been a child prodigy, became the subject of a cruelly revealing *New Yorker* article years after he had withdrawn into obscurity. Abigail Roberson[10] took to her bed suffering from severe nervous shock when her photograph unexpectedly appeared advertising flour. Their interests were unambiguously *personal* interests in privacy. Abigail had an interest in not having public attention focused upon her when she wanted to go about undistinguished. But professional dancers could hardly claim to be shy of the public gaze. The Hendersons' interest was much more akin to property – but property in the intangible assets of name, identity, and reputation, which no one else ought to be able to exploit without permission. The power to endorse products for purposes of advertisement, which for professional sportsmen, for instance, is a commercial asset, has no market value if it can be used freely, and people should not be able to exploit other people's assets except on a proper business footing and with their agreement.

Superficially similar cases of unauthorized publicity may turn out, then, to affect interests of quite different types, to which one should attach rather different weights. Interests of the proprietor-

290

ial/commercial type derive from the requirements of certain kinds of social "games." Their urgency depends on how necessary they are to the proper conduct of those games, and on whether it is important to society that such games be sustained, even to the detriment of other interests, such as the effective and profitable advertisement of records and flour.

Consider the case of credit bureaus. Buying on credit has become so large a part of our commercial practice that its smooth functioning is considered a major public interest. The responsibility for checking the creditworthiness of a buyer rests, however, squarely on the seller, who can reasonably demand freedom to satisfy himself that he has a fair chance of being paid, and this is in the interests of buyers too, since the greater the seller's risk, the more he will charge. It seems unreasonable to complain, therefore, that credit agencies maintain a bank of information on borrowers, supplied for a fee to hire-purchase finance companies, department stores, banks, and so on. Anyone wanting credit on minimal security must accept that, since the lender bears the risk, he must reassure himself as best he can.[11] Of course, players in the commercial game are entitled to protection against false or misleading dossiers, which unfairly deny them borrowing opportunities. But given the social endorsement of the total practice, it is hard to see that the existence of an accurate dossier, and its availability to anyone with whom the borrower seeks to do business, could be an objectionable invasion of privacy. A bad payment record, if true, undercuts any grievance that passing it from one firm to another deprives the borrower of further borrowing opportunities. Reasonable machinery for supplying a person with reasons for a refusal of credit, and opportunities for him to challenge and set the record straight should meet most defensible complaints in this area.

The game analogy helps to distinguish the privacy issues regarding credit information from cases in which a debtor is harassed by intrusive telephone calls from debt collectors, who may also write to his relatives or to his employer, all methods cheaper and swifter than recourse to the courts. If someone fails to pay, it is fair that he should be less favorably placed in the commercial game. After all, no one complains that having his solid commercial *reliability* noised about is a breach of privacy. But a person's debts do not warrant his creditor's seeking, in preference to legal action, a *point d'appui* outside the game, intruding into personal affairs, upsetting his family life, or humiliating him in front of his friends. For that attacks a quite different set of interests deriving not from social games but from the individual's basic interest in the management of his own personality, and therefore of a quite different order of importance. A useful rule of thumb is that no pressure which could not be used in principle against an impersonal corporate enterprise ought to be used in business against an individual; whatever pressure can be put on the proprietorial/commercial interests of the one can be reasonably used against the other; but measures that can exert no pressure on an impersonal agent attack quite other interests when used against individual persons.

## C. Freedom-based interests in privacy

Privacy is frequently referred to as a kind, or a part, of freedom. In a trivial sense it is true: Someone who enjoys privacy is free from observation. But in that sense any valued state, such as health, would be a part of freedom – freedom from its opposite, disease. That is hardly a substantial reason for associating freedom and privacy.

John Stuart Mill's distinction in *On Liberty* between self- and other-regarding actions is sometimes taken as defining the scope of private affairs, in which neither government nor society could have a legitimate interest. So in the debate on victimless crimes, such as (in some jurisdictions) homosexual acts, the private use of narcotic drugs, or pornography, it is often claimed that the criminal law is improperly invading privacy. The famous formulation of a right to privacy, first by Judge Cooley, then by Warren and Brandeis, as "the right to be let alone" has tended to encourage this association.

Yet Mill's essay is not about privacy, in the sense of a right not to have to share information, places, and so on with unwanted intruders. It is about criteria for public regulation of individuals' actions, whether done in private or in public. Victimless crimes do not qualify for regulation by Mill's criteria because they are held not to be "other-regarding"; Mill would claim, on that account, that they are not to be interfered with, that one is at liberty to do as one likes in those matters. He does not claim that one has a special interest in excluding intruders, voyeurs, or reporters when one does such acts. If smoking were a strictly self-damaging vice, legislating to prohibit it would violate not a right to privacy but the general principle of freedom from interference, grounded on the principle of respect for persons.

*Griswold v. Connecticut*[12] illustrates the distinction. The United States Supreme Court struck down the Connecticut law prohibiting the use of contraceptives, because it "operates directly on an intimate relation between husband and wife . . . a right of privacy older than the Bill of Rights." Hyman Gross commented: "In the Griswold situation there had been an attempt by government to regulate personal affairs, not get acquainted with them, and so there was an issue regarding autonomy [that is, noninterference with individual freedom of action] and not privacy."[13] The *Griswold* decision might reasonably be read, however, as invalidating legislation regulating marital intimacy, not because that is intrinsically objectionable, but because it could be done only by resorting to objectionable means of collecting information. Westin asks, with reference to "vice laws" generally, whether "the containment function . . . can justify the spread of surveillance into the large areas of public life that are bound to be involved."[14]

Admittedly, not all the paradigm invasions of privacy (for instance, harassment by debt collectors) could be accurately described as "attempts to get acquainted" with private affairs, but there is a reasonably determinate set of problems having to do with the collection of information by observation or inquiry, and its dissemination, which is not naturally subsumed under considerations of freedom of action, rights of property, or personal security, while having certain things in common with all three. It will be more convenient, therefore, to confine discussion of interests in privacy to this narrower determinate set rather than to adopt a more inclusive interpretation. The analytical edge of the concept of privacy will be blunted if, even in respect of intimate, personal relations and activities, it is invoked to restrain not only access to information, publication, and physical intrusion, but also regulation of the relations and the practices themselves. The problem of determining rights to privacy is complex enough, without subsuming under it the entire question of the limits of state interference.

Nevertheless, a person's freedom may be threatened if someone else has access to information about him making him vulnerable to discrimination, victimization, or blackmail. Not that one has a grievance whenever someone seeks or obtains such information. Prospective employers quite properly ask previous employers about applicants' competence. It is rather that employers, or patrons of various kinds, are likely to discriminate on irrelevant grounds – of race, perhaps, or religion. Someone dependent on them for benefits has an evident interest in revealing only what he chooses about such matters. The power of an influential class to withhold benefits from heretics and dissidents, coupled with the power to pool information electronically, is a real threat to freedom of religious and political opinion. Complaints about employers' questionnaires, personality probes, and polygraph tests rest on the same kind of interest in keeping to oneself facts that might be damaging and are not relevant to the job in question.

The problem of information control is not, of course, new. We have to rely on our doctors, bankers, and lawyers not only not to blackmail us with the information we entrust to them, but also to prevent leakage to others who might. In one respect, replacing files with computer disks has made such information less, not more accessible, since only someone with the necessary technical knowledge can retrieve it. But economy in storage space, the quantity of data that can be banked, the immeasurably greater speed and economy of effort with which expert handlers can retrieve it, and the possibility of sorting through numberless documents in search of someone who will be vulnerable to pressure, present quite new threats to freedom. Police records are particularly sensitive. If a person's criminal past can be readily available to prospective employers, his chance of rehabilitation is very much reduced. It has been alleged that one reason why industrial firms employ retired policemen as security officers is that they are well versed in the technique of obtaining information from the police criminal records office. There are also many different kinds of illegality committed for various reasons, but they may all look much of a muchness on a police file, and those whose brushes with the law have been politically motivated may fairly feel particularly vulnerable. If, as I suppose, perfect leak control is impossible, and a great deal more occurs than we can feel comfortable about, the chance of leakage must always count against the setting up of yet another personal data bank.

## 2. Privacy and competing interests

I remarked earlier that privacy is a latecomer to liberal thought. Despite pointers such as *Prince Albert v. Strange and Others*,[15] English courts have been slow to concede such a right. Possessing, by contrast, a constitutional Bill of Rights in the first ten Amendments, American lawyers are more accustomed than English lawyers to seeking support for their clients' claims in broad statements of universal rights. Though no right of privacy is explicitly included in the Bill of Rights, they have learned to extend proclaimed rights to areas relatively remote from the classic paradigms. But even in the United States the right to privacy gained recognition only at the turn of the century. Of course, interests that would now be called interests in privacy were protected alike by English and American laws well before that. Rights of property defended a person's interest in excluding uninvited people from his house, and Prince Albert's case extended protection to a list of his etchings. The law of defamation protected a person's honor and reputation; his personal security was protected by laws against assault; various torts, like passing off, guarded other interests that are now grouped together in discussions of privacy. But it was exceptional, though not absolutely unheard of, for anyone to refer to a specific right of privacy. I attribute the emergent awareness of this right to social changes of two kinds, the first cultural, the second technological.

If privacy interests have long been protected by other branches of the law, that is because they were seen under different descriptions. One was entitled to exclude unwanted people from one's house because one owned it or had corresponding user rights as tenant in legal possession, just as one might exclude someone from one's barnyard or workshop. Post-Renaissance individualism provided the ideological ground for the interest in privacy, and growing social complexity generated the need for it, but not until relative affluence enabled people to enjoy exclusive places – personal bedrooms in nuclear-family houses, personal studies – were interests in privacy as such articulated. Technological changes highlighted these new-found interests, however, by threatening them in hitherto unimaginable ways. If one could exclude neighbors' or police curiosity by closing the front door and drawing the curtains, property rights were sufficient to preserve one's interest in "being let alone." But electronic devices make it possible for inquisitive people to let one's property alone while still intruding on one's privacy. Again, mass literacy, cheap mass newspapers, and the electronic media have made one's private affairs potentially the subject of gossip at several million breakfast tables. Interests once perceived variously under other descriptions now came to be perceived under a new collective description, "privacy," as a new *telos* or set of closely related *telé* brought together what were formerly seen as unrelated.

As a newcomer, however, privacy has to insert itself into the community of acknowledged and established rights, and others are required to make way. Freedom of the press – a very well-respected right, which its subjects have been valiant to defend –

295

must give ground if everyone has the right to control journalists' attempts to obtain and disseminate information about him. So too would acknowledged public interests in the control of crime and in the efficient and economical administration of social welfare and fiscal policies. The problem is frequently said to be one of "balancing," "the process of compromise between competing needs and demands, which is the normal business of *legislatures*."[16] Yet the diversity of interests claiming protection from a newly proclaimed right to privacy, and the complex impact of such a right on existing interests, make it virtually impossible to legislate comprehensively and in detail for all the many different kinds of conflict. An alternative is to present the courts with a statute recognizing a new general principle of law, breach of which would constitute a tort, but not attempting to settle substantive conflicts in advance. That would leave the judges to do the "balancing." Many authorities are reluctant however to leave so much to the courts; balancing values, they maintain, is a political, not a judicial task. Though judges are accustomed to resolving conflicts of claims in other areas, here there would be no guidance from a tradition of interpretation, embodied in a wealth of precedent fleshing out the basic principles. For the principles of property, protection of reputation, and so forth which inform existing precedents would not be the ones on which plaintiffs in explicitly privacy cases would now be relying. Some jurisdictions have temporized, setting up exploratory committees empowered to negotiate settlements for particular grievances, and to make recommendations piecemeal for quite specific legislation as experience recommends, while encouraging the development of voluntary professional codes.

The metaphor of "balancing" or "weighing," with its image of weights held in a balance or in the hands, is not altogether perspicuous when applied to arguments and claims. For one thing, weighing and balancing suggest the achievement of a state of equilibrium – equal weights – while judgment requires the determination of an outcome because some reasons "outweigh" others. More important than this, however, is the consideration that judging claims and reasons generally proceeds *seriatim*. There is commonly a presumption of right, which counterclaims are then designed to override. These in turn may be undercut or overridden, as may be those adduced against them in their turn. Admittedly, deciding whether a claim has indeed been undercut or whether a counterclaim overrides may itself demand judgment, and secondary disputes employing precisely similar tactics can develop at each point in the argument. It will always help in settling such disputes to understand precisely what kind of argument is going on. To describe it as one in which "considerations are being weighed" or "balanced" is not helpful, because the metaphor does not really illumine the process.[17]

## A. Undercutting arguments

**a. Forfeiting by abuse.** A subject might forfeit protection of his interest in privacy by abusing it to commit a criminal act. A prima facie case against someone may fairly justify the issue of a search warrant for his arrest and search and for forcing a way into private premises to execute it. Again, abuse of another person's legally protected interests can undercut a privacy claim, to justify forcing an entry to save a victim from serious bodily harm. Legislation to protect children from cruel abuse by their parents is only slightly more problematic. If there is disagreement about the propriety of interfering in particular cases, that may not be because a principle is in question, but because the amount of violence used in, say, physical chastisement is differently assessed. Child battering and wife bashing, however, are abuses that uncontroversially undercut the claim to the privacy of the family home.

There is no need in such a case to resort to the puzzling metaphor of "balancing." The claim to privacy is undercut because this is not what the right to privacy is for. The grounds suggested earlier for viewing privacy as an interest or set of interests warranting protection did not include having the opportunity to bash anyone, nor does such an opportunity count as a condition for developing personal relations. Rights are important in relation to their *telé*. When rights *R* and *R'* conflict, it is useful to ask whether, should *R* defeat *R'*, the *telé* would really be promoted, or whether this would be a case of converting to an improper use the normative resource that *R* confers.

Admittedly, this doctrine has practical dangers. A common enough way of attacking exercises of important political freedoms is to say that they are being abused. Claiming that the workers are using industrial action for political ends, to protect, say, the national health service from financial cutbacks, is a way of limiting or even attacking the right to strike: The *telos* of that right, some might say, is to secure better conditions of work and higher wages, not to secure political ends. Precisely what a right is for may be highly controversial, and when it is, the general interest in a free and tolerant society counsels that our interpretations be as little restrictive as may be. Nevertheless, the *procedure* of inquiry is correct; though we may not always agree about *telé*, or about what counts as abuse, deciding upon the extent of a right, where the interests it protects impinges on other rights or on public interests, must involve asking whether this interest is of the kind that the right ought to be understood to protect. If not, the claim to protection, to the exercise of the right in these circumstances, is undercut.

This dialectical process is illustrated by Hyman Gross's treatment of the conflict between the individual interest in privacy and the "basic social interest in making available information about people, in exploring the personal aspects of human affairs, in stimulating and satisfying curiosity about others." His object is to sustain "the privilege to compromise privacy for news and other material whose primary purpose is to impart information, but to deny such privileged status to literary and other art, to entertainment, and generally to any appropriation for commercial purposes," such as the unauthorized use of a portrait in advertising. The criterion, he suggests, is that "[u]nauthorized *use* of another person – whether for entertainment, artistic creation, or economic gain – is offensive. . . . We . . . suffer a loss of autonomy whenever the power to place us in free circulation is exercised by others, but we consider such loss offensive only when another person assumes the control of which we are deprived, when we are used and not merely exposed. . . . The difference is between managing another person as a means to one's own ends, which is offensive, and acting merely as a vehicle of presentation (though not gratuitously) to satisfy established social needs, which is not offensive."[18]

What Gross refers to as "the basic social interest" in the imparting of information about people, is the *telos* of the right to make private information public. This interest is manifold. There is, for instance, the specific interest of any citizen in knowing about candidates for public office. But there is also a broad social interest in making available a great diversity of experience. We need to know about many kinds of person, many life-styles, about the vicissitudes of other people's lives, if we are not to be confined each within the narrow limits of his own experience, with sympathies restricted to his immediate family and acquaintances. Something can be done to preserve anonymity in reporting, but if news stories could not generally be backed by identification, we should have no way of telling truth from titillating fantasies. To say that privacy ought only to be breached in the public interest does not help, for we do not know in advance what is in the public interest and what is not. Only after a number of cases have been reported, each for the sake only of its individual newsworthiness, may we find that we have stumbled on a social problem.

That is the case for the privilege to publicize, overriding the claim to privacy. But the case may still be partially undercut. We do not need to sacrifice everything to the god of news. Anything reported more with a view to the entertainment of the reader, listener, or viewer than for his enlightenment, and which disregards the feelings and personal dignity of the subject in a manner or to a degree unwarranted by the end of informing the public about *this* matter, cannot claim privilege on the grounds of society's interest in being informed. Many close-up shots of unsuspecting spectators in televised games, giving prominence to personal features or behavior that a person might well feel embarrassed to have highlighted in this way, would fall within Gross's excluded area, as the *use* of a person for entertainment.

b. **Surrendering privacy by consent.** A claim to privacy can be undercut by a plea of consent to publicity. Anyone appearing in a public place wearing strange clothes must expect to be stared at: If he wants privacy while wearing them, he should stay indoors. If someone openly and indiscriminately publishes facts about himself, he cannot complain if someone extends the publication. Someone who goes into public life or adopts a profession, such as the stage, which unavoidably attracts public notice, can be said, reasonably (and sometimes literally), to have asked for it. A candidate for high public office must expect inquiries into his finances and even into his mental health record, both relevant to his fitness for the job. And so long as the road to the top in the mass entertainment industry involves wide exposure of one's intimate life, anyone embarking on that road may be judged, perhaps, to have agreed to the price, though the practices of a society that exacts that price may be thought objectionable.

Still, implied consent to publicity may not be total, whether as to subject matter, duration, or the extent of the public. Someone entering a picture in an art competition can be taken to have agreed to the public's interesting itself in his life as an artist, his art school training, the artists who have influenced him, perhaps even in his relations with his models, since that may have something to do with his artistic vision, but not in the diseases from which he suffers, unless (as with El Greco's alleged astigmatism) they also affect his artistic vision. Or again, entering a competition in 1978 need not imply agreeing to renewed publicity in 1988 in an article entitled "The Forgotten Winner of the 1978 Competition." The consent implied should be to a waiver of privacy claims naturally and relevantly consequential upon the act in question, not to infringements after the occasion is well and truly past. Again, if someone with a medical history so singular that his identity could hardly be concealed, agreed nevertheless to his doctor's breaking medical confidence and writing up his case for a professional medical journal for the sake of the advancement of medical science, his agreement need not be taken as consent to its further publication in the popular Sunday press. More precisely, if he had not withheld consent even though he knew that he could not restrict publication thereafter, one might be forced to say that he had consented to the wider publication too as the natural consequence of the narrower, but there would be some point in seeking a way in law of leaving him the choice as to the first, without committing him willy-nilly to the second.

A classification of privacy interests proposed by Professor Hubman, and followed by the German Supreme Court, might be helpful here. Hubman distinguishes two spheres, one comprising "all those facts . . . which a person has an interest in keeping strictly for himself and for the person or persons immediately concerned," the other, "that which is shared with a person's family, colleagues and collaborators, neighbours and, generally speaking, those members of the community among whom the person concerned leads his daily family, business, or professional life."[19] There may be room for a more elaborate theory of "spheres," with the object of establishing that some consideration, such as implied consent, which undercuts a claim to privacy in a narrower sphere, need not imply an undercutting in respect of a broader sphere. Something of this kind already applies in respect of confidentiality and privileged communications, for example, between a candidate for an academic post, an appointing committee, its administrative and secretarial staff, and referees. A candidate is taken to authorize free communications about himself between members of this privileged group, but the latter are barred from spreading such information more widely. Close attention to a person's interests and intentions in making disclosures about his personal affairs may enable

300

us to determine within what limits he has undercut his claim to have those affairs kept private. Of course, restriction of implied consent would not rule out subsequent counterclaims. There might be further overriding reasons for free general publication in a particular case, even though the undercutting condition of consent to publication applied only in a restricted sphere.

**c. Undercutting a presumption of consent.** In general, if one can be said to have a free choice between participating and not participating in a practice which involves loss of privacy, choosing to participate counts as waiving one's claims. But as we saw in Chapters 7 and 8, what counts as a free choice is often contextually relative, depending on variable standards. If it were the case that starlets find advancement in the film industry a great deal easier if they are prepared to sleep with their directors, do they have a free choice? Are the conditions for advancement costs that are natural, reasonable, or necessarily attached to that option? Or are they unnecessarily attached to it by someone able and willing to exploit a powerful bargaining position? If it became the general practice of corporations to require recruits to their executive cadres to submit to regular urine tests for drug abuse, should we say that someone who objected on grounds of privacy need not choose to be a corporation executive, or should we say that these were unreasonably burdensome requirements that a person ought not to have to submit to in order to succeed in business?

It would be difficult to devise legislative measures that could be readily and flexibly applied to protect the employee's legitimate interest against other interests that, in *some* contexts, might indeed be overriding. After all, it is at least arguable that tests for drug abuse might quite properly be required of airline pilots. Legal remedies are not, however, the only solution to the protection of rights. Problems of this kind are often better settled by negotiation or public debate. It is true that the negotiator with the weaker bargaining power in such transactions may have little real choice. White-collar professional unionism might be one solution, either as a strengthening of the negotiator's hand by the threat of collective action or by generating wide publicity and public debate in which the competing values can be openly matched and disinterested support mobilized for the weaker party. Democratic forums for settlement of public-value conflicts are by no means restricted to parliaments, cabinet rooms, or law courts.

## B. *"Overriding" arguments*

Professor Lusky condemns the presumption which places the onus of justification on a would-be intruder. "Biases of this kind," he says, "are the enemy of a just balance. They distort by loading the scale in favor of the value for which recognition is asserted as a broad proposition, subject only to occasional exceptions. Perhaps, in our hierarchy of values, certain values do enjoy a 'preferred position' . . . [but] if any such priorities do or should exist, it is not privacy, but freedom of thought and speech . . . that rank first."[20]

If such "biases" were arbitrary or nonrational, Lusky's first assertion would be correct. But I have claimed that there are reasons for respecting someone's privacy deriving from a very basic concept of our moral phenomenology: the understanding that someone has of himself as a person in a world of persons, which commits him to extending a consideration to other persons corresponding to the consideration he expects from them, and provides reasons not only for a principle of noninterference, but also for a principle of privacy that sets a limit on the noninterference principle. However, I claim no more for these principles than that they settle an onus of justification; any interest that could in principle be seen by the beneficiary of the principle of privacy as a reason for action for someone else might override the presumption. A consideration, such as an interest in profiting from the sale of newspapers to people keen to take a peep into other people's lives, would be enough to meet that onus, if the project of making a profit is accepted as reasonable for anyone to undertake. But this "reasonableness" might be overridden by counterclaims resting on substantive interests, such as the interest in personal development and autonomy, or in forming intimate relations, which may, indeed, rest on the same principle of respect for persons and their interests from which the principle of privacy derives.

There are considerations, however, that will override substantive interests in privacy too. There is no algorithm for determining which these are. There might be practical disagreement on whether the sociological knowledge to be obtained by discreet eavesdropping on bedrooms is more important than the privacy of personal relations. But arguments are available to advocates on both sides to pursue the dispute further, with the possibility of agreement emerging. That claims are contested does not imply that they are irreconcilable.

There are, in any case, other ways of contesting a claim that a

302

certain consideration overrides the interest in privacy, often more conclusive than a flat denial that the value invoked is in all cases more important than privacy. One way is to concede that the value informing the counterclaim would override privacy if the intrusion proposed or committed were strictly necessary to realize the value, but to deny that necessity. It is no longer controversial, for instance, that doctors should provide health authorities with confidential details of cases of "notifiable diseases," in order to reduce the spread of infection. But a proposal to publicize the names of people infected with venereal disease or AIDS in order to protect possible contacts might be resisted not only as an invasion of personal privacy, but also because the threat of disclosure would deter sufferers from seeking medical treatment. The privacy-invasive means would then be not only unnecessary but actually ill-adapted to the valued end. The argument against the preservation of privacy is thus undercut.

A different kind of rebutting argument is less drastically undercutting but still persuasive. Someone claiming that an alleged rape victim's previous sexual experiences should not be submitted as evidence for the defense might allow that were such information necessary to a fair trial, this consideration would be overriding, but since the witness's past experience is not directly relevant to the truth of her present allegation, her right to privacy stands. The argument would then shift to the issue of relevance, for instance, to whether evidence of a woman's past sexual promiscuity tends to rebut her charge that she has been raped. The objection to the invasion of privacy might be strengthened by the further claim that because additional publicity would deter rape victims from reporting offenses, not only would the case for overriding privacy not be sustained, because irrelevant to the question of justice, but publicity would lead to a loss of personal security. The rebuttal would then be reinforced by invoking a value different from privacy in support of the preeminence of privacy in this particular case.

A related argument may concede that a countervailing value would override privacy were the intrusion to make a large difference to the outcomes but claim that in the particular instance the difference would be small or that the claim to its being significant had not been made out. Hyman Gross questions whether an easing of restrictions on wire-tapping and searches by the police would indeed have the desirable effect of increasing security against crime. He casts doubt on the implicit assumption that "the greater the ability to watch what is going on, or obtain evidence of what has gone on, the greater the ability to prevent crime. . . . There is . . . much to be said for the conflicting proposition that once a generally efficient system of law enforcement exists an increase in its efficiency does not result in a corresponding reduction in crime, but only in an increase in punishments."[21] This outcome would not alone justify, in Gross's view, the overriding of privacy rights. Someone who believed that the punishment of offenders was intrinsically good might take a different view – but the justification of punishment is itself a contested subject, to which the discussion would then have to turn.

Analogous cases occur in discussions of sifting processes, such as means tests for welfare services. Inquiries by officials into the truth of gossip that Ms. S, an abandoned wife or widow with children, is "cohabiting" with a man not her husband, thereby disqualifying herself from benefits, are commonly thought particularly offensive and degrading to the applicant. It may be argued from the administration's side, however, that if social welfare payments are to be administered with reasonable economy, benefits should be paid only to the needy; public money is squandered if adequate checks are not made on the merits of each case. However, if the extra cost of investigating rather than of accepting information freely given turned out to exceed the probable losses by making payments to cheats, the overriding case in terms of economy would be undercut.

The administrator of welfare services might invoke, however, not economy but fairness. Supposing the gossip to be true, it is unfair that Ms. S should receive welfare benefits making her better off than someone in the normal or standard situation of a wife and mother living in a conjugal home. At all relevant points, the welfare needs of these two women would be indistinguishable. Providing the intrusion was not conducted in the unnecessarily humiliating and degrading style that some investigators are said to adopt, the argument justifying it, as a condition for the fair administration of a welfare system, is one that Ms. S herself, as a rational person, may well be committed to endorse.

Each party in such a confrontation, however, while possibly endorsing the values relied on by the other side, will tend to have a value orientation related to his social role. So though administrators and research workers will accept the importance of privacy in a general way, their roles equip them with value orderings, at least in their professional performances, in which information collection, whether for the sake of fairness or of truth, will rate above privacy in situations in which someone with other functional commitments might order them otherwise. Each will tend to believe, with or without good reasons, in the importance of his function, or at least of the activity in which he plays his part, and deplore as obscurantist, corrupt, or soft headed the defense of interests likely to impede it.

Privacy is particularly vulnerable; in any given case it is the interest of one individual or of a relatively small group, while against it are set the interests of the public in being fully informed, in being secure from criminal attack, in having policy makers and administrators work with full and up-to-date information. Consequently, in any given instance, the public interest can seem overriding, because it is the interest of so many people. Yet in the long run, protection of the interest of every individual in privacy will have gone by default. The piecemeal erosion of the privilege may never have been halted to take account of the total consequences. In this, privacy resembles environmental values. The particular damage never seems sufficient to outweigh the promised benefits of extra jobs and enlarged national income, but the cumulative consequences can be disastrous. The cumulative erosion of privacy might be checked if every new government proposal for an investigation or an obligatory questionnaire touching personal affairs, for consolidating data in computer banks or for personal surveillance, for the scrutiny of private mail or the tapping of phone lines, had to be tested against clear and strict policy guidelines. These would need to be drawn up appropriately for every class of intrusive activity, but each proposed intrusion would need to be justified by explicit reference to the immediate importance of the information sought, with reasons for supposing that it will be both forthcoming and reliable, and for supposing that it cannot be reliably obtained in less offensive ways. As a police officer seeking a search warrant is required to satisfy the issuing official or magistrate that there is reason to suppose that the search will turn up incriminating evidence, so designers of questionnaires and the like might be required to submit their privacy "impact statements" to curators of privacy rights who are not necessarily committed to the professional values of administrators and researchers.

305

# 16

## Conclusion: A semantic theory of freedom

### 1. Freedom as a complex-structured concept

The title I have given to this book claims that it presents a theory of freedom. What sort of a theory is it? There have been psychological, sociological, economic, and historical theories of freedom in plenty, which attempt to explain the emergence of free institutions, or to specify the empirical conditions for free choice, or to focus on the causal relations between political and economic freedom. And ever since the sixteenth century there have been political, constitutional, or legal theories, such as Harrington's in *Oceana*, Locke's in the *Two Treatises of Government*, Montesquieu's in *The Spirit of the Laws*, and Lord Dicey's in *The Law of the Constitution*, which have aimed at prescribing the legal arrangements to safeguard freedom. After World War II, in the aftermath of logical positivism, and in the spirit of the kind of linguistic analysis that for a time dominated Anglo-Saxon epistemology and philosophical psychology through the works of Wittgenstein, Gilbert Ryle, and J.L. Austin, there emerged a fashion for works in the same genre in social and political philosophy too. These were heavily influenced by the "ordinary language school of philosophy." A theory of freedom was taken to be a theory of "freedom": that is to say, it would have as its object the construction of a theory which would identify necessary and sufficient conditions for the correct use of the word "freedom" and its correlates "free," "unfree," "freely," and so on, in all the diversity of ordinary usage. It was counted a strike against such a theory that some common usage could not be made to comply with it. Alternatively, it was allowed that the meanings of "freedom" were diverse, disparate, and sometimes inconsistent, and that for useful employment in systematic scholarly studies they needed to be cleaned up – as "cause," "space," and "mass" were being cleaned up and transformed into technical terms in theoretical physics. "Freedom" was thus to be "rationalized" or "reconstructed."[1]

My own theory of freedom resembles none of these. It comes

306

closest in intention among the classics to Rousseau's *Social Contract*, but with a somewhat Kantian epistemology to underpin the key concept of rationality. Though much of the *Social Contract* is concerned with institutional arrangements to safeguard freedom, its principal focus is on a semantic theory of freedom, to make a coherent connection between freedom understood as the absence of constraints and freedom as obedience to a law, both moral and positive, which we prescribe to ourselves, in contrast to obedience to the mere impulse of appetite. But the success of the theory does not depend only on the successful exploration of these internal connections. Freedom is very closely connected with other concepts, such as authority, rights, will, autonomy, and so on, such that the sense one ascribes to any one of these is going to affect the meaning of freedom itself. What is needed for this enterprise is not a set of conditions for the use of a word, but a theory displaying the structure of this very complex concept, one which explores the way in which the understanding moves, by steps which may be ideological rather than strictly logical, from conditions for one application to conditions for another.[2]

Diversity of meaning might, of course, be simply a case of ambiguity. Words with the same symbolic form can have meanings so different that we call them homonyms – different words which, for what may be purely contingent philological reasons, come to have the same literal and vocable forms, though they have no semantic connections with each other. I observed in Chapter 7 that *tense* is such a word – or rather, such a pair of words. For one meaning derives from *tempus* (time), the other from *tendere* (to stretch). This convergence into one symbolic form has no semantic significance at all.

But "freedom" is not like this. The freedom of a pendulum to swing is not semantically unrelated to the freedom of a person to choose. Nor is it simply that freedom is a three-term relation, such that to grasp the conditions for its proper application in a given context one must first grasp what impediment *I* must be absent if agent *A* is to be free to Φ.[3] According to that account, freedom would be an abstraction awaiting the assignment of determinate values to its three variables: Without them, it would be quite empty, no more capable of being cashed as a thought-token in actual discourse than an unsigned blank check made out to no payee would be capable of being cashed in a regular commercial transaction.

In a limited way this is true. A complete analysis of any standard employment of 'freedom' would indeed supply the three values.

But freedom stands for ideals and principles; no attempt to supply all-purpose determinants for the variables could make intelligible why it is that interference with the free action of a free agent should constitute, as I claim it does, a prima facie breach of a moral principle.

A semantic theory of freedom is not about words but about the structure and relations of concepts. Our capacity to think, to apprehend reality as intelligible, depends on our having available appropriate conceptual frames into which our experiences will fit, so that we recognize an experience as a case of a $P$, and we have beliefs that enable us to move from the $P$-ness of this experience to its also being $Q$, where $Q$ is a related concept. So the possibility of comprehending our world efficiently depends on these concepts and on our beliefs about their relations with each other. Together they provide a set of ways of interpreting raw phenomena, converting them into meaningful experiences with which and about which it is possible to think, speak, and plan our projects.

When, therefore, I call freedom a complex-structured concept, I mean that in employing and applying it by forming existential propositions in which it figures, we establish relations, partly logical, partly analogical, between our diverse experiences which, to be comprehended and thought about, need to be understood, not as disparate, random events, each *sui generis* or as pure particularities, but as instances of universal ideas or forms, themselves constituents of a pattern or web. Freedom, therefore, is a subsystem of a total structure which so organizes reality that it is accessible to the rational, conscious mind. The arrangement of experiences might be tidier, perhaps, if the complex structure of concepts were broken down into a compound of simpler ones, each with well-defined necessary and sufficient conditions for its use. But what was gained in sharpness would be lost in relatedness. Autonomy, for instance, which, if my semantic theory is correct, is deeply embedded in the concept of freedom, would be snapped apart from, for instance, the freedom to move, from the opportunity to pursue projects within the limits of available resources, and so on, so that the semantic roots of autonomy in the lack of impediment to self-initiated movement would be lost.

## 2. Reasons for action as "action-commitments"

There are two main types of semantic theory of freedom in the Western philosophical tradition; one, perhaps the dominant view, is that freedom of choice and action depends on one's having reasons for what one does. But there is another which treats rationality as a kind of constraint, or which elevates will above reason, so that true freedom consists in the recognition of contingency and the realization that there are ultimately no reasons which can determine the will; consequently, an act might be both free and irrational. Though this book belongs mainly in the first tradition, it takes the other seriously and makes some efforts to explain its attractions and its plausibility. For I do not suppose that there are two *concepts* of freedom, rather, there are many theories which try to delineate the structure of this complex concept, to find room for the many ways in which freedom is intelligibly attributed to persons and things. I take it as a necessary feature of the use of *freedom* in our ordinary forms of discourse that, for any particular context in which determinate values are assigned to the variable terms which are related by the concept of freedom, the proposition "Alan is free" has a truth value.

Free action is more than just undetermined behavior; it requires that the agent knows what he is about and understands his action under some description which gives it a point; that is, he must have some reason for acting. Otherwise, he is no more *acting* than a frog catching a fly. I have little use, therefore, for the concept of the will as a distinct faculty. Chapter 2 develops a theory of practical rationality which makes the concept of the will, while often providing a convenient shortcut in discourse, strictly speaking unnecessary, relying instead on the concept of an *action-commitment* following from belief, which in "willing" we carry into action.

The key idea is that rationality requires that one's beliefs form a coherent and consistent structure and that rational actions are those to which one is committed by such rational beliefs. So epistemic (or theoretical) rationality and practical rationality are fused in a general theory. Just as the principles of logic determine to what conclusions one is committed by holding certain propositions true and entail that to deny the conclusions while adhering to the premises would be irrational, so to hold beliefs that commit one to a certain action and to act otherwise is correspondingly irrational. Of course, people do act irrationally: Some are neurotic or psychotic, others merely akratic. But the account one gives of such behavior is not that it is free from rational restraints, but rather that it is compulsive, or perhaps dazzled by prospects of immediate gratification – in any case, the result of impulse rather than of free choice. Irrationality is a manifestation not of the freedom of will but of constraints on the faculty of reason. One chooses freely when one grasps, and acts in accordance with, the action-commitments implied by one's beliefs.

My theory of freedom denies the Humean doctrine that every explanation of an action must have reference to a desire: Even paradigm instances of desire as a motive for action can be accounted for in terms of beliefs about one's future enjoyments. Consequently, there is room in a theory of rational action not merely for instrumental motivation – relating action to the realization of desired consequences – but also for action for the sake of principles, irrespective of consequences. Chapter 1, entitled "Persons and Values," which sketches the general thrust of the theory, distinguishes reasons of different types. Person-centered reasons rely primarily on the principles of respect for persons and on derivative principles, such as fidelity to truth, noninterference, the equal consideration of interests of persons, and so on. Value-centered reasons invoke valued states of affairs (including, but not wholly constituted by, human well-being) to be maintained or brought about. This distinction might be seen as that between Kantian-style deontology and consequentialist axiology; the theory does indeed rely on something resembling this well-known distinction, but it differs from it in important respects. It differs from theories of either kind in that it accepts both sorts of reasons as carrying action commitments irreducible to commitments of the other kind. Indeed, it canvasses the possibility that there may be reasons of still other kinds, too, such as symbolic reasons, examined at some greater length in Chapter 13. Chapter 3 offers a theory for the resolution of conflicts between apparently competing commitments of whatever sorts, when there is no "common currency" to which they can be reduced and in terms of which they could be held commensurable and when there are no rules assigning lexical priority to one kind or the other. The view that there are "tragic dilemmas" in which one does wrong *whatever* one does is rejected as resulting from a misunderstanding of the nature and purpose of practical reason.

Chapter 4 repudiates moral relativism and subjectivism, insisting that our forms of practical discourse presuppose that practical propositions, including assignments of value, have truth-values, just as much as historical or scientific propositions have truth-values. We may be mistaken in these as with other beliefs; but acceptance of such beliefs does not depend on unreasoned choices or decisions about what we should value. Decisions are, of course, part of the practical life, but in the epistemic life, too, we have to

310

decide what the evidence commits us to believe. The Humean gap between the two forms of life is the result of a false theory of action, and a false logic which rejects the practical syllogism – or at any rate rejects it on the wrong grounds. In Chapter 4 I develop a theory of valuing which depends on the idea of a preference ranking of states of affairs of which the valued object is or is not a feature; but the condition that the ranking be reasoned protects the fundamental cognitive framework of the theory from the treatment of preference and choice as unreasoning and ultimately unreasoned volitions.

## 3. Personality, autarchy, autonomy, and community

The idea of person-centered reasons depends on the concept of the natural person and on the associated concept of the moral person (see Chapters 5 and 6). Both concepts, and the related principle of respect for persons, are fundamental to the complex-structured concept of freedom. There are three principal constituents of this concept. The first, explored in Chapter 7, is a neo-Hobbesian notion of freedom of action, understood as the pursuit of projects without interference. This, of course, required a fairly thorough examination of what can count as an interference and a look at some of the conditions under which the principle of noninterference might be overridden or undermined. Because freedom to act is often confused with power to act, Chapter 7 includes an analysis of *power*, itself a complex-structured concept linked quite tightly to freedom, but organizing reality in importantly different ways, so that to lack the power to $\Phi$ does not necessarily entail that one lacks the freedom to $\Phi$; both concepts involve variables which are highly contested, ideologically speaking, but propositions employing them are not on that account subjective, nor are their truth-values necessarily culture- or agent-relative.

The second constituent of the concept of freedom is that of the free agent, presupposed by the notion of free action. The free agent is the minimally rational chooser, characterized by *autarchy*, the capacity to make decisions in the light of reasons and to act on them. Chapter 8 explores the conditions for autarchy, and the kinds of defects of personality that impair it, such as neurotic and psychotic disorders. These I call *inner-impulsions*, to distinguish them from impulsion induced by other people, which I term *heterarchy;* this includes forms of submissiveness induced, for instance, by hypnotism, brainwashing, or a dominated upbringing. The dis-

311

tinction between autarchy, heterarchy, and impulsion, and between all of these and autarchy abused, for instance, by coercion
and duress, is clearly of first importance in deciding whether a
person's being unfree is evidence of his having been wronged, and
in assessing its consequence for his responsibility for what he does.

Chapter 9 introduces a personality ideal, *autonomy*, to which
one may aspire but the full realization of which goes well beyond
autarchy. In exploring this concept, I have tried, in the first place,
to capture Rousseau's conception of a person subject to "a law
which he prescribes to himself, which is freedom," contrasted with
"the mere impulse of appetite," which Rousseau calls slavery. This
comes close to one idea of freedom as positive (there is another, less
interesting idea of "positive freedom," in which freedom is more or
less identified with opportunity). This ideal raises the question,
also dealt with in this chapter, of how a person socialized into a
culture, without which no one would have the conceptual resources to undertake the quest for autonomy, could claim to prescribe a law, a *nomos*, to himself. What reasons could he have for
adopting one rather than another? The answer lies in the notion of
autonomy as a critical process carried out *within* a multicultural
heritage. The tradition into which one is inducted by upbringing
and education will rarely be so coherent that the thing to do is
always and immediately apparent. The conflicts within a plural
culture provide the occasions and the opportunities for the criticism from within and for the rational reconstruction of the traditional belief structure which makes it intelligibly one's own. Chapters 10 and 11 examine the relation between autonomy and other
personality ideals, such as self-realization, self-development, and
instinctual freedom, showing that some of these are in part consistent with autonomy, even required by it, others are not.

Chapter 12 repudiates the charge that the theory of freedom
thus far expounded is overly and unrealistically individualist. The
chapter begins with a typology of associative relations. This ranges
from the standoff relations of members of a joint-stock company in
which, while respect for persons is preserved, the interaction between agents is kept to a minimum consistent with the conditions
necessary for collaboration for mutual advantage. The chapter re-
views transcendent collective enterprises, such as orchestras, of
which the *telos* is not the advantage of individual members, sepa-
rate or collective, but some otherwise intrinsically valued activity,
and arrives ultimately at fully fledged total communities. Only the
total community would turn out to be necessarily unacceptable to

someone committed to autonomy as a personal and social ideal. The model that seems to combine respect for persons and the ideal of autonomy most fully with the mutual concern which marks the community ideal is the one I term *mutuality*. But I argue that this ideal is practically and psychologically inappropriate to a group of more than some dozen people, imposing otherwise an impossible information overload. *Comradeships,* such as kibbutzim, or some religious communities, have resources enabling them to survive without the degree of interpersonal concern called for by mutualities, but their success depends largely on their being also transcendent collective enterprises, directed, for example, to a national or cultural renaissance, or perhaps to the glory of God, giving the community something of the additional cohesiveness of a regiment, an orchestra, a choral society, or a hospital, whose members have an interest in the joint enterprise itself which can override the centrifugality of their particular interests. If the comradeship grows beyond a certain size without generating or discovering such a transcendent source of community, it is likely either to disintegrate or to overcompensate by becoming a total community.

## 4. The rights of natural persons in society

Chapters 13 to 15 are concerned with different aspects of individual rights. The first examines the conditions for the enjoyment of any rights at all, distinguishing reasons of right from other reasons, principally from need. The action commitments implied by the needs of valued objects, human beings included, derive from consequentialist value considerations. Rights belong to the area of person-centered reasons, being in the first place conditions safeguarding the freedom of persons as project makers to pursue their projects without interference. Rights are thus normative resources which are at the disposal of autarchic persons; in the absence of autarchy, the rights will be converted into the powers of trustees, guardians, and so on. But it is in the light of the subject's being a person, albeit a defective one, that he or she can be regarded as a subject of rights at all. As a valuable object he may have, in addition, needs which can count as reasons for action by other people. Welfare rights, however, combine the two by making each person's interests subjects for consideration equal to the consideration given to anyone else's interests.

In Chapter 14 I derive a general principle of privacy from the principle of respect for persons. The principle of privacy is a fairly weak reason for action, placing an onus of justification for interference with privacy on the intruder. In this respect it reverses the usual onus, argued for in Chapters 6 and 7, which presumes any form of action permissible until reason is shown to the contrary. The argument here depends on a person's interest in forms of self-presentation, as part of his self-awareness as a maker of projects. In Chapter 15 further and stronger, though more specific, arguments are developed deriving from the needs of human beings, and their interests in personal security from persecution, their interest in developing intimate personal relations, and so on. These are the ends, or *telé*, of privacy rights, and the strength of any claim to such rights will depend on whether their recognition will support such *telé* or undermine them. So the right to the privacy of one's home does not extend to a right to bash one's wife and children behind closed doors without interference, since that is not a way of cultivating family intimacies.

Chapter 15 provides then a theory about how to handle conflicts of rights, without resorting to the meaningless metaphor, favored by many jurists, of "balancing" interests. This theory is an application of the more general theory of rational conflict resolution propounded in Chapter 3. It is a theme that has recurred in a large number of ways in the course of this book. The apparent ability of single-valued consequentialist and preferentialist theories to arbitrate in such conflicts by resorting to a common cost-benefit algorithm is, in my view, an illusion, attractive only because of the Humean presuppositions of the form in which these dilemmas are posed. If all reasons for action relate to prior unreasoned desires, deciding on the thing to do, once one has settled the empirical facts of the matter, will depend on how one orders these desires. If the states resulting from satisfying these desires can be made to order themselves (e.g., as quanta of consequential happiness), there is little work left to do. Someone, however, who is not afraid to assume the practical burden of rational decision making will recognize that decision making is not really like that at all. He is left with the very considerable task of pursuing a discursive argument in which principles and values undercut and undermine one another within his belief system, one reason prevailing against another not because it is in some sense (but in what sense?) weightier, but because not to acknowledge it as the best reason for action would be to harbor an inconsistency among one's beliefs.

# Notes

## Chapter 1

1. For Jim and Pedro, see J.J.C. Smart and Bernard Williams, *Utilitarianism: For and Against* (Cambridge, 1973), 98–9. See also B. Williams, "Conflicts of Value," in A. Ryan, ed., *The Idea of Freedom* (Oxford, 1979), 221–32; S. Hampshire, "Public and Private Morality," in Stuart Hampshire, ed., *Public and Private Morality*, (Cambridge, 1978), 23–53; B. Williams, "Politics and Moral Character," in Hampshire, ed., *Public and Private Morality*, 55–73; Michael Walzer, "Political Action: The Problem of Dirty Hands," *Philosophy and Public Affairs* 2 (1973): 160–80; S.I. Benn, "Private and Public Morality – Clean Living and Dirty Hands," in S.I. Benn and G.F. Gaus, eds., *Public and Private in Social Life* (London and New York, 1983), 159–69; A. MacIntyre, *After Virtue* (London, 1981), 134.
2. This is R.M. Hare's strategy in his *Moral Thinking* (Oxford, 1981).
3. See Terrance C. McConnell, "Consistency in Ethics," *Canadian Journal of Philosophy* 8 (1978): 269, 270.
4. For an exposition of Hare's views, see his *Moral Thinking* (Oxford, 1981); "Moral Conflicts," in Sterling McMurrin, ed., *The Tanner Lectures on Human Values*, vol. 1 (Cambridge, 1980), 169–93; and "Ethical Theory and Utilitarianism," in Amartya Sen and B. Williams, eds., *Utilitarianism and Beyond* (Cambridge, 1982), 23–38.
5. Hare, *Moral Thinking*, 91.
6. Ibid., 49–50.
7. Ibid., 6.
8. Hare, "Ethical Theory and Utilitarianism," 27.
9. Hare, *Moral Thinking*, 105.
10. MacIntyre, *After Virtue*.
11. Consider, for instance, J.-P. Sartre's *Les Mains sales*. See also Arlene Saxonhouse, "Classical Greek Conceptions of Public and Private," in Benn and Gaus, eds., *Public and Private in Social Life*, 363–84.
12. MacIntyre, *After Virtue*, 134. The passage continues:

> There are indeed crucial conflicts in which different virtues appear as making rival and incompatible claims upon us. But our situation is tragic in that we have to recognise the authority of both claims. There *is* an objective moral order, but our perceptions of it are such that we cannot bring rival moral truths into complete harmony with each other and yet the acknowledgement of the moral order and of moral truth

makes the kind of choice which a Weber or a Berlin urges upon us out of the question. For to choose does not exempt me from the authority of the claim which I chose to go against. (p. 134)

The Sophoclean self transcends the limitations of social roles . . . but it remains accountable . . . precisely for the way in which it handles itself in those conflicts. . . . Thus the presupposition of the Sophoclean self's existence is that . . . there is an order which requires from us the pursuit of certain ends. . . . (pp. 135–6)

13. MacIntyre, *After Virtue*, 236.

## Chapter 2

1. This chapter is a revised version of a paper having the same title prepared by my colleague Gerald F. Gaus and myself in joint authorship, and which appeared in *American Philosophical Quarterly* 23 (1986): 255–66. Jerry Gaus has most generously agreed to its inclusion in the present version in this book. In that paper, he and I acknowledged with gratitude the help we had received from Fred D'Agostino, Jim Evans, Peter Forrest, John Kleinig, Thomas Nagel, Philip Pettit, David A. J. Richards, J.J.C. Smart, and Albert Weale. I repeat that acknowledgment here.

2. E.J. Bond, *Reason and Value* (Cambridge, 1983), 3. Bond cites Bernard Williams, J. L. Mackie, Richard Taylor, Gilbert Harman, and Roger Beehler as proponents of this view.

3. Ibid. 3.

4. As is often the case, it is not clear that Hume himself subscribed to the Humean orthodoxy. At times, Hume seems to explain desires in terms of the enjoyment-related beliefs which ground them, much as Gans and I did (see section 4 in this chapter). See *A Treatise of Human Nature*, L.A. Selby-Bigge, ed. (Oxford, 1978), 414.

5. My discussion will focus on the "desire"-formulation of the Humean theory. For the "pro-attitude" version, see Donald Davidson, *Essays on Actions and Events* (Oxford, 1980); essays 1, 2 and 5.

6. David A.J. Richards, *A Theory of Reasons for Action* (Oxford, 1971), Chs. 5, 6, 13, 14. For a similar thesis relating to beliefs about goodness and action, see Philippa Foot, *Virtues and Vices* (Berkeley and Los Angeles, 1978), 132ff. Foot, however, is much closer to the Humean position than is Richards; see ibid., 156. See also Ronald D. Milo, *Immorality* (Princeton, 1984), Ch. 6, on 'moral indifference.'

7. See William K. Frankena's discussion of internalism and externalism in his "Obligation and Motivation in Recent Moral Philosophy," in K.E. Goodpaster, ed., *Perspectives on Morality* (Notre Dame, 1976), 49–73.

8. Amartya K. Sen is also interested in using the language of commitment, and for broadly similar reasons. See his "Rational Fools," in Frank Hahn and Martin Hollis, eds., *Philosophy and Economic Theory* (Oxford, 1979), 87–109. Michael H. Robins also suggests focusing on the notion of commitment rather than on reasons for action, in "Practical Reasoning, Commitment and Rational Action," *American Philosophical Quarterly* 21 (1984): 55–68.

9. See, for instance, Bond, *Reason and Value*, 40, 77; T.M. Scanlon, "Rights, Goals, and Fairness," in Stuart Hampshire, ed., *Public and Private Morality* (Cambridge, 1978), 98–101; S.I. Benn, "The Problematic Rationality of Political Participation," in Stanley Benn et al., eds., *Political Participation* (Canberra, 1978), 1–22; reprinted in P. Laslett and J. Fishkin, eds., *Philosophy, Politics and Society: Fifth Series* (Oxford, 1979); S.I. Benn, "Rejoinder," in Benn et al., *Political Participation*, 61–88. See also Chapter 1 this volume.

10. See Roger Trigg, *Reason and Commitment* (Cambridge, 1973). See also Frederic Schick, *Having Reasons* (Princeton, 1984), Ch. 6.

11. Passions, volitions, and actions, Hume asserted, cannot "be pronounced either true or false." *Treatise*, Book 3, Part 1, Section 1, 458.

12. See Robins, "Practical Reasoning," 64.

13. Bernard Williams, "Deciding to Believe," in *Problems of the Self* (Cambridge, 1973), 136–51.

14. This helps explain why some forms of consequentialist ethics seem so counterintuitive when they direct us to believe things that are false but beneficial. As Derek Parfit notes, "We would have to be made to forget how and why we acquired our new beliefs. . . ." (*Reasons and Persons* [Oxford, 1984], 41).

15. See Bernard Williams, "Internal and External Reasons," in Ross Harrison, ed., *Rational Action* (Cambridge, 1979), 17–28.

16. Julius Kovesi, "Descriptions and Reasons," *Proceedings of the Aristotelian Society* (1979–80): 110.

17. Thomas Nagel, *The Possibility of Altruism* (Princeton, 1970), 29.

18. Ibid.

19. These two cases are similar to the continent man and the temperate man discussed by John McDowell. However, whereas McDowell believes that in some cases a 'prospective enjoyment' will not count as any reason for a temperate man, I have suggested that his other commitments may undermine his belief that he would enjoy the experience. "Are Moral Requirements Hypothetical Imperatives?" *Proceedings of the Aristotelian Society* 52 (Suppl.) (1978): 13–19, 26–27.

20. For a defense of these accounts, see Gilbert Ryle, *The Concept of Mind* (London, 1949), 108. See also Richard B. Brandt, *A Theory of the Good and the Right* (Oxford, 1979), 38–42.

21. Sigmund Freud, *Introductory Lectures on Psychoanalysis*, James Strachey, ed. (Harmondsworth, 1973), 297.

22. But see Stuart Hampshire, *Freedom of the Individual* (London, 1975), Ch. 2; Richards, *Reasons for Action*, 32ff.
23. See Parfit, *Reasons and Persons*, 12ff.

## Chapter 3

1. B. Williams, "Conflicts of Value," in A. Ryan, ed., *The Idea of Freedom* (Oxford, 1979), 221–32. See also B. Williams, "Ethical Consistency," in his *Problems of the Self* (Cambridge, 1973), 166–86, on Agamemnon's dilemma.
2. S. Hampshire, "Public and private morality," in S. Hampshire, ed., *Public and Private Morality* (Cambridge, 1978), 34.
3. Ibid., 44.
4. Ibid., 45.

## Chapter 4

1. See J.L. Mackie, *Ethics: Inventing Right and Wrong* (Harmondsworth, 1977), Ch. 1.
2. Thomas Nagel, "The Limits of Objectivity," in S. MacMurrin, ed., *The Tanner Lectures on Human Values*, vol. 1 (Salt Lake City, 1980), 77–139.
3. Given the subtle strategies of collective consequentialism, where one's reasons for action depend crucially on what one expects others' reasons to be, such questions are not mere quibbles. See, for instance, the discussion in Derek Parfit, *Reasons and Persons* Part 1.
4. J.L. Mackie, *Ethics*, 30.
5. Ibid., 35.
6. Ibid., 105–6.
7. The phrase is John McDowell's; "Non-cognitivism and rule-following," in S.H. Holtzman and C.M. Leich, eds., *Wittgenstein: To Follow a Rule* (London, 1981), 154.
8. David Wiggins, "Truth, Invention, and the Meaning of Life," *Proceedings of the British Academy* 62 (1976): 331–78.
9. Ibid., 357.
10. Ibid., 368.
11. Ibid., 369.
12. Ibid., 366–7.
13. Ibid., 341.
14. Nagel, "The Limits of Objectivity," 77.
15. Philippa Foot, "Moral Realism and Moral Dilemma." *Journal of Philosophy* 80 (1983): 396.
16. Wiggins, "Truth, Invention, and the Meaning of Life," 341.
17. Ibid., 366.
18. This argument approximates to one put by my colleague Gerald F. Gaus in *Value and Justification* (in preparation). We have spent many

hours discussing these questions, and the position I adopt here, in opposition to his, is still partly of his devising, though he finds it unacceptable.

19. H. Rashdall, *The Theory of Good and Evil*, vol. 2 (Oxford, 1907), 65.
20. Wiggins, "Truth, Invention, and the Meaning of Life," 373.

## Chapter 5

1. See R.D. Laing, *The Divided Self* (Harmondsworth, 1965), 41–2, 47, 124, 162–4.
2. John Plamenatz, "Persons as Moral Beings," presented posthumously to the World Congress on Freedom and Equality, St. Louis, 1975, and published in Gray Dorsey, ed., *Equality and Freedom; International and Comparative Jurisprudence*, vol. I (New York and Leiden, 1977), 30–1.
3. P.F. Strawson, "Freedom and resentment," in *Freedom and Resentment and Other Essays* (London, 1974), Ch. 1.
4. Thomas Hobbes, *Leviathan*, Michael Oakeshott, ed. (Oxford, 1946), 111, Ch. 17.
5. Ibid., 99, Ch. 15.
6. John Rawls, *A Theory of Justice* (Cambridge, Mass., 1971), Sect. 77, esp. pp. 505–6.

## Chapter 6

1. Philippa Foot, *Virtues and Vices* (Berkeley, 1978), Ch. X.

## Chapter 7

1. I have included in this chapter some passages from S. I. Benn and W. L. Weinstein, "Being Free to Act and Being a Free Man," *Mind* 80 (1971): 194–211, which was a first shot at the theory of freedom elaborated in this book. I wish to acknowledge the contribution Mr. Weinstein made to the early stages of development of this theory, and his generous agreement to my using some of our joint material here.
2. Thomas Hobbes, "Of Liberty and Necessity," in Sir William Molesworth, ed., *English Works*, vol. 4 (London, 1840), 273–4.
3. Genesis 25: 29–34.
4. David Hume, "Of the First Principles of Government," in *Essays Moral, Political and Literary* (Oxford, 1963), 31.
5. *Nicomachean Ethics*, III, 1, 1110ff.
6. Thomas Hobbes, *Leviathan*, Michael Oakeshott, ed. (Oxford, 1961), 137, Ch. 21.
7. Ibid., 130.
8. Cp. W.A. Parent, "Some Recent Work on the Concept of Liberty," *American Philosophical Quarterly* 11 (1974): 160.

## Chapter 8

1. My special interest in the philosophical problems of freedom was first awakened when I tried to distinguish forms of persuasion consistent with it from others that were not; see my "Freedom and Persuasion," *Australasian Journal of Philosophy* 45 (1967): 259–75.
2. David M. Walker, *The Oxford Companion to Law* (Oxford, 1980), 228: ". . . the hypothetical person commonly taken as the standard for judging whether the conduct of the defendant in a negligence action comes up to or falls short of the standard of care which the law requires in the circumstances."
3. Ibid. The quotation concludes with the words, ". . . though Lord Bramwell occasionally attributed to him the agility of an acrobat and the foresight of a Hebrew prophet."
4. Bruno Bettelheim, *The Informed Heart* (New York, 1960), 151ff. The term *Muselmänner* (Moslems) was applied by their fellow inmates to the "walking corpses" – the prisoners "who came to feel that their environment was one over which they could exercise no influence whatsoever. . . . [They] were called 'moslems' . . . because of what was erroneously viewed as a fatalistic surrender to the environment, as Mohammedans are supposed blandly to accept their fate."

## Chapter 9

1. David Hume, *A Treatise of Human Nature*, L.A. Selby-Bigge, ed. (Oxford, 1978), 415.
2. Romans, VII:15–23, in *The New English Bible* (1961), 265.
3. Jean-Jacques Rousseau, *The Social Contract*, G.D.H. Cole, trans. and ed., in *The Social Contract and Discourses* (London, 1973), 177–8.
4. Ibid., 177.
5. Ibid., 174.
6. *Hegel's Philosophy of Right*, T. M. Knox, trans., (Oxford, 1942), 92, section 138.
7. Ibid., section 139.

## Chapter 10

1. S. Freud, "On the History of the Psycho-Analytic Movement," in James Strachey, ed., *Standard Edition of the Complete Psychological Works of Sigmund Freud*, vol. 14 (London, 1957), 16.
2. "A neurosis is thus the result of a conflict between the ego and the id, upon which the ego has embarked because . . . it wishes at all costs to

retain its adaptability in relation to the external world. . . . [It] is because the ego, loyal to its inmost nature, takes sides with the external world that it becomes involved in conflict with the id. . . . What creates the determinant for the illness is not the fact of this conflict . . . but the circumstance that the ego has made use of the inefficient instrument of repression for dealing with conflict." S. Freud, "Inhibitions, Symptoms, and Anxiety," *Standard Edition*, vol. 20, 203–4.

3. S. Freud, "Repression," *Standard Edition*, vol. 14, 146.

4. S. Freud, *A General Introduction to Psychoanalysis*, W.J.H. Sprott, trans. (London, 1922), 255.

5. S. Freud, "A Disturbance of Memory on the Acropolis," *Collected Papers*, vol. 5, Joan Riviere, trans. (London, 1950), 309–10.

6. See S. Freud, *New Introductory Lectures on Psychoanalysis* (New York, 1933), 117–19.

7. Heinz Hartmann, *Ego Psychology and the Problem of Adaptation*, David Rapaport, trans. (London, 1958), 70, 72. First published in German as "Ich-Psychologie und Anpassungsproblem," in *Internationale Zeitschrift für Psychoanalyse und Imago* (1939).

8. David Rapaport, "Dynamic Psychology and Kantian Epistemology," in Merton M. Gill, ed., *Collected Papers*, (New York, 1967), 364, 297.

9. Stuart Hampshire, "Spinoza and the Idea of Freedom," *British Academy Proceedings* (1960): 195–215. Also in "Spinoza's Theory of Freedom," *The Monist* (1971): 554–66, and in *Spinoza* (Harmondsworth, 1951).

10. Eric Erickson, *Identity: Youth and Crisis* (New York, 1968), Ch. 2.

11. Ibid., 50.

12. Ibid., 87.

13. Ibid., 88, 90.

14. Ibid., 110, 89.

15. Bruno Bettelheim, *The Informed Heart* (New York, 1960).

16. Ibid., 257.

17. Ibid., 140ff.

18. Ibid., 68.

19. David Riesman, *The Lonely Crowd* (Yale, 1950); Jean-Jacques Rousseau, *A Discourse on the Origin and Foundation of the Inequality of Mankind*, in G.D.H. Cole, trans. and ed., *The Social Contract and Discourses* (London, 1973), 104.

20. Bettelheim, *The Informed Heart*, 76.

### Chapter 11

1. T.H. Green, "On the Different Senses of 'Freedom' as Applied to Will and the Moral Progress of Man" (1879), in *Lectures on the Principles of Political Obligation* (London, 1941), 21, section 22.

2. Erich Fromm, *The Fear of Freedom* (London, 1942, rep. 1960), 233.

3. Ibid., 247, 250.

4. Ibid., 232.

5. Solomon Asch, *Social Psychology* (New York, 1952), 276, 278, quoted by Christian Bay, *The Structure of Freedom* (New York, 1958), 172.

6. Cf. Stephen E. Toulmin, "Self-knowledge and knowledge of the Self," in Theodore Mischel, ed., *The Self* (Oxford, 1977).

7. Bay, *Structure of Freedom*, 173.

8. Ibid., 187.

9. Ibid., 175.

10. Ibid., 188.

11. Karen Horney, *Neurosis and Human Growth* (London, 1951).

12. Bruno Bettelheim, *The Children of the Dream* (London, 1971).

13. Bruno Bettelheim, "Personality Formation in the Kibbutz," *American Journal of Psychoanalysis* 29 (1969): 3–9.

14. Horney, *Neurosis and Human Growth*, 15.

15. Abraham H. Maslow, *Motivation and Personality*, 2d ed. (New York, 1970), 134.

16. Ibid., 133–4.

17. Ibid., 137.

18. Ibid., 159.

19. Herbert Marcuse, *Eros and Civilization* (London, 1969), 203. The passage cited by Marcuse as a quotation is not assigned to a specific source.

## Chapter 12

1. Sheldon S. Wolin, *Politics and Vision* (Boston, 1960), 357. Wolin "collects under a single roof" nostalgic conservatives like de Maistre and Bonald, radical utopians like Rousseau and Fourier, sociologists and social psychologists like Durkheim, Elton, Mayo, and Fromm, and revolutionary ideologists like Marx, Proudhon, and Lenin. See also Robert A. Nesbit, *The Quest for Community* (London, 1953), Ch. 10, and R.P. Wolff, *The Poverty of Liberalism* (Boston, 1968).

2. Judson Jerome, *Families of Eden* (London, 1975), ix.

3. Students of game theory and other kinds of rational-choice theory in political science – international relations, strategic studies – and economics will be familiar with modern applications of the model. See S.I. Benn and G.W. Mortimore, eds., *Rationality and the Social Sciences* (London, 1976), Chs. 7–10, for discussions of such theories. See also W. Riker, *Theory of Political Coalition* (New Haven, 1965), and Robert Goodin, *The Politics of Rational Man* (London, 1976), as typical instances.

4. Herbert Marcuse, while recognizing that the welfare state is "capable of raising the standard of *administered* living," "of making the administered life secure and comfortable," decries it nevertheless because it

was at the expense of the spontaneous, unrepressed life he valued (*One-Dimensional Man* [London, 1968], 52–7). Marcuse made more, however, of libidinal self-expression, albeit esthetically sublimated through transcendent collective enterprises, and of "solidarity," a sentiment that members of such enterprises (e.g., revolutionary movements) might share, than of the reciprocal concern of persons for one another in communities. His *Eros and Civilization* has remarkably little to say about love!

5. R.M. Kanter, *Commitment and Community* (Cambridge, Mass., 1972).
6. Ibid., 53.
7. C.H. Cooley, *Social Organization: A Study of the Larger Mind* (New York, 1962), quoted in Kanter, *Commitment and Community*, 32.
8. Kanter, *Commitment and Community*, 73.
9. Ibid., 74.
10. Cf. Léopold Sédar Senghor, *On African Socialism*, Mercer Cook, trans. (London, 1964), where a professed aim is "to attempt to define an ideal society that will integrate the contributions of European socialism with our traditional values." Senghor claims that

> collectivist European society . . . is an *assembly of individuals*. The collectivist society inevitably places the emphasis on the individual, on his original activity and his needs. . . . Negro-African society puts more stress on the group than on the individual, more on *solidarity* than on the activity and needs of the individual, more on the *communion* of persons than on their autonomy. Ours is a *community* society. . . . The individual is, in Europe, the man who distinguishes himself from the other and claims his autonomy to affirm himself in his basic originality. The member of the community society also claims his autonomy to affirm himself as a being. But he feels, he thinks that he can develop his potential, his originality, only in and by society, in unison with all other men – indeed, with all other beings in the universe: God, animal, tree, or pebble. (pp. 93–4)

Also Sekou Touré, quoted by Ehud Springzak, "African Traditional Socialism," in *Journal of Modern African Studies* 11 (1973):

> . . . our solidarity, better known under its aspect of social fraternity, the pre-eminence of group interests over the personal interest, the sense of common responsibilities, the practice of a formal democracy which rules and governs village life . . . that is what forms what we call our communocratic realities. (p. 637)

11. Martin Buber, *Paths in Utopia* (London, 1949): 1.
12. Ibid., 136.
13. Jay and Heather Ogilvie make a distinction between monistic and pluralistic communes analogous to mine between total community and comradeship. Because the latter recruit people who are "attracted more by the idea of living with a group of *people* than by the idea of

joining a cadre for a cause," they have "no *raison d'être* other than the processes of personal development." "A pluralistic commune may attempt to increase the sense of community [however] by creating some common task which will help to define the in-group positively rather than negatively: in short, a pluralistic commune may try to become monistic. . . . [They] may find the best way of remaining together to be as a monistic commune united by an agreed upon task." Jay Ogilvie and Heather Ogilvie, "Commune and the Reconstruction of Reality," in Sallie Teselle, ed., *The Family, Communes, and Utopian Societies* (New York, 1972), 90, 96–7, 98.

## Chapter 13

1. H.L.A. Hart, "Are There Any Natural Rights?" in Jeremy Waldron, ed., *Theories of Rights* (Oxford, 1984), 77–90.
2. Richard Wasserstrom calls human rights "moral commodities." See his "Rights, Human Rights, and Racial Discrimination," *Journal of Philosophy* 61 (1964): 628–41.
3. Hart, "Natural Rights?" 88.
4. John Rawls, *A Theory of Justice* (Cambridge, Mass., 1971), Section 19. Rawls says little about natural or human rights.
5. *Universal Declaration of Human Rights* (1948), cited hereafter as *UDHR*, Art. 16.
6. See Hart, "Natural Rights?"
7. Carl Wellman, "A New Conception of Human Rights," in Eugene Kamenka and Alice Ehr-Soon Tay, eds., *Human Rights* (London, 1978), 48–58. W.N. Hohfeld's seminal work, *Fundamental Legal Conceptions as Applied in Judicial Reasoning*, appeared in 1919; Albert Kocourek's *Jural Relations* in 1927.
8. *UDHR*, Arts. 26, 24, and 27.
9. John Kleinig, "Human Rights, Legal Rights, and Social Change," in Eugene Kamenka and Alice Erh-Soon Tay, eds., *Human Rights* (London, 1978), 46. Compare Hume's view that justice arises only on account of the selfishness and limited generosity of men, conjoined with scarcity in comparison with the resources necessary to satisfy their wants: "Encrease to a sufficient degree the benevolence of men, or the bounty of nature, and you render justice useless, by supplying its place with much nobler virtues, and more valuable blessings." David Hume, *A Treatise of Human Nature*, L.A. Selby-Bigge, ed. (Oxford, 1978), 494–5 (Bk. III, Part II, sec. ii).
10. Kleinig virtually concedes the point in a footnote in which he allows that where love and care stifle, "they are defective *as* love and care." (Kleinig, "Human Rights," 46, n. 27) This looks like an acknowledgment of the need for recognition of human rights in a mutuality. However, Kleinig claims that this recognition is of "the other's welfare

interests, including the other's welfare interest in freedom," whereas I want to say that what is at stake is not a welfare interest, which would be an object of concern, but the respect due to a person.

11. Michael J. Sandel, *Liberalism and the Limits of Justice* (Cambridge, 1982), 179.
12. Karl Marx, "On the Jewish Question," in *Early Writings of Karl Marx*, translated by R. Livingstone and G. Benton (Harmondsworth, 1975), 229.
13. Karl Marx, "Excerpts from James Mill's *Elements of Political Economy*," *Early Writings*, 265.
14. K. Wojtyla, "The Person: Subject and Community," *Review of Metaphysics* 33 (1979): 304.
15. Ibid., 306.
16. See L.T. Hobhouse, *Elements of Social Justice* (London, 1922), and Sir Ernest Barker, *Principles of Social and Political Theory* (Oxford, 1951). See also A.D. Lindsay, *The Modern Democratic State* (London, 1943).
17. Ronald Dworkin, *Taking Rights Seriously* (London, 1977), 272.

## Chapter 14

1. S.D. Warren and L.D. Brandeis, "The Right to Privacy," *Harvard Law Review* 4, (1890): 193.
2. A.F. Westin, *Privacy and Freedom* (New York, 1967), 7.
3. L. Lusky, "Invasion of Privacy: A Clarification of Concepts," *Columbia Law Review* 72 (1972): 709.
4. New South Wales Parliamentary Papers, No. 170 (1972–73); W.L. Morison, *Report on the Law of Privacy* (Sydney, 1973), 3.
5. Lusky, "Invasion of Privacy," 709.
6. Cp. Lusky's reference to privacy as "the area of individual non-accountability, in which one can think and speak and act without having to *justify* to Big Brother or anyone else." Ibid., 707.
7. John Buxton relates how, in a prisoner-of-war camp in Germany, he organized a dawn-to-dusk vigil to observe the nesting and mating behavior of a pair of redstarts. A fellow prisoner, A.N.L. Munby, put the redstarts' point of view:

> *When your mind is set on mating*
> *It is highly irritating*
> *To see an ornithologist below:*
> *Though it may be nature-study,*
> *To a bird it's merely bloody*
> *Awful manners. Can't he see that he's de trop!*

From *Lyra Catenata* (printed privately, 1948), quoted in John Buxton, *The Redstart* (London, 1950).

8. G.B. Shaw, *Pygmalion*, Act 1 (Shaw's idiosyncratic punctuation).
9. J.-P. Sartre, *L'être et le néant* (Paris, 1953), Part 3, "Le pour-autrui."
10. R.D. Laing, *The Divided Self* (Harmondsworth, 1965).
11. See W.L. Prosser, "Privacy," *California Law Review*, vol. 48 (1960): 416–17.

## Chapter 15

1. Paul Halmos quotes *The Times*, London, July 20, 1949: "According to the newspaper *Szabad Nép*, some members of the Communist Party in Hungary have not a single working man among their friends, and they are censured in a way that implies that they had better quickly make a friend of a worker or it will be the worse for them." *Solitude and Privacy* (London, 1952), 167.
2. Charles Fried, "Privacy," in G. Hughes, ed., *Law, Reason, and Justice* (New York, 1969), 56.
3. See A.F. Westin, *Privacy and Freedom* (New York, 1967), 18, for references to evidence of this point.
4. Bruno Bettelheim, *Children of the Dream* (London, 1971), 38 ff.
5. E. Leach, *A Runaway World*, The 1967 Reith Lectures, (London, 1968), 44.
6. Halmos, *Solitude and Privacy*, 121–2.
7. See Barrington Moore, Jr., *Privacy: Studies in Social and Cultural History* (London, 1984).
8. In *Henderson v. Radio Corporation Pty. Ltd.*, S.R. (N.S.W.) 576 (1960), the Full Court of the Supreme Court of New South Wales restrained the defendant from publishing such a cover. Cited by Morison, *Report on the Law of Privacy*, 18.
9. *Sidis v. F.R. Publ. Co.*, 113 F.2d 806 (1940).
10. *Roberson v. Rochester Folding Box Co.*, 171 N.Y. 538 (1902).
11. Michael F. Mayer, after citing a number of American cases in which judgments were given for plaintiffs in "abrasive" debt collection cases, remarks that in "the area of credit the courts are less sensitive to plaintiff's anguish. . . . Credit, it is held, is up to the extender to determine and his mode of operation is largely at his discretion. The law appears laggard in this area." *Rights of Privacy* (1972), 133–4.
12. *Griswold v. Connecticut*, 381 U.S. 479 (1965), quoted in Westin, *Privacy and Freedom*, 353, n. 3.
13. Hyman Gross, "Privacy and Autonomy," in J.R. Pennock and J.W. Chapman, eds., *Privacy – NOMOS XIII* (New York, 1971), 169–81.
14. Westin, *Privacy and Freedom*, 371, n. 3.
15. *Prince Albert v. Strange and Others*, 1 Mac. & G., 24 (41 E.R., 1171, 1849).

16. L. Lusky, "Invasion of Privacy: A Clarification of Concepts," *Columbia Law Review* 72 (1972): 700. Lusky refers to Justice Hugo L. Black's opinion that

> . . . "balancing," by vesting unlimited discretion in the balancers (ulti-mately the Justices of the Supreme Court), abrogates law. . . . [A] consti-tutional liberty predicated on "balancing" rests on the shifting sands of membership on the Court. . . . The balancing approach is too dangerous to be used in preference to an available *rule* that does the required job. If and to the extent that the line between the allowed and the forbidden, between the required and the optional, is susceptible of demarcation by words that would be understood the same way by all or nearly all reason-able men, that is what should be done. Such is the connotation of the . . . phrase, "a government of laws and not of men."

On balancing generally, see G. Gottlieb, *The Logic of Choice* (London, 1968), Ch. 10. On the balancing of privacy against other interests, see also A.F. Westin, *Privacy and Freedom*, Ch. 14; Gross, "Privacy and Autonomy," 179–80.
17. See R. Dworkin, *Taking Rights Seriously* (London 1977), 90–4, 197–204, and passim, for discussions of "weighing" and "balancing" proce-dures which, while not in my view satisfactory as solutions, exhibit the problems.
18. Gross, "Privacy and Autonomy," 177–9. Emphasis in original.
19. The quotation is from Stig Stromholm, *Rights of Privacy and Rights of Personality*, working paper prepared for the Nordic Conference on Pri-vacy of the International Commission of Jurists, Stockholm, May 1967, 69–71.
20. Lusky, "Invasion of Privacy," 706, n. 2.
21. Gross, "Privacy and Autonomy," 179–80.

## Chapter 16

1. E.g., Maurice Cranston, *Freedom – A New Analysis* (London, 1953), Fe-lix Oppenheim, *The Dimensions of Freedom* (New York, 1961), and T.D. Weldon, *The Vocabulary of Politics* (Harmondsworth, 1953).
2. G.F. Gaus and I explained our understanding of "a complex-structured concept" in "The Public and the Private: Concepts and Action," in S.I. Benn and G.F. Gaus, eds. *Public and Private in Social Life* (London and New York, 1983), 3–27.
3. See Gerald MacCallum, "Negative and Positive Freedom," in P. Las-lett, W.G. Runciman, and Q. Skinner, eds., *Philosophy, Politics and Society*, 4th Series (Oxford, 1972), 174–93.

# Index

331